lonely planet

Eastern
Europe

PHRASEBOOK & DICTIONARY

P9-CJZ-872

Acknowledgments
Associate Publisher Mina Patria
Managing Editor Bruce Evans
Editors Kate Mathews, Mardi O'Connor
Series Designer Mark Adams
Managing Layout Designer Chris Girdler
Layout Designer Carol Jackson
Production Support Larissa Frost

Thanks

Sasha Baskett, Melanie Dankel, Brendan Dempsey, Ben Handicott, James Hardy, Nic Lehman, Annelies Mertens, Wayne Murphy, Naomi Parker, Trent Paton, Piers Pickard, Mazzy Prinsep, Branislava Vladisavljevic

Published by Lonely Planet Publications Pty Ltd
ABN 36 005 607 983

5th Edition – February 2013
ISBN 978 1 74179 005 4
Text © Lonely Planet 2013
Cover Image Traders and stalls at city market, Zagreb, Croatia
Richard I'Anson/Lonely Planet Images
Printed in China 10 9 8 7 6 5 4 3 2 1

Contact lonelyplanet.com/contact

MIX
Paper from
responsible sources
FSC™ C021741

acknowledgments

This book is based on existing editions of Lonely Planet's phrasebooks as well as new content. It was developed with the help of the following people:

- Anila Mayhew for the Albanian chapter
- Ronelle Alexander for the Bulgarian chapter
- Gordana Ivetac and Ivan Ivetac for the Croatian chapter
- Richard Nebeský for the Czech chapter
- Christina Mayer for the Hungarian chapter
- Liljana Mitkovska for the Macedonian chapter
- Piotr Czajkowski for the Polish chapter
- Anamaria Beligan and Dana Lovinesku for the Romanian chapter
- James Jenkin and Grant Taylor for the Russian chapter
- Katarina Nodrovicziova for the Slovak chapter
- Urška Pajer for the Slovene chapter

Thank you to Hunor Csutoros (Hungarian), Leif Pettersen and Monica Zavoianu (Romanian) and Eugene Terentev (Russian) for additional language expertise.

contents

Eastern Europe

- Albanian
- Bulgarian
- Croatian
- Czech
- Hungarian
- Macedonian
- Polish
- Romanian

RUSSIA

Mosco

Ukraine

Belarus

Latvia

Lithuania

Kaliningrad (RUSSIA)

⊕ Warsaw

Vistula

POLAND

Gulf of Gdansk

BALTIC SEA

Pomeranian Bay

Sweden

Denmark

Germany

Oder

CZECH REPUBLIC

Prague ⊛

language map

eastern europe – at a glance

One of the most rewarding things about travelling through Eastern Europe is the rich variety of cuisine, customs, architecture and history. The flipside of course is that you'll encounter a number of very different languages. Most languages spoken in Eastern Europe belong to what's known as the Indo-European language family, believed to have originally developed from one language spoken thousands of years ago. Luckily for English speakers, most of these languages also use Roman script.

The Slavic languages are a branch of the Indo-European language family and share a large amount of basic vocabulary. They originated north of the Carpathians and are now divided into Eastern (Russian), Western (Czech, Slovak and Polish) and Southern (Bulgarian, Croatian, Macedonian and Slovene) subgroups. The languages traditionally associated with the Orthodox Church (Russian, Bulgarian and Macedonian) use Cyrillic alphabet, while those influenced by the Catholic Church (Czech, Slovak, Polish, Croatian and Slovene) use Roman alphabet. Romanian, the only representative of the Romance languages in Eastern Europe, is more closely related to French, Italian or Spanish. The freedom with which English has borrowed Latin-based vocabulary means you'll quickly recognise many words from Romanian. Albanian forms a single branch of the Indo-European language family. Finally, Hungarian is part of the Ural-Altaic language family, which includes languages spoken from Europe to northeast Asia. Its closest European relative is Finnish.

did you know?

- The European Union (EU) was established by the Maastricht Treaty in 1992. It developed from the European Economic Community, founded by the Treaty of Rome in 1957. Since the 2007 enlargement, it has 27 member states and 23 official languages.
- The EU flag is a circle of 12 gold stars on a blue background — the number 12 representing wholeness.
- The EU anthem is the 'Ode to Joy' from Beethoven's Ninth Symphony.
- Europe Day, 9 May, commemorates the 1950 declaration by French Foreign Minister Robert Schuman which marked the creation of the European Union.
- The euro has been in circulation since E-Day, 1 January 2002. The euro's symbol (€) was inspired by the Greek letter epsilon (ε) – Greece being the cradle of European civilisation and ε being the first letter of the word 'Europe'.
- The Eurovision Song Contest, held each May, has been running since 1956. For the larger part of the competition's history, the performers were only allowed to sing in their country's national language, but that's no longer the case.

Albanian

albanian alphabet

A a a	B b b	C c ts	Ç ç ch	D d d	Dh dh dh
E e e	Ë ë uh	F f f	G g g	Gj gj dy	H h h
I i ee	J j y	K k k	L l l	Ll ll ll	M m m
N n n	Nj nj ny	O o o	P p p	Q q ty	R r r
Rr rr rr	S s s	Sh sh sh	T t t	Th th th	U u oo
V v v	X x dz	Xh xh j	Y y ew	Z z z	Zh zh zh

albanian

introduction

Albanian (*gjuha shqipe* dyoo·ha shtyee·pe) is one of the oldest Indo-European languages, generally considered the only descendant of Illyrian, the language of the ancient inhabitants of the Balkans. With no close relatives and constituting a branch of its own, it's a proud survivor of the Roman, Slavic and Ottoman influxes and a European linguistic oddity on a par with Basque.

Albanian's position on the edge of the turbulent and multilingual Balkans means that it's been influenced by many languages. Some similarities with Romanian, for example, suggest that the two languages were closely related and that their speakers interacted even in pre-Roman times. The Romans, who established control over the present-day Albania by 167 BC and ruled for the next five centuries, left their mark on the vocabulary and structure of the language. After the division of the Roman Empire in AD 395, Albanians fell within the realm of Byzantium and Greek Orthodox culture. The interaction with Bulgarian and Serbian began after the arrival of the Slavs to the Balkans in the 6th century. With the Ottoman conquest in 1479 Turkish and Arabic influences were added to the mix.

There are two main dialects of Albanian – Tosk (with about 3 million speakers in southern Albania, Greece, Italy and Turkey) and Gheg (spoken by about 2.8 million people in northern Albania, Kosovo and the surrounding areas of Serbia, Montenegro and Macedonia). Tosk is the official language of Albania and is also the variety used in this phrasebook.

Not surprisingly, Albanian has been written in various alphabets since the earliest written records from the 15th century. A single-sentence baptismal formula dating from 1462 and a Catholic prayer book from 1555 were both written in the Roman alphabet, which was mainly used for the Gheg dialect during the 17th and 18th centuries. The Tosk dialect, on the other hand, was originally written in the Greek alphabet. However, during the Ottoman rule, texts in both varieties were often in Arabic script (also used for Turkish). Even Cyrillic script was occasionally in use. This orthographic confusion was finally settled by the Manastir Congress in 1908, which adopted a modified Roman alphabet as the standard written form of Albanian.

Even though many Albanians speak English, you'll find attempts to communicate in Albanian are welcomed. Discovering some of the mysteries of this intriguing language will be rewarding – try learning a few of the 27 words Albanian has for 'moustache' or the other 27 used for 'eyebrows'!

introduction – ALBANIAN

pronunciation

vowel sounds

The Albanian vowel system is relatively easy to master, as the sounds mostly have equivalents in English.

symbol	english equivalent	albanian example	transliteration
a	f**a**ther	*pak*	pak
ai	**ai**sle	*çaj*	chai
e	b**e**t	*pse*	pse
ee	s**ee**	*klima*	*klee*·ma
ew	**ee** pronounced with rounded lips	*dy*	dew
ia	t**ia**ra	*djali*	*dia*·lee
o	p**o**t	*mosha*	*mo*·sha
oo	z**oo**	*jug*	yoog
uh	**a**go	*vëlla*	vuh·*lla*

word stress

For the vast majority of words in Albanian, the main stress falls on the last syllable of a word (or the last stem of a compound word). In a sentence, the main stress generally falls on the last word of a phrase. In our coloured pronunciation guides, the stressed syllable is always in italics.

consonant sounds

The Albanian consonant sounds shouldn't present many problems for English speakers. Note that 'rr' and 'll' are pronounced stronger than when they're written as single letters.

symbol	english equivalent	albanian example	transliteration
b	**bed**	*bukë*	*boo*·kuh
ch	**cheat**	*çaj, qen*	chai, chen
d	**dog**	*disa*	dee·*sa*
dh	**that**	*bardhë*	*bar*·dhuh
dy	**joke**	*gjalpë, xhami*	*dyal*·puh, *dya*·mee
dz	**adds**	*nxehtë*	n·*dzeh*·tuh
f	**fat**	*frenat*	*fre*·nat
g	**go**	*gisht*	geesht
h	**hat**	*hundë*	*hoon*·duh
k	**kit**	*raki*	ra·*kee*
l	**lot**	*omletë*	om·*le*·tuh
ll	**strong l**	*llum*	lloom
m	**man**	*muze*	moo·*ze*
n	**not**	*sapun*	sa·*poon*
ny	**canyon**	*një*	nyuh
p	**pet**	*po*	po
r	**run**	*ari*	a·*ree*
rr	**strong r**	*rrotë*	*rro*·tuh
s	**sun**	*sot*	sot
sh	**shot**	*shesh*	shesh
t	**top**	*tani*	ta·*nee*
th	**thin**	*uthull*	*oo*·thooll
ts	**hats**	*cili*	*tsee*·lee
v	**very**	*veri*	ve·*ree*
y	**yes**	*jo*	yo
z	**zero**	*zarf*	zarf
zh	**pleasure**	*bizhuteri*	bee·*zhoo*·te·*ree*

basics

language difficulties

Do you speak English?
A flisni anglisht? — a flees·nee ang·leesht

Do you understand?
A kuptoni? — a koop·to·nee

I (don't) understand.
Unë (nuk) kuptoj. — oo·nuh (nook) koop·toy

What does (*vrapoj*) mean?
Ç'do të thotë fjala (vrapoj)? — chdo tuh tho·tuh fya·la (vra·poy)

How do you ...?   *Si ...?*   see ...
  pronounce this   *shqiptohet kjo*   shcheep·to·het kyo
  write (*atje*)   *shkruhet fjala (atje)*   shkroo·het fya·la (at·ye)

Could you please ...?   *..., ju lutem.*   ... yoo loo·tem
  repeat that   *Përsëriteni*   puhr·suh·ree·te·nee
  speak more slowly   *Flisni më*   flees·nee muh
    ngadalë   nga·da·luh
  write it down   *Shkruajeni*   shkroo·a·ye·nee

essentials

Yes.	*Po.*	po
No.	*Jo.*	yo
Please.	*Ju lutem.*	yoo loo·tem
Thank you	*Faleminderit*	fa·le·meen·de·reet
(very much).	*(shumë).*	(shoo·muh)
You're welcome.	*S'ka përse.*	ska puhr·se
Excuse me.	*Më falni.*	muh fal·nee
Sorry.	*Më vjen keq.*	muh vyen kech

numbers

0	*zero*	ze·ro	17	*shtatëmbëdhjetë*	shta·tuhm·buh·dhye·tuh
1	*një*	nyuh			
2	*dy*	dew	18	*tetëmbëdhjetë*	te·tuhm·buh·dhye·tuh
3	*tre/tri* m/f	tre/tree			
4	*katër*	ka·tuhr	19	*nëntëmbëdhjetë*	nuhn·tuhm·buh·dhye·tuh
5	*pesë*	pe·suh			
6	*gjashtë*	dyash·tuh	20	*njëzet*	nyuh·zet
7	*shtatë*	shta·tuh	21	*njëzet e një*	nyuh·zet e nyuh
8	*tetë*	te·tuh	30	*tridhjetë*	tree·dhye·tuh
9	*nëntë*	nuhn·tuh	40	*dyzet*	dew·zet
10	*dhjetë*	dhye·tuh	50	*pesëdhjetë*	pe·suh·dhye·tuh
11	*njëmbëdhjetë*	nyuhm·buh·dhye·tuh	60	*gjashtëdhjetë*	dyash·tuh·dhye·tuh
12	*dymbëdhjetë*	dewm·buh·dhye·tuh	70	*shtatëdhjetë*	shta·tuh·dhye·tuh
13	*trembëdhjetë*	trem·buh·dhye·tuh	80	*tetëdhjetë*	te·tuh·dhye·tuh
14	*katërmbëdhjetë*	ka·tuhrm·buh·dhye·tuh	90	*nëntëdhjetë*	nuhn·tuh·dhye·tuh
15	*pesëmbëdhjetë*	pe·suhm·buh·dhye·tuh	100	*njëqind*	nyuh·cheend
16	*gjashtëmbëdhjetë*	dyash·tuhm·buh·dhye·tuh	1000	*një mijë*	nyuh mee·yuh

time & dates

What time is it?	*Sa është ora?*	sa uhsh·tuh o·ra
It's one o'clock.	*Ora është një.*	o·ra uhsh·tuh nyuh
It's (two) o'clock.	*Ora është (dy).*	o·ra uhsh·tuh (dew)
Quarter past (one).	*(Një) e një çerek.*	(nyuh) e nyuh che·rek
Half past (one).	*(Një) e gjysmë.*	(nyuh) e dyews·muh
Quarter to (eight).	*(Tetë) pa një çerek.*	(te·tuh) pa nyuh che·rek
At what time ...?	*Në çfarë ore ...?*	nuh chfa·ruh o·re ...
At ...	*Në ...*	nuh ...
am	*paradite*	pa·ra·dee·te
pm	*mbasdite*	mbas·dee·te

Monday	e hënë	e huh-nuh
Tuesday	e martë	e mar-tuh
Wednesday	e mërkurë	e muhr-koo-ruh
Thursday	e enjte	e eny-te
Friday	e premte	e prem-te
Saturday	e shtunë	e shtoo-nuh
Sunday	e diel	e dee-el

January	janar	ya-nar
February	shkurt	shkoort
March	mars	mars
April	prill	preell
May	maj	mai
June	qershor	cher-shor
July	korrik	ko-rreek
August	gusht	goosht
September	shtator	shta-tor
October	tetor	te-tor
November	nëntor	nuhn-tor
December	dhjetor	dhye-tor

What date is it today?	Sa është data sot?	sa uhsh-tuh da-ta sot
It's (10 October).	Është (dhjetë tetor).	uhsh-tuh (dhye-tuh te-tor)

since (May)	që në (maj)	chuh nuh (mai)
until (June)	deri në (qershor)	de-ree nuh (cher-shor)

next week	javën e ardhshme	ya-vuhn e ardh-shme
next month	muajin e ardhshëm	moo-a-yeen e ardh-shuhm
next year	vitin e ardhshëm	vee-teen e ardh-shuhm

last ...	... e kaluar	... e ka-loo-ar
night	mbrëmjen	mbruhm-yen
week	javën	ya-vuhn
month	muajin	moo-a-yeen
year	vitin	vee-teen

yesterday/tomorrow ...	dje/nesër ...	dee-e/ne-suhr ...
morning	në mëngjes	nuh muhn-dyes
afternoon	mbasdite	mbas-dee-te
evening	në mbrëmje	nuh mbruhm-ye

weather

What's the weather like?	*Si është koha?*	see *uhsh*·tuh *ko*·ha
It's ...	*Koha është ...*	*ko*·ha *uhsh*·tuh ...
cold	*e ftohtë*	e *ftoh*·tuh
hot	*e nxehtë*	e *ndzeh*·tuh
raining	*me shi*	me shee
snowing	*me borë*	me *bo*·ruh
sunny	*me diell*	me *dee*·ell
warm	*e ngrohtë*	e *ngroh*·tuh
windy	*me erë*	me *e*·ruh
spring	*pranverë* f	pran·*ve*·ruh
summer	*verë* f	*ve*·ruh
autumn	*vjeshtë* f	*vyesh*·tuh
winter	*dimër* m	*dee*·muhr

border crossing

I'm here ...	*Jam këtu ...*	yam kuh·*too* ...
on business	*me punë*	me *poo*·nuh
on holiday	*me pushime*	me poo·*shee*·me
I'm here for ...	*Do të qëndroj për ...*	do tuh chuhn·*droy* puhr ...
(10) days	*(dhjetë) ditë*	*(dhye*·tuh) *dee*·tuh
(two) months	*(dy) muaj*	(dew) *moo*·ai
(three) weeks	*(tri) javë*	(tree) *ya*·vuh

I'm going to (Tirana).
Do të shkoj në (Tiranë).
do tuh shkoy nuh (tee·*ra*·nuh)

I'm staying at the (Hotel Tirana).
Po qëndroj te (hotel Tirana).
po chuhn·*droy* te (ho·*tel* tee·*ra*·na)

I have nothing to declare.
S'kam asgjë për të deklaruar.
skam as·*dyuh* puhr tuh de·kla·*roo*·ar

I have something to declare.
Dua të deklaroj diçka.
doo·a tuh de·kla·*roy* deech·ka

That's (not) mine.
(Nuk) Është e imja.
(nook) *uhsh*·tuh e *eem*·ya

transport

tickets & luggage

Where can I buy a ticket?
Ku mund të blej një biletë? koo moond tuh bley nyuh bee-*le*-tuh

Do I need to book a seat?
A duhet të bëj rezervim? a *doo*-het tuh buhy re-zer-*veem*

One ... ticket	*Një biletë ...*	nyuh bee-*le*-tuh ...
(to Shkodër),	*(për në Shkodër),*	(puhr nuh *shko*-duhr)
please.	*ju lutem.*	yoo *loo*-tem
one-way	*për vajtje*	puhr *vai*-tye
return	*kthimi*	*kthee*-mee

I'd like to ... my	*Dua ta ... biletën*	*doo*-a ta ... bee-*le*-tuhn
ticket, please.	*time, ju lutem.*	*tee*-me yoo *loo*-tem
cancel	*anuloj*	a-noo-*loy*
change	*ndryshoj*	ndrew-*shoy*
collect	*marr*	marr
confirm	*konfirmoj*	kon-feer-*moy*

I'd like a ... seat,	*Dua një vend ...,*	*doo*-a nyuh vend ...
please.	*ju lutem.*	yoo *loo*-tem
nonsmoking	*ku s'pihet duhan*	koo *spee*-het doo-*han*
smoking	*ku pihet duhan*	koo *pee*-het doo-*han*

How much is it?
Sa kushton? sa koosh-*ton*

Is there air conditioning?
A ka ajër të kondicionuar? a ka *a*-yuhr tuh kon-*dee*-tsee-o-noo-ar

Is there a toilet?
A ka banjë? a ka *ba*-nyuh

How long does the trip take?
Sa zgjat udhëtimi? sa zdyat oo-dhuh-*tee*-mee

Is it a direct route?
A është linjë direkte? a *uhsh*-tuh *lee*-nyuh dee-*rek*-te

I'd like a luggage locker.
Dua një kyç për valixhet. *doo*-a nyuh kewch puhr va-*lee*-dyet

My luggage has been ...	Valixhet e mia ...	va·lee·dyet e mee·a ...
damaged	janë dëmtuar	ya·nuh duhm·too·ar
lost	kanë humbur	ka·nuh hoom·boor
stolen	i kanë vjedhur	ee ka·nuh vye·dhoor

getting around

Where does flight (728) arrive/depart?
Ku mbërrin/niset linja (728)?
koo *mbuh·*rreen/*nee·*set *lee·*nya (shta·tuh·*cheend* e *nyuh·*zet e *te·*tuh)

Where's (the) ...?	Ku është ...?	koo *uhsh·*tuh ...
arrivals hall	salla e mbërritjes	sa·lla e mbuh·rree·tyes
departures hall	salla e nisjes	sa·lla e nee·syes
duty-free shop	dyqani pa taksa	dew·cha·nee pa tak·sa
gate (12)	hyrja (dymbëdhjetë)	hew·rya (dewm·buh·dhye·tuh)

Is this the ... to (Durrës)?	Është ... për në (Durrës)?	uhsh·tuh ... puhr nuh (doo·rruhs)
boat	kjo anija	kyo a·nee·ya
bus	ky autobusi	kew a·oo·to·boo·see
plane	ky aeroplani	kew a·e·ro·pla·nee
train	ky treni	kew tre·nee

What time's the ... bus?	Në ç'orë vjen autobusi ...?	nuh cho·ruh vyen a·oo·to·boo·see ...
first	i parë	e pa·ruh
last	i fundit	e foon·deet
next	tjetër	tye·tuhr

At what time does it arrive/leave?
Në ç'orë arrin/niset?
nuh cho·ruh a·rreen/nee·set

How long will it be delayed?
Sa do të vonohet?
sa do tuh vo·no·het

What station/stop is this?
Cili stacion është ky?
tsee·lee sta·tsee·on uhsh·tuh kew

What's the next station/stop?
Cili është stacioni tjetër?
tsee·lee uhsh·tuh sta·tsee·o·nee tye·tuhr

Does it stop at (Vora)?
A ndalon në (Vorë)?
a nda·lon nuh (vo·ruh)

Please tell me when we get to (Kruja).
Ju lutem më tregoni kur të arrijmë në (Krujë).
yoo *loo*·tem muh tre·*go*·nee koor tuh a·*rreey*·muh nuh (*kroo*·yuh)

How long do we stop here?
Për sa kohë do ndalojmë këtu?
puhr sa *ko*·huh do nda·*loy*·muh kuh·*too*

Is this seat available?
I lirë është ky vendi?
ee *lee*·ruh *uhsh*·tuh kew *ven*·dee

That's my seat.
Ky është vendi im.
kew *uhsh*·tuh *ven*·dee eem

I'd like a taxi …	*Dua një taksi …*	*doo*·a nyuh tak·*see* …
at (9am)	në orën (nëntë paradite)	nuh o·*ruhn* (*nuhn*·tuh pa·ra·*dee*·te)
now	tani	ta·*nee*
tomorrow	nesër	ne·suhr

Is this taxi available?
Është bosh kjo taksia?
uhsh·tuh bosh kyo tak·*see*·a

How much is it to …?
Sa kushton për të vajtur në …?
sa koosh·*ton* puhr tuh *vai*·toor nuh …

Please put the meter on.
Ju lutem ndizeni matësin e kilometrave.
yoo *loo*·tem *ndee*·ze·nee *ma*·tuh·seen e kee·lo·*me*·tra·ve

Please take me to (this address).
Ju lutem më çoni te (kjo adresë).
yoo *loo*·tem muh *cho*·nee te (kyo a·*dre*·suh)

Please …	*Ju lutem …*	yoo *loo*·tem …
slow down	uleni	oo·le·nee
	shpejtësinë	shpey·tuh·*see*·nuh
stop here	ndaloni këtu	nda·*lo*·nee kuh·*too*
wait here	prisni këtu	*prees*·nee kuh·*too*

car, motorbike & bicycle hire

I'd like to hire a …	*Dua të marr me qira një …*	*doo*·a tuh marr me chee·*ra* nyuh …
bicycle	biçikletë	bee·chee·*kle*·tuh
car	makinë	ma·*kee*·nuh
motorbike	motor	mo·*tor*

with ...	me ...	me ...
a driver	*shofer*	sho·*fer*
air conditioning	*ajër të*	*a*·yuhr tuh
	kondicionuar	kon·*dee*·tsee·o·noo·ar
antifreeze	*kundërngrirës*	koon·duhr·*ngree*·ruhs
snow chains	*zinxhira për borë*	zeen·*dyee*·ra puhr bo·ruh

How much for	*Sa kushton*	sa koosh·*ton*
... hire?	*për një ...?*	puhr nyuh ...
hourly	*orë*	o·ruh
daily	*ditë*	*dee*·tuh
weekly	*javë*	*ya*·vuh

air	*ajër* m	*a*·yuhr
oil	*vaj* m	vai
petrol	*benzinë* f	ben·*zee*·nuh
tyres	*goma* f	*go*·ma

I need a mechanic.
Më duhet një mekanik.   muh *doo*·het nyuh me·ka·*neek*

I've run out of petrol.
Më ka mbaruar benzina.   muh ka mba·*roo*·ar ben·*zee*·na

I have a flat tyre.
Më ka rënë goma.   muh ka *ruh*·nuh *go*·ma

directions

Where's the ...?	*Ku është ...?*	koo *uhsh*·tuh ...
bank	*banka*	*ban*·ka
city centre	*qendra e qytetit*	*chen*·dra e chew·*te*·teet
hotel	*hoteli*	ho·*te*·lee
market	*tregu*	*tre*·goo
police station	*rajoni i policisë*	ra·*yo*·nee ee po·lee·*tsee*·suh
post office	*posta*	*pos*·ta
public toilet	*banja publike*	*ba*·nya poo·*blee*·ke
tourist office	*zyra turistike*	*zew*·ra too·rees·*tee*·ke

Is this the road to (Berat)?
A është kjo rruga për në (Berat)?   a *uhsh*·tuh kyo *rroo*·ga puhr nuh (be·*rat*)

Can you show me (on the map)?
A mund të ma tregoni (në hartë)?   a moond tuh ma tre·*go*·nee (nuh *har*·tuh)

What's the address?
Cila është adresa?   tsee-la *uhsh*-tuh a-*dre*-sa

How far is it?
Sa larg është?   sa larg *uhsh*-tuh

How do I get there?
Si mund të shkoj atje?   see moond tuh shkoy at-*ye*

Turn ...	*Kthehuni ...*	kthe-hoo-nee ...
at the corner	*te qoshja e rrugës*	te *chosh*-ya e *rroo*-guhs
at the traffic lights	*te semafori*	te se-ma-*fo*-ree
left/right	*majtas/djathtas*	*mai*-tas/*diath*-tas
It's ...	*Është ...*	*uhsh*-tuh ...
behind ...	*prapa ...*	*pra*-pa ...
far away	*larg*	larg
here	*këtu*	kuh-*too*
in front of ...	*përpara ...*	puhr-*pa*-ra ...
left	*majtas*	*mai*-tas
near (to ...)	*afër ...*	*a*-fuhr ...
next to ...	*ngjitur me ...*	ndyee-toor me ...
on the corner	*te qoshja*	te *chosh*-ya
opposite ...	*përballë ...*	puhr-*ba*-lluh ...
right	*djathtas*	*diath*-tas
straight ahead	*drejt*	dreyt
there	*atje*	at-*ye*
by bus	*me autobus*	me a-oo-to-*boos*
by taxi	*me taksi*	me tak-*see*
by train	*me tren*	me tren
on foot	*në këmbë*	nuh *kuhm*-buh
north	*veri*	ve-*ree*
south	*jug*	yoog
east	*lindje*	*leen*-dye
west	*perëndim*	pe-ruhn-*deem*

22

Hyrje/Dalje	*hewr·ye/dal·ye*	**Entrance/Exit**
Hapur/Mbyllur	*ha·poor/mbew·lloor*	**Open/Closed**
Ka vende	ka *ven*·de	**Rooms Available**
Nuk ka vende	nook ka *ven*·de	**No Vacancies**
Informacion	een·for·ma·tsee·*on*	**Information**
Rajoni i policisë	ra·yo·nee ee po·lee·*tsee*·suh	**Police Station**
E ndaluar	e nda·*loo*·ar	**Prohibited**
Banjat	*ba*·nyat	**Toilets**
Burra	*boo*·rra	**Men**
Gra	gra	**Women**
Nxehtë/Ftohtë	ndzeh·tuh/ftoh·tuh	**Hot/Cold**

accommodation

finding accommodation

Where's a ...?	*Ku ka një ...?*	koo ka nyuh ...
camping ground	*vend kampimi*	vend kam·*pee*·mee
guesthouse	*bujtinë*	booy·*tee*·nuh
hotel	*hotel*	ho·*tel*
youth hostel	*fjetore për të rinj*	fye·*to*·re puhr tuh reeny
Can you	*A mund të më*	a moond tuh muh
recommend	*rekomandoni*	re·ko·man·*do*·nee
somewhere ...?	*një vend ...?*	nyuh vend ...
cheap	*të lirë*	tuh *lee*·ruh
good	*të mirë*	tuh *mee*·ruh
nearby	*këtu afër*	kuh·*too* a·fuhr

I'd like to book a room, please.
Dua të rezervoj një dhomë,   *doo*·a tuh re·zer·*voy* nyuh *dho*·muh
ju lutem.   yoo *loo*·tem

I have a reservation.
Kam bërë rezervim.   kam *buh*·ruh re·zer·*veem*

My name is ...
Unë quhem ...   *oo*·nuh *choo*·hem ...

Do you have a ... room?	*A keni një dhomë ...?*	a *ke*·nee nyuh *dho*·muh ...
single	teke	*te*·ke
double	dopjo	*dop*·yo
twin	dyshe	*dew*·she

How much is it per ...?	*Sa kushton për një ...?*	sa koosh·*ton* puhr nyuh ...
night	natë	*na*·tuh
person	njeri	nye·*ree*

Can I pay ...?	*A mund të paguaj me ...?*	a moond tuh pa·*goo*·ai me ...
by credit card	kartë krediti	*kar*·tuh kre·*dee*·tee
with a travellers cheque	çek udhëtimi	chek oo·dhuh·*tee*·mee

I'd like to stay for (two) nights.
Dua të qëndroj (dy) net.   *doo*·a tuh chuhn·*droy* (dew) net

From (2 July) to (6 July).
Nga (dy korriku) deri më (gjashtë korrik).   nga (dew ko·*rree*·koo) *de*·ree muh (*dyash*·tuh ko·*rreek*)

Can I see it?
A mund ta shoh?   a moond ta shoh

Am I allowed to camp here?
A mund të bëj kampim këtu?   a moond tuh buhy kam·*peem* kuh·*too*

Is there a camp site nearby?
A ka vend kampimi këtu afër?   a ka vend kam·*pee*·mee kuh·*too* a·fuhr

requests & queries

When/Where is breakfast served?
Kur/Ku shërbehet mëngjesi?   koor/koo shuhr·*be*·het muhn·*dye*·see

Please wake me at (seven).
Më zgjoni në orën (shtatë), ju lutem.   muh *zdyo*·nee nuh *o*·ruhn (*shta*·tuh) yoo *loo*·tem

Could I have my key, please?
Dua çelësin, ju lutem.   *doo*·a *che*·luh·seen yoo *loo*·tem

Can I get another (blanket)?
A mund të më jepni një (batanije) tjetër?   a moond tuh muh *yep*·nee nyuh (ba·ta·*nee*·ye) *tye*·tuhr

Is there a/an ...?	A ka ...?	a ka ...
elevator	ashensor	a·shen·*sor*
safe	kasafortë	ka·sa·*for*·tuh

The room is too ...	Dhoma është shumë e ...	*dho*·ma uhsh·tuh *shoo*·muh e ...
expensive	shtrenjtë	*shtreny*·tuh
noisy	zhurmshme	*zhoorm*·shme
small	vogël	*vo*·guhl

The ... doesn't work.	Është prishur ...	uhsh·tuh *pree*·shoor ...
air conditioning	ajri i kondicionuar	*ai*·ree ee kon·*dee*·tsee·o·noo·ar
fan	ventilatori	ven·tee·la·*to*·ree
toilet	banja	*ba*·nya

This ... isn't clean.	Ky ... nuk është i pastër.	kew ... nook uhsh·tuh ee *pas*·tuhr
pillow	jastëk	*yas*·tuhk
sheet	çarçaf	char·*chaf*
towel	peshqir	pesh·*cheer*

checking out

What time is checkout?
Në çfarë ore është çrregjistrimi?
nuh *chfa*·ruh *o*·re uhsh·tuh chrre·dyees·*tree*·mee

Can I leave my luggage here?
A mund t'i lë valixhet këtu?
a moond tee luh va·*lee*·dyet kuh·*too*

Could I have my ..., please?
A mund të më jepni ..., ju lutem?
a moond tuh muh *yep*·nee ... yoo *loo*·tem

deposit	paratë e depozituara	pa·*ra*·tuh e de·po·zee·*too*·a·ra
passport	pasaportën	pa·sa·*por*·tuhn
valuables	gjërat e mia	*dyuh*·rat e *mee*·a

communications & banking

the internet

Where's the local Internet café?
Ku është qendra lokale
e internetit?
koo *uhsh*·tuh *chen*·dra lo·*ka*·le
e een·*ter*·ne·teet

How much is it per hour?
Sa kushton për një orë?
sa koosh·*ton* puhr nyuh *o*·ruh

I'd like to ...	*Dua të ...*	*doo*·a tuh ...
check my email	*kontrolloj postën*	kon·tro·*lloy pos*·tuhn
	time elektronike	*tee*·me e·lek·tro·*nee*·ke
get Internet access	*futem në internet*	*foo*·tem nuh een·*ter*·net
use a printer	*përdor një printer*	puhr·*dor* nyuh *preen*·ter
use a scanner	*përdor një skaner*	puhr·*dor* nyuh *ska*·ner

mobile/cell phone

I'd like a mobile/cell phone for hire.
Dua të marr me qira një
telefon celular.
doo·a tuh marr me qee·*ra* nyuh
te·le·*fon* tse·loo·*lar*

I'd like a SIM card for your network.
Dua të blej një kartë SIM
për rrjetin tuaj.
doo·a tuh bley nyuh *kar*·tuh seem
puhr *rrye*·teen *too*·ai

What are the rates?
Sa është tarifa?
sa *uhsh*·tuh ta·*ree*·fa

telephone

What's your phone number?
Sa e ke numrin e telefonit?
sa e ke *noom*·reen e te·le·*fo*·neet

The number is ...
Numri është ...
noom·ree *uhsh*·tuh ...

Where's the nearest public phone?
Ku ka telefon publik këtu afër?
koo ka te·le·*fon* poob·*leek* kuh·*too* a·fuhr

I'd like to buy a phonecard.
Dua të blej një kartë telefonike.
doo·a tuh bley nyuh *kar*·tuh te·le·fo·*nee*·ke

I want to ...	Dua të ...	doo·a tuh ...
call (Singapore)	telefonoj (Singaporin)	te·le·fo·noy (seen·ga·po·reen)
make a local call	bëj një telefonatë lokale	buhy nyuh te·le·fo·na·tuh lo·ka·le
reverse the charges	anuloj tarifat	a·noo·loy ta·ree·fat

How much does a (three)-minute call cost?

Sa kushtojnë (tri) minuta në telefon?	sa koosh·toy·nuh (tree) mee·noo·ta nuh te·le·fon

How much does each extra minute cost?

Sa kushton çdo minutë shtesë?	sa koosh·ton chdo mee·noo·tuh shte·suh

(100) lek per minute.

(Njëqind) lekë minuta.	(nya·cheend) le·kuh mee·noo·ta

post office

I want to send a ...	Dua të dërgoj një ...	doo·a tuh duhr·goy nyuh ...
fax	faks	faks
letter	letër	le·tuhr
parcel	pako	pa·ko
postcard	kartolinë	kar·to·lee·nuh

I want to buy a/an ...	Dua të blej një ...	doo·a tuh bley nyuh ...
envelope	zarf	zarf
stamp	pullë	poo·lluh

Please send it (to Australia) by ...	Ju lutem dërgojeni (në Australi) me ...	yoo loo·tem duhr·go·ye·nee (nuh a·oos·tra·lee) me ...
airmail	postë ajrore	pos·tuh ai·ro·re
express mail	postë ekspres	pos·tuh eks·pres
registered mail	letër rekomande	le·tuhr re·ko·man·de
surface mail	postë të rregullt	pos·tuh tuh rre·goollt

Is there any mail for me?

A më ka ardhur ndonjë letër?	a muh ka ar·dhoor ndo·nyuh le·tuhr

bank

Where's a/an ...?	*Ku ka një ...?*	koo ka nyuh ...
automated teller machine	*makinë automatike për të holla*	ma-*kee*-nuh a-oo-to-ma-*tee*-ke puhr tuh *ho*-lla
foreign exchange office	*zyrë për këmbim valute*	*zew*-ruh puhr kuhm-*beem* va-*loo*-te
I'd like to ...	*Dua të ...*	*doo*-a tuh ...
Where can I ...?	*Ku mund të ...?*	koo moond tuh ...
arrange a transfer	*të bëj një transferim*	tuh buhy nyuh trans-fe-*reem*
cash a cheque	*thyej një çek*	*thew*-ey nyuh chek
change a travellers cheque	*thyej një çek udhëtimi*	*thew*-ey nyuh chek oo-dhuh-*tee*-mee
change money	*këmbej valutën*	kuhm-*bey* va-*loo*-tuhn
get a cash advance	*marr para në avancë*	marr pa-*ra* nuh a-*van*-tsuh
withdraw money	*bëj tërheqje parash*	buhy tuhr-*hech*-ye pa-*rash*

What's the ...?	*Sa është ...?*	sa *uhsh*-tuh ...
charge for that	*tarifa për këtë*	ta-*ree*-fa puhr kuh-*tuh*
commission	*komisioni*	ko-mee-see-*o*-nee
exchange rate	*kursi i këmbimit*	*koor*-see ee kuhm-*bee*-meet
It's ...	*Është ...*	*uhsh*-tuh ...
(12) lek	*(dymbëdhjetë) lekë*	(dewm-buh-*dhye*-tuh) *le*-kuh
free	*falas*	*fa*-las

What time does the bank open?
Në ç'orë hapet banka? nuh *cho*-ruh *ha*-pet *ban*-ka

Has my money arrived yet?
A kanë mbërritur paratë e mia? a *ka*-nuh mbuh-*rree*-toor pa-*ra*-tuh e *mee*-a

sightseeing

getting in

What time does it open/close?
Në ç' orë hapet/mbyllet?   nuh *cho*·ruh ha·pet/*mbew*·llet

What's the admission charge?
Sa kushton bileta e hyrjes?   sa koosh·*ton* bee·*le*·ta e *hewr*·yes

Is there a discount for students/children?
A bëni zbritje për   a *buh*·nee *zbree*·tye puhr
studentët/fëmijët?   stoo·*den*·tuht/fuh·*mee*·yuht

I'd like a ...	*Desha një ...*	*de*·sha nyuh ...
catalogue	*broshurë*	bro·*shoo*·ruh
guide	*manual*	ma·noo·*al*
local map	*hartë lokale*	*har*·tuh lo·*ka*·le

I'd like to see ...	*Dua të shikoj ...*	*doo*·a tuh shee·*koy* ...
What's that?	*Ç'është ajo?*	*chuhsh*·tuh *a*·yo
Can I take a photo?	*A mund të bëj*	a moond tuh buhy
	fotografi?	fo·to·gra·*fee*

tours

When's the next ...?	*Kur është ...?*	koor *uhsh*·tuh ...
day trip	*udhëtimi tjetër*	oo·dhuh·*tee*·mee *tye*·tuhr
	ditor	dee·*tor*
tour	*udhëtimi tjetër*	oo·dhuh·*tee*·mee *tye*·tuhr
	turistik	too·rees·*teek*

Is ... included?	*A përfshihet ...?*	a puhr·*fshee*·het ...
accommodation	*fjetja*	*fye*·tya
the admission	*tarifa e*	ta·*ree*·fa e
charge	*regjistrimit*	re·dyees·*tree*·meet
food	*ushqimi*	oosh·*chee*·mee
transport	*transporti*	trans·*por*·tee

How long is the tour?
Sa zgjat udhëtimi turistik?   sa zdyat oo·dhuh·*tee*·mee too·rees·*teek*

What time should we be back?
Në ç'orë duhet të kthehemi?   nuh *cho*·ruh *doo*·het tuh *kthe*·he·mee

sightseeing

castle	*kështjellë* f	kuhsh-*tye*-lluh
church	*kishë* f	*kee*-shuh
main square	*shesh kryesor* m	shesh krew-e-*sor*
monastery	*manastir* m	ma-nas-*teer*
monument	*monument* m	mo-noo-*ment*
mosque	*xhami* f	dya-*mee*
museum	*muze* m	moo-*ze*
old city	*qytet i vjetër* m	chew-*tet* ee *vye*-tuhr
ruins	*rrënoja* f	rruh-*no*-ya
stadium	*stadium* m	sta-dee-*oom*
statue	*statujë* f	sta-*too*-yuh

shopping

enquiries

Where's a ... ?	*Ku është ...?*	koo *uhsh*-tuh ...
bank	*banka*	*ban*-ka
bookshop	*libraria*	lee-bra-*ree*-a
camera shop	*dyqani i aparatëve fotografikë*	dew-*cha*-nee ee a-pa-*ra*-tuh-ve fo-to-gra-*fee*-kuh
department store	*dyqani i veshjeve*	dew-*cha*-nee ee *vesh*-ye-ve
grocery store	*ushqimorja*	oosh-chee-*mor*-ya
market	*tregu*	*tre*-goo
newsagency	*agjencia e lajmeve*	a-dyen-*tsee*-a e *lai*-me-ve
supermarket	*supermarketi*	soo-per-*mar*-ke-tee

Where can I buy (a padlock)?
Ku mund të blej (një dry)?   koo moond tuh bley (nyuh drew)

I'm looking for ...
Po kërkoj për ...   po kuhr-*koy* puhr ...

Can I look at it?
Ta shikoj pak?   ta shee-*koy* pak

Do you have any others?
A keni të tjera?   a *ke*-nee tuh *tye*-ra

Does it have a guarantee?
A ka garanci? a ka ga·ran·*tsee*

Can I have it sent abroad?
A mund ta dërgoj jashtë shtetit? a moond ta duhr·*goy* yash·tuh *shte*·teet

Can I have my ... repaired?
A mund të ma riparoni ...? a moond tuh ma ree·pa·*ro*·nee ...

It's faulty.
Është prishur. uhsh·tuh *pree*·shoor

I'd like ..., please. *Desha ..., ju lutem.* de·sha ... yoo loo·tem
  a bag *një çantë* nyuh *chan*·tuh
  a refund *kthim të parave* ktheem tuh pa·*ra*·ve
  to return this *ta kthej këtë* ta kthey kuh·*tuh*

paying

How much is it?
Sa kushton? sa koosh·*ton*

Can you write down the price?
A mund ta shkruani çmimin? a moond ta *shkroo*·a·nee chmee·meen

That's too expensive.
Është shumë shtrenjtë. uhsh·tuh *shoo*·muh *shtreny*·tuh

What's your lowest price?
Cili është çmimi më i *tsee*·lee uhsh·tuh chmee·mee muh ee
ulët që ofroni? *oo*·luht chuh o·*fro*·nee

I'll give you (five) lek.
Do t'ju jap (pesë) lekë. do tyoo yap (*pe*·suh) *le*·kuh

There's a mistake in the bill.
Është gabim fatura. uhsh·tuh ga·*beem* fa·*too*·ra

Do you accept ...? *A pranoni ...?* a pra·*no*·nee ...
  credit cards *karta krediti* *kar*·ta kre·*dee*·tee
  debit cards *karta debitore* *kar*·ta de·bee·*to*·re
  travellers cheques *çeqe udhëtimi* *che*·che oo·dhuh·*tee*·mee

I'd like ..., please. *Dua ..., ju lutem.* *doo*·a ... yoo loo·tem
  a receipt *një faturë* nyuh fa·*too*·ruh
  my change *kusurin* koo·*soo*·reen

clothes & shoes

Can I try it on?	A mund ta provoj?	a moond ta pro-*voy*
My size is (40).	Numri im është (dyzet).	*noom*-ree eem uhsh-tuh (dew-*zet*)
It doesn't fit.	Nuk më nxë.	nook muh ndzuh
small	e vogël	e *vo*-guhl
medium	mesatare	me-sa-*ta*-re
large	e madh	e *ma*-dhe

books & music

I'd like a ...	Dua një ...	*doo*-a nyuh ...
newspaper	gazetë	ga-*ze*-tuh
(in English)	(në anglisht)	(nuh an-*gleesht*)
pen	stilolaps	stee-lo-*laps*

Is there an English-language bookshop?
A ka ndonjë librari të   a ka *ndo*-nyuh lee-bra-*ree* tuh
gjuhës angleze?   *dyoo*-huhs an-*gle*-ze

Can I listen to this?
A mund ta dëgjoj këtë?   a moond ta duh-*dyoy* kuh-*tuh*

photography

Can you ...?	A mund ...?	a moond ...
burn a CD from	të djeg një	tuh *dee*-eg nyuh
my memory card	CD nga karta	tsuh duh nga *kar*-ta
	ime e memorjes	*ee*-me e me-*mor*-yes
develop this film	ta laj këtë film	ta lai kuh-*tuh* feelm
load my film	fus filmin	foos *feel*-meen
I need a ... film	Më duhet një film ...	muh *doo*-het nyuh feelm ...
for this camera.	për këtë aparat	puhr kuh-*tuh* a-pa-*rat*
	fotografik.	fo-to-gra-*feek*
colour	me ngjyra	me *ndyew*-ra
slide	diapozitiv	dee-a-po-zee-*teev*
(200) speed	me shpejtësi	me shpey-tuh-*see*
	(dyqind)	(dew-cheend)

When will it be ready?   Kur do të jetë gati?   koor do tuh *ye*-tuh *ga*-tee

meeting people

greetings, goodbyes & introductions

Hello.	*Tungjatjeta.*	toon·dya·*tye*·ta
Hi.	*Ç'kemi.*	chke·mee
Good night.	*Natën e mirë.*	na·tuhn e *mee*·ruh
Goodbye/Bye.	*Mirupafshim.*	mee·roo·*paf*·sheem
See you later.	*Shihemi më vonë.*	shee·*he*·mee muh *vo*·nuh
Mr	*Zotëri*	zo·tuh·*ree*
Mrs	*Zonjë*	zo·nyuh
Miss	*Zonjushë*	zo·*nyoo*·shuh
How are you?	*Si jeni/je?* pol/inf	see ye·nee/ye
Fine, thanks.	*Mirë, faleminderit.*	*mee*·ruh fa·le·meen·*de*·reet
And you?	*Po ju/ti?* pol/inf	po yoo/tee
What's your name?	*Si quheni?*	see *choo*·he·nee
My name is …	*Unë quhem …*	*oo*·nuh *choo*·hem …
I'm pleased to	*Gëzohem që u*	guh·*zo*·hem chuh oo
meet you.	*njohëm.*	*nyo*·huhm
This is my …	*Ky është …*	kew *uhsh*·tuh …
boyfriend	*i dashuri im*	ee da·*shoo*·ree eem
brother	*vëllai im*	vuh·*lla*·ee eem
daughter	*vajza ime*	*vai*·za ee·me
father	*babai im*	ba·*ba*·ee eem
friend	*shoku im* m	*sho*·koo eem
	shoqja ime f	*sho*·chya ee·me
girlfriend	*e dashura ime*	e da·*shoo*·ra ee·me
husband	*burri im*	*boo*·rree eem
mother	*nëna ime*	*nuh*·na ee·me
partner (intimate)	*partneri im* m	part·*ne*·ree eem
	partnerja ime f	part·*ne*·rya ee·me
sister	*motra ime*	*mot*·ra ee·me
son	*djali im*	*dia*·lee eem
wife	*gruaja ime*	groo·a·ya ee·me
Here's my …	*Ja …*	ya …
address	*adresa ime*	ad·*re*·sa ee·me
email address	*adresa ime e*	ad·*re*·sa ee·me e
	emailit	ee·*mey*·leet

What's your ...?	Cila është ...?	tsee·la uhsh·tuh ...
address	adresa juaj	ad·re·sa yoo·ai
email address	adresa juaj e emailit	ad·re·sa yoo·ai ee ee·mey·leet

Here's my ...	Ja ...	ya ...
fax number	numri im i faksit	noom·ree eem ee fak·seet
phone number	numri im i	noom·ree eem ee
	telefonit	te·le·fo·neet

What's your ...?	Cili është ...?	tsee·lee uhsh·tuh ...
fax number	numri juaj i faksit	noom·ree yoo·ai ee fak·seet
phone number	numri juaj i	noom·ree yoo·ai ee
	telefonit	te·le·fo·neet

occupations

What's your occupation?	Ç' punë bëni?	chpoo·nuh buh·nee
I'm a/an ...	Jam ...	yam ...
artist	artist/artiste m/f	ar·teest/ar·tees·te
businessperson	biznesmen m	beez·nes·men
	biznesmene f	beez·nes·me·ne
manual worker	punëtor/punëtore m/f	poo·nuh·tor/poo·nuh·to·re
office worker	nëpunës m	nuh·poo·nuhs
	nëpunëse f	nuh·poo·nuh·se
student	student/studente m/f	stoo·dent/stoo·den·te
tradesperson	tregtar/tregtare m/f	treg·tar/treg·ta·re

background

Where are you from?	Nga jeni?	nga ye·nee
I'm from ...	Jam nga ...	yam nga ...
Australia	Australia	a·oos·tra·lee·a
Canada	Kanadaja	ka·na·da·ya
England	Anglia	an·glee·a
New Zealand	Zelanda e Re	ze·lan·da e re
the USA	Shtetet e Bashkuara	shte·tet e bash·koo·a·ra
Are you married?	A jeni i martuar? m	a ye·nee ee mar·too·ar
	A je e martuar? f	a ye e mar·too·ar
I'm married.	Jam i/e martuar. m/f	yam ee/e mar·too·ar
I'm single.	Jam beqar/beqare. m/f	yam be·char/be·cha·re

age

How old ...?	Sa vjeç ...?	sa vyech ...
are you	jeni/je pol/inf	ye-nee/ye
is your daughter	është vajza	uhsh-tuh vai-za
	juaj/jote pol/inf	yoo-ai/yo-te
is your son	djali juaj/yt pol/inf	dia-lee yoo-ai/ewt

I'm ... years old.
Jam ... vjeç.   yam ... vyech

He/She is ... years old.
Ai/Ajo është ... vjeç.   a-ee/a-yo uhsh-tuh ... vyech

feelings

I'm (not) ...	(Nuk) Kam ...	(nook) kam ...
Are you ...?	Po ju a keni ...?	po yoo a ke-nee ...
cold	ftohtë	ftoh-tuh
hot	vapë	va-puh
hungry	uri	oo-ree
thirsty	etje	et-ye

I'm (not) ...	(Nuk) Jam ...	(nook) yam ...
Are you ...?	Po ju a jeni ...?	po yoo a ye-nee ...
happy	i/e gëzuar m/f	ee/e guh-zoo-ar
OK	mirë	mee-ruh
sad	i/e mërzitur m/f	ee/e muhr-zee-toor
tired	i/e lodhur m/f	ee/e lo-dhoor

entertainment

going out

Where can I find ...?	Ku mund të gjej ...?	koo moond tuh dyey ...
clubs	një klub	nyuh kloob
gay venues	vendtakim për	vend-ta-keem puhr
	homoseksualë	ho-mo-sek-soo-a-luh
pubs	një bar	nyuh bar

I feel like going to a/the ...	*Dua të shkoj në ...*	doo-a tuh shkoy nuh ...
concert	*koncert*	kon-tsert
movies	*kinema*	kee-ne-ma
restaurant	*restorant*	res-to-rant
theatre	*teatër*	te-a-tuhr

interests

Do you like ...?	*A ju pëlqen ...?*	a yoo puhl-chen ...
I (don't) like ...	*(Nuk) Më pëlqen ...*	(nook) muh puhl-chen ...
art	*arti*	ar-tee
cooking	*gatimi*	ga-tee-mee
movies	*kinemaja*	kee-ne-ma-ya
reading	*leximi*	le-dzee-mee
sport	*sporti*	spor-tee
travelling	*udhëtimi*	oo-dhuh-tee-mee

Do you like to ...?	*A ju pëlqen të ...?*	a yoo puhl-chen tuh ...
dance	*vallëzoni*	va-lluh-zo-nee
go to concerts	*shkoni në koncerte*	shko-nee nuh kon-tser-te
listen to music	*dëgjoni muzikë*	duh-dyo-nee moo-zee-kuh

food & drink

finding a place to eat

Can you recommend a ...?	*A mund të më rekomandoni një ...?*	a moond tuh muh re-ko-man-do-nee nyuh ...
bar	*bar*	bar
café	*kafene*	ka-fe-ne
restaurant	*restorant*	res-to-rant

I'd like ..., please.	*Dua ..., ju lutem.*	doo-a ... yoo loo-tem
a table for (four)	*një tavolinë për (katër veta)*	nyuh ta-vo-lee-nuh puhr (ka-tuhr ve-ta)
the nonsmoking section	*një vend ku ndalohet duhani*	nyuh vend koo nda-lo-het doo-ha-nee
the smoking section	*një vend ku lejohet duhani*	nyuh vend koo le-yo-het doo-ha-nee

ordering food

breakfast	*mëngjes* m	muhn-*dyes*
lunch	*drekë* f	dre-kuh
dinner	*darkë* f	dar-kuh
snack	*zemër* f	ze-muhr

| What would you recommend? | *Çfarë më rekomandoni?* | chfa-ruh muh re-ko-man-*do*-nee |

I'd like (the) ..., please.	*Më sillni ..., ju lutem.*	muh *seell*-nee ... yoo *loo*-tem
bill	*faturën*	fa-*too*-ruhn
drink list	*listën e pijeve*	*lees*-tuhn e pee-ye-ve
menu	*menunë*	me-*noo*-nuh
that dish	*atë gjellën*	a-*tuh* dye-lluhn

drinks

(cup of) coffee/tea ...	*(filxhan) kafe/çaj ...*	(feel-*dyan*) ka-fe/chai ...
with milk	*me qumësht*	me *choo*-muhsht
without sugar	*pa sheqer*	pa she-*cher*

| (orange) juice | *lëng (portokalli)* m | luhng (por-to-*ka*-llee) |
| soft drink | *pije joalkolike* f | pee-ye yo-al-koo-*lee*-ke |

... water	*ujë ...*	*oo*-yuh ...
boiled	*i valuar*	ee va-*loo*-ar
mineral	*gline mineral*	*glee*-ne mee-ne-*ral*

in the bar

I'll have ...	*Dua ...*	*doo*-a ...
I'll buy you a drink.	*Do t'ju/të të qeras me një pije.* pol/inf	do tyoo/tuh tuh che-*ras* me nyuh *pee*-ye
What would you like?	*Çfarë dëshironi?*	chfa-ruh duh-shee-*ro*-nee
Cheers!	*Gëzuar!*	guh-*zoo*-ar

a bottle/glass of beer	*një shishe/gotë birrë*	nyuh *shee*-she/go-tuh *bee*-rruh
cocktail	*koktej* m	kok-*tey*
cognac	*konjak* m	ko-*nyak*
a shot of (whisky)	*një gllënjkë (uiski)*	nyuh *glluhny*-kuh (*oo*-ees-kee)

a bottle/glass	një shishe/gotë	nyuh *shee*·she/*go*·tuh
of ... wine	verë ...	*ve*·ruh ...
red	të kuqe	tuh *koo*·che
sparkling	me shkumë	me *shkoo*·muh
white	të bardhë	tuh *bar*·dhuh

self-catering

What's the local speciality?
    Cili është specialiteti vendas?   tsee·lee *uhsh*·tuh spe·tsee·a·lee·*te*·tee *ven*·das

How much is (a kilo of cheese)?
    Sa kushton (një kilogram djathë)?   sa koosh·*ton* (nyuh kee·lo·*gram* dia·thuh)

I'd like ...	Dua ...	*doo*·a ...
(100) grams	(njëqind) gram	(nyuh·*cheend*) gram
(two) kilos	(dy) kile	(dew) *kee*·le
(three) pieces	(tri) copa	(tree) *tso*·pa
(six) slices	(gjashtë) feta	(*dyash*·tuh) *fe*·ta

Less.	Më pak.	muh pak
Enough.	Mjaft.	myaft
More.	Më shumë.	muh *shoo*·muh

special diets & allergies

Is there a vegetarian restaurant near here?
    A ka ndonjë restorant   a ka *ndo*·nyuh res·to·*rant*
    vegjetarian këtu afër?   ve·dye·ta·ree·*an* kuh·*too* a·fuhr

Could you prepare	A mund të përgatisni	a moond tuh puhr·ga·*tees*·nee
a meal without ...?	një gjellë pa ...?	nyuh *dye*·lluh pa ...
butter	gjalpë	*dyal*·puh
eggs	vezë	*ve*·zuh
meat stock	lëng mishi	luhng *mee*·shee

I'm allergic to ...	Kam alergji ndaj ...	kam a·ler·*dyee* ndai ...
dairy produce	bulmetrave	bool·*me*·tra·ve
gluten	glutenit	gloo·*te*·neet
MSG	msg·së	*muh*·suh·guh·suh
nuts	arrave	*a*·rra·ve
seafood	prodhimeve të detit	pro·*dhee*·me·ve tuh *de*·teet

menu decoder

burani f	boo·ra·*nee*	*dish of spinach, rice & other greens*
byrek m	bew·*rek*	*filo pastry stuffed with cheese or spinach*
çomlek m	chom·*lek*	*meat & onion stew*
djathë i fërguar m	dia·thuh ee fuhr·*goo*·ar	*fried cheese*
dollma me lakër f	doll·*ma* me *la*·kuhr	*stuffed cabbage leaves*
fërgesë f	fuhr·*ge*·suh	*rich beef stew with cheese*
fërgesë Tirane f	fuhr·*ge*·suh tee·*ra*·ne	*dish of offal, eggs & tomatoes*
filetë peshku me arra f	fee·*le*·tuh *pesh*·koo me *a*·rra	*fish fillet with nuts*
gjel deti m	dyel *de*·tee	*turkey*
hallvë f	*hall*·vuh	*dessert with fried almonds in syrup*
jani me fasule f	ya·*nee* me fa·*soo*·le	*thick bean soup*
japrakë me mish m pl	ya·*pra*·kuh me meesh	*vine leaves stuffed with meat & rice*
kadaif m	ka·da·*eef*	*pastry soaked in sugar syrup & flavoured with nuts*
kukurec m	koo·koo·*rets*	*roasted entrails of sheep or goat*
kurabie f	koo·ra·*bee*·e	*oval-shaped biscuits*
lakror misri m	lak·*ror* mees·ree	*corn pie*
midhje në verë të bardhë f pl	mee·dhye nuh *ve*·ruh tuh *bar*·dhuh	*mussels in white wine*
mish qingji m	meesh *cheen*·dyee	*fried veal with walnuts*
musaka me patate f	moo·sa·*ka* me pa·*ta*·te	*potato casserole*
omëletë me djathë f	om·*le*·tuh me *dia*·thuh	*cheese omelette*
paidhaqe f	pai·*dha*·che	*grilled lamb ribs*
pastiço me djathë f	pas·*tee*·cho me *dia*·thuh	*pie with noodles, cheese, eggs & meat*

patate të skuqura f pl	pa-*ta*-te tuh *skoo*-choo-ra	fried potatoes
patëllxhane të mbushura m pl	pa-tuhll-*dya*-ne tuh *mboo*-shoo-ra	stuffed eggplants
peshk i pjekur m	peshk ee *pye*-koor	grilled fish
petulla me kos f pl	pe-too-lla me kos	pancakes with yogurt
pulë e pjekur me oriz f	*poo*-luh e *pye*-koor me o-*reez*	fried chicken with rice
pulë me arra f	*poo*-luh me *a*-rra	fried chicken with walnuts
qefull i furrës m	*che*-fooll ee *foo*-rruhs	baked mullet
qofte f	*chof*-te	meatballs
romstek m	rom-*stek*	mincemeat patties
rosto me salcë kosi f	*ros*-to me *sal*-tsuh *ko*-see	roast beef with sour cream
sallatë me fasule f	sa-*lla*-tuh me fa-*soo*-le	bean salad
shishqebap m	sheesh-che-*bap*	grilled meat on a skewer
speca të mbushur m pl	*spe*-tsa tuh *mboo*-shoor	stuffed peppers
spinaq me kos m	spee-*nach* me kos	spinach with yogurt
supë me barishte f	*soo*-puh me ba-*reesh*-te	vegetable soup
supë me patate e lakër f	*soo*-puh me pa-*ta*-te e *la*-kuhr	potato & cabbage soup
tarator m	ta-ra-*tor*	yogurt & cucumber salad
tavë Elbasani f	*ta*-vuh el-ba-*sa*-nee	baked lamb with yogurt, eggs & rice
tavë kosi f	*ta*-vuh *ko*-see	baked lamb with yogurt
tavë me peshk f	*ta*-vuh me peshk	fish casserole
tavë me presh f	*ta*-vuh me presh	baked leeks with ground meat
turli perimesh m pl	toor-*lee* pe-*ree*-mesh	sautéed vegetables (potatoes, tomatoes, eggplant & peppers)

emergencies

basics

Help!	Ndihmë!	ndeeh·muh
Stop!	Ndal!	ndal
Go away!	Ik!	eek
Thief!	Hajdut!	hai·doot
Fire!	Zjarr!	zyarr
Watch out!	Kujdes!	kooy·des

Call ...!	Thirrni ...!	theerr·nee ...
a doctor	doktorin	dok·to·reen
an ambulance	ambulancën	am·boo·lan·tsuhn
the police	policinë	po·lee·tsee·nuh

It's an emergency!
Është urgjente! · uhsh·tuh oor·dyen·te

Could you help me, please?
A mund të më ndihmoni, ju lutem? · a moond tuh muh ndeeh·mo·nee yoo loo·tem

I have to use the telephone.
Më duhet të përdor telefonin. · muh doo·het tuh puhr·dor te·le·fo·neen

I'm lost.
Kam humbur rrugën. · kam hoom·boor rroo·guhn

Where are the toilets?
Ku janë banjat? · koo ya·nuh ba·nyat

police

Where's the police station?
Ku është rajoni i policisë? · koo uhsh·tuh ra·yo·nee ee po·lee·tsee·suh

I want to report an offence.
Dua të bëj një denoncim. · doo·a tuh buh·ey nyuh de·non·tseem

I have insurance.
Kam sigurim. · kam see·goo·reem

I've been ...	Më kanë ...	muh ka·nuh ...
assaulted	sulmuar	sool·moo·ar
raped	përdhunuar	puhr·dhoo·noo·ar
robbed	plaçkitur	plach·kee·toor

I've lost my ...	Kam humbur ...	kam *hoom*·boor ...
My ... was/were stolen.	Ma/M'i vodhën ...sg/pl	ma/mee vo·dhuhn ...
backpack	çantën e shpinës sg	*chan*·tuhn e *shpee*·nuhs
bags	çantat pl	*chan*·tat
credit card	kartën e kreditit sg	*kar*·tuhn e kre·*dee*·teet
handbag	çantën e dorës sg	*chan*·tuhn e *do*·ruhs
jewellery	bizhuteritë pl	bee·zhoo·te·*ree*·tuh
money	paratë pl	pa·*ra*·tuh
passport	pasaportën sg	pa·sa·*por*·tuhn
travellers cheques	çeqet e udhëtimit pl	*che*·chet e oo·dhuh·*tee*·meet
wallet	kuletën sg	koo·*le*·tuhn

I want to contact my ...	Dua të lidhem me ... time.	*doo*·a tuh *lee*·dhem me ... *tee*·me
consulate	konsullatën	kon·soo·*lla*·tuhn
embassy	ambasadën	am·ba·*sa*·duhn

health

medical needs

Where's the nearest ...?	Ku është ... më i afërt?	koo *uhsh*·tuh ... muh ee *a*·fuhrt
dentist	dentisti	den·*tees*·tee
doctor	doktori	dok·*to*·ree
hospital	spitali	spee·*ta*·lee
(night) pharmacist	farmacisti (i natës)	far·ma·*tsees*·tee (ee *na*·tuhs)

I need a doctor (who speaks English).
Kam nevojë për një mjek (që flet anglisht).
kam ne·*vo*·yuh puhr nyuh myek (chuh flet an·*gleesht*)

Could I see a female doctor?
A mund të vizitohem te një mjeke?
a moond tuh vee·zee·*to*·hem te nyuh *mye*·ke

I've run out of my medication.
Më është mbaruar ilaçi.
muh *uhsh*·tuh mba·*roo*·ar ee·*la*·chee

symptoms, conditions & allergies

I'm sick.	Jam i/e sëmurë. m/f	yam ee/e suh·*moo*·ruh
It hurts here.	Më dhemb këtu.	muh dhemb kuh·*too*

I have (a) ...		
asthma	Jam me azëm.	yam me *a*·zuhm
bronchitis	Jam me bronkit.	yam me bron·*keet*
constipation	Jam bërë kaps.	yam *buh*·ruh kaps
cough	Jam me kollë.	yam me *ko*·lluh
diarrhoea	Më shkon bark.	muh shkon bark
fever	Kam temperaturë.	kam tem·pe·ra·*too*·ruh
headache	Kam dhimbje koke.	kam *dheem*·bye *ko*·ke
heart condition	Jam me zemër.	yam me *ze*·muhr
nausea	Më përzihet.	muh puhr·*zee*·het
pain	Kam dhimbje.	kam *dheem*·bye
sore throat	Më dhembin grykët.	muh *dhem*·been *grew*·kuht
toothache	Më dhemb dhëmbi.	muh dhemb *dhuhm*·bee

I'm allergic to ...	Kam alergji ndaj ...	kam a·ler·*dyee* ndai ...
antibiotics	antibiotikëve	an·tee·bee·o·*tee*·kuh·ve
anti- inflammatories	ilaçeve antipezmatuese	ee·*la*·che·ve an·tee·pez·ma·*too*·e·se
aspirin	aspirinës	as·pee·*ree*·nuhs
bees	bletëve	*ble*·tuh·ve
codeine	kodinës	ko·*dee*·nuhs
penicillin	penicilinës	pe·nee·tsee·*lee*·nuhs

antiseptic	antiseptik m	an·tee·sep·*teek*
bandage	fasho f	*fa*·sho
condoms	prezervativ m	pre·zer·va·*teev*
contraceptives	kontraceptiv m	kon·tra·tsep·*teev*
diarrhoea medicine	ilaç për diarrenë m	ee·*lach* puhr dee·a·*rre*·nuh
insect repellent	ilaç insektlargues m	ee·*lach* een·sekt·lar·*goo*·es
laxatives	laksativ m	lak·sa·*teev*
painkillers	ilaç kundër dhimbjes m	ee·*lach* koon·duhr *dheem*·byes
rehydration salts	kripëra rihidruese f pl	kree·*puh*·ra ree·hee·*droo*·e·se
sleeping tablets	hape gjumi f pl	*ha*·pe *dyoo*·mee

english–albanian dictionary

Albanian nouns in this dictionary have their gender indicated by ⓜ (masculine) or ⓕ (feminine). If it's a plural noun, you'll also see pl. Adjectives are given in the masculine form only. Words are also marked as a (adjective), v (verb), sg (singular), pl (plural), inf (informal) or pol (polite) where necessary.

A

accident aksident ⓜ ak-see-dent
accommodation vend për të fjetur ⓜ
   vend puhr tuh fye-toor
adaptor adaptor ⓜ a-dap-tor
address adresë ⓕ ad-re-suh
after pas pas
air-conditioned me ajër të kondicionuar
   me a-yuhr tuh kon-dee-tsee-o-noo-ar
airplane aeroplan ⓜ a-e-ro-plan
airport aeroport ⓜ a-e-ro-port
Albania Shqipëri ⓕ shchee-puh-ree
Albanian (language) gjuha shqipe ⓕ dyoo-ha shchee-pe
Albanian a shqip shcheep
alcohol alkool ⓜ al-kol
all gjithë dyee-thuh
allergy alergji ⓕ a-ler-dyee
ambulance ambulancë ⓕ am-boo-lan-tsuh
and dhe dhe
ankle thembër ⓕ them-buhr
arm krah ⓜ krah
ashtray tavëll duhani ⓕ ta-vuhll doo-ha-nee
ATM makinë automatike për të holla ⓕ
   ma-kee-nuh a-oo-to-ma-tee-ke puhr tuh ho-lla

B

baby bebe ⓕ be-be
back (body) shpinë ⓕ shpee-nuh
backpack çantë shpine ⓕ chan-tuh shpee-ne
bad keq kech
bag çantë ⓕ chan-tuh
baggage claim tërheqje e bagazhit ⓕ
   tuhr-hech-ye e ba-ga-zheet
bank bankë ⓕ ban-kuh
bar bar ⓜ bar
bathroom banjë ⓕ ba-nyuh
battery bateri ⓕ ba-te-ree
beautiful i bukur ee boo-koor
bed krevat ⓜ kre-vat
beer birrë ⓕ bee-rruh

before përpara puhr-pa-ra
behind mbrapa mbra-pa
bicycle biçikletë ⓕ bee-chee-kle-tuh
big i madh ee madh
bill faturë ⓕ fa-too-ruh
black i zi ee zee
blanket batanije ⓕ ba-ta-nee-ye
blood group grup gjaku ⓜ groop dya-koo
blue blu bloo
boat anije ⓕ a-nee-ye
book (make a reservation) v rezervoj re-zer-voy
bottle shishe ⓕ shee-she
bottle opener hapës shishesh ⓜ ha-puhs shee-shesh
boy djalë ⓜ dia-luh
brakes (car) frena ⓜ pl fre-na
breakfast mëngjes ⓜ muhn-dyes
broken (faulty) i prishur ee pree-shoor
bus autobus ⓜ a-oo-to-boos
business biznes ⓜ beez-nes
buy blej bley

C

café kafene ⓕ ka-fe-ne
camera aparat fotografik ⓜ a-pa-rat fo-to-gra-feek
camp site vend kampimi ⓜ vend kam-pee-mee
cancel anuloj a-noo-loy
can opener hapës konservash ⓜ ha-puhs kon-ser-vash
car makinë ⓕ ma-kee-nuh
cash të holla ⓕ pl tuh ho-lla
cash (a cheque) v thyej (një çek) thew-ey (nyuh chek)
cell phone telefon celular ⓜ te-le-fon tse-loo-lar
centre qendër ⓕ chen-duhr
change (money) v këmbej (para) kuhm-bey (pa-ra)
cheap i lirë ee lee-ruh
check (bill) faturë ⓕ fa-too-ruh
check-in regjistrohem re-dyees-tro-hem
chest kraharor ⓜ kra-ha-ror
child fëmijë ⓕ fuh-mee-yuh
cigarette cigare ⓕ tsee-ga-re
city qytet ⓜ chew-tet
clean a i pastër ee pas-tuhr

closed *mbyllur* mbew-lloor
coffee *kafe* ① ka-fe
coins *monedha* ① pl mo-ne-dha
cold a *i ftohtë* ee ftoh-tuh
collect call *telefonatë e paguar nga marrësi* ①
  te-le-fo-na-tuh e pa-goo-ar nga ma-rruh-see
come *vij* veey
computer *kompjuter* ⑩ kom-pyoo-ter
condom *prezervativ* ⑩ pre-zer-va-teev
contact lenses *lente kontakti* ① pl len-te kon-tak-tee
cook v *gatuaj* ga-too-ai
cost *kosto* ⑩ kos-to
credit card *kartë krediti* ① kar-tuh kre-dee-tee
cup *gotë* ① go-tuh
currency exchange *këmbim valute* ⑩
  kuhm-beem va-loo-te
customs (immigration) *doganë* ① do-ga-nuh

D

dangerous *i rrezikshëm* ee rre-zeek-shuhm
date *datë* ① da-tuh
day *ditë* ① dee-tuh
delay *vonesë* ① vo-ne-suh
dentist *dentist* ⑩ den-teest
depart *nisem* nee-sem
diaper *pelenë* ① pe-le-nuh
dictionary *fjalor* ⑩ fya-lor
dinner *darkë* ① dar-kuh
direct *direkt* dee-rekt
dirty *i pistë* ee pees-tuh
disabled *invalid* een-va-leed
discount *zbritje* ① zbree-tye
doctor *doktor* ⑩ dok-tor
double bed *krevat dopjo* ⑩ kre-vat dop-yo
double room *dhomë dopjo* ① dho-muh dop-yo
drink *pije* ① pee-ye
drive v *jap makinës* yap ma-kee-nuhs
drivers licence *patentë shoferi* ① pa-ten-tuh sho-fe-ree
drug (illicit) *drogë* ① dro-guh
dummy (pacifier) *biberon* ⑩ bee-be-ron

E

ear *vesh* ⑩ vesh
east *lindje* ① leen-dye
eat *ha* ha
economy class *klasë ekonomike* ①
  kla-suh e-ko-no-mee-ke
electricity *elektricitet* ⑩ e-lek-tree-tsee-tet
elevator *ashensor* ⑩ a-shen-sor

email *email • postë elektronike*
  ee-meyl • pos-tuh e-lek-tro-nee-ke
embassy *ambasadë* ① am-ba-sa-duh
emergency *urgjencë* ① oor-dyen-tsuh
English (language) *anglisht* ang-leesht
entrance *hyrje* ① hewr-ye
evening *mbrëmje* ① mbruhm-ye
exchange rate *kurs këmbimi* ⑩ koors kuhm-bee-mee
exit *dalje* ① dal-ye
expensive *i shtrenjtë* ee shtreny-tuh
express mail *postë ekspres* ① pos-tuh eks-pres
eye *sy* ⑩ sew

F

far *larg* larg
fast *shpejt* shpeyt
father *baba* ⑩ ba-ba
film (camera) *film* ⑩ feelm
finger *gisht* ⑩ geesht
first-aid kit *kuti e ndihmës së shpejtë* ①
  koo-tee e ndeeh-muhs suh shpey-tuh
first class *klas i parë* ⑩ klas ee pa-ruh
fish *peshk* ⑩ peshk
food *ushqim* ⑩ oosh-cheem
foot *këmbë* ① kuhm-buh
fork *pirun* ① pee-roon
free (of charge) *falas* fa-las
friend *shok/shoqe* ⑩/① shok/sho-che
fruit *frutë* ① froo-tuh
full *plot* plot
funny *për të qeshur* puhr tuh che-shoor

G

gift *dhuratë* ① dhoo-ra-tuh
girl *vajzë* ① vai-zuh
glass (drinking) *gotë* ① go-tuh
glasses *syze* ① pl sew-ze
go *shkoj* shkoy
good *mirë* mee-ruh
green *jeshil* ye-sheel
guide *shoqërues* sho-chuh-roo-es

H

half *gjysmë* ① dyews-muh
hand *dorë* ① do-ruh
handbag *çantë dore* ① chan-tuh do-re
happy *i gëzuar* ee guh-zoo-ar
have *kam* kam

he *ai* a-ee
head *kokë* ① ko-kuh
heart *zemër* ① ze-muhr
heat *nxehtësi* ① ndzeh-tuh-see
heavy *i rëndë* ee ruhn-duh
help v *ndihmoj* ndeeh-moy
here *këtu* kuh-too
high *lart* lart
highway *rrugë kryesore automobilistike* ①
   rroo-guh krew-e-so-re a-oo-to-mo-bee-lees-tee-ke
hike v *eci në natyrë* e-tsee nuh na-tew-ruh
holiday *pushime* ⑰ pl poo-shee-me
homosexual *homoseksual* ho-mo-sek-soo-al
hospital *spital* ⑫ spee-tal
hot *i nxehtë* ee ndzeh-tuh
hotel *hotel* ⑫ ho-tel
hungry *i uritur* ee oo-ree-toor
husband *burrë* ⑫ boo-rruh**

I

I *unë* oo-nuh
identification (card) *kartë identifikimi* ①
   kar-tuh ee-den-tee-fee-kee-mee
ill *i sëmurë* ee suh-moo-ruh
important *i rëndësishëm* ee ruhn-duh-see-shuhm
included *përfshihet* puhr-fshee-het
injury *lëndim* luhn-deem
insurance *sigurim* ① see-goo-reem
Internet *internet* ⑫ een-ter-net
interpreter *përkthyes* puhr-kthew-es

J

jewellery *bizhuteri* ① pl bee-zhoo-te-ree
job *punë* ① poo-nuh

K

key *çelës* ⑫ che-luhs
kilogram *kilogram* ⑫kee-lo-gram
kitchen *kuzhinë* ① koo-zhee-nuh
knife *thikë* ① thee-kuh
Kosovo *Kosovë* ① ko-so-vuh

L

laundry (place) *lavanteri* ① la-van-te-ree
lawyer *avokat* ⑫ a-vo-kat
left (direction) *majtas* mai-tas

left-luggage office *zyra për lënien e valixheve* ①
   zew-ra puhr luh-nee-en e va-lee-dye-ve
leg *këmbë* ① kuhm-buh
lesbian *lezbiane* lez-bee-a-ne
less *më pak* muh pak
letter (mail) *letër* ① le-tuhr
lift (elevator) *ashensor* ⑫ a-shen-sor
light *dritë* ① dree-tuh
like v *pëlqej* puhl-chey
lock *kyç* ⑫ kewch
long *i gjatë* ee dya-tuh
lost *i humbur* ee hoom-boor
lost-property office *zyra e sendeve të humbura* ①
   zew-ra e sen-de-ve tuh hoom-boo-ra
love v *dashuroj* da-shoo-roy
luggage *valixhe* ① va-lee-dye
lunch *drekë* ① dre-kuh

M

mail *postë* ① pos-tuh
man *burrë* ⑫ boo-rruh
map *hartë* ① har-tuh
market *treg* ⑫ treg
matches *shkrepëse* ① shkre-puh-se
meat *mish* ⑫ meesh
medicine *ilaç* ⑫ ee-lach
menu *menu* ① me-noo
message *mesazh* ⑫ me-sazh
milk *qumësht* ⑫ choo-muhsht
minute *minutë* ① mee-noo-tuh
mobile phone *telefon celular* ⑫ te-le-fon tse-loo-lar
money *para* ① pa-ra
month *muaj* ⑫ moo-ai
morning *mëngjes* ⑫ muhn-dyes
mother *nënë* ① nuh-nuh
motorcycle *motor* ⑫ mo-tor
motorway *autostradë* ① a-oo-tos-tra-duh
mouth *gojë* ① go-yuh
music *muzikë* ① moo-zee-kuh

N

name *emër* ⑫ e-muhr
napkin *pecetë* ① pe-tse-tuh
nappy *pelenë* ① pe-le-nuh
near *afër* a-fuhr
neck *qafë* ① cha-fuh
new *i ri* ee ree
news *lajm* ⑫ laim
newspaper *gazetë* ① ga-ze-tuh

night *natë* ① na-tuh
no *jo* yo
noisy *i zhurmshëm* ee zhoorm-shuhm
nonsmoking *ku ndalohet duhani*
koo nda-lo-het doo-ha-nee
north *veri* ① ve-ree
nose *hundë* ① hoon-duh
now *tani* ta-nee
number *numër* ① noo-muhr

O

oil (engine) *vaj* ⓜ vai
old *i vjetër* ee vye-tuhr
one-way ticket *biletë vetëm për vajtje* ①
bee-le-tuh ve-tuhm puhr vai-tye
open a *i hapur* ee ha-poor
outside *jashtë* yash-tuh

P

package *pako* ① pa-ko
paper *letër* ① le-tuhr
park (car) v *parkoj* par-koy
passport *pasaportë* ① pa-sa-por-tuh
pay *paguaj* pa-goo-ai
pen *stilolaps* ⓜ stee-lo-laps
petrol *benzinë* ① ben-zee-nuh
pharmacy *farmaci* ① far-ma-tsee
phonecard *kartë telefonike* ① kar-tuh te-le-fo-nee-ke
photo *fotografi* ① fo-to-gra-fee
plate *pjatë* ① pya-tuh
police *polici* ① po-lee-tsee
postcard *kartolinë* ① kar-to-lee-nuh
post office *postë* ① pos-tuh
pregnant *shtatzënë* shtat-zuh-nuh
price *çmim* ⓜ chmeem

Q

quiet *i qetë* i che-tuh

R

rain *shi* ⓜ shee
razor *brisk* ⓜ breesk
receipt *faturë* ① fa-too-ruh
red *i kuq* ee kooch
refund *kthim parash* ⓜ ktheem pa-rash
registered mail *letër rekomande* ①
le-tuhr re-ko-man-de

rent v *marr me qira* marr me chee-ra
repair v *riparoj* ree-pa-roy
reservation *rezervim* ⓜ re-zer-veem
restaurant *restorant* ⓜ res-to-rant
return v *kthej* kthey
return ticket *biletë kthimi* ① bee-le-tuh kthee-mee
right (direction) *djathtas* diath-tas
road *rrugë* ① rroo-guh
room *dhomë* ① dho-muh

S

safe a *i sigurt* ee see-goort
sanitary napkin *pecetë higjienike* ①
pe-tse-tuh hee-dyee-e-nee-ke
seat *vend* ⓜ vend
send *dërgoj* duhr-goy
service station *pikë karburanti* ①
pee-kuh kar-boo-ran-tee
sex *seks* ⓜ seks
shampoo *shampo* ① sham-po
share (a dorm) *marr (dhomë) bashkë*
marr (dho-muh) bash-kuh
shaving cream *pastë rroje* ① pas-tuh rro-ye
she *ajo* a-yo
sheet (bed) *çarçaf* ⓜ char-chaf
shirt *këmishë* ① kuh-mee-shuh
shoes *këpucë* ① kuh-poo-tsuh
shop *dyqan* ⓜ dew-chan
short *i shkurtër* ee shkoor-tuhr
shower *dush* ⓜ doosh
single room *dhomë teke* ① dho-muh te-ke
skin *lëkurë* ① luh-koo-ruh
skirt *fund* ⓜ foond
sleep v *fle* fle
slowly *me ngadalë* me nga-da-luh
small *i vogël* ee vo-guhl
smoke (cigarettes) v *pij cigare* peey tsee-ga-re
soap *sapun* ⓜ sa-poon
some *disa* dee-sa
soon *së shpejti* suh shpey-tee
south *jug* ⓜ yoog
souvenir shop *dyqan suveniresh* ⓜ
dew-chan soo-ve-nee-resh
speak *flas* flas
spoon *lugë* ① loo-guh
stamp *pullë* ① poo-lluh
stand-by ticket *biletë rezervë* ① bee-le-tuh re-zer-vuh
station (train) *stacion (treni)* ⓜ sta-tsee-on (tre-nee)
stomach *stomak* ⓜ sto-mak
stop v *ndaloj* nda-loy

(bus) stop *stacion (autobusi)* ⓜ sta-tsee-*on* (a-oo-to-*boo*-see)

street *rrugë* ⓕ rroo-guh

student *student/studente* ⓜ / ⓕ stoo-*dent*/stoo-*den*-te

sun *diell* ⓜ dee-ell

sunscreen *krem mbrojtës* ⓜ krem *mbroy*-tuhs

swim v *notoj* no-*toy*

T

tampons *tampona* ⓕ pl tam-*po*-na

taxi *taksi* ⓕ tak-*see*

teaspoon *lugë caji* ⓕ loo-guh *cha*-yee

teeth *dhëmbë* ⓕ pl *dhuhm*-buh

telephone *telefon* ⓜ te-le-*fon*

television *televizor* ⓜ te-le-vee-*zor*

temperature (weather) *temperaturë* ⓕ tem-pe-ra-*too*-ruh

tent *çadër* ⓕ *cha*-duhr

that (one) *atë* a-*tuh*

they *ata* a-*ta*

thirsty *i etur* ee e-*toor*

this (one) *këtë* kuh-*tuh*

throat *grykë* ⓕ *grew*-kuh

ticket *biletë* ⓕ bee-*le*-tuh

time *kohë* ⓕ *ko*-huh

tired *i lodhur* ee lo-*dhoor*

tissues *shami letre* ⓕ sha-*mee* le-tre

today *sot* sot

toilet *banjë* ⓕ *ba*-nyuh

tomorrow *nesër* ne-*suhr*

tonight *sonte* son-te

toothbrush *furçë dhëmbësh* ⓕ *foor*-chuh *dhuhm*-buhsh

toothpaste *pastë dhëmbësh* *pas*-tuh *dhuhm*-buhsh

torch (flashlight) *elektrik dore* e-lek-*treek* do-re

tour *vizitë* ⓕ vee-*zee*-tuh

tourist office *zyrë turistike* ⓕ *zew*-ruh too-rees-*tee*-ke

towel *peshqir* ⓜ pesh-*cheer*

train *tren* ⓜ tren

translate *përkthej* puhr-*kthey*

travel agency *agjenci udhëtimi* ⓕ a-dyen-*tsee* oo-dhuh-*tee*-mee

travellers cheque *çek udhëtimi* ⓜ chek oo-dhuh-*tee*-mee

trousers *pantallona* ⓕ pl pan-ta-*llo*-na

twin beds *krevatë dyshë* ⓜ pl kre-va-tuh *dew*-shuh

tyre *gomë* ⓕ *go*-muh

U

underwear ⓕ pl *mbathje* mba-thye

urgent *urgjent* oor-*dyent*

V

vacant *bosh* bosh

vacation *pushime* ⓜ pl poo-*shee*-me

vegetable *zarzavate* ⓕ zar-za-*va*-te

vegetarian a *vegjetarian* ve-dye-ta-ree-*an*

visa *vizë* ⓕ vee-*zuh*

W

waiter *kamarier* ka-ma-*ree*-er

walk v *eci* e-*tsee*

wallet *kuletë* ⓕ koo-*le*-tuh

warm a *i ngrohtë* ee ngroh-tuh

wash (something) *laj* lai

watch *orë dore* ⓕ o-ruh do-re

water *ujë* ⓕ oo-yuh

we *ne* ne

weekend *fundjavë* ⓕ foond-ya-vuh

west *perëndim* pe-ruhn-*deem*

wheelchair *karrocë invalidi* ⓕ ka-*rro*-tsuh een-va-lee-dee

when *kur* koor

where *ku* koo

white *i bardhë* ee *bar*-dhuh

who *kush* koosh

why *pse* pse

wife *grua* ⓕ *groo*-a

window *dritare* ⓕ dree-*ta*-re

wine *verë* ⓕ *ve*-ruh

with *me* me

without *pa* pa

woman *grua* ⓕ *groo*-a

write *shkruaj* shkroo-ai

Y

yellow *i verdhë* ee *ver*-dhuh

yes *po* po

yesterday *dje* dee-*e*

you sg inf *ti* tee

you sg pol & pl *ju* yoo

Bulgarian

bulgarian alphabet

А а a	**Б б** buh	**В в** vuh	**Г г** guh	**Д д** duh
Е е e	**Ж ж** zhuh	**З з** zuh	**И и** ee	**Й й** ee *krat*-ko
К к kuh	**Л л** luh	**М м** muh	**Н н** nuh	**О о** o
П п puh	**Р р** ruh	**С с** suh	**Т т** tuh	**У у** oo
Ф ф fuh	**Х х** huh	**Ц ц** tsuh	**Ч ч** chuh	**Ш ш** shuh
Щ щ shtuh	**Ъ ъ** uh	**ь** er *ma*-luhk	**Ю ю** yoo	**Я я** ya

bulgarian

БЪЛГАРСКИ

introduction

Surprisingly, the name of the oldest South Slavic literary language, Bulgarian (български *buhl-*gar-skee), isn't of Slavic origin. It's one of a handful of words remaining in Bulgarian from the language of the Bulgars, a Turkic people who invaded the eastern Balkans in the late 7th century. Together with their language, they were assimilated by the local Slavs, who had crossed the Danube and settled in the peninsula at the start of the 6th century.

As a member of the South Slavic group of languages, Bulgarian has Macedonian and Serbian as its closest relatives. However, it also shows similarities with the non-Slavic languages in the so-called Balkan linguistic union (Romanian, Albanian and Greek), as a result of multilingualism and interaction among the Balkan nations. These foreign influences explain many of its grammatical features – for example, the lack of noun cases, which sets Bulgarian (and Macedonian) apart from the other Slavic languages. In addition, numerous Turkish words entered the Bulgarian vocabulary during five centuries of Ottoman rule. During the 19th century, many of the loanwords from Turkish were eliminated from the language. Their place was partially filled by Russian words, as Russian has influenced Bulgarian through both Bulgaria's ties with the Orthodox Church and long-standing cultural ties with Russia.

Old Bulgarian (also known as Old Church Slavonic) was the first Slavic language recorded in written form, in religious literature from the 9th century. The central figures in the development of the Slavic literary language were Saints Cyril and Methodius, Byzantine Orthodox missionaries who invented the Glagolitic alphabet around 863 AD and used it to translate Greek liturgical texts into Old Church Slavonic. Their disciples devised the Cyrillic alphabet (based on Greek and Glagolitic) in which Bulgarian has been written ever since. In its modern version, standardised after the last spelling reform in 1945, it's very similar to the Russian Cyrillic alphabet. Today, Bulgarians celebrate St Cyril and Methodius Day as a national holiday on 24 May (also known as the Day of Bulgarian Culture or the Cyrillic Alphabet Day).

Modern Bulgarian has about 9 million speakers and is the official language of Bulgaria, with Bulgarian-speaking minorities in Ukraine, Moldova, Romania, Serbia, Hungary, Greece and Turkey. The literary standard is based on the northeastern dialects. The transitional dialects spoken around the borders between Bulgaria, Serbia and Macedonia are very similar and the political issues arising from this linguistic similarity have been sensitive throughout history.

pronunciation

vowel sounds

The vowels in Bulgarian all have equivalents in English, so you shouldn't have any problems. To make yourself sound like a native, just remember that in Bulgarian, vowels in unstressed syllables are generally pronounced shorter and weaker than they are in stressed syllables.

symbol	english equivalent	bulgarian example	transliteration
a	**father**	дата	*da*·ta
ai	**aisle**	май	mai
e	**bet**	лек	lek
ee	**see**	бира	*bee*·ra
o	**pot**	вода	vo·*da*
oo	**zoo**	тук	took
uh	**ago**	къде	kuh·*de*

word stress

There's no general rule regarding word stress in Bulgarian – it can fall on any syllable and sometimes changes in different grammatical forms of the same word. Just follow our coloured pronunciation guides, in which the stressed syllable is always in italics.

consonant sounds

The consonant sounds in Bulgarian are pretty straightforward, as they all have equivalents in English. The only sound you might trip over is ts, which can occur at the start of words. Try saying 'cats', then 'ats', then 'ts' to get the idea.

symbol	english equivalent	bulgarian example	transliteration
b	**bed**	брат	brat
ch	**ch**eat	чист	cheest
d	**d**og	душ	doosh
f	**f**at	фенерче	fe-*ner*-che
g	**g**o	гума	*goo*-ma
h	**h**at	хотел	ho-*tel*
k	**k**it	карта	*kar*-ta
l	**l**ot	билет	bee-*let*
m	**m**an	масло	*mas*-lo
n	**n**ot	нула	*noo*-la
p	**p**et	грип	greep
r	**r**un	утро	*oot*-ro
s	**s**un	син	seen
sh	**sh**ot	шест	shest
t	**t**op	сто	sto
ts	ha**ts**	крадец	kra-*dets*
v	**v**ery	вчера	vche-*ra*
y	**y**es	брой	broy
z	**z**ero	зад	zad
zh	plea**s**ure	плаж	plazh

basics

language difficulties

Do you speak English?
Говорите ли английски?   go·*vo*·ree·te lee ang·*lees*·kee

Do you understand?
Разбирате ли?   raz·*bee*·ra·te lee

I (don't) understand.
(Не) разбирам.   (ne) raz·*bee*·ram

What does (механа) mean?
Какво значи (механа)?   kak·*vo zna*·chee (me·ha·*na*)

How do you ...?	Как се ...?	kak se ...
pronounce this	произнася това	pro·eez·*nas*·ya to·*va*
write (спирка)	пише (спирка)	*pee*·she (*speer*·ka)

Could you please ...?	Моля ...?	*mol*·ya ...
repeat that	повторете това	pov·to·*re*·te to·*va*
speak more slowly	говорете бавно	go·vo·*re*·te *bav*·no
write it down	напишете това	na·pee·*she*·te to·*va*

БЪЛГАРСКИ – basics

essentials

Yes.	Да.	da
No.	Не.	ne
Please.	Моля.	*mol*·ya
Thank you	Благодаря	bla·go·dar·*ya*
(very much).	(много).	(*mno*·go)
You're welcome.	Няма защо.	*nya*·ma zash·*to*
Excuse me.	Извинете.	iz·vee·*ne*·te
Sorry.	Съжалявам.	suh·zhal·*ya*·vam

numbers

0	нула	*noo*·la	15	петнайсет	pet·*nai*·set	
1	един/една m/f	ed·*een*/ed·*na*	16	шеснайсет	shes·*nai*·set	
	едно n	ed·*no*	17	седемнайсет	se·dem·*nai*·set	
2	два/две m/f&n	dva/dve	18	осемнайсет	o·sem·*nai*·set	
3	три	tree	19	деветнайсет	de·vet·*nai*·set	
4	четири	*che*·tee·ree	20	двайсет	*dvai*·set	
5	пет	pet	21	двайсет и едно	*dvai*·set ee ed·*no*	
6	шест	shest	22	двайсет и две	*dvai*·set ee dve	
7	седем	*se*·dem	30	трийсет	*tree*·set	
8	осем	*o*·sem	40	четирийсет	che·*tee*·ree·set	
9	девет	*de*·vet	50	петдесет	pet·de·*set*	
10	десет	*de*·set	60	шестдесет	shest·de·*set*	
11	единайсет	e·dee·*nai*·set	70	седемдесет	se·dem·de·*set*	
12	дванайсет	dva·*nai*·set	80	осемдесет	o·sem·de·*set*	
13	тринайсет	tree·*nai*·set	90	деветдесет	de·vet·de·*set*	
14	четири-найсет	che·tee·ree·*nai*·set	100	сто	sto	
			1000	хиляда	hee·*lya*·da	

time & dates

What time is it?	Колко е часът?	*kol*·ko e cha·*suht*
It's one o'clock.	Часът е един.	cha·*suht* e e·*deen*
It's (two) o'clock.	Часът е (два).	cha·*suht* e (dva)
Quarter past (one).	(Един) и петнайсет.	(e·*deen*) ee pet·*nai*·set
Half past (one).	(Един) и половина.	(e·*deen*) ee po·lo·*vee*·na
Quarter to (eight).	(Осем) без петнайсет.	(o·sem) bez pet·*nai*·set
At what time ...?	В колко часа ...?	v *kol*·ko cha·*suh* ...
At ...	В ...	v ...
am	сутрин	*soo*·treen
pm	следобед	sle·*do*·bed
Monday	понеделник	po·ne·*del*·neek
Tuesday	вторник	*vtor*·neek
Wednesday	сряда	*srya*·da
Thursday	четвъртък	chet·*vuhr*·tuhk
Friday	петък	*pe*·tuhk
Saturday	събота	*suh*·bo·ta
Sunday	неделя	ne·*del*·ya

January	януари	ya-noo-*a*-ree
February	февруари	fev-roo-*a*-ree
March	март	mart
April	април	ap-*reel*
May	май	mai
June	юни	*yoo*-nee
July	юли	*yoo*-lee
August	август	*av*-goost
September	септември	sep-*tem*-vree
October	октомври	ok-*tom*-vree
November	ноември	no-*em*-vree
December	декември	de-*kem*-vree

What date is it today?
   Коя дата е днес?   ko-*ya da*-ta e dnes

It's (15 December).
   Днес е (петнайсти декември).   dnes e (pet-*nai*-stee de-*kem*-vree)

| **since (May)** | от (май) | ot (mai) |
| **until (June)** | до (юни) | do (*yoo*-nee) |

last/	миналата/	*mee*-na-la-ta/
next ...	следващата ...	*sled*-vash-ta-ta ...
night	вечер	*ve*-cher
week	седмица	*sed*-mee-tsa
year	година	go-*dee*-na

| **last month** | миналия месец | *mee*-na-lee-ya *me*-sets |
| **next month** | следващия месец | *sled*-vash-tee-ya *me*-sets |

yesterday/	вчера/утре ...	*vche*-ra/*oot*-re ...
tomorrow ...		
morning	сутринта	soot-reen-*ta*
afternoon	следобед	sle-*do*-bed
evening	вечерта	ve-cher-*ta*

weather

What's the weather like?	Какво е времето?	kak·*vo* e *vre*·me·to
It's ...	... e.	... e
cloudy	Облачно	*ob*·lach·no
cold	Студено	stoo·*de*·no
hot	Горещо	go·*resh*·to
raining	Дъждовно	duhzh·*dov*·no
snowing	Снеговито	sne·go·*vee*·to
sunny	Слънчево	*sluhn*·che·vo
warm	Топло	*top*·lo
windy	Ветровито	vet·tro·*vee*·to

spring	пролет f	*pro*·let
summer	лято n	*lya*·to
autumn	есен f	*e*·sen
winter	зима f	*zee*·ma

border crossing

I'm here ...	Тука съм ...	*too*·ka suhm ...
on business	по работа	po *ra*·bo·ta
on holiday	във ваканция	vuhv va·*kan*·tsee·ya

I'm here for ...	Тука съм за ...	*too*·ka suhm za ...
(10) days	(десет) дена	(*de*·set) *de*·na
(two) months	(два) месеца	(dva) me·*se*·tsa
(three) weeks	(три) седмици	(tree) *sed*·mee·tsee

I'm going to (Gabrovo).
Отивам в (Габрово). — o·*tee*·vam v (*gab*·ro·vo)

I'm staying at the (Serdika).
Отседнал/Отседнала — ot·*sed*·nal/ot·*sed*·na·la
съм в (Сердика). m/f — suhm v (*ser*·dee·ka)

I have nothing to declare.
Нямам нищо да декларирам. — *nya*·mam *neesh*·to da dek·la·*ree*·ram

I have something to declare.
Имам нещо да декларирам. — *ee*·mam *nesh*·to da dek·la·*ree*·ram

That's (not) mine.
Това (не) е мое. — to·*va* (ne) e *mo*·ye

transport

tickets & luggage

Where can I buy a ticket?
Къде мога да си купя билет?   kuh·*de mo*·ga da see *koop*·ya bee·*let*

Do I need to book a seat?
Трябва ли да запазя място?   *tryab*·va lee da za·*paz*·ya *myas*·to

One ... ticket	Един билет ...	e·*deen* bee·*let* ...
(to Varna), please.	(за Варна), моля.	(za *var*·na) *mol*·ya
one-way	в едната посока	v ed·*na*·ta po·*so*·ka
return	за отиване	za o·*tee*·va·ne
	и връщане	ee *vruhsh*·ta·ne

I'd like to ... my	Искам да ...	*ees*·kam da ...
ticket, please.	своя билет, моля.	*svo*·ya bee·*let mol*·ya
cancel	върна	*vuhr*·na
change	сменя	smen·*ya*
collect	взема	*vze*·ma
confirm	потвърдя	pot·*vuhr*·*dya*

I'd like a ... seat,	Искам място ...,	*ees*·kam *myas*·to ...
please.	моля.	*mol*·ya
nonsmoking	за непушачи	za ne·poo·*sha*·chee
smoking	за пушачи	za poo·*sha*·chee

How much is it?
Колко струва?   *kol*·ko *stroo*·va

Is there air conditioning?
Има ли климатична   *ee*·ma lee klee·ma·*teech*·na
инсталация?   een·sta·*la*·tsee·ya

Is there a toilet?
Има ли тоалетна?   *ee*·ma lee to·a·*let*·na

How long does the trip take?
Колко трае пътуването?   *kol*·ko *tra*·ye puh·*too*·va·ne·to

Is it a direct route?
Има ли прекачване?   *ee*·ma lee pre·*kach*·va·ne

I'd like a luggage locker.
Искам да оставя багажа   *ees*·kam da os·*tav*·ya ba·*ga*·zha
си на гардероб.   see na gar·de·*rob*

My luggage has been ...	Багажът ми е ...	ba-*ga*-zhuht mee e ...
damaged	повреден	po-vre-*den*
lost	загубен	za-*goo*-ben
stolen	откраден	ot-*kra*-den

getting around

Where does flight (355) arrive?
Къде пристига полет (355)? kuh-*de* prees-*tee*-ga *po*-let (tree pet pet)

Where does flight (355) depart?
Откъде тръгва полет (355)? ot-kuh-*de* *truhg*-va *po*-let (tree pet pet)

Where's (the) ...?	Къде се намира ...?	kuh-*de* se na-*mee*-ra ...
arrivals hall	терминал	ter-mee-*nal*
	'пристигане'	pree-*stee*-ga-ne
departures hall	терминал	ter-mee-*nal*
	'заминаване'	za-mee-*na*-va-ne
duty-free shop	безмитен магазин	bez-*mee*-ten ma-ga-*zeen*
gate (12)	изход (дванайсет)	*ees*-hod (dva-*nai*-set)

Is this the ...	Това ли е ...	to-*va* lee e ...
to (Burgas)?	за (Бургас)?	za (boor-*gas*)
boat	корабът	ko-*ra*-buht
bus	автобусът	av-to-*boo*-suht
plane	самолетът	sa-mo-*le*-tuht
train	влакът	*vla*-kuht

What time's	В колко часа	v *kol*-ko cha-*suh*
the ... bus?	е ... автобус?	e ... av-to-*boos*
first	първият	*puhr*-vee-yat
last	последният	po-*sled*-nee-yat
next	следващият	*sled*-vash-tee-yat

At what time does it arrive/leave?
В колко часа пристига/тръгва? v *kol*-ko cha-*suh* prees-*tee*-ga/*truhg*-va

How long will it be delayed?
Колко закъснение има? *kol*-ko za-kuhs-*ne*-nee-ye *ee*-ma

What station/stop is this?
Коя е тази гара/спирка? ko-*ya* e *ta*-zee *ga*-ra/*speer*-ka

Does it stop at (Plovdiv)?
Спира ли в (Пловдив)? *spee*-ra lee v (*plov*-deev)

Please tell me when we get to (Smoljan).

Кажете ми моля когато
пристигнем в (Смолян).

ka·*zhe*·te mee *mol*·ya ko·*ga*·to
prees·*teeg*·nem v (*smol*·yan)

How long do we stop here?

След колко време тръгваме оттук?

sled *kol*·ko *vre*·me *truhg*·va·me ot·*took*

Is this seat available?

Това място свободно ли е?

to·*va myas*·to svo·*bod*·no lee e

That's my seat.

Това е моето място.

to·*va* e *mo*·ye·to *myas*·to

I'd like a taxi ...

Искам да поръчам
такси ...

ees·kam da po·*ruh*·cham
tak·*see* ...

at (9am)	в (девет часа сутринта)	v (*de*·vet cha·*sa* soo·treen·*ta*)
now	сега	se·*ga*
tomorrow	за утре	za *oot*·re

Is this taxi available?

Таксито свободно ли е?

tak·*see*·to svo·*bod*·no lee e

How much is it to ...?

Колко струва до ...?

kol·ko *stroo*·va do ...

Please put the meter on.

Моля да включите таксиметъра.

mol·ya da *vklyoo*·chee·te tak·see·*me*·tuh·ra

Please take me to (this address).

Моля да ме докарате
до (този адрес).

mol·ya da me do·*ka*·ra·te
do (*to*·zi ad·*res*)

Please ...	Моля ...	*mol*·ya ...
slow down	намалете	na·ma·*le*·te
stop here	спрете тук	*spre*·te took
wait here	чакайте тук	*cha*·kai·te took

car, motorbike & bicycle hire

I'd like to hire a ...	Искам да взема под наем ...	*ees*·kam da *vze*·ma pod *na*·em ...
bicycle	един велосипед	e·*deen* ve·lo·see·*ped*
car	една кола	e·*dna* ko·*la*
motorbike	един мотопед	e·*deen* mo·to·*ped*

with …	с …	s …
a driver	шофьор	sho-*fyor*
air conditioning	климатична инсталация	klee-ma-*teech*-na een-sta-*la*-tsee-ya
antifreeze	антифриз	an-tee-*freez*
snow chains	вериги за сняг	ve-*ree*-gee za snyag

How much for	Колко струва на …	*kol*-ko *stroo*-va na …
… hire?	да се наеме?	da se na-*e*-me
hourly	час	chas
daily	ден	den
weekly	седмица	*sed*-mee-tsa

air	въздух m	*vuhz*-dooh
oil	масло n	*mas*-lo
petrol	бензин m	ben-*zeen*
tyres	гуми f pl	*goo*-mee

I need a mechanic.
Трябва ми монтьор. *tryab*-va mee mon-*tyor*

I've run out of petrol.
Нямам бензин. *nya*-mam ben-*zeen*

I have a flat tyre.
Пукнала ми се е гумата. *pook*-na-la mee se e *goo*-ma-ta

directions

Where's the …?	Къде се намира …?	kuh-*de* se na-*mee*-ra …
bank	банката	*ban*-ka-ta
city centre	центърът на града	*tsen*-tuh-ruht na gra-*duh*
hotel	хотелът	ho-*te*-luht
market	пазарът	pa-*za*-ruht
police station	полицейският участък	po-lee-*tsey*-skee-uht oo-*chas*-tuhk
post office	пощата	*po*-shta-ta
public toilet	една градска тоалетна	ed-*na* grad-ska to-a-*let*-na
tourist office	бюрото за туристическа информация	byoo-*ro*-to za too-*ree*-stee-ches-ka een-for-*ma*-tsee-ya

Is this the road to (Rila)?

Това ли е пътят за (Рила)? — to-*va* lee e *puh*-tyat za (*ree*-la)

Can you show me (on the map)?

Можете ли да ми покажете (на картата)? — *mo*-zhe-te lee da mee po-*ka*-zhe-te (na *kar*-ta-ta)

What's the address?

Какъв е адресът? — ka-*kuhv* e ad-*re*-suht

How far is it?

На какво разстояние е? — na kak-*vo* ras-to-*ya*-nee-e e

How do I get there?

Как се ходи до там? — kak se *ho*-dee do tam

Turn ...	Завийте ...	za-*veey*-te ...
at the corner	на следващия ъгъл	na *sled*-vash-tee-ya *uh*-guhl
at the traffic lights	при светофара	pree sve-to-*fa*-ra
left/right	наляво/надясно	na-*lya*-vo/na-*dyas*-no

It's ...	Това е ...	to-*va* e ...
behind ...	зад ...	zad ...
far away	далече	da-*le*-che
here	тука	*too*-ka
in front of ...	пред ...	pred ...
left	наляво	na-*lya*-vo
near (to ...)	близо (до ...)	*blee*-zo (do ...)
next to ...	до ...	do ...
on the corner	на ъгъла	na *uh*-guh-luh
opposite ...	срещу ...	*sresh*-too ...
right	надясно	na-*dyas*-no
straight ahead	право	*pra*-vo
there	там	tam

by bus	с автобус	s av-to-*boos*
by taxi	с такси	s tak-*see*
by train	с влак	s vlak
on foot	пеша	pe-*sha*

north	север	*se*-ver
south	юг	yoog
east	изток	*ees*-tok
west	запад	*za*-pad

Вход/Изход	vhod/*ees*·hod	**Entrance/Exit**
Отворено/Затворено	ot·*vo*·re·no/zat·*vo*·re·no	**Open/Closed**
Свободни стаи	svo·*bod*·nee *sta*·yee	**Rooms Available**
Няма стаи	*nya*·ma *sta*·yee	**No Vacancies**
Информация	een·for·*ma*·tsee·ya	**Information**
Полиция	po·*lee*·tsee·ya	**Police Station**
Забранено	za·bra·*ne*·no	**Prohibited**
Тоалетни	to·a·*let*·nee	**Toilets**
Мъже	muh·*zhe*	**Men**
Жени	zhe·*nee*	**Women**
Горещо/Студено	go·*resh*·to/stoo·*de*·no	**Hot/Cold**

accommodation

finding accommodation

Where's a ...?	Къде има ...?	kuh·*de ee*·ma ...
camping ground	къмпинг	*kuhm*·peeng
guesthouse	пансион	pan·see·*on*
hotel	хотел	ho·*tel*
youth hostel	общежитие	ob·shte·*zhee*·tee·ye
Can you	Можете ли	*mo*·zhe·te lee
recommend	да препоръчате	da pre·po·*ruh*·cha·te
somewhere ...?	нещо ...?	*nesh*·to ...
cheap	евтино	*ev*·tee·no
good	хубаво	*hoo*·ba·vo
nearby	наблизо	na·*blee*·zo

I have a reservation.
Имам резервация.   *ee*·mam re·zer·*va*·tsee·ya

My name's ...
Казвам се ...   *kaz*·vam se ...

I'd like to book a room, please.
Искам да взема една стая, моля.   *ees*·kam da *vze*·ma ed·*na sta*·ya *mol*·ya

Do you have a ... room?	Имате ли стая с ...?	ee·ma·te lee sta·ya s ...
single	едно легло	ed·no leg·lo
double	едно голямо легло	ed·no go·lya·mo leg·lo
twin	две легла	dve leg·la

How much is it per ...?	Колко е на ...?	kol·ko e na ...
night	вечер	ve·cher
person	човек	cho·vek

Can I pay ...?	Мога ли да платя ...?	mo·ga lee da pla·tya ...
by credit card	с кредитна карта	s kre·deet·na kar·ta
with a travellers cheque	с пътнически чекове	s puht·nee·ches·kee che·ko·ve

I'd like to stay for (two) nights.
Искам стаята за (две) нощи.
ees·kam sta·ya·ta za (dve) nosh·ti

From (2 July) to (6 July).
От (втори юли) до (шести юли).
ot (vto·ree yoo·lee) do (shes·tee yoo·lee)

Can I see it?
Мога ли да я видя?
mo·ga lee da ya vee·dya

Am I allowed to camp here?
Мога ли да си сложа палатката тук?
mo·ga lee da see slo·zha pa·lat·ka·ta took

Is there a camp site nearby?
Има ли къмпинг наблизо?
ee·ma lee kuhm·peeng na·blee·zo

requests & queries

When/Where is breakfast served?
Кога/Къде сервират закуската?
ko·ga/kuh·de ser·vee·rat za·koos·ka·ta

Please wake me at (seven).
Моля събудете ме в (седем).
mol·ya suh·boo·de·te me v (se·dem)

Could I have my key, please?
Дайте ми ключа, моля.
dai·te mee klyoo·cha mol·ya

Can I get another (blanket)?
Дайте ми моля още едно (одеяло).
dai·te mee mol·ya osh·te ed·no (o·de·ya·lo)

Is there an elevator/a safe?
Има ли асансьор/сейф?
ee·ma lee a·san·syor/seyf

The room is too ...	Стаята е прекалено ...	*sta*·ya·ta e pre·ka·*le*·no ...
expensive	скъпа	*skuh*·pa
noisy	шумна	*shoom*·na
small	малка	*mal*·ka

The ... doesn't work.	Не работи ...	ne ra·*bo*·tee ...
air conditioning	климатичната	klee·ma·*teech*·na·ta
	инсталация	een·sta·*la*·tsee·ya
fan	вентилаторът	ven·tee·*la*·to·ruht
toilet	тоалетната	to·a·*let*·na·ta

This ... isn't clean.	Тази ... не е чиста.	*ta*·zee ... ne e *chees*·ta
pillow	възглавница	vuhz·*glav*·nee·tsa
towel	кърпа	*kuhr*·pa

| This sheet isn't clean. | Този чаршаф не е чист. | *to*·zee char·*shaf* ne e cheest |

checking out

What time is checkout?
Кога трябва да напусна стаята?
ko·*ga* tryab·va da na·*poos*·na *sta*·ya·ta

Can I leave my luggage here?
Мога ли да оставя своя
багаж тук?
mo·ga lee da os·*tav*·ya *svo*·ya
ba·*gazh* took

Could I have my ...?	Дайте ми ..., моля.	*dai*·te mee ... *mol*·ya
deposit	моя депозит	*mo*·ya de·*po*·zeet
passport	моя паспорт	*mo*·ya pas·*port*
valuables	моите ценности	*mo*·yee·te *tsen*·nos·tee

communications & banking

the internet

Where's the local Internet café?
Къде се намира най-близкият
интернет?
kuh·*de* se na·*mee*·ra nai·*blees*·kee·yat
een·ter·*net*

How much is it per hour?
Колко се плаща на час?
kol·ko se *pla*·shta na chas

I'd like to ...	Искам да ...	*ees*·kam da ...
check my email	проверя и-мейла си	pro·*ver*·ya ee·*mey*·la see
get Internet access	използвам интернета	iz·*polz*·vam een·ter·*ne*·ta
use a printer	използвам принтер	iz·*polz*·vam *preen*·ter
use a scanner	използвам скенер	iz·*polz*·vam *ske*·ner

mobile/cell phone

I'd like a ...	Искам ...	*ees*·kam ...
mobile/cell phone for hire	да взема под наем един мобилен телефон	da *vze*·ma pod *na*·em e·*deen* mo·*bee*·len te·le·*fon*
SIM card for your network	предплатена карта за мобилни телефони за вашата мрежа	pred·pla·*te*·na *kar*·ta za mo·*beel*·nee te·le·*fo*·nee za *va*·sha·ta *mre*·zha
What are the rates?	Какви са цените?	kak·*vee* sa tse·*nee*·te

telephone

What's your phone number?
Какъв е вашият телефонен номер?
ka·*kuhv* e *va*·shee·yat te·le·*fo*·nen *no*·mer

The number is ...
Номерът е ...
no·me·ruht e ...

Where's the nearest public phone?
Къде се намира най-близката телефонна будка?
kuh·*de* se na·*mee*·ra nai·*blees*·ka·ta te·le·*fon*·na *bood*·ka

I'd like to buy a phonecard.
Искам да си купя една телефонна карта.
ees·kam da see *koop*·ya ed·*na* te·le·*fon*·na *kar*·ta

I want to ...	Искам да ...	*ees*·kam da ...
call (Singapore)	се обадя в (Сингапур)	se o·*bad*·ya v (seen·ga·*poor*)
make a local call	се обадя някъде в града	se o·*bad*·ya *nya*·kuh·de v gra·*duh*
reverse the charges	се обадя на тяхната сметка	se o·*bad*·ya na *tyah*·na·ta *smet*·ka

How much does ... cost?	Колко струва ...?	*kol*-ko *stroo*-va ...
a (three)-minute	разговор от	*raz*-go-vor ot
call	(три) минути	(tree) mee-*noo*-tee
each extra minute	всяка допълнителна	*vsya*-ka do-puhl-*nee*-tel-na
	минута	mee-*noo*-ta

(Five) leva per minute.
(Пет) лева една минута.   (pet) *le*-va ed-*na* mee-*noo*-ta

post office

I want to send a ...	Искам да изпратя ...	*ees*-kam da eez-*prat*-ya ...
letter	едно писмо	ed-*no* pees-*mo*
parcel	един колет	e-*deen* ko-*let*
postcard	една пощенска	ed-*na* posh-*ten*-ska
	картичка	*kar*-teech-ka

I want to buy a/an ...	Искам да купя ...	*ees*-kam da *koop*-ya ...
envelope	един плик	e-*deen* pleek
stamp	една марка	ed-*na* mar-ka

Please send it	Моля да се изпрати	*mol*-ya da se eez-*pra*-tee
(to Australia) by ...	(в Австралия) ...	(v av-*stra*-lee-ya) ...
airmail	с въздушна поща	s *vuhz*-doosh-na *posh*-ta
express mail	с бърза поща	s *buhr*-za *posh*-ta
registered mail	препоръчано	pre-po-*ruh*-cha-no
surface mail	с обикновена поща	s o-beek-no-*ve*-na *posh*-ta

Is there any mail for me?
Има ли писма за мене?   *ee*-ma lee pees-*ma* za *me*-ne

bank

Where's a/an ...?	Къде има ...?	kuh-*de ee*-ma ...
ATM	банкомат	ban-ko-*mat*
foreign exchange	обмяна на валута	ob-*mya*-na na va-*loo*-ta
office		

I'd like to …	Искам да …	*ees*·kam da …
Where can I …?	Къде мога да …?	kuh·*de mo*·ga da …
arrange a transfer	уредя да ми се	oo·red·*ya* da mee se
	изпратят пари	eez·*prat*·yat pa·*ree*
	чрез банков превод	chrez *ban*·kov pre·*vod*
cash a cheque	осребря чек	os·reb·*ryuh* chek
change a travellers cheque	осребря пътнически чек	os·reb·*ryuh* puht·*nee*·ches·kee chek
change money	обменя пари	ob·men·*ya* pa·*ree*
get a cash advance	изтегля пари от кредитната си карта	eez·*teg*·lya pa·*ree* ot kre·*deet*·na·ta see *kar*·ta
withdraw money	тегля пари в брой	*teg*·lya pa·*ree* v broy

What's the …?	Каква е …?	kak·*va* e …
charge for that	таксата	ko·mee·see·*on*·na
commission	комисионна	*tak*·sa·ta

It's …	… е.	… e
(10) leva	(Десет) лева	(*de*·set) *le*·va
free	Безплатно	bez·*plat*·no

What's the exchange rate?
Какъв е валутен курс?   ka·*kuhv* e va·*loo*·ten koors

What time does the bank open?
В колко часа се отваря банката?   v *kol*·ko cha·*suh* se ot·*var*·ya *ban*·ka·ta

Has my money arrived yet?
Парите ми пристигнаха ли вече?   pa·*ree*·te mee prees·*teeg*·na·ha lee *ve*·che

sightseeing

getting in

What time does it open/close?
В колко часа се отваря/затваря?   v *kol*·ko cha·*suh* se ot·*var*·ya/zat·*var*·ya

What's the admission charge?
Каква е входната такса?   kak·*va* e *vhod*·na·ta *tak*·sa

Is there a discount for students/children?
Има ли намаление за студенти/деца?   *ee*·ma lee na·ma·*le*·nee·ye za stoo·*den*·tee/det·*sa*

I'd like a ...	Искам ...	*ees*-kam ...
catalogue	един каталог	e-*deen* ka-ta-*log*
guide	един гид	e-*deen* geed
map	една карта на района	ed-*na kar*-ta na ra-*yo*-na

I'd like to see ...	Искам да видя ...	*ees*-kam da *veed*-ya ...
What's that?	Какво е онова?	kak-*vo* e o-no-*va*
Can I take a photo?	Мога ли да направя снимка?	*mo*-ga lee da na-*prav*-ya *sneem*-ka

tours

When's the next ...?	Кога тръгва следващата ...?	ko-*ga truhg*-va *sled*-vash-ta-ta ...
day trip	еднодневна екскурзия	ed-no-*dnev*-na eks-*koor*-zee-ya
tour	обиколка	o-bee-*kol*-ka

Is ... included?	Включена ли е ...?	vklyoo-che-*na* lee e ...
accommodation	нощувката	nosh-*toov*-ka-ta
the admission charge	входната такса	*vhod*-na-ta *tak*-sa
food	храната	hra-*na*-ta

Is transport included?
Включен ли е транспортът? — vklyoo-*chen* lee e trans-*por*-tuht

How long is the tour?
Колко трае екскурзията? — *kol*-ko *tra*-e eks-*koor*-zee-ya-ta

What time should we be back?
В колко часа ще се върнем? — v *kol*-ko cha-*suh* shte se *vuhr*-nem

sightseeing

church	църква f	*tsuhrk*-va
main square	централен площад m	tsen-*tra*-len plosh-*tad*
monastery	манастир m	ma-nas-*teer*
monument	паметник m	*pa*-met-nik
museum	музей m	moo-*zey*
old city	старият град m	*sta*-ree-yuht grad
palace	дворец m	dvo-*rets*
ruins	развалини f pl	raz-va-lee-*nee*
stadium	стадион m	sta-dee-*on*
statue	статуа f	*sta*-too-a

shopping

enquiries

Where's a ... ?	Къде има ...?	kuh-de ee-ma ...
bank	банка	ban-ka
bookshop	книжарница	knee-zhar-nee-tsa
camera shop	магазин за	ma-ga-zeen za
	фотоапарати	fo-to-a-pa-ra-tee
department store	универсален	oo-nee-ver-sa-len
	магазин	ma-ga-zeen
grocery store	гастроном	gas-tro-nom
market	пазар	pa-zar
newsagency	киоск	kee-osk
supermarket	супермаркет	soo-per-mar-ket

Where can I buy ...?
Къде мога да си купя
(един катинар)?
kuh-de mo-ga da see koop-ya
(e-deen ka-nee-tar)

I'm looking for ...
Търся ...
tuhr-sya ...

Can I look at it?
Мога ли да го разгледам?
mo-ga lee da go raz-gle-dam

Do you have any others?
Имате ли още?
ee-ma-te lee osh-te

Does it have a guarantee?
Има ли гаранция?
ee-ma lee ga-ran-tsee-ya

Can I have it sent abroad?
Можете ли да го изпратите
в чужбина?
mo-zhe-te lee da go eez-pra-tee-te
v choozh-bee-na

Can I have my ... repaired?
Можете ли да поправите
моя ...?
mo-zhe-te lee da po-pra-vee-te
mo-ya ...

It's faulty.
Не е на ред.
ne e na red

I'd like ..., please.	Искам ..., моля.	ees·kam ... mol·ya
a bag	един плик	e·deen pleek
a refund	да ми се вратят	da mee se vrat·yuht
	парите	pa·ree·te
to return this	да върна това нещо	da vuhr·na to·va nesh·to

paying

How much is it?
Колко струва? — *kol·ko stroo·va*

Can you write down the price?
Моля, напишете цената. — *mol·ya na·pee·she·te tse·na·ta*

That's too expensive.
Скъпо е. — *skuh·po e*

What's your lowest price?
Каква е най-низката ви цена? — *kak·va e nai·neez·ka·ta vee tse·na*

I'll give you (five) euros.
Ще ви дам (пет) евро. — *shte vee dam (pet) ev·ro*

I'll give you (15) leva.
Ще ви дам (петнайсет) лева. — *shte vee dam (pet·nai·set) le·va*

There's a mistake in the bill.
Има грешка в сметката. — *ee·ma gresh·ka v smet·ka·ta*

Do you accept ...?	Приемате ли ...?	pree·e·ma·te lee ...
credit cards	кредитни карти	kre·deet·nee kar·tee
debit cards	дебитни карти	de·beet·nee kar·tee
travellers cheques	пътнически	puht·nee·ches·kee
	чекове	che·ko·ve

I'd like ..., please.	Дайте ми моля ...	dai·te mee mol·ya ...
a receipt	квитанция	kvee·tan·tsee·ya
my change	ресто	res·to

clothes & shoes

Can I try it on?	Мога ли да го пробвам?	mo·ga lee da go prob·vam
My size is (42).	Номерът ми е	no·me·ruht mee e
	(четирийсет и два).	(che·tee·ree·set ee dva)
It doesn't fit.	Не ми става.	ne mee sta·va

small	малко	*mal*·ko
medium	средно	*sred*·no
large	голямо	gol·*ya*·mo

books & music

I'd like a ...	Искам ...	*ees*·kam ...
newspaper	един вестник	e·*deen vest*·neek
(in English)	(на английски)	(na an·*glee*·skee)
pen	една писалка	ed·*na* pee·*sal*·ka

Is there an English-language bookshop?
Има ли книжарница с   *ee*·ma lee knee·*zhar*·nee·tsa s
книги на английски?   *knee*·gee na ang·*lees*·kee

I'm looking for something by (Ivan Vazov).
Търся нещо от (Иван Вазов).   *tuhr*·sya *nesh*·to ot (ee·*van* va·zov)

Can I listen to this?
Мога ли да слушам това?   *mo*·ga lee da *sloo*·sham to·*va*

photography

Can you ...?	Можете ли да ...?	*mo*·zhe·te lee da ...
burn a CD from	запишете на	za·*pee*·she·te na
my memory card	компактен диск от	kom·*pak*·ten deesk ot
	моя флешдрайв	*mo*·ya *flesh*·draiv
develop this film	проявите този филм	pro·*ya*·vee·te *to*·zee film
load my film	заредите моя филм	za·*re*·dee·te *mo*·ya film

I need a ... film	Трябви ми ... филм	*tryab*·va mee ... film
for this camera.	за този фотоапарат.	za *to*·zee fo·to·a·pa·*rat*
APS	АПС	a puh suh
B&W	черно-бял	cher·no·*byal*
colour	цветен	*tsve*·ten

I need a ... film	Трябви ми филм ...	*tryab*·va mee film ...
for this camera.	за този фотоапарат.	za *to*·zee fo·to·a·pa·*rat*
slide	за диапозитиви	za dee·a·po·zee·*tee*·vee
(200) speed	за скорост (двеста)	za *sko*·rost (*dve*·sta)

When will it be ready?
Кога ще бъде готов?   ko·*ga* shte *buh*·de go·*tov*

meeting people

greetings, goodbyes & introductions

Hello/Hi.	Здравейте/Здравей.	zdra·*vey*·te/zdra·*vey*
Good night.	Лека нощ.	*le*·ka nosht
Goodbye/Bye.	Довиждане./Чао.	do·*veezh*·da·ne/*cha*·o
Mr/Mrs	господин/госпожа	gos·po·*deen*/gos·*po*·zha
Miss	госпожица	gos·*po*·zhee·tsa
How are you?	Как си/сте? inf/pol	kak si/ste
Fine, thanks.	Добре, благодаря.	do·*bre* bla·go·da·*rya*
And you?	А ти/вие? inf/pol	a te/*vee*·e
What's your name?	Как се казваш/ казвате? inf/pol	kak se *kaz*·vash/ *kaz*·va·te
My name is ...	Казвам се ...	*kaz*·vam se ...
I'm pleased to meet you.	Приятно ми е да се запозная с вас.	pree·*yat*·no mee e da se za·poz·*na*·ya s vas
This is my ...	Това е ...	to·*va* e ...
boyfriend	моят приятел	*mo*·yat pree·*ya*·tel
brother	моят брат	*mo*·yat brat
daughter	моята дъщеря	*mo*·ya·ta duh·*shter*·ya
father	моят баща	*mo*·yat bash·*ta*
friend	мой приятел m	moy pree·*ya*·tel
	моя приятелка f	*mo*·ya pree·*ya*·tel·ka
girlfriend	моята приятелка	*mo*·ya·ta pree·*ya*·tel·ka
husband	моят съпруг	*mo*·yat suh·*proog*
mother	моята майка	*mo*·ya·ta *mai*·ka
partner (intimate)	моят приятел m	*mo*·ya·ta pree·*ya*·tel
	моята приятелка f	*mo*·ya·ta pree·*ya*·tel·ka
sister	моята сестра	*mo*·ya·ta ses·*tra*
son	моят син	*mo*·yat seen
wife	моята съпруга	*mo*·ya·ta suh·*proo*·ga
Here's my ...	Ето моя ...	e·to *mo*·ya ...
What's your ...?	Какъв е вашият ...?	ka·*kuhv* e va·shee·yat ...
(email) address	(и-мейл) адрес	(ee·meyl) a·*dres*
fax number	факс	faks
phone number	телефонен номер	te·le·*fo*·nen *no*·mer

occupations

What's your occupation?	Какво работите?	kak-vo ra-bo-tee-te
I'm a/an ...	Аз съм ...	az suhm ...
artist	художник m	hoo-*dozh*-neek
	художничка f	hoo-*dozh*-neech-ka
businessperson	бизнесмен m	beez-nes-*men*
	бизнесменка f	beez-nes-*men*-ka
farmer	фермер m	*fer*-mer
	фермерка f	*fer*-mer-ka
office worker	чиновник m	chee-*nov*-neek
	чиновничка f	chee-*nov*-neech-ka
scientist	учен m&f	*oo*-chen

background

Where are you from?	Откъде сте?	ot-kuh-*de* ste
I'm from ...	Аз съм от ...	az suhm ot ...
Australia	Австралия	av-*stra*-lee-ya
Canada	Канада	*ka*-na-da
England	Англия	*ang*-lee-ya
New Zealand	Нова Зеландия	*no*-va ze-*lan*-dee-ya
the USA	Съединените	suh-e-dee-*ne*-nee-te
	Щати	*sha*-tee
Are you married?	Женен/Омъжена ли сте? m/f	*zhe*-nen/o-*muh*-zhe-na lee ste
I'm married.	Женен/Омъжена съм. m/f	*zhe*-nen/o-*muh*-zhe-na suhm
I'm single.	Не съм женен/омъжена. m/f	ne suhm *zhe*-nen/o-*muh*-zhe-na

age

How old ...?	На колко години ...?	na *kol*-ko go-*dee*-nee ...
are you	си/сте inf/pol	si/ste
is your daughter	е дъщеря	e duhsh-ter-*ya*
	ти/ви inf/pol	tee/vee
is your son	е синът ти/ви inf/pol	e see-*nuht* tee/vee

| I'm ... years old. | На ... години съм. | na ... go-*dee*-nee suhm |
| He/She is ... years old. | Той/Тя е на ... години. | toy/tya e na ... go-*dee*-nee |

feelings

I'm ...	Аз съм ...	az suhm ...
I'm not ...	Не съм ...	ne suhm ...
happy	щастлив	shtast-*leev*
hungry	гладен	*gla*-den
sad	тъжен	*tuh*-zhen
thirsty	жаден	*zha*-den
tired	уморен	oo-mo-*ren*

I'm ...	На мене ми е ...	na *me*-ne mee e ...
I'm not ...	Не ми е ...	ne mee e ...
cold	студено	stoo-*de*-no
hot	топло	*top*-lo
OK	добре	do-*bre*

Are you ...?	... ли ви е?	... lee vee e
cold	Студено	stoo-*de*-no
hot	Топло	*top*-lo
OK	Добре	do-*bre*

entertainment

going out

Where can I find ...?	Къде има ...?	kuh-*de* ee-*ma* ...
clubs	нощни заведения	*nosht*-nee za-ve-*de*-nee-ya
gay venues	гей клубове	gey *kloo*-bo-ve
pubs	кръчми	*kruhch*-mee

I feel like going	Ходи ми се	*ho*-dee mee se
to a/the ...	на ...	na ...
concert	концерт	kon-*tsert*
movies	кино	*kee*-no
party	един купон	e-*deen* koo-*pon*
restaurant	ресторант	res-to-*rant*
theatre	театър	te-*a*-tuhr

interests

Do you like ...?	Харесвате ли ...?	ha-*res*-va-te lee ...
I (don't) like ...	(Не) Харесвам ...	(ne) ha-*res*-vam ...
art	изкуството	iz-*koost*-vo-to
movies	киното	*kee*-no-to
reading	четенето	*che*-te-ne-to
sport	спорта	*spor*-tuht
travelling	пътуването	puh-*too*-va-ne-to
Do you like to ...?	Обичате ли да ...?	o-*bee*-cha-te lee da ...
dance	танцувате	tan-*tsoo*-va-te
go to concerts	ходите на концерти	*ho*-dee-te na kon-*tser*-tee
listen to music	слушате музика	*sloo*-sha-te *moo*-zee-ka

food & drink

finding a place to eat

Can you recommend a ...?	Можете ли да препоръчате ...?	*mo*-zhe-te lee da pre-po-*ruh*-cha-te ...
bar	един бар	e-*deen* bar
café	едно кафене	ed-*no* ka-fe-*ne*
restaurant	един ресторант	e-*deen* res-to-*rant*
I'd like ..., please.	Искам ..., моля.	*ees*-kam ... *mol*-ya
a table for (four)	една маса за (четирма)	ed-*na* *ma*-sa za (che-*teer*-ma)
the (non)smoking section	в залата за (не)пушачи	v *za*-la-ta za (ne-)poo-*sha*-chee

ordering food

breakfast	закуска f	za-*koos*-ka
lunch	обед m	*o*-bed
dinner	вечеря f	ve-*cher*-ya
snack	закуска f	za-*koos*-ka
What would you recommend?	Какво ще препоръчате?	kak-*vo* shte pre-po-*ruh*-cha-te

I'd like (the) ..., please.	Дайте ми ..., моля.	*dai*·te mee ... *mol*·ya
bill	сметката	*smet*·ka·ta
drink list	листата с напитките	*lees*·ta·ta s na·*peet*·kee·te
menu	менюто	men·*yoo*·to
that dish	онова блюдо	o·*no*·va blyoo·do

drinks

(cup of) coffee/tea ...	(чаша) кафе/чай ...	(*chas*·ha) ka·*fe*/chai ...
with milk	с мляко	s *mlya*·ko
without sugar	без захар	bez *za*·har
(orange) juice	(портокалов) сок m	(por·to·*ka*·lov) sok
soft drink	безалкохолна напитка f	bez·al·ko·*hol*·na na·*peet*·ka
... water	... вода	... vo·*da*
boiled	преварена	pre·va·*re*·na
mineral	минерална	mee·ne·*ral*·na

in the bar

I'll have ...	Ще взема ...	shte *vze*·ma ...
I'll buy you a drink.	Ще ти/ви	shte tee/vee
	почерпя. inf/pol	po·*cher*·pya
What would you like?	Какво ще вземеш/	kak·*vo* shte *vze*·mesh/
	вземете? inf/pol	*vze*·me·te
Cheers!	Наздраве!	na·*zdra*·ve
brandy	ракия f	ra·*kee*·ya
cocktail	коктейл m	kok·*teyl*
cognac	коняк m	kon·*yak*
a shot of (whisky)	едно малко (уиски)	ed·*no mal*·ko (oo·*ees*·kee)
a ... of beer	... бира	... *bee*·ra
bottle	едно шише	ed·*no* shee·*she*
glass	една чаша	ed·*na* cha·sha
a bottle of ... wine	едно шише ... вино	ed·*no* shee·*she* ... *vee*·no
a glass of ... wine	една чаша ... вино	ed·*na* cha·sha ... *vee*·no
red	червено	cher·*ve*·no
sparkling	шумящо	shoo·*myash*·to
white	бяло	*bya*·lo

food & drink – BULGARIAN

self-catering

What's the local speciality?
Има ли някакъв
местен специалитет?
ee-ma lee *nya*-ka-kuhv
mes-ten spe-*tsee*-a-lee-*tet*

How much is (a kilo of cheese)?
Колко струва (един
килограм кашкавал)?
kol-ko *stroo*-va (e-*deen*
kee-lo-*gram* kash-ka-*val*)

I'd like ...	Дайте ми ...	*dai*-te mee ...
(100) grams	(сто) грама	(sto) *gra*-ma
(two) kilos	(два) килограма	(dva) kee-lo-*gra*-ma
(three) pieces	(три) парчета	(tree) par-*che*-ta
(six) slices	(шест) парчета	(shest) par-*che*-ta

Less.	По-малко.	*po*-mal-ko
Enough.	Достатъчно.	dos-*ta*-tuch-no
More.	Повече.	*po*-ve-che

special diets & allergies

Is there a vegetarian restaurant near here?
Има ли наблизо
вегетериански ресторант?
ee-ma lee nab-*lee*-zo
ve-ge-te-ree-*an*-skee res-to-*rant*

Do you have vegetarian food?
Имате ли вегетерианска храна?
ee-ma-te lee ve-ge-te-ree-*an*-ska hra-*na*

Could you	Можете ли да	*mo*-zhe-te lee da
prepare a meal	приготвите	pree-*got*-vee-te
without ...?	яденето без ...?	*ya*-de-ne-to bez ...
butter	краве масло	*kra*-ve *mas*-lo
eggs	яйца	yai-*tsa*
meat stock	месен бульон	*me*-sen bool-*yon*

I'm allergic to ...	Алергичен/Алергична съм към ... m/f	a-ler-*gee*-chen/a-ler-*geech*-na suhm *kuhm* ...
dairy produce	млечни продукти	*mlech*-nee pro-*dook*-tee
gluten	глутен	*gloo*-ten
MSG	МСГ	muh suh guh
nuts	ядки	*yad*-kee
seafood	морски продукти	*mor*-skee pro-*dook*-tee

menu decoder

агнешка курбан-чорба f	*ag-nesh-ka koor-ban chor-ba*	*boiled lamb, cut into cubes with chopped onion, paprika, rice, parsley & eggs*
баница f	*ba-nee-tsa*	*flaky pasties stuffed with white cheese*
боб m	*bob*	*seasoned bean soup*
бъркани яйца с печени чушки n	*buhr-ka-nee yai-tsa s pe-che-nee choosh-kee*	*scrambled eggs with diced roasted peppers & grated white cheese*
друсан кебап m	*droo-san ke-bap*	*large cubes of meat fried in fat, then boiled, with spices, onions & parsley*
градинарска чорба f	*gra-dee-nar-ska chor-ba*	*soup of celery, carrots, parsley, cabbage & potatoes, with white cheese & milk*
гювеч m	*gyoo-vech*	*peppers, tomatoes, aubergine, onions, potatoes, zucchini, carrots & sometimes meat, cooked in the oven*
зрял фасул m	*zryal fa-sool*	*boiled kidney beans with onions, carrots, celery, dried red peppers & mint*
каварма f	*ka-var-ma*	*meat or vegetable stew (usually pork or chicken), served in an earthenware pot*
кебапчета на скара n	*ke-bap-che-ta na ska-ra*	*grilled, sausage-shaped pork meatballs, mixed with finely chopped onion*
кюфтета n	*kyoof-te-ta*	*round meatballs, similar to the above*
кюфте татарско n	*kyoof-te ta-tar-sko*	*pork burger filled with melted cheese*
луканка f	*loo-kan-ka*	*flat sausage, usually made from dried pork, beef & spices*
миш-маш m	*meesh-mash*	*scrambled eggs with baked peppers, onions, tomatoes & cheese*
млечна баница f	*mlech-na ba-nee-tsa*	*sweet pastry made with milk & eggs*
мусака от телешко месо f	*moo-sa-ka ot te-lesh-ko me-so*	*minced beef, sliced eggplant & tomatoes, covered in white sauce & oven-baked*

овнешко-пилаф m	*ov*-nesh-ko pee-*laf*	cubed mutton fried with rice, onions, seasonings & tomatoes, then cooked
палачинки f	pa-la-*cheen*-kee	pancakes
пататник m	pa-*tat*-neek	hearty cheese & potato omelette
печено пиле с домати n	*pe*-che-no *pee*-le s do-*ma*-tee	chicken with tomatoes roasted in the oven & served with rice
пълнена риба на фурна n	*puhl*-ne-na *ree*-ba na *foor*-na	carp, sea bass or pike stuffed with rice, hazelnuts, basil & rosemary, then baked
пълнени пиперки с месо f	*puhl*-ne-nee pee-*per*-kee s me-*so*	peppers stuffed with minced veal or pork, paprika & rice, then cooked in the oven
риба-плакия f	*ree*-ba pla-*kee*-ya	baked fish (usually carp) with paprika & tomato paste
сирене по шопски n	*see*-re-ne po *shop*-skee	white cheese, eggs & tomatoes baked in a clay pot
спанак загора m	spa-*nak* za-*go*-ra	spinach baked with sour cream, walnuts, parmesan, garlic, onions & spices
сърми f	suhr-*mee*	vine leaves stuffed with minced lamb or veal & rice, then cooked in a sauce of tomatoes, with sour cream or yogurt
таратор m	ta-ra-*tor*	chilled soup made with finely chopped cucumber, yogurt, walnuts & spices
тюрлюгювеч m	tyoor-lyoo-gyoo-*vech*	diced mutton stewed with tomatoes, peppers & potatoes
халва f	hal-*va*	dessert of melted butter, sugar & water, served with crushed walnuts & cinnamon
чорба от зрял фасул f	chor-*ba* ot zryal fa-*sool*	boiled beans with tomato puree, paprika & mint
чорба от пиле f	chor-*ba* ot *pee*-le	soup made by cooking rice in chicken stock, with yogurt, flour & egg yolks

emergencies

basics

Help!	Помощ!	*po*-mosht
Stop!	Стоп!	stop
Go away!	Махайте се!	*ma*-hai-te se
Thief!	Крадец!	kra-*dets*
Fire!	Пожар!	po-*zhar*
Watch out!	Внимавайте!	vnee-*ma*-vai-te

Call ...!	Повикайте ...!	po-*vee*-kai-te ...
a doctor	лекар	*le*-kar
an ambulance	бърза помощ	*buhr*-za po-mosht
the police	полицията	po-*lee*-tsee-ya-ta

It's an emergency!
Има спешен случай!
ee-ma *spe*-shen *sloo*-chai

Could you help me, please?
Бихте ли ми помогнали?
beeh-te lee mee po-*mog*-na-lee

I have to use the telephone.
Трябва да телефонирам.
tryab-va da te-le-fo-*nee*-ram

I'm lost.
Загубих се.
za-*goo*-beeh se

Where are the toilets?
Къде има тоалетни?
kuh-*de* ee-ma to-a-*let*-nee

police

Where's the police station?
Къде е полицейският участък?
kuh-*de* e po-lee-*tsey*-skee-yat oo-*chas*-tuhk

I want to report an offence.
Искам да съобщя за едно
нарушение.
ees-kam da suh-obsh-*tya* ed-*no*
na-roo-*she*-nee-ye

I have insurance.
Имам застраховка.
ee-mam za-stra-*hov*-ka

I've been ...	... ме.	... me
assaulted	Нападнаха	na-*pad*-na-ha
raped	Изнасилиха	eez-na-*see*-lee-ha
robbed	Ограбиха	o-*gra*-bee-ha

I've lost my ...	Изгубих си ...	eez·goo·beeh see ...
My ... was/were stolen.	Откраднаха ми ...	ot·krad·na·ha mee ...
backpack	раница	ra·nee·tsa
bags	чантите	chan·tee·te
credit card	кредитната карта	kre·deet·na·ta kar·ta
handbag	чантата	chan·ta·ta
jewellery	бижутата	bee·zhoo·ta·ta
money	парите	pa·ree·te
passport	паспорта	pas·por·ta
travellers cheques	пътническите чекове	puht·nee·ches·kee·te che·ko·ve
wallet	портфейла	port·fey·la

I want to contact my ...	Искам да се свържа с нашето ...	ees·kam da se svuhr·zha s na·she·to ...
consulate	консулство	kon·sools·tvo
embassy	посолство	po·sols·tvo

health

medical needs

Where's the nearest ...?	Къде е най-близкият/ най-близката ...? m/f	kuh·de e nai·bleez·kee·yat/ nai·bleez·ka·ta ...
dentist	зъболекар m	zuh·bo·le·kar
doctor	лекар m	le·kar
hospital	болница f	bol·nee·tsa
(night) pharmacist	(нощна) аптека f	(nosht·na) a·po·te·ka

I need a doctor (who speaks English).
Трябва ми лекар
(говорещ английски).
tryab·va mee le·kar
(go·vo·resht ang·lees·kee)

Could I see a female doctor?
Може ли да ме прегледа лекарка?
mo·zhe lee da me pre·gle·da le·kar·ka

I've run out of my medication.
Свърши ми се е лекарството.
svuhr·shee mee se e le·karst·vo·to

conditions, symptoms & allergies

I'm sick.	Болен/Болна съм. m/f	bo-len/bol-na suhm
It hurts here.	Тук ме боли.	took me bo-lee
I have a headache/ toothache.	Боли ме глава/ зъб.	bo-lee me gla-va/ zuhb

I have (a) ...	Имам ...	ee-mam ...
asthma	астма	ast-ma
bronchitis	бронхит	bron-heet
constipation	запек	za-pek
cough	кашлица	kash-lee-tsa
diarrhoea	диария	dee-a-ree-ya
fever	температура	tem-pe-ra-too-ra
heart condition	болно сърце	bol-no suhr-tse
pain	болки	bol-kee
sore throat	възпалено гърло	vuhz-pa-le-no guhr-lo

I'm allergic to ...	Алергичен/Алергична съм на ... m/f	a-ler-gee-chen/a-ler-geech-na suhm na ...
antibiotics	антибиотици	an-tee-bee-o-tee-tsee
anti- inflammatories	противо- възпалителни лекарства	pro-tee-vo- vuhz-pa-lee-tel-nee le-karst-va
aspirin	аспирин	as-pee-reen
bees	пчели	pche-lee
codeine	кодеин	ko-de-een
penicillin	пеницилин	pe-nee-tsee-leen

antiseptic	антисептичен m	an-tee-sep-tee-chen
bandage	бинт m	beent
condoms	презервативи m pl	pre-zer-va-tee-vee
contraceptives	противозачатъчни средства n pl	pro-tee-vo-za-cha-tuhch-nee sred-stva
diarrhoea medicine	лекарство против разтройство n	le-karst-vo pro-teev raz-troyst-vo
insect repellent	средство срещу насекоми n	sredst-vo pro-teev na-se-ko-mee
laxatives	пургатив m	poor-ga-teev
painkillers	обезболяващо n	o-bez-bo-lya-va-shto
rehydration salts	соли за оводняване f pl	so-lee za o-vod-nya-va-ne
sleeping tablets	приспивателно n	pree-spee-va-tel-no

english–bulgarian dictionary

Bulgarian nouns in this dictionary have their gender indicated by ⓜ (masculine), ⓕ (feminine) or ⓝ (neuter). If it's a plural noun, you'll also see pl. Adjectives are given in the masculine form only. Words are also marked as a (adjective), v (verb), sg (singular), pl (plural), inf (informal) or pol (polite) where necessary.

A

accident катастрофа ⓕ ka-tas-tro-fa
accommodation нощувка ⓕ nosh-toov-ka
adaptor адаптер ⓜ a-dap-ter
address адрес ⓜ ad-res
after след sled
air-conditioned с климатична инсталация
s klee-ma-teech-na een-sta-la-tsee-ya
airplane самолет ⓜ sa-mo-let
airport летище ⓝ le-teesh-te
alcohol алкохол ⓜ al-ko-hol
all всичко vseech-ko
allergy алергия ⓕ a-ler-gee-ya
ambulance линейка ⓕ lee-ney-ka
and и ee
ankle глезен ⓜ gle-zen
arm ръка ⓕ ruh-ka
ashtray пепелница ⓕ pe-pel-nee-tsa
ATM банкомат ⓜ ban-ko-mat

B

baby бебе ⓝ be-be
back (body) гръб ⓜ gruhb
backpack раница ⓕ ra-nee-tsa
bad лош losh
bag чанта ⓕ chan-ta
baggage claim подаване на багаж ⓝ
po-da-va-ne na ba-gazh
bank банка ⓕ ban-ka
bar бар ⓜ bar
bathroom баня ⓕ ban-ya
battery батерия ⓕ ba-te-ree-ya
beautiful красив kra-seev
bed легло ⓝ leg-lo
beer бира ⓕ bee-ra
before пред pred
behind зад zad
bicycle колело ⓝ ko-le-lo
big голям gol-yam
bill банкнота ⓕ bank-no-ta

black черен che-ren
blanket одеяло ⓝ o-de-ya-lo
blood group кръвна група ⓕ kruhv-na groo-pa
blue син seen
boat кораб ⓜ ko-rab
book (make a reservation) v запазвам za-paz-vam
bottle шише ⓝ shee-she
bottle opener отварачка ⓕ ot-va-rach-ka
boy момче ⓝ mom-che
brakes (car) спирачки ⓕ pl spee-rach-kee
breakfast закуска ⓕ za-koos-ka
broken (faulty) развален raz-va-len
Bulgaria България ⓕ buhl-ga-ree-ya
Bulgarian (language) български ⓜ buhl-gar-skee
Bulgarian а български buhl-gar-skee
bus автобус ⓜ av-to-boos
business търговия ⓕ tuhr-go-vee-ya
buy купувам koo-poo-vam

C

café кафене ⓝ ka-fe-ne
camera фотоапарат ⓜ fo-to-a-pa-rat
camp site къмпинг ⓜ kuhm-peeng
cancel отказвам ot-kaz-vam
can opener отварачка ⓕ ot-va-rach-ka
car кола ⓕ ko-la
cash пари ⓝ pa-ree
cash (a cheque) v осребрявам os-reb-rya-vam
cell phone мобилен телефон ⓜ mo-bee-len te-le-fon
centre център ⓜ tsen-tuhr
change (money) v сменям smen-yam
cheap евтин ev-teen
check (bill) сметка ⓕ smet-ka
check-in регистрация ⓕ re-gees-tra-tsee-ya
chest гърди ⓕ guhr-dee
child дете ⓝ de-te
cigarette цигара ⓕ tsee-ga-ra
city град ⓜ grad
clean а чист cheest
closed затворен zat-vo-ren
coffee кафе ⓝ ka-fe
coins монети ⓕ pl mo-ne-tee

cold a студен stoo-*den*
collect call обаждане за тяхна цметка ⓝ
o-*bazh*-da-ne na *tyah*-na *smet*-ka
come идвам *eed*-vam
computer компютър ⓜ kom-*pyoo*-tuhr
condom презерватив ⓜ pre-zer-va-*teev*
contact lenses контактни лещи ⓕ pl
kon-*takt*-nee *lesh*-tee
cook v готвя *got*-vya
cost цена ⓕ tse-*na*
credit card кредитна карта ⓕ *kre*-deet-na *kar*-ta
cup чаша ⓕ *cha*-sha
currency exchange обмяна на валута ⓕ
ob-*mya*-na na va-*loo*-ta
customs (immigration) митница ⓕ *meet*-neet-sa

D

dangerous опасен o-*pa*-sen
date (time) дата ⓕ *da*-ta
day ден den
delay закъснение ⓝ za-kuhs-*ne*-nee-ye
dentist зъболекар ⓜ zuh-bo-*le*-kar
depart тръгвам *truhg*-vam
diaper пелена ⓕ pe-le-*na*
dictionary речник ⓜ *rech*-neek
dinner вечеря ⓕ ve-*cher*-ya
direct пряк pryak
dirty мръсен *mruh*-sen
disabled (person) инвалид ⓜ een-va-*leed*
discount намаление ⓝ na-ma-*le*-nee-ye
doctor лекар ⓜ *le*-kar
double bed двойно легло ⓝ *dvoy*-no leg-*lo*
double room стая с две легла ⓕ *sta*-ya s dve leg-*la*
drink пиене ⓝ *pee*-ya
drive v карам *ka*-ram
drivers licence шофьорска книжка ⓕ
sho-*fyor*-ska *kneesh*-ka
drug (illicit) наркотик ⓜ nar-ko-*teek*
dummy (pacifier) биберон ⓜ bee-be-*ron*

E

ear ухо ⓝ oo-*ho*
east изток ⓜ *eez*-tok
eat ям yam
economy class втора класа ⓕ *vto*-ra *kla*-sa
electricity електричество ⓝ e-lek-*tree*-chest-vo
elevator асансьор ⓜ a-san-*syor*
email и-мейл ⓜ *ee*-meyl
embassy посолство ⓝ po-*sols*-tvo

emergency спешен случай ⓜ *spe*-shen *sloo*-chai
English (language) английски ⓜ ang-*lees*-kee
entrance вход ⓜ vhod
evening вечер ⓕ *ve*-cher
exchange rate валутен курс ⓜ va-*loo*-ten *koors*
exit изход ⓜ *eez*-hod
expensive скъп skuhp
express mail бърза поща ⓕ *buhr*-za *posh*-ta
eye око ⓝ o-*ko*

F

far далече da-*le*-che
fast бърз buhrz
father баща ⓜ bash-*ta*
film (camera) филм ⓜ feelm
finger пръст ⓜ pruhst
first-aid kit първа помощ ⓕ *puhr*-va po-*mosht*
first class първа класа ⓕ *puhr*-va *kla*-sa
fish риба ⓕ *ree*-ba
food храна ⓕ hra-*na*
foot крак ⓜ krak
fork вилица ⓕ *vee*-lee-tsa
free (of charge) безплатно bez-*plat*-no
friend приятел/приятелка ⓜ/ⓕ
pree-*ya*-tel/pree-*ya*-tel-ka
fruit плод ⓜ plod
full пълен *puh*-len
funny смешен *sme*-shen

G

gift подарък ⓜ po-*da*-ruhk
girl момиче ⓝ mo-*mee*-che
glass (drinking) чаша ⓕ *cha*-sha
glasses очила ⓝ pl o-chee-*la*
go отивам o-*tee*-vam
good добър do-*buhr*
green зелен ze-*len*
guide гид ⓜ geed

H

half половина ⓕ po-lo-*vee*-na
hand ръка ⓕ ruh-*ka*
handbag дамска чанта ⓕ *dam*-ska chan-*ta*
happy щастлив shtast-*leev*
have имам ee-*mam*
he той toy
head глава ⓕ gla-*va*

heart сърце ⑩ suhr-*tse*
heat горещина ① go-resh-tee-*na*
heavy тежък *te*-zhuhk
help ∨ помагам po-*ma*-gam
here тука *too*-ka
high висок vee-*sok*
highway шосе sho-*se*
hike ∨ ходя пеш *hod*-ya pesh
holiday ваканция ① va-*kan*-tsee-ya
homosexual ⓐ хомосексуален ho-mo-sek-soo-*a*-len
hospital болница ① *bol*-nee-tsa
hot горещ go-*resht*
hotel хотел ⑩ ho-*tel*
hungry гладен *gla*-den
husband мъж ⑩ muhzh

I

I аз az
identification (card) легитимация ①
le-*gee*-tee-*ma*-tsee-ya
ill болен *bo*-len
important важен *va*-zhen
included включен *vklyoo*-chen
injury щета ① shte-*ta*
insurance застраховка ① za-stra-*hov*-ka
Internet интернет ⑩ een-ter-*net*
interpreter преводач ⑩ pre-vo-*dach*

J

jewellery бижутерия ① bee-zhoo-*te*-ree-ya
job работа ① *ra*-bo-ta

K

key ключ ⑩ klyooch
kilogram килограм ⑩ kee-lo-*gram*
kitchen кухня ① *kooh*-nya
knife нож ⑩ nozh

L

laundry (place) пералня ① pe-*ral*-nya
lawyer адвокат ⑩ ad-vo-*kat*
left (direction) ляво *lya*-vo
left-luggage office гардероб ⑩ gar-de-*rob*
leg крак ⑩ krak
lesbian ⓐ лезбийски lez-*bee*-skee

less по-малко po-mal-ko
letter (mail) писмо ⑩ pees-*mo*
lift (elevator) асансьор ⑩ a-san-*syor*
light светлина ① svet-lee-*na*
like ∨ харесвам ha-*res*-vam
lock брава ① bra-*va*
long дълъг *duh*-luhg
lost загубен za-*goo*-ben
lost-property office бюро за загубени вещи ⑩
byoo-ro za za-*goo*-be-nee *vesh*-tee
love ∨ обичам o-*bee*-cham
luggage багаж ⑩ ba-*gazh*
lunch обяд o-*byad*

M

mail поща ① *posh*-ta
man мъж ⑩ muhzh
map карта ① *kar*-ta
market пазар ⑩ pa-*zar*
matches кибрит ⑩ kee-*breet*
meat месо ⑩ me-*so*
medicine лекарство ⑩ le-*karst*-vo
menu меню ⑩ men-*yoo*
message съобщение ⑩ suh-ob-*shte*-nee-ye
milk мляко ⑩ *mlya*-ko
minute минута ① mee-*noo*-ta
mobile phone мобилен телефон ⑩
mo-*bee*-len te-le-*fon*
money пари ① pa-*ree*
month месец ⑩ *me*-sets
morning сутрин ① *soot*-reen
mother майка ① *mai*-ka
motorcycle мотоциклет ⑩ mo-to-tseek-*let*
motorway магистрала ① ma-gee-*stra*-la
mouth уста ① oos-*ta*
music музика ① *moo*-zee-ka

N

name име ⑩ *ee*-me
napkin салфетка ① sal-*fet*-ka
nappy пелена ① pe-le-*na*
near близък *blee*-zuhk
neck врат ⑩ vrat
new нов nov
news новина ① no-vee-*na*
newspaper вестник ⑩ *vest*-neek
night нощ ① nosht
no не ne

noisy шумен *shoo*-men
nonsmoking за непушачи za ne-*poo*-sha-chee
north север ⓜ *se*-ver
nose нос ⓜ nos
now сега *se*-ga
number число ① *chees*-lo

O

oil (engine) масло ① *mas*-lo
old стар star
one-way ticket еднопосочен билет ⓜ
    ed-no-po-*so*-chen bee-*let*
open а отворен ot-*vo*-ren
outside навън na-*vuhn*

P

package колет ⓜ ko-*let*
paper хартия ① har-*tee*-ya
park (car) v паркирам par-*kee*-ram
passport паспорт ⓜ pas-*port*
pay плащам *plash*-tam
pen писалка ① pee-*sal*-ka
petrol бензин ⓜ ben-*zeen*
pharmacy аптека ① ap-*te*-ka
phonecard телефонна карта ① te-le-*fon*-na *kar*-ta
photo снимка ① *sneem*-ka
plate чиния ① chee-*nee*-ya
police полиция ① po-*leet*-see-ya
postcard пощенска карта ① *posh*-ten-ska *kar*-ta
post office поща ① *posh*-ta
pregnant бременна *bre*-men-na
price цена ① *tse*-na

Q

quiet тих teeh

R

rain дъжд ⓜ duhzhd
razor самобръсначка ① sa-mo-bruhs-*nach*-ka
red червен cher-*ven*
refund връщане на парите ①
    vruhsh-ta-ne na pa-*ree*-te
registered mail препоръчано писмо ⓜ
    pre-po-*ruh*-cha-no pees-*mo*
rent v вземам под наем vze-mam pod *na*-em

repair v поправям po-*prav*-yam
reservation резервация ① re-zer-*va*-tsee-ya
restaurant ресторант ⓜ res-to-*rant*
return v връщам *vruhsh*-tam
return ticket билет за отиване и връщане ⓜ
    bee-*let* za o-*tee*-va-ne ee *vruhsh*-ta-ne
right (direction) дясно *dyas*-no
road път ⓜ puht
room стая ① *sta*-ya

S

safe а безопасен be-zo-*pa*-sen
sanitary napkin дамска превръзка ①
    dam-ska pre-*vruhz*-ka
seat място ⓝ *myas*-to
send пращам *prash*-tam
service station бензиностанция ①
    ben-zee-no-*stan*-tsee-ya
sex секс ⓜ seks
shampoo шампоан ⓜ sham-po-*an*
share a room живея в една стая с
    zhee-ve-ya v ed-na *sta*-ya s
shaving cream крем за бръснене ⓜ
    krem za *bruhs*-ne-ne
she тя tya
sheet (bed) чаршаф ⓜ char-*shaf*
shirt риза ① *ree*-za
shoes обувки ① pl o-*boov*-kee
shop магазин ⓜ ma-ga-*zeen*
short къс kuhs
shower душ ⓜ doosh
single room стая с едно легло ① *sta*-ya s ed-*no* leg-*lo*
skin кожа ① *ko*-zha
skirt пола ① po-*la*
sleep v сля spyuh
slowly бавно *bav*-no
small малък *mal*-uhk
smoke (cigarettes) v пуша *poo*-sha
soap сапун ⓜ sa-*poon*
some някои *nya*-ko-yee
soon скоро *sko*-ro
south юг ⓜ yoog
souvenir shop магазин за сувенири ⓜ
    ma-ga-*zeen* za soo-ve-*nee*-ree
speak говоря go-*vor*-ya
spoon лъжица ① luh-*zhee*-tsa
stamp марка ① *mar*-ka
stand-by ticket билет на търси се ⓜ
    bee-*let* na *tuhr*-see se
station (train) гара ① *ga*-ra
stomach стомах ⓜ sto-*mah*

stop v спря spryuh
stop (bus) спирка ① speer-ka
street улица ① oo-leet-sa
student студент/студентка ⑩/①
stoo-dent/stoo-dent-ka
sun слънце ⑩ sluhn-tse
sunscreen крем против загаряне ⑩
krem pro-teev za-ga-rya-ne
swim v плувам ploo-vam

T

tampons тампони ⑩ pl tam-po-nee
taxi такси ① tak-see
teaspoon лъжичка ① luh-zheech-ka
teeth зъби ⑩ pl zuh-bee
telephone телефон ⑩ te-le-fon
television телевизия ① te-le-vee-zee-ya
temperature (weather) температура ①
tem-pe-ra-too-ra
tent палатка ① pa-lat-ka
that (one) онова o-no-va
they те te
thirsty жаден zha-den
this (one) това to-va
throat гърло ⑩ guhr-lo
ticket билет ⑩ bee-let
time време ⑩ vre-me
tired уморен oo-mo-ren
tissues хартийни носни кърпички ① pl
har-teey-nee nos-nee kuhr-peech-kee
today днес dnes
toilet тоалетна ① to-a-let-na
tomorrow утре oot-re
tonight довечера do-ve-che-ra
toothbrush четка за зъби ① chet-ka za zuh-bee
toothpaste паста за зъби ① pas-ta za zuh-bee
torch (flashlight) фенерче ⑩ fe-ner-che
tour екскурзия eks-koor-zee-ya
tourist office бюро за туристическа информация ⑩
byoo-ro za too-rees-tee-ches-ka een-for-ma-tsee-ya
towel кърпа ① kuhr-pa
train влак ⑩ vlak
translate превеждам pre-vezh-dam
travel agency туристическа агенция ①
too-rees-tee-ches-ka a-gen-tsee-ya
travellers cheque пътнически чек ⑩
puht-nee-ches-kee chek
trousers панталони ⑩ pl pan-ta-lo-nee
twin beds двойни легла ⑩ pl dvoy-nee leg-la
tyre гума ① goo-ma

U

underwear бельо ⑩ bel-yo
urgent спешен spe-shen

V

vacant свободен svo-bo-den
vacation ваканция ① va-kan-tsee-ya
vegetable зеленчук ⑩ ze-len-chook
vegetarian a вегетериански ve-ge-te-ree-an-skee
visa виза ① vee-za

W

waiter сервитьор ⑩ ser-vee-tyor
walk v ходя ho-dya
wallet портфейл ⑩ port-feyl
warm a топъл to-puhl
wash (something) мия mee-ya
watch часовник ⑩ cha-sov-neek
water вода ① vo-da
we ние nee-ye
weekend събота и неделя ① suh-bo-ta ee ne-del-ya
west запад ⑩ za-pad
wheelchair инвалидна количка ①
een-va-leed-na ko-leech-ka
when кога ko-ga
where къде kuh-de
white бял byal
who кой koy
why защо zash-to
wife жена ① zhe-na
window прозорец ⑩ pro-zo-rets
wine вино ① vee-no
with с/със s/suhs
without без bez
woman жена ① zhe-na
write пиша pee-sha

Y

yellow жълт zhult
yes да da
yesterday вчера vche-ra
you sg inf ти tee
you sg pol & pl вие vee-ye

88

Croatian

croatian & serbian alphabets

croatian	serbian	croatian	serbian	croatian	serbian	croatian	serbian
A a a	А а	*E e* e	Е е	*Lj lj* l'	Љ љ	*Š š* sh	Ш ш
B b be	Б б	*F f* ef	Ф ф	*M m* em	М м	*T t* te	Т т
C c tse	Ц ц	*G g* ge	Г г	*N n* en	Н н	*U u* u	У у
Č č tch	Ч ч	*H h* ha	Х х	*Nj nj* n'	Њ њ	*V v* ve	В в
Ć ć ch	Ћ ћ	*I i* i	И и	*O o* o	О о	*Z z* zed	З з
D d de	Д д	*J j* y	J j	*P p* pe	П п	*Ž ž* zh	Ж ж
Dž dž dzh	Џ џ	*K k* ka	К к	*R r* er	Р р		
Đ đ j	Ђ ђ	*L l* el	Л л	*S s* es	С с		

croatian/serbian

HRVATSKI

introduction

Did you know that the words *Dalmatian* and *cravat* come from Croatian (*hrvatski* hr·vat·ski), which is also referred to as Serbo-Croatian? Linguists commonly refer to the varieties spoken in Croatia, Bosnia-Hercegovina, Montenegro and Serbia with the umbrella term 'Serbo-Croatian' while acknowledging dialectical differences between them. Croats, Serbs, Bosnians and Montenegrins themselves generally maintain that they speak different languages, however – a reflection of their desire to retain separate ethnic identities.

As the language of about 5 million people in one of the world's newest countries, Croatian has an intriguing, cosmopolitan and at times fraught history. Its linguistic ancestor was brought to the region in the 6th and 7th centuries by the South Slavs, who may have crossed the Danube from the area now known as Poland. This ancestral language split off into two branches: East South Slavic, which later evolved into Bulgarian and Macedonian, and West South Slavic, of which Slovene, Serbian and Croatian are all descendants.

Croatia may be a peaceful country today but the Balkan region to which it belongs has a long history of invasion and conflict. These upheavals have enriched and politicised the language. The invasion by Charlemagne's armies and the conversion of Croats to the Roman Church in AD 803 left its mark on Croatian in the form of words borrowed from Latin and the adoption of the Latin alphabet rather than the Cyrillic alphabet (with which Serbian is written). Subsequent invasions by the Hapsburg, Ottoman and Venetian empires added vibrancy to the language through an influx of German, Turkish and Venetian dialect words. Many words from the standard Italian of Croatia's neighbour Italy have also been absorbed.

The good news is that if you venture into Serbia, Bosnia or Montenegro, you'll be able to enrich your travel experience there by using this chapter. In case of the most common differences between Croatian and Serbian, both translations are given and indicated with ©/®. The Cyrillic alphabet (used alternatively with the Latin alphabet in Serbia, Bosnia and Montenegro) is also included on the page opposite. Croatian is a handy lingua franca in any of the other states that made up part of the former Yugoslavia, as it's an official language in Bosnia-Hercegovina as well as Montenegro (along with Serbian and Bosnian) and people in Macedonia and Slovenia, who speak closely related languages, generally understand Croatian. In other words (often heard throughout this region) – *nema problema* ne·ma pro·ble·ma (no problem)!

pronunciation

vowel sounds

In written Croatian, vowels that appear next to each other don't run together as in English. When you see two or more vowels written next to each other in a Croatian word, pronounce them separately.

symbol	english equivalent	croatian example	transliteration
a	father	*zdravo*	*zdra*·vo
ai	aisle	*ajvar*	*ai*·var
e	bet	*pet*	pet
i	hit	*sidro*	*si*·dro
o	pot	*brod*	brod
oy	toy	*tvoj*	tvoy
u	put	*skupo*	*sku*·po

word stress

As a general rule, in two-syllable words in Croatian stress usually falls on the first syllable. In words of three or more syllables, stress may fall on any syllable except the last. In our pronunciation guides, the stressed syllable is italicised.

Croatian also has what's known as 'pitch accent'. A stressed vowel may have either a rising or a falling pitch and be long or short. The combination of stress, pitch and vowel length in a given syllable occasionally affects the meaning of a word, but you don't need to worry about reproducing this feature of Croatian and we haven't indicated it in this book. In the few cases where it's important, it should be clear from the context what's meant. You may notice though that the speech of native speakers has an appealing musical lilt to it.

consonant sounds

Croatian consonant sounds all have close equivalents in English. The rolled r sound can be pronounced in combination with other consonants as a separate syllable – eg *Hrvat* hr-vat (Croat). If the syllables without vowels look a bit intimidating, try inserting a slight 'uh' sound before the r to help them run off your tongue more easily.

symbol	english equivalent	croatian example	transliteration
b	bed	*glazba*	*glaz*-ba
ch	cheat	*četiri, ćuk*	*che*-ti-ri, chuk
d	dog	*doručak*	*do*-ru-chak
f	fat	*fotograf*	fo-*to*-graf
g	go	*jagoda*	ya-go-da
h	hat	*hodnik*	*hod*-nik
j	joke	*džep, đak*	jep, jak
k	kit	*krov*	krov
l	lot	*lutka*	*lut*-ka
ly	million	*nedjelja*	ned-ye-**lya**
m	man	*mozak*	*mo*-zak
n	not	*nafta*	*naf*-ta
ny	canyon	*kuhinja*	ku-hi-**nya**
p	pet	*petak*	*pe*-tak
r	run (rolled)	*radnik*	*rad*-nik
s	sun	*sastanak*	*sas*-ta-nak
sh	shot	*košta*	*kosh*-ta
t	top	*sat*	sat
ts	hats	*prosinac*	*pro*-si-nats
v	very	*viza*	*vi*-za
y	yes	*svjetlost*	svyet-lost
z	zero	*zec*	zets
zh	pleasure	*koža*	*ko*-zha
'	a slight y sound	*kašalj, siječanj*	ka-shal', si-ye-chan'

basics

language difficulties

Do you speak English?
Govorite/Govoriš li engleski? pol/inf   *go*-vo-ri-te/*go*-vo-rish li *en*-gle-ski

Do you understand?
Da li razumijete/razumiješ? pol/inf   da li ra-*zu*-mi-ye-te/ra-*zu*-mi-yesh

I (don't) understand.
Ja (ne) razumijem.   ya (ne) ra-*zu*-mi-yem

What does (*dobro*) mean?
Što znači (dobro)?   shto *zna*-chi (*do*-bro)

How do you ...?	*Kako se ...?*	*ka*-ko se ...
pronounce this	*ovo izgovara*	*o*-vo iz-*go*-va-ra
write (*dobro*)	*piše (dobro)*	*pi*-she (*do*-bro)

Could you please ...?	*Možete li ...?* pol	*mo*-zhe-te li ...
	Možeš li ...? inf	*mo*-zhesh li ...
repeat that	*to ponoviti*	to po-*no*-vi-ti
speak more slowly	*govoriti sporije*	go-*vo*-ri-ti *spo*-ri-ye
write it down	*to napisati*	to na-*pi*-sa-ti

essentials

Yes.	*Da.*	da
No.	*Ne.*	ne
Please.	*Molim.*	*mo*-lim
Thank you (very much).	*Hvala vam/ti (puno).* pol/inf	*hva*-la vam/ti (*pu*-no)
You're welcome.	*Nema na čemu.*	*ne*-ma na *che*-mu
Excuse me.	*Oprostite.*	o-*pro*-sti-te
Sorry.	*Žao mi je.*	*zha*-o mi ye

numbers

0	nula	nu·la	14	četrnaest	che·tr·na·est	
1	jedan m	ye·dan	15	petnaest	pet·na·est	
	jedna f	yed·na	16	šesnaest	shes·na·est	
	jedno n	yed·no	17	sedamnaest	se·dam·na·est	
2	dva m&n	dva	18	osamnaest	o·sam·na·est	
	dvije f	dvi·ye	19	devetnaest	de·vet·na·est	
3	tri	tri	20	dvadeset	dva·de·set	
4	četiri	che·ti·ri	21	dvadeset jedan	dva·de·set ye·dan	
5	pet	pet	30	trideset	tri·de·set	
6	šest	shest	40	četrdeset	che·tr·de·set	
7	sedam	se·dam	50	pedeset	pe·de·set	
8	osam	o·sam	60	šezdeset	shez·de·set	
9	devet	de·vet	70	sedamdeset	se·dam·de·set	
10	deset	de·set	80	osamdeset	o·sam·de·set	
11	jedanaest	ye·da·na·est	90	devedeset	de·ve·de·set	
12	dvanaest	dva·na·est	100	sto	sto	
13	trinaest	tri·na·est	1000	tisuću/hiljadu ©/⑤	ti·su·chu/hi·lya·du	

time & dates

What time is it?	Koliko je sati?	ko·li·ko ye sa·ti
It's one o'clock.	Jedan je sat.	ye·dan ye sa·t
It's (10) o'clock.	(Deset) je sati.	(de·set) ye sa·ti
Quarter past (10).	(Deset) i petnaest.	(de·set) i pet·na·est
Half-past (10).	(Deset) i po.	(de·set) i po
Quarter to (10).	Petnaest do (deset).	pet·na·est do (de·set)
At what time?	U koliko sati?	u ko·li·ko sa·ti
At ...	U ...	u ...
am	prijepodne	pri·ye·pod·ne
pm	popodne	po·pod·ne
Monday	ponedjeljak	po·ne·dye·lyak
Tuesday	utorak	u·to·rak
Wednesday	srijeda	sri·ye·da
Thursday	četvrtak	chet·vr·tak
Friday	petak	pe·tak
Saturday	subota	su·bo·ta
Sunday	nedjelja	ne·dye·lya

January	siječanj	si·ye·chan'
February	veljača	ve·lya·cha
March	ožujak	o·zhu·yak
April	travanj	tra·van'
May	svibanj	svi·ban'
June	lipanj	li·pan'
July	srpanj	sr·pan'
August	kolovoz	ko·lo·voz
September	rujan	ru·yan
October	listopad	li·sto·pad
November	studeni	stu·de·ni
December	prosinac	pro·si·nats

What date is it today?	Koji je danas datum?	ko·yi ye da·nas da·tum
It's (18 October).	(Osamnaesti listopad).	(o·sam·na·e·sti li·sto·pad)
since (May)	od (svibnja)	od (svib·nya)
until (June)	do (lipnja)	do (lip·nya)
last night	sinoć	si·noch
last week	prošlog tjedna Ⓒ	prosh·log tyed·na
	prošle nedelje Ⓢ	prosh·le ne·de·lye
last month	prošlog mjeseca	prosh·log mye·se·tsa
last year	prošle godine	prosh·le go·di·ne
next week	iduću tjedna Ⓒ	i·du·cheg tyed·na
	iduće nedelje Ⓢ	i·du·che ne·de·lye
next month	idućeg mjeseca	i·du·cheg mye·se·tsa
next year	iduće godine	i·du·che go·di·ne
yesterday/	jučer/	yu·cher/
tomorrow ...	sutra ...	su·tra ...
morning	ujutro	u·yu·tro
afternoon	popodne	po·pod·ne
evening	uvečer	u·ve·cher

weather

What's the weather like?	Kakvo je vrijeme?	kak·vo ye vri·ye·me
It's ...	... je.	... ye
cloudy	Oblačno	o·blach·no
cold	Hladno	hlad·no
hot	Vruće	vru·che
raining	Kišovito	ki·sho·vi·to
snowing	Snjegovito	snye·go·vi·to
sunny	Sunčano	sun·cha·no
warm	Toplo	to·plo
windy	Vjetrovito	vye·tro·vi·to
spring	proljeće n	pro·lye·che
summer	ljeto n	lye·to
autumn	jesen f	ye·sen
winter	zima f	zi·ma

border crossing

I'm here ...	Ja sam ovdje ...	ya sam ov·dye ...
in transit	u prolazu	u pro·la·zu
on business	poslovno	po·slov·no
on holiday	na odmoru	na od·mo·ru
I'm here for ...	Ostajem ovdje ...	o·sta·yem ov·dye ...
(10) days	(deset) dana	(de·set) da·na
(two) months	(dva) mjeseca	(dva) mye·se·tsa
(three) weeks	(tri) tjedna ⓒ	(tri) tyed·na
	(tri) nedelje ⓢ	(tri) ne·de·lye

I'm going to (Zagreb).
Ja idem u (Zagreb).　　　　ya i·dem u (za·greb)

I'm staying at the (Intercontinental).
Odsjesti ću u (Interkontinentalu).　　od·sye·sti chu u (in·ter·kon·ti·nen·ta·lu)

I have nothing to declare.
Nemam ništa za prijaviti.　　ne·mam nish·ta za pri·ya·vi·ti

I have something to declare.
Imam nešto za prijaviti.　　i·mam nesh·to za pri·ya·vi·ti

That's (not) mine.
To (ni)je moje.　　to (ni·)ye mo·ye

transport

tickets & luggage

Where can I buy a ticket?
Gdje mogu kupiti kartu?   gdye *mo*·gu *ku*·pi·ti *kar*·tu

Do I need to book a seat?
Trebam li rezervirati mjesto?   tre·bam li re·zer·*vi*·ra·ti *myes*·to

One ... ticket (to Split), please.	*Jednu ... kartu* *(do Splita), molim.*	*yed*·nu ... *kar*·tu (do *spli*·ta) *mo*·lim
one-way	*jednosmjernu*	*yed*·no·smyer·nu
return	*povratnu*	*po*·vrat·nu

I'd like to ... my ticket, please.	*Želio/Željela bih ...* *svoju kartu, molim.* m/f	zhe·li·o/zhe·lye·la bih ... *svoy*·u *kar*·tu *mo*·lim
cancel	*poništiti*	*po*·ni·shti·ti
change	*promijeniti*	pro·mi·*ye*·ni·ti
collect	*uzeti*	*u*·ze·ti
confirm	*potvrditi*	pot·*vr*·di·ti

I'd like a ... seat, please.	*Želio/Željela bih ...* *sjedište, molim.* m/f	zhe·li·o/zhe·lye·la bih ... *sye*·dish·te *mo*·lim
nonsmoking	*nepušačko*	*ne*·pu·shach·ko
smoking	*pušačko*	*pu*·shach·ko

How much is it?
Koliko stoji?   ko·*li*·ko *stoy*·i

Is there air conditioning?
Imate li klima-uređaj?   *i*·ma·te li *kli*·ma·u·re·jai

Is there a toilet?
Imate li zahod/toalet? ©/ⓢ   *i*·ma·te li *za*·hod/to·a·*let*

How long does the trip take?
Koliko traje putovanje?   ko·*li*·ko *trai*·e pu·to·*va*·nye

Is it a direct route?
Je li to direktan pravac?   ye li to di·*rek*·tan *pra*·vats

Where can I find a luggage locker?
Gdje se nalazi pretinac/sanduče
za odlaganje prtljage? ©/ⓢ   gdye se *na*·la·zi *pre*·ti·nats/*san*·du·che
za od·*la*·ga·nye prt·*lya*·ge

My luggage has been ...	Moja prtljaga je ...	moy·a prt·lya·ga ye ...
damaged	oštećena	osh·te·che·na
lost	izgubljena	iz·gub·lye·na
stolen	ukradena	u·kra·de·na

getting around

Where does flight (10) arrive?
Gdje stiže let (deset)? gdye *sti*·zhe let (*de*·set)

Where does flight (10) depart?
Odakle kreće let (deset)? o·dak·le *kre*·che let (*de*·set)

Where's (the) ...?	Gdje se nalazi ...?	gdye se *na*·la·zi ...
arrivals hall	dvorana za dolaske	dvo·*ra*·na za do·las·ke
departures hall	dvorana za odlaske	dvo·*ra*·na za od·las·ke
duty-free shop	duty-free	dyu·ti·fri
	prodavaonica	pro·da·va·o·ni·tsa
gate (12)	izlaz (dvanaest)	iz·laz (dva·na·est)

Which ... goes	Koji ... ide	koy·i ... i·de
to (Dubrovnik)?	za (Dubrovnik)?	za (du·brov·nik)
boat	brod	brod
bus	autobus	a·u·to·bus
plane	zrakoplov/avion ©/Ⓢ	zra·ko·plov/a·vi·on
train	vlak/voz ©/Ⓢ	vlak/voz

What time's the ... bus?	Kada ide ... autobus?	ka·da i·de ... a·u·to·bus
first	prvi	pr·vi
last	zadnji	zad·nyi
next	slijedeći	sli·ye·de·chi

At what time does it arrive/leave?
U koliko sati stiže/kreće? u ko·*li*·ko *sa*·ti sti·zhe/kre·che

How long will it be delayed?
Koliko kasni? ko·*li*·ko *kas*·ni

What station/stop is this?
Koja stanica je ovo? koy·a *sta*·ni·tsa ye o·vo

What's the next station/stop?
Koja je slijedeća stanica? koy·a ye sli·*ye*·de·cha *sta*·ni·tsa

Does it stop at (Zadar)?
Da li staje u (Zadru)? da li *sta*·ye u (zad·ru)

Please tell me when we get to (Pula).
*Molim vas recite mi
kada stignemo u (Pulu).*
mo·lim vas re·tsi·te mi
ka·da stig·ne·mo u (pu·lu)

How long do we stop here?
Koliko dugo ostajemo ovdje?
ko·li·ko du·go o·stai·e·mo ov·dye

Is this seat available?
Da li je ovo sjedište slobodno?
da li ye o·vo sye·dish·te slo·bod·no

That's my seat.
Ovo je moje sjedište.
o·vo ye moy·e sye·dish·te

I'd like a taxi …
at (9am)
now
tomorrow
*Trebam taksi …
u (devet prijepodne)
sada
sutra*
tre·bam tak·si …
u (de·vet pri·ye·pod·ne)
sa·da
su·tra

Is this taxi available?
Da li je ovaj taksi slobodan?
da li ye o·vai tak·si slo·bo·dan

How much is it to …?
Koliko stoji prijevoz do …?
ko·li·ko stoy·i pri·ye·voz do …

Please put the meter on.
Molim uključite taksimetar.
mo·lim uk·lyu·chi·te tak·si·me·tar

Please take me to (this address).
*Molim da me odvezete
na (ovu adresu).*
mo·lim da me od·ve·ze·te
na (o·vu a·dre·su)

Please …
slow down
stop here
wait here
*Molim vas …
usporite
stanite ovdje
pričekajte ovdje*
mo·lim vas …
u·spo·ri·te
sta·ni·te ov·dye
pri·che·kai·te ov·dye

car, motorbike & bicycle hire

I'd like to
hire a …
bicycle
car
motorbike
*Želio/Željela
bih iznajmiti … m/f
bicikl
automobil
motocikl*
zhe·li·o/zhe·lye·la
bih iz·nai·mi·ti …
bi·tsi·kl
a·u·to·mo·bil
mo·to·tsi·kl

with …
a driver
air conditioning
*sa …
vozačem
klima-uređajem*
sa …
vo·za·chem
kli·ma·u·re·jai·em

How much for ... hire?	*Koliko stoji najam po ...?*	ko·li·ko *stoy*·i *nai*·am po ...
hourly	*satu*	*sa*·tu
daily	*danu*	*da*·nu
weekly	*tjednu/nedelji* ©/⑤	*tyed*·nu/*ne*·de·lyi

air	*zrak/vazduh* m ©/⑤	zrak/*vaz*·duh
oil	*ulje* n	*u*·lye
petrol	*benzin* m	*ben*·zin
tyres	*gume* f pl	*gu*·me

I need a mechanic.
Trebam automehaničara. — tre·bam a·u·to·me·ha·ni·cha·ra

I've run out of petrol.
Nestalo mi je benzina. — ne·sta·lo mi ye ben·zi·na

I have a flat tyre.
Imam probušenu gumu. — i·mam pro·bu·she·nu gu·mu

directions

Where's the ...?	*Gdje je ...?*	gdye ye ...
bank	*banka*	*ban*·ka
city centre	*gradski centar*	*grad*·ski *tsen*·tar
hotel	*hotel*	*ho*·tel
market	*tržnica/pijaca* ©/⑤	*trzh*·ni·tsa/*pi*·ya·tsa
police station	*policijska stanica*	po·*li*·tsiy·ska *sta*·ni·tsa
post office	*poštanski ured*	*po*·shtan·ski *u*·red
public toilet	*javni zahod/toalet* ©/⑤	*yav*·ni za·hod/to·a·*let*
tourist office	*turistička agencija*	tu·*ris*·tich·ka a·*gen*·tsi·ya

Is this the road to (Pazin)?
Je li ovo cesta/put za (Pazin)? ©/⑤ — ye li o·vo *tse*·sta/put za (*pa*·zin)

Can you show me (on the map)?
Možete li mi to — *mo*·zhe·te li mi to
pokazati (na karti)? — po·*ka*·za·ti (na *kar*·ti)

What's the address?
Koja je adresa? — *koy*·a ye a·*dre*·sa

How far is it?
Koliko je udaljeno? — ko·*li*·ko ye u·da·lye·no

How do I get there?
Kako mogu tamo stići? — *ka*·ko *mo*·gu *ta*·mo *sti*·chi

Turn ...	Skrenite ...	skre·ni·te ...
at the corner	na uglu	na u·glu
at the traffic lights	na semaforu	na se·ma·fo·ru
left/right	lijevo/desno	li·ye·vo/de·sno

It's ...	Nalazi se ...	na·la·zi se ...
behind ...	iza ...	i·za ...
far away	daleko	da·le·ko
here	ovdje	ov·dye
in front of ...	ispred ...	i·spred ...
left	lijevo	li·ye·vo
near ...	blizu ...	bli·zu ...
next to ...	pored ...	po·red ...
on the corner	na uglu	na u·glu
opposite ...	nasuprot ...	na·su·prot ...
right	desno	de·sno
straight ahead	ravno naprijed	rav·no na·pri·yed
there	tamo	ta·mo

by bus	autobusom	a·u·to·bu·som
by taxi	taksijem	tak·si·yem
by train	vlakom/vozom ©/⑤	vla·kom/vo·zom
on foot	pješke	pyesh·ke

north	sjever m	sye·ver
south	jug m	yug
east	istok m	is·tok
west	zapad m	za·pad

signs

Ulaz/Izlaz	u·laz/iz·laz	Entrance/Exit
Otvoreno/Zatvoreno	ot vo·re·no/zat vo·re·no	Open/Closed
Slobodna Mjesta	slo·bod·na mye·sta	Rooms Available
Bez Slobodnih Mjesta	bez slo·bod·nih mye·sta	No Vacancies
Informacije	in·for·ma·tsi·ye	Information
Policijska Stanica	po·li·tsiy·ska sta·ni·tsa	Police Station
Zabranjeno	za·bra·nye·no	Prohibited
WC	ve·tse	Toilets
Muški	mush·ki	Men
Ženski	zhen·ski	Women
Toplo/Hladno	to·plo/hlad·no	Hot/Cold

accommodation

finding accommodation

Where's a ...?	Gdje se nalazi ...?	gdye se na·la·zi ...
camping ground	kamp	kamp
guesthouse	privatni smještaj	pri·vat·ni smyesh·tai
	za najam	za nai·am
hotel	hotel	ho·tel
youth hostel	prenoćište za	pre·no·chish·te za
	mladež	mla·dezh

Can you recommend	Možete li	mo·zhe·te li
somewhere ...?	preporučiti negdje ...?	pre·po·ru·chi·ti neg·dye ...
cheap	jeftino	yef·ti·no
good	dobro	do·bro
nearby	blizu	bli·zu

I'd like to book a room, please.
Želio/Željela bih rezervirati   zhe·li·o/zhe·lye·la bih re·zer·vi·ra·ti
sobu, molim. m/f   so·bu mo·lim

I have a reservation.
Imam rezervaciju.   i·mam re·zer·va·tsi·yu

My name's ...
Moje ime je ...   moy·e i·me ye ...

Do you have a ...	Imate li ...?	i·ma·te li ...
room?		
single	jednokrevetnu sobu	yed·no·kre·vet·nu so·bu
double	sobu sa duplim	so·bu sa dup·lim
	krevetom	kre·ve·tom
twin	dvokrevetnu sobu	dvo·kre·vet·nu so·bu

How much is it per ...?	Koliko stoji po ...?	ko·li·ko sto·yi po ...
night	noći	no·chi
person	osobi	o·so·bi

Can I pay by ...?	Mogu li platiti sa ...?	mo·gu li pla·ti·ti sa ...
credit card	kreditnom	kre·dit·nom
	karticom	kar·ti·tsom
travellers cheque	putničkim čekom	put·nich·kim che·kom

For (three) nights.
Na (tri) noći.
na (tri) *no*·chi

From (2 July) to (6 July).
Od (drugog srpnja) do
(šestog srpnja).
od (*dru*·gog *srp*·nya) do
(*she*·stog *srp*·nya)

Can I see it?
Mogu li je vidjeti?
mo·gu li ye *vi*·dye·ti

Am I allowed to camp here?
Mogu li ovdje kampirati?
mo·gu li *ov*·dye kam·*pi*·ra·ti

Where can I find the nearest camp site?
Gdje se nalazi najbliže
mjesto za kampiranje?
gdye se *na*·la·zi *nai*·bli·zhe
mye·sto za kam·*pi*·ra·nye

requests & queries

When/Where is breakfast served?
Kada/Gdje služite doručak?
ka·da/gdye *slu*·zhi·te *do*·ru·chak

Please wake me at (seven).
Probudite me u (sedam), molim.
pro·*bu*·di·te me u (*se*·dam) *mo*·lim

Could I have my key, please?
Mogu li dobiti moj
ključ, molim?
mo·gu li *do*·bi·ti moy
klyuch *mo*·lim

Could I have another (blanket)?
Mogu li dobiti jednu dodatnu
(deku)?
mo·gu li *do*·bi·ti *yed*·nu *do*·dat·nu
(*de*·ku)

Is there a/an ...?	*Imate li ...?*	*i*·ma·te li ...
elevator	*dizalo/lift* ©/Ⓢ	*di*·za·lo/lift
safe	*sef*	sef

The room is too ...	*Suviše je ...*	*su*·vi·she ye ...
expensive	*skupo*	*sku*·po
noisy	*bučno*	*buch*·no
small	*malo*	*ma*·lo

The ... doesn't work.	*... je neispravan.*	... ye *ne*·i·spra·van
air conditioning	*Klima-uređaj*	*kli*·ma·u·re·jai
fan	*Ventilator*	ven·ti·*la*·tor
toilet	*Zahod/Toalet* ©/Ⓢ	*za*·hod/to·a·let

This ... isn't clean.	Ova ... nije čista.	o·va ... ni·ye chis·ta
blanket	deka	de·ka
sheet	plahta ©	plah·ta

This ... isn't clean.	Ovaj ... nije čist.	o·va ... ni·ye chist
sheet	čaršav ⑤	char·shav
towel	ručnik/peškir ©/⑤	ruch·nik/pesh·kir

checking out

What time is checkout?
U koliko sati treba napustiti sobu?   u ko·li·ko sa·ti tre·ba na·pu·sti·ti so·bu

Can I leave my luggage here?
Mogu li ovdje ostaviti svoje torbe?   mo·gu li ov·dye o·sta·vi·ti svoy·e tor·be

Could I have my ..., please?	Mogu li dobiti ..., molim?	mo·gu li do·bi·ti ... mo·lim
deposit	svoj depozit	svoy de·po·zit
passport	svoju putovnicu/ pasoš ©/⑤	svoy·u pu·tov·ni·tsu/ pa·sosh
valuables	svoje dragocjenosti	svo·ye dra·go·tsye·no·sti

communications & banking

the internet

Where's the local Internet café?
Gdje je mjesni internet kafić?   gdye ye mye·sni in·ter·net ka·fich

How much is it per hour?
Koja je cijena po satu?   koy·a ye tsi·ye·na po sa·tu

I'd like to ...	Želio/Željela bih ... m/f	zhe·li·o/zhe·lye·la bih ...
check my email	provjeriti svoj email	pro·vye·ri·ti svoy i·meyl
get Internet access	pristup internetu	pri·stup in·ter·ne·tu
use a printer	koristiti pisač/ štampač ©/⑤	ko·ri·sti·ti pi·sach/ shtam·pach
use a scanner	koristiti skener	ko·ri·sti·ti ske·ner

mobile/cell phone

I'd like a ...	Trebao/Trebala bih ... m/f	tre·ba·o/tre·ba·la bih ...
mobile/cell phone for hire	iznajmiti mobilni telefon	iz·nai·mi·ti mo·bil·ni te·le·fon
SIM card for your network	SIM karticu za vašu mrežu	sim kar·ti·tsu za va·shu mre·zhu

What are the rates?
Koje su cijene telefoniranja?
ko·ye su tsi·ye·ne te·le·fo·ni·ra·nya

telephone

What's your phone number?
Koji je vaš/tvoj broj telefona? pol/inf
koy·i ye vash/tvoy broy te·le·fo·na

The number is ...
Broj je ...
broy ye ...

Where's the nearest public phone?
Gdje je najbliži javni telefon?
gdye ye nai·bli·zhi yav·ni te·le·fon

I'd like to buy a phonecard.
Želim kupiti telefonsku karticu.
zhe·lim ku·pi·ti te·le·fon·sku kar·ti·tsu

I want to ...	Želim ...	zhe·lim ...
call (Singapore)	nazvati (Singapur)	naz·va·ti (sin·ga·pur)
make a (local) call	obaviti (lokalni) poziv	o·ba·vi·ti (lo·kal·ni) po·ziv
reverse the charges	obaviti poziv na račun pozvanog	o·ba·vi·ti po·ziv na ra·chun poz·va·nog

How much does ... cost?	Koliko košta ...?	ko·li·ko kosh·ta ...
a (three)-minute call	poziv od (tri) minute	po·ziv od (tri) mi·nu·te
each extra minute	svaka naknadna minuta	sva·ka nak·nad·na mi·nu·ta

(3 kuna) per (30) seconds.	(3 kune) po (30) sekundi.	(tri ku·ne) po (tri·de·set) se·kun·di

post office

I want to send a ...	Želim poslati ...	zhe·lim po·sla·ti ...
fax	telefaks	te·le·faks
letter	pismo	pi·smo
parcel	paket	pa·ket
postcard	dopisnicu	do·pi·sni·tsu

I want to buy a/an ...	Želim kupiti ...	zhe·lim ku·pi·ti ...
envelope	omotnicu/koverat ©/⑤	o·mot·ni·tsu/ko·ve·rat
stamp	poštansku marku	posh·tan·sku mar·ku

Please send it by ... to (Australia).	Molim da pošaljete to ... u (Australiju).	mo·lim da po·sha·lye·te to ... u (a·u·stra·li·yu).
airmail	zračnom/vazdušnom poštom ©/⑤	zrach·nom/vaz·dush·nom posh·tom
express mail	ekspres poštom	eks·pres posh·tom
registered mail	preporučenom poštom	pre·po·ru·che·nom posh·tom
surface mail	običnom poštom	o·bich·nom posh·tom

Is there any mail for me?
Ima li bilo kakve pošte za mene?   i·ma li bi·lo kak·ve posh·te za me·ne

bank

Where's a/an ...?	Gdje se nalazi ...?	gdye se na·la·zi ...
ATM	bankovni automat	ban·kov·ni a·u·to·mat
foreign exchange office	mjenjačnica za strane valute	mye·nyach·ni·tsa za stra·ne va·lu·te

Where can I ...?	Gdje mogu ...?	gdye mo·gu ...
I'd like to ...	Želio/Željela bih ... m/f	zhe·li·o/zhe·lye·la bih ...
arrange a transfer	obaviti prijenos novca	o·ba·vi·ti pri·ye·nos nov·tsa
cash a cheque	unovčiti ček	u·nov·chi·ti chek
change a travellers cheque	zamijeniti putnički ček	za·mi·ye·ni·ti put·nich·ki chek
change money	zamijeniti novac	za·mi·ye·ni·ti no·vats
get a cash advance	uzeti predujam/avans u gotovini ©/⑤	u·ze·ti pre·du·yam/a·vans u go·to·vi·ni
withdraw money	podignuti novac	po·dig·nu·ti no·vats

What's the ...?	Koji/Kolika je ...? m/f	koy·i/ko·li·ka ye ...
charge for that	pristojba/tarifa	pri·stoy·ba/ta·ri·fa
	za to f ©/⑤	za to
exchange rate	tečaj/kurs	te·chai/kurs
	razmjene m ©/⑤	raz·mye·ne

It's ...	To je ...	to ye ...
(50) kuna	(pedeset) kuna	(pe·de·set) ku·na
free	besplatno	bes·plat·no

What time does the bank open?
U koliko sati se otvara banka? u ko·li·ko sa·ti se ot·va·ra ban·ka

Has my money arrived yet?
Da li je moj novac stigao? da li ye moy no·vats sti·ga·o

sightseeing

getting in

What time does it open/close?
U koliko sati se otvara/zatvara? u ko·li·ko sa·ti se ot·va·ra/zat·va·ra

What's the admission charge?
Koliko stoji ulaznica? ko·li·ko stoy·i u·laz·ni·tsa

Is there a discount for students/children?
Imate li popust za i·ma·te li po·pust za
studente/djecu? stu·den·te/dye·tsu

I'd like a ...	Želio/Željela bih ... m/f	zhe·li·o/zhe·lye·la bih ...
catalogue	katalog	ka·ta·log
guide	turistički vodič	tu·ri·stich·ki vo·dich
local map	kartu mjesta	kar·tu mye·sta

I'd like to see ...
Želio/Željela bih vidjeti ... m/f zhe·li·o/zhe·lye·la bih vi·dye·ti ...

What's that?
Što je to? shto ye to

Can I take a photo?
Mogu li slikati? mo·gu li sli·ka·ti

tours

When's the next ...?	*Kada je idući/ iduća ...?* m/f	*ka*·da ye *i*·du·chi/ *i*·du·cha ...
day trip	*dnevni izlet* m	*dnev*·ni *iz*·let
tour	*turistička ekskurzija* f	tu·*ri*·stich·ka ek·*skur*·zi·ya
Is ... included?	*Da li je ... uključen/ uključena?* m/f	da li ye ... *uk*·lyu·chen/ *uk*·lyu·che·na
accommodation	*smještaj* m	*smye*·shtai
the admission charge	*ulaznica* f	u·*laz*·ni·tsa
food	*hrana* f	*hra*·na
transport	*prijevoz* m	pri·*ye*·voz

How long is the tour?
Koliko traje ekskurzija?   ko·*li*·ko *trai*·e ek·*skur*·zi·ya

What time should we be back?
U koje bi se vrijeme   u *koy*·e bi se vri·*ye*·me
trebali vratiti?   *tre*·ba·li *vra*·ti·ti

sightseeing

castle	*dvorac* m	*dwa*·rats
cathedral	*katedrala* f	ka·te·*dra*·la
church	*crkva* f	*tsr*·kva
main square	*glavni trg* m	*glav*·ni trg
monastery	*samostan/manastir* m ©/⑤	*sa*·mo·stan/*ma*·nas·tir
monument	*spomenik* m	*spo*·me·nik
museum	*muzej* m	*mu*·zey
old city	*stari grad* m	*sta*·ri grad
palace	*palača* f	*pa*·la·cha
ruins	*ruševine* f pl	*ru*·she·vi·ne
stadium	*stadion* m	*sta*·di·on
statue	*kip* m	kip

shopping

enquiries

Where's a ...?	Gdje je ...?	gdye ye ...
bank	banka	ban·ka
bookshop	knjižara	knyi·zha·ra
camera shop	prodavaonica	pro·da·va·o·ni·tsa
	fotoaparata	fo·to·a·pa·ra·ta
department store	robna kuća	rob·na ku·cha
grocery store	prodavaonica	pro·da·va·o·ni·tsa
	namirnica	na·mir·ni·tsa
market	tržnica/pijaca ©/©	tr·zhni·tsa/pi·ya·tsa
newsagency	prodavaonica	pro·da·va·o·ni·tsa
	novina	no·vi·na
supermarket	supermarket	su·per·mar·ket

Where can I buy (a padlock)?
Gdje mogu kupiti (lokot)? — gdye *mo*·gu *ku*·pi·ti (*lo*·kot)

I'm looking for ...
Tražim ... — *tra*·zhim

Can I look at it?
Mogu li to pogledati? — *mo*·gu li to po·*gle*·da·ti

Do you have any others?
Imate li bilo kakve druge? — *i*·ma·te li *bi*·lo *kak*·ve *dru*·ge

Does it have a guarantee?
Ima li ovo garanciju? — *i*·ma li *o*·vo ga·*ran*·tsi·yu

Can I have it sent abroad?
Možete li mi to — *mo*·zhe·te li mi to
poslati u inozemstvo? — po·*sla*·ti u i·no·*zemst*·vo

Can I have my (backpack) repaired?
Mogu li popraviti svoj (ranac)? — *mo*·gu li po·*pra*·vi·ti svoy (*ra*·nats)

It's faulty.
Neispravno je. — ne·*is*·prav·no ye

I'd like ..., please. *Želio/Željela bih ... m/f* — *zhe*·li·o/*zhe*·lye·la bih ...
a bag	vrećicu	*vre*·chi·tsu
a refund	povrat novca	*pov*·rat *nov*·tsa
to return this	ovo vratiti	*o*·vo *vra*·ti·ti

paying

How much is it?
Koliko stoji/košta? ©/⑤   ko·*li*·ko *sto*·yi/*kosh*·ta

Can you write down the price?
Možete li napisati cijenu?   mo·zhe·te li na·*pi*·sa·ti tsi·*ye*·nu

That's too expensive.
To je preskupo.   to ye *pre*·sku·po

Do you have something cheaper?
Imate li nešto jeftinije?   i·ma·te li *nesh*·to yef·*ti*·ni·ye

I'll give you (five kuna).
Dati ću vam (pet kuna).   *da*·ti chu vam (pet *ku*·na)

There's a mistake in the bill.
Ima jedna greška na računu.   i·ma yed·na *gresh*·ka na ra·*chu*·nu

Do you accept …?   *Da li prihvaćate …?*   da li *pri*·hva·cha·te …
    credit cards   *kreditne kartice*   kre·dit·ne *kar*·ti·tse
    debit cards   *debitne kartice*   de·bit·ne *kar*·ti·tse
    travellers cheques   *putničke čekove*   put·nich·ke *che*·ko·ve

I'd like …, please.   *Želio/Željela bih …* m/f   zhe·li·o/zhe·lye·la bih …
    a receipt   *račun*   ra·chun
    my change   *moj ostatak novca*   moy o·*sta*·tak nov·tsa

clothes & shoes

Can I try it on?   *Mogu li to probati?*   mo·gu li to *pro*·ba·ti
My size is (40).   *Moja veličina je*   moy·a ve·li·*chi*·na ye
    (četrdeset).   (che·tr·*de*·set)
It doesn't fit.   *Ne odgovara mi to.*   ne od·*go*·va·ra mi to

small   *sitna*   sit·na
medium   *srednja*   sred·nya
large   *krupna*   krup·na

books & music

I'd like (a) ...	Želio/Željela bih ... m/f	zhe·li·o/zhe·lye·la bih ...
newspaper	novine	no·vi·ne
(in English)	(na engleskom)	(na en·gles·kom)
pen	kemijsku	ke·miy·sku

Is there an English-language bookshop?
Postoji li knjižara za — po·stoy·i li knyi·zha·ra za
engleski jezik? — en·gle·ski ye·zik

I'm looking for something by (Oliver Dragojević).
Tražim nešto od — tra·zhim nesh·to od
(Olivera Dragojevića). — (o·li·ve·ra dra·goy·e·vi·cha)

Can I listen to this?
Mogu li ovo poslušati? — mo·gu li o·vo po·slu·sha·ti

photography

Can you ...?	Možete li ...?	mo·zhe·te li ...
develop this film	razviti ovaj film	raz·vi·ti o·vai film
load my film	staviti moj film	sta·vi·ti moy film
	u foto-aparat	u fo·to·a·pa·rat
transfer photos	prebaciti	pre·ba·tsi·ti
from my	fotografije sa	fo·to·gra·fi·ye sa
camera to CD	mog aparata na CD	mog a·pa·ra·ta na tse de

I need a/an ... film	Trebam ... film	tre·bam ... film
for this camera.	za ovaj foto-aparat.	za o·vai fo·to·a·pa·rat
APS	APS	a pe es
B&W	crno-bijeli	tsr·no·bi·ye·li
colour	kolor	ko·lor

I need a ... film	Trebam film ...	tre·bam film ...
for this camera.	za ovaj foto-aparat.	za o·vai fo·to·a·pa·rat
slide	za dijapozitive	za di·ya·po·zi·ti·ve
(200) speed	brzine (dvijesto)	br·zi·ne (dvi·ye·sto)

When will it	Kada će to biti	ka·da che to bi·ti
be ready?	gotovo?	go·to·vo

meeting people

greetings, goodbyes & introductions

Hello.	*Dobar dan.*	*do-*bar dan
Hi.	*Ćao.*	*cha-*o
Good night.	*Laku noć.*	*la-*ku noch
Goodbye.	*Zbogom.*	*zbo-*gom
Bye.	*Ćao.*	*cha-*o
See you later.	*Doviđenja.*	do-vi-*je-*nya
Mr	*Gospodin*	go-*spo-*din
Mrs	*Gospođa*	go-*spo-*ja
Miss	*Gospođica*	go-*spo-*ji-tsa
How are you?	*Kako ste/si?* pol/inf	*ka-*ko ste/si
Fine. And you?	*Dobro. A vi/ti?* pol/inf	*do-*bro a vi/ti
What's your name?	*Kako se zovete/zoveš?* pol/inf	*ka-*ko se zo-ve-te/zo-vesh
My name is ...	*Zovem se ...*	*zo-*vem se ...
I'm pleased to meet you.	*Drago mi je da smo se upoznali.*	*dra-*go mi ye da smo se u-*poz-*na-li

This is my ...	*Ovo je moj/moja ...* m/f	*o-*vo ye moy/*moy-*a ...
boyfriend	*dečko*	*dech-*ko
brother	*brat*	brat
daughter	*ćerka*	*cher-*ka
father	*otac*	*o-*tats
friend	*prijatelj/prijateljica* m/f	pri-ya-*tel'/*pri-ya-*te-*lyi-tsa
girlfriend	*cura/devojka* ©/©	*tsu-*ra/de-*voy-*ka
husband	*muž*	muzh
mother	*majka*	*mai-*ka
partner (intimate)	*suprug/supruga* m/f	*su-*prug/*su-*pru-ga
sister	*sestra*	*ses-*tra
son	*sin*	sin
wife	*žena*	*zhe-*na

Here's my ...	*Ovo je moj/moja ...* m/f	*o-*vo ye moy/*moy-*a ...
What's your ...?	*Koji je tvoj ...?* m	*koy-*i ye tvoy ...
	Koja je tvoja ...? f	*koy-*a ye *tvoy-*a ...
(email) address	*(email) adresa* f	(*i-*meyl) a-*dre-*sa
fax number	*broj faksa* m	broy *fak-*sa
phone number	*broj telefona* m	broy te-le-*fo-*na

occupations

What's your occupation?	*Čime se bavite?*	chi·me se ba·vi·te
I'm a/an ...	*Ja sam ...*	ya sam ...
artist	*umjetnik* m	um·yet·nik
	umjetnica f	um·yet·ni·tsa
businessperson	*poslovna osoba*	po·slo·vna o·so·ba
farmer	*poljodjelac* ©	po·lyo·dye·lats
	zemljoradnik ⑤	zem·lyo·rad·nik
office worker	*službenik* m	sluzh·be·nik
	službenica f	sluzh·be·ni·tsa
scientist	*znanstvenik* ©	znans·tve·nik
	naučnik ⑤	na·uch·nik
tradesperson	*zanatlija*	za·nat·li·ya

background

Where are you from?	*Odakle ste?*	o·da·kle ste
I'm from ...	*Ja sam iz ...*	ya sam iz ...
Australia	*Australije*	a·u·stra·li·ye
Canada	*Kanade*	ka·na·de
England	*Engleske*	en·gles·ke
New Zealand	*Novog Zelanda*	no·vog ze·lan·da
the USA	*Amerike*	a·me·ri·ke
Are you married?	*Jeste li vi vjenčani?*	ye·ste li vi vyen·cha·ni
I'm married.	*Ja sam u braku.*	ya sam u bra·ku
I'm single.	*Ja sam neoženjen.* m	ya sam ne·o·zhe·nyen
	Ja sam neudata. f	ya sam ne·u·da·ta

age

How old ...?	*Koliko ... godina?*	ko·li·ko ... go·di·na
are you	*imate/imaš* pol/inf	i·ma·te/i·mash
is your daughter	*vaša kći ima*	va·sha k·chi i·ma
is your son	*vaš sin ima*	vash sin i·ma
I'm ... years old.	*Imam ... godina.*	i·mam ... go·di·na
He/She is ... years old.	*On/Ona ima ... godina.*	on/o·na i·ma ... go·di·na

feelings

I'm (not) ...	Ja (ni)sam ...	ya (ni·)sam ...
Are you ...?	Jeste li ...?	ye·ste li ...
happy	sretni	sret·ni
hungry	gladni	glad·ni
OK	dobro	dob·ro
sad	tužni	tuzh·ni
thirsty	žedni	zhed·ni
tired	umorni	u·mor·ni

Are you hot/cold?
Je li vam toplo/hladno?   ye li vam to·plo/hlad·no

I'm (not) hot/cold.
Meni (ni)je toplo/hladno.   me·ni (ni·)ye to·plo/hlad·no

entertainment

going out

Where can	Gdje mogu	gdye mo·gu
I find ...?	pronaći ...?	pro·na·chi ...
clubs	noćne klubove	noch·ne klu·bo·ve
gay venues	gay lokale	gey lo·ka·le
pubs	gostionice	go·sti·o·ni·tse

I feel like going	Želim otići ...	zhe·lim o·ti·chi ...
to a/the ...		
concert	na koncert	na kon·tsert
movies	u kino/bioskop ©/ⓢ	u ki·no/bi·os·kop
party	na zabavu	na za·ba·vu
restaurant	u restoran	u re·sto·ran
theatre	u kazalište	u ka·za·lish·te

interests

Do you like ...?	*Volite li ...?*	*vo·li·te li ...*
I (don't) like ...	*Ja (ne) volim ...*	*ya (ne) vo·lim ...*
art	*umjetnost*	*um·yet·nost*
cooking	*kuhanje*	*ku·ha·nye*
movies	*filmove*	*fil·mo·ve*
reading	*čitanje*	*chi·ta·nye*
shopping	*kupovanje*	*ku·po·va·nye*
sport	*sport*	*sport*
travelling	*putovanja*	*pu·to·va·nya*
Do you like to ...?	*Da li volite da ...?*	*da li vo·li·te da ...*
dance	*plešete*	*ple·she·te*
listen to music	*slušate glazbu/*	*slu·sha·te glaz·bu/*
	muziku ©/Ⓢ	*mu·zi·ku*

food & drink

finding a place to eat

Can you	*Možete li preporučiti*	*mo·zhe·te li pre·po·ru·chi·ti*
recommend a ...?	*neki ...?*	*ne·ki ...*
bar	*bar*	*bar*
café	*kafić*	*ka·fich*
restaurant	*restoran*	*re·sto·ran*
I'd like ...	*Želim ...*	*zhe·lim ...*
a table for (five)	*stol za (petoro)*	*stol za (pe·to·ro)*
the (non)smoking	*(ne)pušačko*	*(ne·)pu·shach·ko*
section	*mjesto*	*mye·sto*

ordering food

breakfast	*doručak* m	*do·ru·chak*
lunch	*ručak* m	*ru·chak*
dinner	*večera* f	*ve·che·ra*
snack	*užina* f	*u·zhi·na*
today's special	*specijalitet dana* m	*spe·tsi·ya·li·tet da·na*

What would you recommend?	*Što biste nam preporučili?*	shto *bi*·ste nam pre·po·*ru*·chi·li
I'd like (the) ..., please.	*Mogu li dobiti ..., molim?*	*mo*·gu li *do*·bi·ti ... *mo*·lim
bill	*račun*	*ra*·chun
drink list	*cjenik pića*	*tsye*·nik *pi*·cha
menu	*jelovnik*	ye·*lov*·nik
that dish	*ono jelo*	*o*·no *ye*·lo

drinks

coffee/tea ...	*kava/čaj ...*	*ka*·va/chai ...
with milk	*sa mlijekom*	sa mli·*ye*·kom
without sugar	*bez šećera*	bez *she*·che·ra
(orange) juice	*sok (od naranče)* m	sok (od *na*·ran·che)
mineral water	*mineralna voda* f	*mi*·ne·ral·na *vo*·da
soft drink	*bezalkoholno piće* m	be·zal·ko·hol·no *pi*·che
(hot) water	*(topla) voda* f	(*to*·pla) *vo*·da

in the bar

I'll have ...	*Želim naručiti ...*	*zhe*·lim na·*ru*·chi·ti ...
I'll buy you a drink.	*Častim vas/te pićem.* pol/inf	*cha*·stim vas/te *pi*·chem
What would you like?	*Što želite/želiš?* pol/inf	shto *zhe*·li·te/*zhe*·lish
Cheers!	*Živjeli!*	*zhi*·vye·li
brandy	*rakija* f	*ra*·ki·ya
champagne	*šampanjac* m	sham·*pa*·nyats
cocktail	*koktel* m	kok·*tel*
plum brandy	*šljivovica* f	*shlyi*·vo·vi·tsa
a bottle/glass of beer	*boca/čaša piva*	*bo*·tsa/*cha*·sha *pi*·va
a shot of (whiskey)	*jedna čašica (viskija)*	*yed*·na *cha*·shi·tsa (*vi*·ski·ya)
a bottle/glass of ... wine	*boca/čaša ... vina*	*bo*·tsa/*cha*·sha ... *vi*·na
red	*crnog*	*tsr*·nog
sparkling	*pjenušavog*	pye·*nu*·sha·vog
white	*bijelog*	bi·*ye*·log

self-catering

What's the local speciality?
Što je ovdje područni/lokalni ©/⑤
specijalitet?

shto ye *ov*·dye *po*·druch·ni/*lo*·kal·ni
spe·tsi·ya·*li*·tet

What's that?
Što je to?

shto ye to

How much is (a kilo of cheese)?
Koliko stoji/košta (kila sira)? ©/⑤

ko·*li*·ko *sto*·yi/*kosh*·ta (*ki*·la *si*·ra)

I'd like ...	*Želim ...*	*zhe*·lim ...
(200) grams	*(dvijesto) grama*	(dvi·ye·sto) *gra*·ma
(two) kilos	*(dvije) kile*	(dvi·ye) *ki*·le
(three) pieces	*(tri) komada*	(tri) ko·*ma*·da
(six) slices	*(šest) krišaka*	(shest) *kri*·sha·ka

Less.	*Manje.*	*ma*·nye
Enough.	*Dosta.*	*do*·sta
More.	*Više.*	*vi*·she

special diets & allergies

Is there a vegetarian restaurant near here?
Da li znate za vegetarijanski
restoran ovdje blizu?

da li *zna*·te za ve·ge·ta·*ri*·yan·ski
re·*sto*·ran *ov*·dye *bli*·zu

Do you have vegetarian food?
Da li imate vegetarijanski obrok?

da li *i*·ma·te ve·ge·ta·*ri*·yan·ski *o*·brok

Could you prepare a	*Možete li prirediti*	*mo*·zhe·te li pri·*re*·di·ti
meal without ...?	*obrok koji ne sadrži ...?*	*o*·brok koy·i ne *sa*·dr·zhi ...
butter	*maslac*	*ma*·slats
eggs	*jaja*	*yai*·a
meat stock	*mesni bujon*	*mes*·ni *bu*·yon

I'm allergic	*Ja sam alergičan/*	ya sam a·*ler*·gi·chan/
to ...	*alergična na ... m/f*	a·*ler*·gich·na na ...
dairy produce	*mliječne proizvode*	mli·*yech*·ne pro·*iz*·vo·de
gluten	*gluten*	*glu*·ten
MSG	*glutaminat*	glu·ta·mi·*nat*
nuts	*razne orahe*	*raz*·ne *o*·ra·he
seafood	*morske plodove*	*mor*·ske *plo*·do·ve

menu decoder

baklava f	ba·*kla*·va	pastry with layers of nuts, sugar & cinnamon, soaked in syrup
bečki odrezak m	*bech*·ki o·dre·zak	Wiener schnitzel
burek m	*bu*·rek	flaky pastry stuffed with cheese or meat
čevapčići m pl	che·*vap*·chi·chi	skinless minced beef & lamb sausages
džuveč m	ju·vech	tomatoey casserole made from mixed vegetables, pork cutlets & rice
gulaš od divljači m	*gu*·lash od *div*·lya·chi	game goulash
hladetina f	*hla*·de·ti·na	pork brawn with vegetables, boiled eggs, garlic, parsley & paprika
hladni pladanj m	*hlad*·ni *pla*·dan'	cold cuts
janjeća čorba f	ya·*nye*·cha *chor*·ba	lamb stew
janjetina na ražnju f	ya·*nye*·ti·na na *razh*·nyu	lamb cooked on a spit
japraci m pl	ya·*pra*·tsi	mincemeat parcels rolled in vine or silver beet leaves (also called **arambašići** a·ram·*ba*·shi·chi)
juha od graha f	*yu*·ha od *gra*·ha	soup made from dried kidney or borlotti beans, smoked bacon bones (or smoked pork hock), onion, carrot, bay leaf & garlic
kiseli kupus m	*ki*·se·li *ku*·pus	sauerkraut – prepared from whole cored cabbage heads layered with horseradish, bay leaves, garlic, dried red pepper & salt
kobasica f	ko·*ba*·si·tsa	sausage
kotlovina f	*kot*·lo·vi·na	fried pork chops simmered in a piquant sauce

ledene kocke f pl	*le·de·ne kots·ke*	coffee- or chocolate-flavoured sponge cake layered with chocolate cream
lička kisela čorba f	*lich·ka ki·se·la chor·ba*	stew prepared with cubed meat, mixed vegetables & cabbage
mađarica f	*ma·ja·ri·tsa*	layers of a rich sweet baked dough interspersed with a chocolate cream filling & topped with melted chocolate
miješano meso n	*mi·ye·sha·no me·so*	mixed grill
musaka f	*mu·sa·ka*	layered lasagne-style dish containing meat & vegetables
odojak na ražnju m	*o·doy·ak na razh·nyu*	suckling pig roasted on a spit
paprikaš m	*pa·pri·kash*	beef or fish stew flavoured with paprika
pastičada f	*pa·sti·cha·da*	beef rounds larded with smoked bacon & stewed with fried vegetables – served with a white wine sauce
pastirska juha f	*pa·stir·ska yu·ha*	soup made from cubed lamb, veal chops & pork neck
pita sa špinatom f	*pi·ta sa shpi·na·tom*	spinach pie & cottage cheese pie
pršut m	*pr·shut*	smoke-dried ham
punjene paprike f pl	*pu·nye·ne pa·pri·ke*	capsicums stuffed with rice, tomato paste, parsley, onion & mincemeat then oven baked
ražnjići m pl	*razh·nyi·chi*	shish kebabs
riblja juha f	*rib·lya yu·ha*	fish chowder made of freshwater fish
sarma f	*sar·ma*	sour cabbage leaves stuffed with a mixture of ground meat, rice & garlic
štrudla f	*shtru·dla*	strudel with a sweet or savoury filling
tartuf m	*tar·tuf*	truffle – sometimes served shaved over scrambled eggs or risotto

emergencies

basics

Help!	Upomoć!	u·po·moch
Stop!	Stanite!	sta·ni·te
Go away!	Maknite se!	mak·ni·te se
Thief!	Lopov!	lo·pov
Fire!	Požar!	po·zhar
Watch out!	Pazite!	pa·zi·te
Call ...!	Zovite ...!	zo·vi·te ...
a doctor	liječnika/lekara ©/⑤	li·yech·ni·ka/le·ka·ra
an ambulance	hitnu pomoć	hit·nu po·moch
the police	policiju	po·li·tsi·yu

It's an emergency!
Imamo hitan slučaj. i·ma·mo hi·tan slu·chai

Could you help me, please?
Molim vas, možete li mi pomoći? mo·lim vas mo·zhe·te li mi po·mo·chi

Can I use your phone?
Mogu li koristiti vaš telefon? mo·gu li ko·ri·sti·ti vash te·le·fon

I'm lost.
Izgubio/Izgubila sam se. m/f iz·gu·bi·o/iz·gu·bi·la sam se

Where are the toilets?
Gdje se nalaze zahodi/toaleti? ©/⑤ gdye se na·la·ze za·ho·di/to·a·le·ti

police

Where's the police station?
Gdje se nalazi policijska stanica? gdye se na·la·zi po·li·tsiy·ska sta·ni·tsa

I want to report an offence.
Želim prijaviti prekršaj. zhe·lim pri·ya·vi·ti pre·kr·shai

I have insurance.
Imam osiguranje. i·mam o·si·gu·ra·nye

I've been ...	Ja sam bio/bila ... m/f	ya sam bi·o/bi·la ...
assaulted	napadnut/napadnuta m/f	na·pad·nut/na·pad·nu·ta
raped	silovan/silovana m/f	si·lo·van/si·lo·va·na
robbed	opljačkan m	op·lyach·kan
	opljačkana f	op·lyach·ka·na

My ... was/were stolen.	Ukrali su mi ...	u·kra·li su mi ...
I've lost my ...	Izgubio/Izgubila	iz·gu·bi·o/iz·gu·bi·la
	sam ... m/f	sam ...
backpack	svoj ranac	svoy ra·nats
bags	svoje torbe	svoy·e tor·be
credit card	svoju kreditnu	svoy·oo kre·dit·nu
	karticu	kar·ti·tsu
jewellery	svoj nakit	svoy na·kit
money	svoj novac	svoy no·vats
passport	svoju putovnicu ©	svoy·oo pu·tov·ni·tsu
	svoj pasoš ⑤	svoy pa·sosh
travellers cheques	svoje putničke	svoy·e put·nich·ke
	čekove	che·ko·ve
I want to contact	Želim stupiti u	zhe·lim stu·pi·ti u
my ...	kontakt sa ...	kon·takt sa ...
consulate	svojom ambasadom	svoy·om am·ba·sa·dom
embassy	svojim konzulatom	svoy·im kon·zu·la·tom

health

medical needs

Where's the	Gdje je najbliži/	gdye ye nai·bli·zhi/
nearest ...?	najbliža ...? m/f	nai·bli·zha ...
dentist	zubar m	zu·bar
doctor	liječnik/lekar m ©/⑤	li·yech·nik/le·kar
hospital	bolnica f	bol·ni·tsa
(night) pharmacist	(noćna) ljekarna/	(noch·na) lye·kar·na
	apoteka f ©/⑤	a·po·te·ka

I need a doctor (who speaks English).
Trebam liječnika/lekara   tre·bam li·yech·ni·ka/le·ka·ra
(koji govori engleski). ©/⑤   (koy·i go·vo·ri en·gle·ski)

Could I see a female doctor?
Mogu li dobiti ženskog   mo·gu li do·bi·ti zhen·skog
liječnika/lekara? ©/⑤   li·yech·ni·ka/le·ka·ra

I've run out of my medication.
Nestalo mi je lijekova.   ne·sta·lo mi ye li·ye·ko·va

symptoms, conditions & allergies

I'm sick.	Ja sam bolestan/ bolesna. m/f	ya sam bo·le·stan/ bo·le·sna
It hurts here.	Boli me ovdje.	bo·li me ov·dye
I have ...	Imam ...	i·mam ...

asthma	astma f	ast·ma
bronchitis	bronhitis m	bron·hi·tis
constipation	zatvorenje n	zat·vo·re·nye
cough	kašalj m	ka·shal'
diarrhoea	proljev m	pro·lyev
fever	groznica f	gro·zni·tsa
headache	glavobolja f	gla·vo·bo·lya
heart condition	poremećaj srca m	po·re·me·chai sr·tsa
nausea	mučnina f	much·ni·na
pain	bol m	bol
sore throat	grlobolja f	gr·lo·bo·lya
toothache	zubobolja f	zu·bo·bo·lya

| I'm allergic to ... | Ja sam alergičan/ alergična na ... m/f | ya sam a·ler·gi·chan/ a·ler·gich·na na ... |

antibiotics	antibiotike	an·ti·bi·o·ti·ke
anti-inflammatories	lijekove protiv upale	li·ye·ko·ve pro·tiv u·pa·le
aspirin	aspirin	a·spi·rin
bees	pčele	pche·le
codeine	kodein	ko·de·in
penicillin	penicilin	pe·ni·tsi·lin

antiseptic	antiseptik m	an·ti·sep·tik
bandage	zavoj m	za·voy
contraceptives	sredstva za spriječavanje trudnoće n pl	sreds·tva za spri·ye·cha·va·nye trud·no·che
diarrhoea medicine	lijekovi protiv proljeva m pl	li·ye·ko·vi pro·tiv pro·lye·va
insect repellent	sredstvo za odbijanje insekata n	sreds·tvo za od·bi·ya·nye in·se·ka·ta
laxatives	laksativi m pl	lak·sa·ti·vi
painkillers	tablete protiv bolova f pl	ta·ble·te pro·tiv bo·lo·va
rehydration salts	soli za rehidrataciju f	so·li za re·hi·dra·ta·tsi·yu
sleeping tablets	tablete za spavanje f pl	ta·ble·te za spa·va·nye

english–croatian dictionary

Croatian nouns in this dictionary have their gender indicated by ⓜ (masculine), ⓕ (feminine) or ⓝ (neuter). If it's a plural noun, you'll also see pl. Adjectives are given in the masculine form only. Words are also marked as a (adjective), v (verb), sg (singular), pl (plural), inf (informal), pol (polite), ⓒ (Croatian) or ⓢ (Serbian) where necessary.

A

accident *nezgoda* ⓕ *nez-*go-da
accommodation *smještaj* ⓜ *smye-*shtai
adaptor *konverter* ⓜ kon-*ver-*ter
address *adresa* ⓕ a-*dre-*sa
after *poslije* po-*sli-*ye
air-conditioned *klimatiziran* kli-ma-*ti-*zi-ran
airplane *zrakoplov/avion* ⓜ
     zra-ko-plov/a-vi-on ⓒ/ⓢ
airport *zračna luka* ⓕ*/aerodrom* ⓜ
     zrach-na lu-ka/a-e-ro-drom ⓒ/ⓢ
alcohol *alkohol* ⓜ *al-*ko-hol
all *sve* sve
allergy *alergija* ⓕ a-*ler-*gi-ya
ambulance *hitna pomoć* ⓕ *hit-*na *po-*moch
and *i* i
ankle *gležanj/članak* ⓜ *gle-*zhan'/*chla-*nak ⓒ/ⓢ
arm *ruka* ⓕ *ru-*ka
ashtray *pepeljara* ⓕ pe-*pe-*lya-ra
ATM *bankovni automat* ⓜ *ban-*kov-ni a-u-to-mat

B

baby *beba* ⓕ *be-*ba
back (body) *leđa* ⓝ pl *le-*ja
backpack *ranac* ⓜ *ra-*nats
bad *loš* losh
bag *torba* ⓕ *tor-*ba
baggage claim *šalter za podizanje prtljage* ⓜ
     *shal-*ter za po-di-za-nye prt-*lya-*ge
bank *banka* ⓕ *ban-*ka
bar *bar* ⓜ bar
bathroom *kupaonica* ⓕ ku-pa-o-*ni-*tsa
battery (car) *akumulator* ⓜ a-ku-mu-*la-*tor
battery (general) *baterija* ⓕ ba-*te-*ri-ya
beautiful *lijep* *li-*yep
bed *krevet* ⓜ *kre-*vet
beer *pivo* ⓝ *pi-*vo
before *prije* *pri-*ye
behind *iza* i-za
bicycle *bicikl* li-*yep*
big *velik* *ve-*lik
bill *račun* ⓜ *ra-*chun

black *crn* tsrn
blanket *deka* ⓕ *de-*ka
blood group *krvna grupa* ⓕ *krv-*na *gru-*pa
blue *plav* plav
boat (ship) *brod* ⓜ brod
boat (smaller/private) *čamac* ⓜ *cha-*mats
book (make a reservation) v *rezervirati* re-zer-*vi-*ra-ti
Bosnia-Hercegovina *Bosna i Hercegovina* ⓕ
     bos-na i her-tse-go-*vi-*na
Bosnian (language) *bosanski jezik* ⓜ bo-*san-*ski *ye-*zik
bottle *boca* ⓕ *bo-*tsa
bottle opener *otvarač za boce* ⓜ ot-*va-*rach za *bo-*tse
boy *dječak* ⓜ *dye-*chak
brakes (car) *kočnice* ⓕ pl *koch-*ni-tse
breakfast *doručak* ⓜ *do-*ru-chak
broken (faulty) *pokvaren* po-*kva-*ren
bus *autobus* ⓜ a-u-*to-*bus
business *biznis* ⓜ *biz-*nis
buy *kupiti* ku-*pi-*ti

C

café *kafić/kavana* ⓜ/ⓕ ka-*fich*/ka-*va-*na
camera *foto-aparat* ⓜ *fo-*to-a-*pa-*rat
camp site *mjesto za kampiranje* ⓜ
     *mye-*sto za kam-*pi-*ra-nye
cancel *poništiti* po-*ni-*shti-ti
can opener *otvarač za limenke/konzerve* ⓜ
     ot-*va-*rach za *li-*men-ke/*kon-*zer-ve ⓒ/ⓢ
car *automobil* ⓜ a-u-to-*mo-*bil
cash *gotovina* ⓕ go-to-*vi-*na
cash (a cheque) v *unovčiti* u-nov-*chi-*ti
cell phone *mobilni telefon* ⓜ *mo-*bil-ni te-*le-*fon
centre *centar* ⓜ *tsen-*tar
change (money) v *zamijeniti* za-mi-*ye-*ni-ti
cheap *jeftin* *yef-*tin
check (bill) *račun* ⓜ *ra-*chun
check-in *prijemni šalter* ⓜ pri-*yem-*ni *shal-*ter
chest *prsa/grudi* ⓝ pl *pr-*sa/*gru-*di ⓒ/ⓢ
child *dijete* ⓝ di-*ye-*te
cigarette *cigareta* ⓕ tsi-ga-*re-*ta
city *grad* ⓜ grad
clean a *čist* chist
closed *zatvoren* zat-*vo-*ren
coffee *kava* ⓕ *ka-*va

coins *novčići* ⓜ pl *nov*-chi-chi
cold a *hladan hla*-dan
collect call *poziv na račun nazvane osobe* ⓜ
po-ziv na *ra*-chun *naz*-va-ne o-so-be
come *doći* do-chi
computer *računalo* ⓝ/*kompjuter* ⓜ
ra-chu-na-lo/komp-*yu*-ter ©/⑤
condom *prezervativ* ⓜ pre-zer-va-tiv
contact lenses *kontakt leće* ⓕ pl/*kontaktna sočiva*
ⓝ pl *kon*-takt *le*-che/*kon*-takt-na *so*-chi-va ©/⑤
cook v *kuhati ku*-ha-ti
cost *cijena* ⓕ *tsi*-ye-na
credit card *kreditna kartica* ⓕ *kre*-dit-na *kar*-ti-tsa
Croatia *Hrvatska* ⓕ *hr*-vat-ska
Croatian (language) *hrvatski* ⓜ *hr*-vat-ski
Croatian a *hrvatski hr*-vat-ski
cup *šalica/šoljica* ⓕ *sho*-li-tsa/*sho*-l'i-tsa ©/⑤
currency exchange *tečaj/kurs strana valuta* ⓕ
te-chai/kurs *stra*-nih va-*lu*-ta ©/⑤
customs (immigration) *carinarnica* ⓕ *tsa*-ri-*nar*-ni-tsa

D

dangerous *opasan* o-pa-san
date (time) *datum* ⓜ *da*-tum
day *dan* ⓜ dan
delay *zakašnjenje* ⓝ za-kash-*nye*-nye
dentist *zubar* ⓜ zu-bar
depart *otići* o-ti-chi
diaper *pelene* ⓕ pl *pe*-le-ne
dictionary *rječnik* ⓜ *ryech*-nik
dinner *večera* ⓕ *ve*-che-ra
direct *direktan* di-rek-tan
dirty *prljav* pr-lyav
disabled *onesposobljen* o-ne-spo-*sob*-lyen
discount *popust* ⓜ po-pust
doctor *liječnik/lekar* ⓜ li-*yech*-nik/*le*-kar ©/⑤
double bed *dupli krevet* ⓜ *du*-pli kre-vet
double room *dvokrevetna soba* ⓕ *dvo*-kre-vet-na so-ba
drink *piće* ⓝ *pi*-che
drive v *voziti* vo-zi-ti
drivers licence *vozačka dozvola* ⓕ *vo*-zach-ka *doz*-vo-la
drug (illicit) *droga* ⓕ *dro*-ga
dummy (pacifier) *duda/cucla* ⓕ *du*-da/*tsu*-tsla ©/⑤

E

ear *uho* ⓝ *u*-ho
east *istok* ⓜ *i*-stok
eat *jesti ye*-sti
economy class *drugi razred* ⓜ *dru*-gi raz-red
electricity *struja* ⓕ *stru*-ya
elevator *dizalo* ⓝ/*lift* ⓜ *di*-za-lo/lift ©/⑤

email *e-mail* ⓜ *i*.me-il
embassy *ambasada* ⓕ am-ba-*sa*-da
emergency *hitan slučaj* ⓜ *hi*-tan *slu*-chai
English (language) *engleski* ⓜ *en*-gle-ski
entrance *ulaz* ⓜ *u*-laz
evening *večer* ⓕ *ve*-cher
exchange rate *tečaj/kurs razmjene* ⓜ
te-chai/kurs *raz*-mye-ne©/⑤
exit *izlaz* ⓜ *iz*-laz
expensive *skup* skup
express mail *ekspres pošta* ⓕ *eks*-pres *posh*-ta
eye *oko* ⓝ *o*-ko

F

far *daleko* da-*le*-ko
fast *brz* brz
father *otac* ⓜ *o*-tats
film (camera) *film* ⓜ film
finger *prst* ⓜ prst
first-aid kit *pribor za prvu pomoć* ⓜ
pri-bor za *pr*-vu po-moch
first class *prvi razred* ⓜ *pr*-vi raz-red
fish *riba* ⓕ *ri*-ba
food *hrana* ⓕ *hra*-na
foot *stopalo* ⓝ *sto*-pa-lo
fork *viljuška* ⓕ *vi*-lyush-ka
free (of charge) *besplatan be*-spla-tan
friend *prijatelj/prijateljica* ⓜ/ⓕ
pri-ya-tel'/*pri*-ya-te-lyi-tsa
fruit *voće* ⓝ *vo*-che
full *pun* pun
funny *smješan smye*-shan

G

gift *dar/poklon* ⓜ dar/*pok*-lon ©/⑤
girl *djevojčica* ⓕ dye-*voy*-chi-tsa
glass (drinking) *čaša* ⓕ *cha*-sha
glasses *naočale* ⓕ pl *na*-o-cha-le
go *ići* i-chi
good *dobar* do-bar
green *zelen* ze-len
guide *vodič* ⓜ *vo*-dich

H

half *polovina* ⓕ po-lo-*vi*-na
hand *ruka* ⓕ *ru*-ka
handbag *ručna torbica* ⓕ *ruch*-na *tor*-bi-tsa
happy *sretan sre*-tan
have *imati i*-ma-ti
he *on* on

head *glava* ⓝ *gla*-va
heart *srce* ⓝ *sr*-tse
heat *vrućina* ⓕ vru-*chi*-na
heavy *težak* te-*zhak*
help V *pomoći* po-*mo*-chi
here *ovdje* *ov*-dye
high *visok* vi-*sok*
highway *autoput* *a*-u-to-put
hike V *pješačiti* pye-*sha*-chi-ti
holidays *praznici* ⓜ pl *praz*-ni-tsi
homosexual *homoseksualac/homoseksualka* ⓜ/ⓕ *ho*-mo-sek-su-a-lats/*ho*-mo-sek-su-al-ka
hospital *bolnica* ⓕ *bol*-ni-tsa
hot *vruć* vruch
hotel *hotel* ⓜ ho-*tel*
hungry *gladan/gladna* ⓜ/ⓕ *gla*-dan/*gla*-dna
husband *muž* ⓜ muzh

I

I *ja* ya
identification (card) *osobna iskaznica/lična karta* ⓕ o-*sob*-na i-*skaz*-ni-tsa/*lich*-na *kar*-ta ©/Ⓢ
ill *bolestan* bo-le-*stan*
important *važan* *va*-zhan
included *uključen* uk-*lyu*-chen
injury *povreda* ⓕ po-*vre*-da
insurance *osiguranje* ⓝ o-si-gu-*ra*-nye
Internet *internet* ⓜ *in*-ter-net
interpreter *tumač* ⓜ *tu*-mach

J

jewellery *nakit* ⓜ *na*-kit
job *posao* ⓜ *po*-sa-o

K

key *ključ* ⓜ klyuch
kilogram *kilogram* ⓜ *ki*-lo-gram
kitchen *kuhinja* ⓕ *ku*-hi-nya
knife *nož* ⓜ nozh

L

laundry (place) *praonica* ⓕ pra-*o*-ni-tsa
lawyer *pravnik* ⓜ *prav*-nik
left (direction) *lijevi* *li*-ye-vi
left-luggage office *ured za odlaganje prtljage* ⓜ *u*-red za od-*la*-ga-nye prt-*lya*-ge
leg *noga* ⓕ *no*-ga
lesbian *lezbijka* ⓕ *lez*-biy-ka
less *manje* *ma*-nye

letter (mail) *pismo* ⓝ *pi*-smo
lift (elevator) *dizalo* ⓝ/*lift* di-za-lo/lift ©/Ⓢ
light *svjetlost* ⓕ *svyet*-lost
like V *dopadati se* do-*pa*-da-ti se
lock *brava* ⓕ *bra*-va
long *dugačak* du-*ga*-chak
lost *izgubljen* iz-*gub*-lyen
lost-property office *ured za izgubljene stvari* ⓜ *u*-red za iz-*gub*-lye-ne *stva*-ri
love V *voljeti* vo-*lye*-ti
luggage *prtljaga* ⓕ prt-*lya*-ga
lunch *ručak* ⓜ *ru*-chak

M

mail *pošta* ⓕ *posh*-ta
man *čovjek* ⓜ *cho*-vyek
map (of country) *karta* ⓕ *kar*-ta
map (of town) *plan grada* ⓜ plan *gra*-da
market *tržnica/pijaca* ⓕ *trzh*-ni-tsa ©/Ⓢ
matches *šibice* ⓕ pl *shi*-bi-tse
meat *meso* ⓝ *me*-so
medicine *lijekovi* ⓜ pl li-*ye*-ko-vi
menu *jelovnik* ⓜ ye-*lov*-nik
message *poruka* ⓕ po-*ru*-ka
milk *mlijeko* ⓝ mli-*ye*-ko
minute *minuta* ⓕ mi-*nu*-ta
mobile phone *mobilni telefon* ⓜ mo-bil-ni te-*le*-fon
money *novac* ⓜ *no*-vats
Montenegro *Crna Gora* ⓕ tsr-na *go*-ra
month *mjesec* ⓜ *mye*-sets
morning *jutro* ⓝ *yu*-tro
mother *majka* ⓕ *mai*-ka
motorcycle *motocikl* ⓜ mo-to-*tsi*-kl
motorway *autoput* ⓜ *a*-u-to-put
mouth *usta* ⓝ pl *u*-sta
music *glazba* ⓕ *glaz*-ba

N

name *ime* ⓝ *i*-me
napkin *salveta* ⓕ sal-*ve*-ta
nappy *pelene* ⓕ pl *pe*-le-ne
near *blizu* bli-zu
neck *vrat* ⓜ vrat
new *nov* nov
news *vijesti* ⓕ pl vi-*ye*-sti
newspaper *novine* ⓕ pl *no*-vi-ne
night *noć* ⓕ noch
no *ne* ne
noisy *bučan* bu-*chan*
nonsmoking *nepušački* ⓝ *ne*-pu-shach-ki
north *sjever* ⓜ *sye*-ver

nose *nos* ⓜ nos
now *sada* sa-da
number *broj* ⓜ broy

O

oil (engine) *ulje* ⓝ u-lye
old *star* star
one-way ticket *jednosmjerna karta* ⓕ
  yed-no-smyer-na *kar*-ta
open ⓐ *otvoren* ot-vo-ren
outside *vani/napolju* va-ni/na-po-l'u ⓒ/Ⓢ

P

package *paket* ⓜ *pa*-ket
paper *papir* ⓜ *pa*-pir
park (car) ⱽ *parkirati* par-*ki*-ra-ti
passport *putovnica* ⓕ/*pasoš* ⓜ
  pu-*tov*-ni-tsa/*pa*-sosh ⓒ/Ⓢ
pay *platiti* *pla*-ti-ti
pen *kemijska* ⓕ *ke*-miy-ska
petrol *benzin* ⓜ ben-*zin*
pharmacy *ljekarna/apoteka* ⓕ
  lye-*kar*-na/a-po-*te*-ka ⓒ/Ⓢ
phonecard *telefonska kartica* ⓕ
  te-le-fon-ska *kar*-ti-tsa
photo *fotografija* ⓕ fo-to-*gra*-fi-ya
plate *tanjur* ⓜ *ta*-nyur
police *policija* ⓕ po-*li*-tsi-ya
postcard *dopisnica* ⓕ do-pi-sni-tsa
post office *poštanski ured* ⓜ posh-tan-ski *u*-red
pregnant *trudna* trud-na
price *cijena* ⓕ tsi-*ye*-na

Q

quiet *tih* tih

R

rain *kiša* ⓕ *ki*-sha
razor *brijač* ⓜ *bri*-yach
receipt *račun* ⓜ *ra*-chun
red *crven* tsr-ven
refund *povrat novca* ⓜ *pov*-rat *nov*-tsa
registered mail *preporučena pošta* ⓕ
  pre-po-ru-che-na *posh*-ta
rent ⱽ *iznajmiti* iz-*nai*-mi-ti
repair ⱽ *popraviti* po-*pra*-vi-ti
reservation *rezervacija* ⓕ re-zer-*va*-tsi-ya
restaurant *restoran* ⓜ re-*sto*-ran
return ⱽ *vratiti se* *vra*-ti-ti se

return ticket *povratna karta* ⓕ *po*-*vra*-tna *kar*-ta
right (direction) *desno* de-*sno*
road *cesta* ⓕ/*put* ⓜ *tse*-sta/put ⓒ/Ⓢ
room *soba* ⓕ *so*-ba

S

safe ⓐ *siguran* si-*gu*-ran
sanitary napkin *higijenski uložak* ⓜ
  hi-gi-yen-ski u-lo-zhak
seat *sjedište* ⓝ *sye*-dish-te
send *poslati* po-*sla*-ti
Serbia *Srbija* ⓕ *sr*-bi-ya
Serbian (language) *srpski jezik* ⓜ *srp*-ski *ye*-zik
service station *benzinska stanica* ⓕ
  ben-zin-ska *sta*-ni-tsa
sex *seks* ⓜ seks
shampoo *šampon* ⓜ sham-*pon*
share (a dorm) *dijeliti* di-*ye*-li-ti
shaving cream *pjena za brijanje* ⓕ
  pye-na za bri-ya-nye
she *ona* o-na
sheet (bed) *plahta* ⓕ/*čaršav* ⓜ
  pla-hta/char-shav ⓒ/Ⓢ
shirt *košulja* ⓕ *ko*-shu-lya
shoes *cipele* ⓕ pl *tsi*-pe-le
shop *prodavaonica* ⓕ pro-da-va-o-ni-tsa
short *kratak* *kra*-tak
shower *tuš* ⓜ tush
single room *jednokrevetna soba* ⓕ
  yed-no-kre-vet-na *so*-ba
skin *koža* ⓕ *ko*-zha
skirt *suknja* ⓕ *suk*-nya
sleep ⱽ *spavati* *spa*-va-ti
slowly *sporo* spo-ro
small *mali* *ma*-li
smoke (cigarettes) ⱽ *pušiti* pu-*shi*-ti
soap *sapun* ⓜ *sa*-pun
some *malo* ma-lo
soon *uskoro* u-*sko*-ro
south *jug* ⓜ yug
souvenir shop *prodavaonica suvenira* ⓕ
  pro-da-va-o-ni-tsa su-ve-*ni*-ra
speak *govoriti* go-vo-ri-ti
spoon *žlica/kašika* ⓕ *zhli*-tsa/*ka*-shi-ka ⓒ/Ⓢ
stamp *poštanska marka* ⓕ posh-tan-ska *mar*-ka
stand-by ticket *uvjetna/uslovna karta* ⓕ
  uv-yet-na/us-lov-na *kar*-ta ⓒ/Ⓢ
station (train) *stanica* ⓕ *sta*-ni-tsa
stomach *želudac* ⓜ zhe-*lu*-dats
stop ⱽ *zaustaviti* za-u-sta-vi-ti
stop (bus) *stanica* ⓕ *sta*-ni-tsa
street *ulica* ⓕ *u*-li-tsa

student *student* ⓜ & ⓕ *stu*-dent
sun *sunce* ⓝ *sun*-tse
sunscreen *losion za zaštitu od sunca* ⓜ *lo*-si-on za *zash*-ti-tu od *sun*-tsa
swim v *plivati* pli-*va*-ti

T

tampon *tampon* ⓜ *tam*-pon
taxi *taksi* ⓜ *tak*-si
teaspoon *žličica/kašičica* ⓕ *zhli*-chi-tsa/*ka*-shi-chi-tsa ©/Ⓢ
teeth *zubi* ⓜ pl *zu*-bi
telephone *telefon* ⓜ te-*le*-fon
television *televizija* ⓕ te-le-*vi*-zi-ya
temperature (weather) *temperatura* ⓕ tem-pe-ra-*tu*-ra
tent *šator* ⓜ *sha*-tor
that (one) *ono* o-no
they *oni/one/ona* ⓜ/ⓘ/ⓕ o-ni/o-ne/o-na
thirsty *žedan* zhe-dan
this (one) *ovo* o-vo
throat *grlo* ⓝ *gr*-lo
ticket *karta* ⓕ *kar*-ta
time *vrijeme* ⓝ vri-ye-me
tired *umoran* u-mo-ran
tissues *papirnati rupčići* ⓜ pl *pa*-pir-na-ti *rup*-chi-chi ©
   papirne maramice ⓕ pl *pa*-pir-ne *ma*-ra-mi-tse Ⓢ
today *danas* *da*-nas
toilet *zahod/toalet* ⓜ *za*-hod/to-a-*let* ©/Ⓢ
tomorrow *sutra* su-tra
tonight *večeras* ve-*che*-ras
toothbrush *četkica za zube* ⓕ *chet*-ki-tsa za *zu*-be
toothpaste *pasta za zube* ⓕ *pa*-sta za *zu*-be
torch (flashlight) *ručna svjetiljka* ⓕ *ruch*-na svye-til'-ka
tour *ekskurzija* ⓕ ek-*skur*-zi-ya
tourist office *turistička agencija* ⓕ tu-ri-*stich*-ka a-*gen*-tsi-ya
towel *ručnik/peškir* ⓜ *ruch*-nik/*pesh*-kir ©/Ⓢ
train *vlak/voz* ⓜ vlak/voz ©/Ⓢ
translate *prevesti* pre-ve-sti
travel agency *putna agencija* ⓕ *put*-na a-*gen*-tsi-ya
travellers cheque *putnički ček* ⓜ *put*-nich-ki chek
trousers *hlače/pantalone* ⓕ pl *hla*-che/pan-ta-lo-ne
twin beds *dva kreveta* ⓜ pl dva *kre*-ve-ta
tyre *guma* ⓕ *gu*-ma

U

underwear *donje rublje* ⓝ *do*-nye *rub*-lye
urgent *hitan* *hi*-tan

V

vacant *prazan* *pra*-zan
vacation *praznici* ⓜ pl *praz*-ni-tsi
vegetable *povrće* ⓝ *po*-vr-che
vegetarian a *vegetarijanski* ve-ge-ta-*ri*-yan-ski
visa *viza* ⓕ *vi*-za

W

waiter *konobar* ⓜ *ko*-no-bar
walk v *hodati* ho-da-ti
wallet *novčanik* ⓜ nov-*cha*-nik
warm a *topao* to-pa-o
wash (something) *oprati* o-*pra*-ti
watch *sat* ⓜ sat
water *voda* ⓕ *vo*-da
we *mi* mi
weekend *vikend* ⓜ *vi*-kend
west *zapad* ⓜ *za*-pad
wheelchair *invalidska kolica* ⓕ pl in-*va*-lid-ska ko-*li*-tsa
when *kada* ka-da
where *gdje* gdye
white *bijel* bi-yel
who *tko* tko
why *zašto* zash-to
wife *žena* ⓕ *zhe*-na
window *prozor* ⓜ *pro*-zor
wine *vino* ⓝ *vi*-no
with *sa* sa
without *bez* bez
woman *žena* ⓕ *zhe*-na
write *napisati* na-*pi*-sa-ti

Y

yellow *žut* zhut
yes *da* da
yesterday *jučer* yu-cher
you sg inf *ti* ti
you sg pol & pl *vi* vi

Czech

czech alphabet

A a uh	*Á á* a	*B b* bair	*C c* tsair	*Č č* chair
D d dair	*Ď ď* dyair	*E e* e	*É é* *dloh*-hair air	*Ě ě* e s *hach*-kem
F f ef	*G g* gair	*H h* ha	*Ch ch* cha	*I i* ee
Í í *dloh*-hair ee	*J j* yair	*K k* ka	*L l* el	*M m* em
N n en	*Ň ň* en'	*O o* o	*P p* pair	*Q q* kair
R r er	*Ř ř* erzh	*S s* es	*Š š* esh	*T t* tair
Ť ť tyair	*U u* u	*Ú ú* *dloh*-hair u	*Ů ů* u s *krohzh*-kem	*V v* vair
W w *dvo*-yi-tair vair	*X x* iks	*Y y* *ip*-si-lon	*Ý ý* *dloh*-hee *ip*-si-lon	*Z z* zet
Ž ž zhet				

czech

ČEŠTINA

introduction

Czech (*čeština* chesh-tyi-nuh), the language which gave us words such as *dollar*, *pistol* and *robot*, has a turbulent history. The Czech Republic may now be one of the most stable and well-off Eastern European countries, but over the centuries the land and the language have been regularly swallowed and regurgitated by their neighbours. In 1993 the Velvet Divorce ended the patched-together affair that was Czechoslovakia, and allowed Czech to go its own way after being tied to Slovak for over 70 years.

Both Czech and Slovak belong to the western branch of the Slavic language family, pushed westward with the Slavic people by the onslaught of the Huns, Avars, Bulgars and Magyars in the 5th and 6th centuries. Czech is also related to Polish, though not as closely as to Slovak – adults in Slovakia and the Czech Republic can generally understand one another, although younger people who have not been exposed to much of the other language may have more difficulty.

The earliest written literature dates from the 13th century upswing in Czech political power, which continued for several centuries. In the 17th century, however, the Thirty Years War nearly caused literature in Czech to become extinct. Fortunately, the national revival of the late 18th century brought it to the forefront again, at least until the 20th century, when first Nazi and then Communist rule pressed it into a subordinate position once more.

Many English speakers flinch when they see written Czech, especially words like *prst* prst (finger) and *krk* krk (neck) with no apparent vowels, and the seemingly unpronounceable clusters of consonants in phrases like *čtrnáct dní* chtr-natst dnyee (fortnight). Don't despair! With a little practice and the coloured pronunciation guides in this chapter you'll be enjoying the buttery mouthfeel of Czech words in no time. Czech also has one big advantage in the pronunciation stakes – each Czech letter is always pronounced exactly the same way, so once you've got the hang of the Czech alphabet you'll be able to read any word put before you with aplomb. Thank religious writer and martyr Jan Hus for this – he reformed the spelling system in the 15th and 16th centuries and introduced the *háček* ha-chek (ˇ) and the various other accents you'll see above Czech letters.

So, whether you're visiting the countryside or marvelling at Golden Prague, launch into this Czech chapter and your trip will be transformed into a truly memorable one.

introduction – CZECH

pronunciation

vowel sounds

The Czech vowel system is relatively easy to master and most sounds have equivalents in English.

symbol	english equivalent	czech example	transliteration
a	**father**	*já*	ya
ai	**aisle**	*krajka*	*krai*-kuh
air	**hair**	*veliké*	*ve*-lee-kair
aw	**law**	*balcón*	*bal*-kawn
e	**bet**	*pes*	pes
ee	**see**	*prosím*	pro-*seem*
ey	**hey**	*dej*	dey
i	**bit**	*kolik*	*ko*-lik
o	**pot**	*noha*	*no*-huh
oh	**oh**	*koupit*	*koh*-pit
oo	**zoo**	*ústa*	*oo*-stuh
oy	**toy**	*výstroj*	*vee*-stroy
ow	**how**	*autobus*	*ow*-to-bus
u	**put**	*muž*	muzh
uh	**run**	*nad*	nuhd

word stress

Word stress in Czech is easy — it's always on the first syllable of the word. Stress is marked with italics in the pronunciation guides in this chapter as a reminder.

consonant sounds

The consonants in Czech are mostly the same as in English, with the exception of the kh sound, the r sound (which is rolled as it is in Spanish) and the rzh sound.

symbol	english equivalent	czech example	transliteration
b	bed	*bláto*	*bla*·to
ch	cheat	*odpočinek*	ot·po·chi·nek
d	dog	*nedávný*	ne·dav·nee
f	fat	*vyfotit*	vi·fo·tit
g	go	*vegetarián*	ve·ge·tuh·ri·an
h	hat	*zahrady*	zuh·hruh·di
k	kit	*navěky*	na·vye·ki
kh	loch	*kuchyně*	ku·khi·nye
l	lot	*loni*	lo·nyi
m	man	*menší*	men·shee
n	not	*nízký*	nyeez·kee
p	pet	*dopis*	do·pis
r	run (rolled)	*rok*	rok
rzh	rolled r followed by zh	*řeka*	rzhe·kuh
s	sun	*slovo*	slo·vo
sh	shot	*pošta*	posh·tuh
t	top	*fronta*	fron·tuh
ts	hats	*co*	tso
v	very	*otvor*	ot·vor
y	yes	*již*	yizh
z	zero	*zmiz*	zmiz
zh	pleasure	*už*	uzh
'	a slight y sound	*promiňte*	pro·min'·te

basics

language difficulties

Do you speak English?
Mluvíte anglicky? — mlu·vee·te uhn·glits·ki

Do you understand?
Rozumíte? — ro·zu·mee·te

I understand.
Rozumím. — ro·zu·meem

I don't understand.
Nerozumím. — ne·ro·zu·meem

What does (knedlík) mean?
Co znamená (knedlík)? — tso znuh·me·na (kned·leek)

How do you ...?	*Jak se ...?*	yuhk se ...
pronounce this	*toto vyslovuje*	toh·to vis·lo·vu·ye
write (krtek)	*píše (krtek)*	pee·she (kr·tek)

Could you please ...?	*Prosím, můžete ...?*	pro·seem moo·zhe·te ...
repeat that	*to opakovat*	to o·puh·ko·vuht
speak more slowly	*mluvit pomaleji*	mlu·vit po·muh·le·yi
write it down	*to napsat*	to nuhp·suht

essentials

Yes.	*Ano.*	uh·no
No.	*Ne.*	ne
Please.	*Prosím.*	pro·seem
Thank you (very much).	*(Mnohokrát) Děkuji.*	(mno·ho·krat) dye·ku·yi
You're welcome.	*Prosím.*	pro·seem
Excuse me.	*Promiňte.*	pro·min'·te
Sorry.	*Promiňte.*	pro·min'·te

numbers

0	*nula*	nu·luh		16	*šestnáct*	shest·natst
1	*jeden* m	ye·den		17	*sedmnáct*	se·dm·natst
	jedna f	yed·na		18	*osmnáct*	o·sm·natst
	jedno n	yed·no		19	*devatenáct*	de·vuh·te·natst
2	*dva/dvě* m/f&n	dvuh/dvye		20	*dvacet*	dvuh·tset
3	*tři*	trzhi		21	*dvacet jedna*	dvuh·tset yed·nuh
4	*čtyři*	chti·rzhi			*jednadvacet*	yed·nuh·dvuh·tset
5	*pět*	pyet		22	*dvacet dva*	dvuh·tset dvuh
6	*šest*	shest			*dvaadvacet*	dvuh·uh·dvuh·tset
7	*sedm*	se·dm		30	*třicet*	trzhi·tset
8	*osm*	o·sm		40	*čtyřicet*	chti·rzhi·tset
9	*devět*	de·vyet		50	*padesát*	puh·de·sat
10	*deset*	de·set		60	*šedesát*	she·de·sat
11	*jedenáct*	ye·de·natst		70	*sedmdesát*	se·dm·de·sat
12	*dvanáct*	dvuh·natst		80	*osmdesát*	o·sm·de·sat
13	*třináct*	trzhi·natst		90	*devadesát*	de·vuh·de·sat
14	*čtrnáct*	chtr·natst		100	*sto*	sto
15	*patnáct*	puht·natst		1000	*tisíc*	tyi·seets

time & dates

What time is it?	*Kolik je hodin?*	ko·lik ye ho·dyin
It's one o'clock.	*Je jedna hodina.*	ye yed·nuh ho·dyi·nuh
It's (10) o'clock.	*Je (deset) hodin.*	ye (de·set) ho·dyin
Quarter past (10).	*Čvrt na (jedenáct).*	chtvrt nuh (ye·de·natst)
	(lit: quarter of eleven)	
Half past (10).	*Půl (jedenácté).*	pool (ye·de·nats·tair)
	(lit: half eleven)	
Quarter to (eleven).	*Třičtvrtě na (jedenáct).*	trzhi·chtvr·tye nuh (ye·de·natst)
At what time?	*V kolik hodin?*	f ko·lik ho·dyin
At ...	*V ...*	f ...
am (midnight–8am)	*ráno*	ra·no
am (8am–noon)	*dopoledne*	do·po·led·ne
pm (noon–7pm)	*odpoledne*	ot·po·led·ne
pm (7pm–midnight)	*večer*	ve·cher

Monday	pondělí	pon·dye-lee
Tuesday	úterý	oo-te-ree
Wednesday	středa	strzhe-duh
Thursday	čtvrtek	chtvr·tek
Friday	pátek	pa·tek
Saturday	sobota	so-bo-tuh
Sunday	neděle	ne-dye-le

January	leden	le·den
February	únor	oo-nor
March	březen	brzhe-zen
April	duben	du·ben
May	květen	kvye·ten
June	červen	cher·ven
July	červenec	cher·ve·nets
August	srpen	sr·pen
September	září	za·rzhee
October	říjen	rzhee-yen
November	listopad	li·sto-puht
December	prosinec	pro·si·nets

What date is it today?
Kolikátého je dnes? ko·li·ka·tair·ho ye dnes

It's (18 October).
Je (osmnáctého října). ye (o·sm·nats·tair·ho rzheey·nuh)

last night	včera v noci	fche-ruh v no·tsi
last week/month	minulý týden/měsíc	mi·nu·lee tee-den/mye-seets
last year	vloni	vlo-nyi

next ...	příští ...	przheesh-tyee ...
week	týden	tee-den
month	měsíc	mye-seets
year	rok	rok

tomorrow/yesterday ...	zítra/včera ...	zee-truh/fche-ruh ...
morning (early/late)	ráno/dopoledne	ra·no/do-po-led-ne
afternoon	odpoledne	ot-po-led-ne
evening	večer	ve-cher

weather

What's the weather like?	Jaké je počasí?	yuh-kair ye po-chuh-see
It's ...		
cloudy	Je zataženo.	ye zuh-tuh-zhe-no
cold	Je chladno.	ye khluhd-no
hot	Je horko.	ye hor-ko
raining	Prší.	pr-shee
snowing	Sněží.	snye-zhee
sunny	Je slunečno.	ye slu-nech-no
warm	Je teplo.	ye tep-lo
windy	Je větrno.	ye vye-tr-no
spring	jaro n	yuh-ro
summer	léto n	lair-to
autumn	podzim m	pod-zim
winter	zima f	zi-muh

border crossing

I'm here ...	Jsem zde ...	ysem zde ...
in transit	v tranzitu	f truhn-zi-tu
on business	na služební cestě	nuh slu-zheb-nyee tses-tye
on holiday	na dovolené	nuh do-vo-le-nair
I'm here for ...	Jsem zde na ...	ysem zde nuh ...
(10) days	(deset) dní	(de-set) dnyee
(three) weeks	(tři) týdny	(trzhi) teed-ni
(two) months	(dva) měsíce	(dvuh) mye-see-tse

I'm going to (Valtice).
Jedu do (Valtic).   ye-du do (vuhl-tyits)

I'm staying at the (Hotel Špalíček).
Jsem ubytovaný/á v   ysem u-bi-to-vuh-nee/a v
(Hotelu Špalíček). m/f   (ho-te-lu shpuh-lee-chek)

I have nothing to declare.
Nemám nic k proclení.   ne-mam nyits k prots-le-nyee

I have something to declare.
Mám něco k proclení.   mam nye-tso k prots-le-nyee

That's not mine.
To není moje.   to ne-nyee mo-ye

transport

tickets & luggage

Where can I buy a ticket?
Kde koupím jízdenku?   gde *koh*·peem *yeez*·den·ku

Do I need to book a seat?
Potřebuji místenku?   pot·rzhe·bu·yi *mees*·ten·ku

One ... ticket	... *do (Telče),*	... do (*tel*·che)
to (Telč), please.	*prosím.*	*pro*·seem
one-way	*Jednosměrnou*	*yed*·no·smyer·noh
	jízdenku	*yeez*·den·ku
return	*Zpáteční jízdenku*	*zpa*·tech·nyee *yeez*·den·ku

I'd like to ...	*Chtěl/Chtěla bych ...*	khtyel/*khtye*·luh bikh ...
my ticket, please.	*moji jízdenku, prosím.* m/f	*mo*·yee *yeez*·den·ku *pro*·seem
cancel	*zrušit*	*zru*·shit
change	*změnit*	*zmye*·nyit
collect	*vyzvednout*	*vi*·zved·noht
confirm	*potvrdit*	*pot*·vr·dyit

I'd like a ...	*Chtěl/Chtěla*	khtyel/*khtye*·luh
seat, please.	*bych ...* m/f	bikh ...
nonsmoking	*nekuřácké místo*	*ne*·ku·rzhats·kair *mees*·to
smoking	*kuřácké místo*	*ku*·rzhats·kair *mees*·to

How much is it?
Kolik to stojí?   *ko*·lik to *sto*·yee

Is there a toilet?
Je tam toaleta?   ye tuhm *to*·uh·le·tuh

Is there air conditioning?
Je tam klimatizace?   ye tuhm *kli*·muh·ti·zuh·tse

How long does the trip take?
Jak dlouho trvá cesta?   yuhk *dloh*·ho *tr*·va *tses*·tuh

Is it a direct route?
Je to přímá cesta?   ye to *przhee*·ma *tses*·tuh

Where can I find a luggage locker?
Kde mohu najít   gde *mo*·hu *nuh*·yeet
zavazadlová schránka?   *zuh*·vuh·zuhd·lo·va *skhran*·kuh

My luggage	Moje zavazadlo	mo·ye zuh·vuh·zuhd·lo
has been ...	bylo ...	bi·lo ...
damaged	poškozeno	posh·ko·ze·no
lost	ztraceno	ztruh·tse·no
stolen	ukradeno	u·kruh·de·no

getting around

Where does flight (OK25) arrive?

| Kam přiletí let (OK25)? | kuhm przhi·le·tyee let (aw·ka dvuh·tset pyet) |

Where does flight (OK25) depart?

| Kde odlítá let (OK25)? | gde od·lee·ta let (aw·ka dvuh·tset pyet) |

Where's (the) ...?	Kde je ...?	gde ye ...
arrivals hall	příletová hala	przhee·le·to·va huh·luh
departures hall	odletová hala	od·le·to·va huh·luh
duty-free shop	prodejna	pro·dey·nuh
	bezcelního zboží	bez·tsel·nyee·ho zbo·zhee
gate (12)	východ k letadlu	vee·khod k le·tuhd·lu
	(dvanáct)	(dvuh·natst)

Is this the ...	Jede tento/tato ...	ye·de ten·to/tuh·to ...
to (Mělník)?	do (Mělníka)? m/f	do (myel·nyee·kuh)
bus	autobus m	ow·to·bus
train	vlak m	vluhk
tram	tramvaj f	truhm·vai
trolleybus	trolejbus m	tro·ley·bus

When's the	V kolik jede	f ko·lik ye·de
... bus?	... autobus?	... ow·to·bus
first	první	prv·nyee
last	poslední	po·sled·nyee
next	příští	przhee·shtyee

At what time does the bus/train leave?

| V kolik hodin odjíždí | f ko·lik ho·dyin od·yeezh·dyee |
| autobus/vlak? | ow·to·bus/vluhk |

How long will it be delayed?

| Jak dlouho bude mít zpoždění? | yuhk dloh·ho bu·de meet zpozh·dye·nyee |

What's the next station/stop?

| Která je příští stanice/zastávka? | kte·ra ye przheesh·tyee stuh·nyi·tse/zuhs·taf·kuh |

Does it stop at (Cheb)?
Zastaví to v (Chebu)?   zuhs·tuh·vee to f (khe·bu)

Please tell me when we get to (Přerov).
Prosím vás řekněte mi   pro·seem vas rzhek·nye·te mi
kdy budeme v (Přerově).   kdi bu·de·me f (przhe·ro·vye)

How long do we stop here?
Jak dlouho zde budeme stát?   yuhk dloh·ho zde bu·de·me stat

Is this seat available?
Je toto místo volné?   ye to·to mees·to vol·nair

That's my seat.
To je mé místo.   to ye mair mees·to

I'd like a taxi ...	*Potřebuji taxíka ...*	po·trzhe·bu·yi tuhk·see·kuh ...
at (9am)	*v (devět hodin*	f (de·vyet ho·dyin
	dopoledne)	do·po·led·ne)
now	*teď*	ted'
tomorrow	*zítra*	zee·truh

Is this taxi available?
Je tento taxík volný?   ye ten·to tuhk·seek vol·nee

How much is it to ...?
Kolik stojí jízdenka do ...?   ko·lik sto·yee yeez·den·kuh do ...

Please put the meter on.
Prosím zapněte taxametr.   pro·seem zuhp·nye·te tuhk·suh·me·tr

Please take me to (this address).
Prosím odvezte mě na (tuto adresu).   pro·seem od·ves·te mye na (tu·to uh·dre·su)

Please ...	*Prosím ...*	pro·seem ...
slow down	*zpomalte*	spo·muhl·te
stop here	*zastavte zde*	zuhs·tuhf·te zde
wait here	*počkejte zde*	poch·key·te zde

car, motorbike & bicycle hire

I'd like to hire	*Chtěl/Chtěla bych*	khtyel/khtye·luh bikh
a ...	*si půjčit ... m/f*	si pooy·chit ...
bicycle	*kolo*	ko·lo
car	*auto*	ow·to
motorbike	*motorku*	mo·tor·ku

with ...	s ...	s ...
a driver	*řidičem*	*rzhi*·dyi·chem
air conditioning	*klimatizací*	*kli*·muh·ti·zuh·tsee
antifreeze	*nemrznoucí směsí*	*ne*·mrz·noh·tsee *smye*·see
snow chains	*sněhovými řetězy*	*snye*·ho·vee·mi *rzhe*·tye·zi

How much for	*Kolik stojí*	*ko*·lik *sto*·yee
... hire?	*půjčení na ...?*	*pooy*·che·nyee nuh ...
hourly	*hodinu*	*ho*·dyi·nu
daily	*den*	den
weekly	*týden*	*tee*·den

air	*vzduch* m	*vz*·dukh
oil	*olej* m	*o*·ley
petrol	*benzin* m	*ben*·zin
tyre	*pneumatika* f	*pne*·u·muh·ti·kuh

I need a mechanic.	*Potřebuji*	*pot*·rzhe·bu·yi
	mechanika.	*me*·khuh·ni·kuh
I've run out of petrol.	*Došel mi benzin.*	*do*·shel mi *ben*·zin
I have a flat tyre.	*Mám defekt.*	mam *de*·fekt

directions

Where's the ...?	*Kde je ...?*	gde ye ...
bank	*banka*	*buhn*·kuh
city centre	*centrum*	*tsen*·trum
hotel	*hotel*	*ho*·tel
market	*trh*	trh
police station	*policejní stanice*	*po*·li·tsey·nyee *stuh*·nyi·tse
post office	*pošta*	*posh*·tuh
public toilet	*veřejný záchod*	*ve*·rzhey·nee *za*·khod
tourist office	*turistická*	*tu*·ris·tits·ka
	informační	*in*·for·muhch·nyee
	kancelář	*kuhn*·tse·larzh

Is this the road to (Cheb)?
Vede tato silnice do (Chebu)?   *ve*·de *tuh*·to *sil*·ni·tse do (*khe*·bu)

Can you show me (on the map)?
Můžete mi to ukázat   *moo*·zhe·te mi to *u*·ka·zuht
(na mapě)?   (nuh *muh*·pye)

What's the address?		
Jaká je adresa?		*yuh·ka ye uh·dre·suh*
How far is it?		
Jak je to daleko?		*yuhk ye to duh·le·ko*
How do I get there?		
Jak se tam dostanu?		*yuhk se tuhm dos·tuh·nu*
Turn ...	*Odbočte ...*	*od·boch·te ...*
at the corner	*za roh*	*zuh rawh*
at the traffic lights	*u semaforu*	*u se·muh·fo·ru*
left/right	*do leva/prava*	*do le·vuh/pruh·vuh*
It's ...	*Je to ...*	*ye to ...*
behind ...	*za ...*	*zuh ...*
far away	*daleko*	*duh·le·ko*
here	*zde*	*zde*
in front of ...	*před ...*	*przhed ...*
left	*na levo*	*nuh le·vo*
near	*blízko*	*bleez·ko*
next to ...	*vedle ...*	*ved·le ...*
on the corner	*na rohu*	*nuh ro·hu*
opposite ...	*naproti ...*	*nuh·pro·tyi ...*
right	*na pravo*	*nuh pruh·vo*
straight ahead	*přímo*	*przhee·mo*
there	*tam*	*tuhm*

by bus	*autobusem*	*ow·to·bu·sem*
by taxi	*taxikem*	*tuhk·si·kem*
by train	*vlakem*	*vluh·kem*
on foot	*pěšky*	*pyesh·ki*
north	*sever*	*se·ver*
south	*jih*	*yih*
east	*východ*	*vee·khod*
west	*západ*	*za·puhd*

Vchod/Východ	vkhod/*vee*-khod	**Entrance/Exit**
Otevřeno/Zavřeno	o-te-vrzhe-no/*zuh*-vrzhe-no	**Open/Closed**
Volné pokoje	vol-nair po-ko-ye	**Rooms Available**
Obsazeno	op-suh-ze-no	**No Vacancies**
Informace	in-for-muh-tse	**Information**
Policejní stanice	po-li-tsey-nyee *stuh*-nyi-tse	**Police Station**
Zakázáno	zuh-ka-za-no	**Prohibited**
Záchody	za-kho-di	**Toilets**
Páni	pa-nyi	**Men**
Ženy	zhe-ni	**Women**
Horké/Studené	hor-kair/*stu*-de-nair	**Hot/Cold**

accommodation

finding accommodation

Where's a ...?	Kde je ...?	gde ye ...
camping ground	tábořiště	ta-bo-rzhish-tye
guesthouse	penzion	pen-zi-on
hotel	hotel	ho-tel
youth hostel	mládežnická	mla-dezh-nyits-ka
	ubytovna	u-bi-tov-nuh
Can you recommend	Můžete mi doporučit	moo-zhe-te mi do-po-ru-chit
somewhere ...?	něco ...?	nye-tso ...
cheap	levného	lev-nair-ho
good	dobrého	dob-rair-ho
nearby	nejbližšího	ney-blizh-shee-ho

I'd like to book a room, please.
Chtěl/Chtěla bych   khtyel/*khtye*-luh bikh
rezervovat pokoj, prosím. m/f   re-zer-vo-vuht po-koy pro-seem

I have a reservation.
Mám rezervaci.   mam re-zer-vuh-tsi

My name is ...
Mé jméno je ...   mair ymair-no ye ...

Do you have a double room?
Máte pokoj s manželskou postelí?   ma-te po-koy s muhn-zhels-koh pos-te-lee

Do you have a ... room?	Máte ... pokoj?	ma·te ... po·koy
single	jednolůžkový	yed·no·loozh·ko·vee
twin	dvoulůžkový	dvoh·loozh·ko·vee

How much is it per ...?	Kolik to stojí ...?	ko·lik to sto·yee ...
night	na noc	nuh nots
person	za osobu	zuh o·so·bu

Can I pay ...?	Mohu zaplatit ...?	mo·hu zuh·pluh·tyit ...
by credit card	kreditní kartou	kre·dit·nyee kuhr·toh
with a travellers cheque	cestovním šekem	tses·tov·nyeem she·kem

For (three) nights/weeks.
Na (tři) noci/týdny. nuh (trzhi) no·tsi/teed·ni

From (2 July) to (6 July).
Od (druhého července) od (dru·hair·ho cher·ven·tse)
do (šestého července). do (shes·tair·ho cher·ven·tse)

Can I see it?
Mohu se na něj podívat? mo·hu se na nyey po·dyee·vuht

Am I allowed to camp here?
Mohu zde stanovat? mo·hu zde stuh·no·vuht

Where can I find a camping ground?
Kde mohu najít stanový tábor? gde mo·hu nuh·yeet stuh·no·vee ta·bor

requests & queries

When's breakfast served?
V kolik se podává snídaně? f ko·lik se po·da·va snyee·duh·nye

Where's breakfast served?
Kde se podává snídaně? gde se po·da·va snyee·duh·nye

Please wake me at (seven).
Prosím probuďte mě v (sedm). pro·seem pro·buď·te mye f (se·dm)

Could I have my key, please?
Můžete mi dát můj klíč, prosím? moo·zhe·te mi dat mooy kleech pro·seem

Can I get another (blanket)?
Mohu dostat další (deku)? mo·hu dos·tuht duhl·shee (de·ku)

Do you have a/an ...?	Máte ...?	ma·te ...
elevator	výtah	vee·tah
safe	trezor	tre·zor
The room is too ...	Je moc ...	ye mots ...
expensive	drahý	druh·hee
noisy	hlučný	hluch·nee
small	malý	muh·lee
The ... doesn't work.	... nefunguje.	... ne·fun·gu·ye
air conditioning	Klimatizace	kli·muh·ti·zuh·tse
fan	Větrák	vye·trak
toilet	Toaleta	to·uh·le·tuh
This ... isn't clean.	Tento ... není čistý.	ten·to ... ne·nyi chis·tee
pillow	polštář	pol·shtarzh
towel	ručník	ruch·nyeek

checking out

What time is checkout?
V kolik hodin máme vyklidit pokoj? f ko·lik ho·dyin ma·me vi·kli·dyit po·koy

Can I leave my luggage here?
Mohu si zde nechat zavazadla? mo·hu si zde ne·khuht zuh·vuh·zuhd·luh

Could I have my ..., please?	Můžete mi vrátit ..., prosím?	moo·zhe·te mi vra·tyit ... pro·seem
deposit	zálohu	za·lo·hu
passport	pas	puhs
valuables	cennosti	tse·nos·tyi

communications & banking

the internet

Where's the local Internet café?
Kde je místní internetová kavárna? gde ye meest·nyee in·ter·ne·to·va kuh·var·nuh

How much is it per hour?
Kolik to stojí na hodinu? ko·lik to sto·yee nuh ho·dyi·nu

I'd like to ...	Chtěl/Chtěla bych ... m/f	khtyel/khtye·luh bikh ...
check my email	zkontrolovat	skon·tro·lo·vuht
	můj email	mooy ee·meyl
get Internet	přístup na	przhees·tup nuh
access	internet	in·ter·net
use a printer	použít tiskárnu	po·u·zheet tyis·kar·nu
use a scanner	použít skener	po·u·zheet ske·ner

mobile/cell phone

I'd like a ...	Chtěl/Chtěla bych ... m/f	ktyel/khtye·luh bikh ...
mobile/cell phone for hire	si půjčit mobil	si pooy·chit mo·bil
SIM card for your network	SIM kartu pro vaší síť	sim kuhr·tu pro vuh·shee seet'
What are the rates?	Jaké jsou tarify?	yuh·kair ysoh tuh·ri·fi

telephone

What's your phone number?
Jaké je vaše telefonní číslo? yuh·kair ye vuh·she te·le·fo·nyee chees·lo

The number is ...
Číslo je ... chees·lo ye ...

Where's the nearest public phone?
Kde je nejbližší veřejný telefon? gde ye ney·blizh·shee ve·rzhey·nee te·le·fon

I'd like to buy a phonecard.
Chtěl/Chtěla bych koupit ktyel/khtye·luh bikh koh·pit
telefonní kartu. m/f te·le·fo·nyee kuhr·tu

I want to ...	Chtěl/Chtěla bych ... m/f	ktyel/khtye·luh bikh ...
call (Singapore)	telefonovat do (Singapůru)	te·le·fo·no·vuht do sin·guh·poo·ru
make a local call	si zavolat místně	si zuh·vo·luht meest·nye
reverse the charges	telefonovat na účet volaného	te·le·fo·no·vuht na oo·chet vo·luh·nair·ho

How much does ... cost?	Kolik stojí ...?	ko·lik sto·yee ...
a (three)-minute	(tří) minutový	(trzhee) mi·nu·to·vee
call	hovor	ho·vor
each extra minute	každá další	kuhzh·da duhl·shee
	minuta	mi·nu·tuh

(Seven crowns) per minute.
(Sedm korun) za jednu minutu.   (se·dm ko·run) zuh yed·nu mi·nu·tu

post office

I want to send a ...	Chci poslat ...	khtsi po·sluht ...
fax	fax	fuhks
letter	dopis	do·pis
parcel	balík	buh·leek
postcard	pohled	po·hled

I want to buy a/an ...	Chci koupit ...	khtsi koh·pit ...
envelope	obálku	o·bal·ku
stamp	známku	znam·ku

Please send it by	Prosím vás pošlete	pro·seem vas po·shle·te
... to (Australia).	to ... do (Austrálie).	to ... do (ow·stra·li·ye)
airmail	letecky poštou	le·tets·ki posh·toh
express mail	expresní poštou	eks·pres·nyee posh·toh
registered mail	doporučenou poštou	do·po·ru·che·noh posh·toh
surface mail	obyčejnou poštou	o·bi·chey·noh posh·toh

Is there any mail for me?
Mám zde nějakou poštu?   mam zde nye·yuh·koh posh·tu

bank

I'd like to ...	Chtěl/Chtěla bych ... m/f	kthyel/khtye·luh bikh ...
Where can I ...?	Kde mohu ...?	gde mo·hu ...
arrange a transfer	převést peníze	przhe·vairst pe·nyee·ze
cash a cheque	proměnit šek	pro·mye·nyit shek
change a travellers	proměnit	pro·mye·nyit
cheque	cestovní šek	tses·tov·nyee shek
change money	vyměnit peníze	vi·mye·nyit pe·nyee·ze
get a cash advance	zálohu v hotovosti	za·lo·hu v ho·to·vos·tyi
withdraw money	vybrat peníze	vi·bruht pe·nyee·ze

Where's a/an ...?	Kde je ...?	gde ye ...
ATM	bankomat	buhn·ko·muht
foreign exchange office	směnárna	smye·nar·nuh

What's the ...?	Jaký je ...?	yuh·kee ye ...
charge for that	poplatek za to	po·pluh·tek zuh to
exchange rate	devizový kurz	de·vi·zo·vee kurz

It's ...	Je to ...	ye to ...
(12) crowns	(dvanáct) korun	(dvuh·natst) ko·run
(five) euros	(pět) eur	(pyet) e·ur
free	bez poplatku	bez po·pluht·ku

What time does the bank open?
Jaké jsou úřední hodiny?   yuh·kair ysoh oo·rzhed·nyee ho·dyi·ni

Has my money arrived yet?
Přišly už moje peníze?   przhi·shli uzh mo·ye pe·nyee·ze

sightseeing

getting in

What time does it open/close?
V kolik hodin otevírají/ zavírají?   f ko·lik ho·dyin o·te·vee·ruh·yee/ zuh·vee·ruh·yee

What's the admission charge?
Kolik stojí vstupné?   ko·lik sto·yee vstup·nair

Is there a discount for students/children?
Máte slevu pro studenty/děti?   ma·te sle·vu pro stu·den·ti/dye·tyi

I'd like a ...	Chtěl/Chtěla bych ... m/f	khtyel/khtye·luh bikh ...
catalogue	katalog	kuh·tuh·log
guide	průvodce	proo·vod·tse
local map	mapu okolí	ma·pu o·ko·lee

I'd like to see ...		
*Chtěl/Chtěla bych vidět ... * m/f		khtyel/*khtye*·luh bikh *vi*·dyet ...
What's that?		
Co je to?		tso ye to
Can I take a photo of this?		
Mohu toto fotografovat?		*mo*·hu *to*·to *fo*·to·gruh·fo·vuht
Can I take a photo of you?		
Mohu si vás vyfotit?		*mo*·hu si vas *vi*·fo·tyit

tours

When's the next ...?	*Kdy je příští ...?*	gdi ye *przheesh*·tyee ...
day trip	*celodenní výlet*	*tse*·lo·de·nyee *vee*·let
tour	*okružní jízda*	o·*kruzh*·nyee *yeez*·duh

Is ... included?	*Je zahrnuto/a ...?* n/f	ye *zuh*·hr·nu·to/a ...
accommodation	*ubytování* n	*u*·bi·to·va·nyee
the admission charge	*vstupné* n	*fstup*·nair
food	*strava* f	*struh*·vuh
transport	*doprava* f	*do*·pruh·vuh

How long is the tour?
Jak dlouho bude trvat   yuhk *dloh*·ho *bu*·de *tr*·vuht
tento zájezd?   *ten*·to *za*·yezd

What time should we be back?
V kolik hodin se máme vrátit?   f *ko*·lik *ho*·dyin se *ma*·me *vra*·tyit

sightseeing

castle	*hrad* m	hruhd
cathedral	*katedrála* f	*kuh*·te·dra·luh
church	*kostel* m	*kos*·tel
main square	*hlavní náměstí* n	*hluhv*·nyee *na*·myes·tyee
monastery	*klášter* m	*klash*·ter
monument	*památník* m	*puh*·mat·nyeek
museum	*muzeum* f	*mu*·ze·um
old city	*staré město* n	*stuh*·rair *myes*·to
palace	*palác* m	*puh*·lats
ruins	*zříceniny* f pl	*zrzhee*·tse·nyi·ni
stadium	*stadion* m	*stuh*·di·yon
statue	*socha* f	*so*·khuh

shopping

enquiries

Where's a ...?	Kde je ...?	gde ye ...
bank	banka	buhn·kuh
bookshop	knihkupectví	knyih·ku·pets·tvee
camera shop	foto potřeby	fo·to pot·rzhe·bi
department store	obchodní dům	op·khod·nyee doom
grocery store	smíšené zboží	smee·she·nair zbo·zhee
market	tržnice	tr·zhnyi·tse
newsagency	tabák	tuh·bak
supermarket	samoobsluha	suh·mo·op·slu·huh

Where can I buy (a padlock)?
Kde si mohu koupit (zámek)? gde si mo·hu koh·pit (za·mek)

I'm looking for ....
Hledám ... hle·dam ...

Can I look at it?
Mohu se na to podívat? mo·hu se nuh to po·dyee·vuht

Do you have any others?
Máte ještě jiné? ma·te yesh·tye yi·nair

Does it have a guarantee?
Je na to záruka? ye nuh to za·ru·kuh

Can I have it sent abroad?
Můžete mi to poslat moo·zhe·te mi to pos·luht
do zahraničí? do zuh·hruh·nyi·chee

Can I have my ... repaired?
Můžete zde opravit ...? moo·zhe·te zde o·pruh·vit ...

It's faulty.
Je to vadné. ye to vuhd·nair

I'd like ..., please.	Chtěl/Chtěla bych ..., prosím. m/f	khtyel/khtye·la bikh ... pro·seem
a bag	tašku	tuhsh·ku
a refund	vrátit peníze	vra·tyit pe·nyee·ze
to return this	toto vrátit	to·to vra·tyit

paying

How much is it?
Kolik to stojí?
ko·lik to sto·yee

Can you write down the price?
Můžete mi napsat cenu?
moo·zhe·te mi *nuhp*·suht *tse*·nu

That's too expensive.
To je moc drahé.
to ye mots *druh*·hair

What's your lowest price?
Jaká je vaše konečná cena?
yuh·ka ye vuh·she ko·nech·na *tse*·nuh

I'll give you (200 crowns).
Dám vám (dvěstě korun).
dam vam (*dvye*·stye ko·run)

There's a mistake in the bill.
Na účtu je chyba.
nuh *ooch*·tu ye *khi*·buh

Do you accept ...?	*Mohu platit ...?*	mo·hu *pluh*·tyit ...
credit cards	*kreditními kartami*	kre·dit·nyee·mi *kuhr*·tuh·mi
debit cards	*platebními kartami*	pluh·teb·nyee·mi *kuhr*·tuh·mi
travellers cheques	*cestovními šeky*	tses·tov·nyee·mi *she*·ki
I'd like ..., please.	*Můžete mi dát ..., prosím?*	moo·zhe·te mi dat ... *pro*·seem
a receipt	*účet*	*oo*·chet
my change	*mé drobné*	mair *drob*·nair

clothes & shoes

Can I try it on?	*Mohu si to zkusit?*	mo·hu si to *sku*·sit
My size is (40).	*Mám číslo (čtyřicet).*	mam *chee*·slo (*chti*·rzhi·tset)
It doesn't fit.	*Nepadne mi to.*	ne·*puhd*·ne mi to
small	*malý*	*muh*·le
medium	*střední*	*strzhed*·nyee
large	*velký*	*vel*·keeh

books & music

I'd like a ...	Chtěl/Chtěla bych ... m/f	khtyel/khtye·luh bikh ...
newspaper	noviny	no·vi·ni
(in English)	(v angličtině)	(f uhn·glich·tyi·nye)
pen	propisovací pero	pro·pi·so·vuh·tsee pe·ro

Is there an English-language bookshop?
Je tam knihkupectví
s anglickýma knihama?
ye tuhm knyih·ku·pets·tvee
s uhn·glits·kee·muh knyi·huh·muh

I'm looking for something by (Kabát).
Hledám něco od (Kabátu).
hle·dam nye·tso od (kuh·ba·tu)

Can I listen to this?
Mohu si to poslechnout?
mo·hu si to po·slekh·noht

photography

Can you ...?	Můžete ...?	moo·zhe·te ...
develop this film	vyvolat tento film	vi·vo·luht ten·to film
load my film	vložit můj film	vlo·zhit mooy film
transfer photos	uložit fotografie	u·lo·zhit fo·to·gruh·fi·ye
from my camera	z mého	z mair·ho
to CD	fotoaparátu	fo·to·uh·puh·ra·tu
	na CD	nuh tsair·dairch·ko

I need a/an ... film	Potřebuji ... film	pot·rzhe·bu·yi ... film
for this camera.	pro tento fotoaparát.	pro ten·to fo·to·uh·puh·rat
APS	APS	a·pair·es
B&W	černobílý	cher·no·bee·lee
colour	barevný	buh·rev·nee
slide	diapozitivní	di·uh·po·zi·tiv·nyee
(200) speed	film s citlivostí	film s tsit·li·vos·tyee
	(dvěstě)	(dvye·stye)

| When will it be ready? | Kdy to bude hotové? | gdi to bu·de ho·to·vair |

meeting people

greetings, goodbyes & introductions

Hello/Hi.	*Ahoj/Čau.*	*uh*·hoy/chow
Good night.	*Dobrou noc.*	*do*·broh nots
Goodbye.	*Na shledanou.*	nuh·skhle·duh·noh
Bye.	*Ahoj/Čau.*	*uh*·hoy/chow
See you later.	*Na viděnou.*	nuh *vi*·dye·noh
Mr/Mrs	*pan/paní*	puhn/*puh*·nyee
Miss	*slečna*	*slech*·nuh
How are you?	*Jak se máte/máš?* pol/inf	yuhk se *ma*·te/mash
Fine. And you?	*Dobře. A vy/ty?* pol/inf	*dob*·rzhe a vi/ti
What's your name?	*Jak se jmenujete/*	yuhk se *yme*·nu·ye·te/
	jmenuješ? pol/inf	*yme*·nu·yesh
My name is ...	*Jmenuji se ...*	*yme*·nu·yi se ...
I'm pleased to meet you.	*Těší mě.*	*tye*·shee mye
This is my ...	*To je můj/moje ...* m/f	to ye mooy/*mo*·ye ...
boyfriend	*přítel*	*przhee*·tel
brother	*bratr*	*bruh*·tr
daughter	*dcera*	*dtse*·ruh
father	*otec*	*o*·tets
friend	*přítel* m	*przhee*·tel
	přítelkyně f	*przhee*·tel·ki·nye
girlfriend	*přítelkyně*	*przhee*·tel·ki·nye
husband	*manžel*	*muhn*·zhel
mother	*matka*	*muht*·kuh
partner (intimate)	*partner/partnerka* m/f	*puhrt*·ner/*puhrt*·ner·kuh
sister	*sestra*	*ses*·truh
son	*syn*	sin
wife	*manželka*	*muhn*·zhel·kuh
Here's my ...	*Zde je moje ...*	zde ye *mo*·ye ...
What's your ...?	*Jaké/Jaká je*	yuh·*kair*/yuh·ka ye
	vaše ...? n/f	*vuh*·she ...
(email) address	*(email) adresa* f	(ee·meyl) uh·dre·suh
fax number	*faxové číslo* n	*fuhk*·so·vair *chees*·lo
phone number	*telefonní číslo* n	te·le·fo·nyee *chees*·lo

occupations

What's your occupation?
Jaké je vaše povolání?   yuh·kair ye vuh·she po·vo·la·nyee

I'm a/an ...	Jsem ...	ysem ...
artist	umělec/umělkyně m/f	u·mye·lets/u·myel·ki·nye
businessperson	obchodník m&f	ob·khod·nyeek
farmer	zemědělec m	ze·mye·dye·lets
	zemědělkyně f	ze·mye·dyel·ki·nye
manual worker	dělník m&f	dyel·nyeek
office worker	úředník m	oo·rzhed·nyeek
	úřednice f	oo·rzhed·nyi·tse
scientist	vědec/vědkyně m/f	vye·dets/vyed·ki·nye

background

Where are you from?   *Odkud jste?*   ot·kud yste

I'm from ...	Jsem z ...	ysem s ...
Australia	Austrálie	ow·stra·li·ye
Canada	Kanady	kuh·nuh·di
England	Anglie	uhn·gli·ye
New Zealand	Nového Zélandu	no·vair·ho zair·luhn·du
the USA	Ameriky	uh·meh·ri·ki

Are you married?	*Jste ženatý/vdaná?* m/f	yste zhe·nuh·tee/fduh·na
I'm married.	*Jsem ženatý/vdaná.* m/f	ysem zhe·nuh·tee/fduh·na
I'm single.	*Jsem svobodný/á.* m/f	ysem svo·bod·nee/a

age

How old ...?	Kolik ...?	ko·lik ...
are you	je vám let pol	ye vam let
	ti je let inf	ti je let
is your daughter	let je vaší dceři	let ye vuh·shee dtse·rzhi
is your son	let je vašemu synovi	let ye vuh·she·mu si·no·vi

I'm ... years old.	*Je mi ... let.*	ye mi ... let
He's ... years old.	*Je mu ... let.*	ye mu ... let
She's ... years old.	*Jí je ... let.*	yee ye ... let

feelings

Are you ...?	Jste ...?	yste ...
I'm/I'm not ...	Jsem/Nejsem ...	ysem/ney·sem ...
happy	šťastný/šťastná m/f	shtyuhst·nee/shtyuhst·na
hungry	hladový/hladová m/f	hluh·do·vee/hluh·do·va
sad	smutný/smutná m/f	smut·nee/smut·na
thirsty	žíznivý/žíznivá m/f	zheez·nyi·vee/zheez·nyi·va

Are you ...?	Je vám ...?	ye vam ...
I'm/I'm not ...	Je/Není mi ...	ye/ne·nyi mi ...
cold	zima	zi·muh
hot	horko	hor·ko

entertainment

going out

Where can I find ...?	Kde mohu najít ...?	gde mo·hu nuh·yeet ...
clubs	kluby	klu·bi
gay venues	homosexuální	ho·mo·sek·su·al·nyee
	zábavné podniky	za·buhv·nair pod·ni·ki
pubs	hospody	hos·po·di

I feel like going	Rád bych šel ... m	rad bikh shel ...
to a/the ...	Ráda bych šla ... f	ra·duh bikh shluh ...
concert	na koncert	nuh kon·tsert
movies	do kina	do ki·nuh
party	na mejdan/	nuh mey·duhn/
	večírek	ve·chee·rek
theatre	na hru	nuh hru
restaurant	do restaurace	do res·tow·ruh·tse

interests

Do you like to ...?		
go to concerts	Chodíte na koncerty?	kho·dyee·te nuh kon·tser·ti
dance	Tancujete?	tuhn·tsu·ye·te
listen to music	Posloucháte hudbu?	po·sloh·kha·te hud·bu

Do you like ...?	Máte rád/ráda ...? m/f	*ma*·te rad/*ra*·duh ...
I like ...	Mám rád/ráda ... m/f	mam rad/*ra*·duh ...
I don't like ...	Nemám rád/ráda ... m/f	*ne*·mam rad/*ra*·duh ...
art	umění	*u*·mye·nyee
cooking	vaření	*vuh*·rzhe·nyee
movies	filmy	*fil*·mi
reading	čtení	*chte*·nyee
sport	sport	sport
travelling	cestování	*tses*·to·va·nyee

food & drink

finding a place to eat

Can you	Můžete	*moo*·zhe·te
recommend a ...?	doporučit ...?	*do*·po·ru·chit ...
café	kavárnu	*kuh*·var·nu
pub	hospodu	*hos*·po·du
restaurant	restauraci	*res*·tow·ruh·tsi

I'd like ..., please.	Chtěl/Chtěla bych	khtyel/*khtye*·luh bikh
	..., prosím. m/f	... *pro*·seem
a table for (five)	stůl pro (pět)	stool pro (pyet)
the nonsmoking	nekuřáckou	*ne*·ku·rzhats·koh
section	místnost	*meest*·nost
the smoking section	kuřáckou místnost	*ku*·rzhats·koh *meest*·nost

ordering food

breakfast	snídaně f	*snee*·duh·nye
lunch	oběd m	*o*·byed
dinner	večeře f	*ve*·che·rzhe
snack	občerstvení n	*ob*·cherst·ve·nyee

| What would you | Co byste doporučil/ | tso *bis*·te *do*·po·ru·chil/ |
| recommend? | doporučila? m/f | *do*·po·ru·chi·luh |

I'd like (the) ..., please.	Chtěl/Chtěla bych ..., prosím. m/f	khtyel/khtye·luh bikh ... pro·seem
bill	účet	oo·chet
drink list	nápojový lístek	na·po·yo·vee lees·tek
menu	jídelníček	yee·del·nye·chek
that dish	ten pokrm	ten po·krm

drinks

(cup of) coffee ...	(šálek) kávy ...	(sha·lek) ka·vi ...
(cup of) tea ...	(šálek) čaje ...	(sha·lek) chuh·ye ...
with milk	s mlékem	s mlair·kem
without sugar	bez cukru	bez tsu·kru
(orange) juice	(pomerančový) džus m	(po·me·ruhn·cho·vee) dzhus
soft drink	nealkoholický nápoj m	ne·uhl·ko·ho·lits·kee na·poy
(hot) water	(horká) voda f	(hor·ka) vo·duh
... mineral water	... minerální voda	... mi·ne·ral·nyee vo·duh
sparkling	perlivá	per·li·va
still	neperlivá	ne·per·li·va

in the bar

I'll have a ...	Dám si ...	dam si ...
I'll buy you a drink.	Zvu vás/tě na sklenku. pol/inf	zvu vas/tye nuh sklen·ku
What would you like?	Co byste si přál/přála? m/f	tso bis·te si przhal/przha·la
Cheers!	Na zdraví!	nuh zdruh·vee
brandy	brandy f	bruhn·di
champagne	šampaňské n	shuhm·puhn'·skair
cocktail	koktejl m	kok·teyl
a shot of (whisky)	panák (visky)	puh·nak (vis·ki)
a bottle/jug of beer	láhev/džbán piva	la·hef/dzhban pi·vuh
a bottle/glass of ... wine	láhev/skleničku ... vína	la·hef/skle·nyich·ku ... vee·nuh
red	červeného	cher·ve·nair·ho
sparkling	šumivého	shu·mi·vair·ho
white	bílého	bee·lair·ho

self-catering

What's the local speciality?
Co je místní specialita? — tso ye *meest*·nyee *spe*·tsi·uh·li·tuh

What's that?
Co to je? — tso to ye

How much is (500 grams of cheese)?
Kolik stojí (padesát — *ko*·lik *sto*·yee (puh·de·sat
deka sýra)? — de·kuh see·ruh)

I'd like ...	*Chtěl/Chtěla bych ... m/f*	khtyel/*khtye*·luh bikh ...
200 grams	*dvacet deka*	*dvuh*·tset de·kuh
(two) kilos	*(dvě) kila*	(dvye) *ki*·luh
(three) pieces	*(tři) kusy*	(trzhi) *ku*·si
(six) slices	*(šest) krajíců*	(shest) *kruh*·yee·tsoo

Less.	*Méně.*	*mair*·nye
Enough.	*Stačí.*	*stuh*·chee
More.	*Trochu více.*	*tro*·khu *vee*·tse

special diets & allergies

Is there a vegetarian restaurant near here?
Je zde blízko vegetariánská — ye zde *blees*·ko *ve*·ge·tuh·ri·ans·ka
restaurace? — res·tow·ruh·tse

Do you have vegetarian food?
Máte vegetariánská jídla? — ma·te *ve*·ge·tuh·ri·ans·ka *yeed*·luh

Could you prepare a meal without ...?
Mohl/Mohla by jste — *mo*·hl/*mo*·hluh bi yste
připravit jídlo bez ...? m/f — *przhi*·pruh·vit *yeed*·lo bez ...

butter	*máslo* n	*mas*·lo
eggs	*vejce* n pl	*vey*·tse
meat stock	*bujón* m	*bu*·yawn

I'm allergic to ...	*Mám alergii na ...*	mam *uh*·ler·gi·yi nuh ...
dairy produce	*mléčné výrobky*	*mlair*·chnair *vee*·rob·ki
gluten	*lepek*	*le*·pek
MSG	*glutaman sodný*	*glu*·tuh·muhn *sod*·nee
nuts	*ořechy*	*o*·rzhe·khi
seafood	*plody moře*	*plo*·di *mo*·rzhe

menu decoder

boršč m	*borshch*	*beetroot soup*
bramboračka f	*bruhm-bo-ruhch-kuh*	*thick soup of potatoes & mushrooms*
bramborák m	*bruhm-bo-rak*	*potato cake*
čevapčiči n pl	*che-vuhp-chi-chi*	*fried or grilled minced veal, pork & mutton made into cone-like shapes*
dršťky f pl	*drsht-ki*	*sliced tripe*
dušená roštěnka f	*du-she-na rosh-tyen-kuh*	*braised beef slices in sauce*
fazolová polévka f	*fuh-zo-lo-va po-lairf-kuh*	*bean soup*
guláš m	*gu-lash*	*thick, spicy stew, usually made with beef & potatoes*
gulášová polévka f	*gu-la-sho-va po-lairf-kuh*	*beef goulash soup*
houskové knedlíky m pl	*hohs-ko-vair kned-lee-ki*	*bread dumplings*
hovězí guláš n	*ho-vye-zee gu-lash*	*beef stew, sometimes served with dumplings*
hrachová polévka f	*hra-kho-va po-lairf-kuh*	*thick pea soup with bacon*
hranolky f pl	*hruh-nol-ki*	*French fries*
jablečný závin m	*yuh-blech-nee za-vin*	*apple strudel*
jelito n	*ye-li-to*	*black pudding*
karbanátek m	*kuhr-buh-na-tek*	*hamburger with breadcrumbs, egg, diced bread roll & onions*
klobása f	*klo-ba-suh*	*thick sausage*
koprová polévka f	*kop-ro-va po-lairf-kuh*	*dill & sour cream soup*

krokety f pl	*kro*-ke-ti	deep-fried mashed potato balls
kuřecí polévka s nudlemi f	ku-rzhe-tsee po-lairf-kuh s *nud*-le-mi	chicken noodle soup
kuře na paprice n	ku-rzhe nuh puh-pri-tse	chicken boiled in spicy paprika cream sauce
lečo n	*le*-cho	stewed onions, capsicums, tomatoes, eggs & sausage
míchaná vejce f pl	mee-khuh-na *vey*-tse	scrambled eggs
nudlová polévka f	nud-lo-va po-lairf-kuh	noodle soup made from chicken broth with vegetables
oplatka f	o-pluht-kuh	large paper-thin waffle
ovocné knedlíky m pl	o-vots-nair *kned*-lee-ki	fruit dumplings
palačinka f	puh-luh-chin-kuh	crepe • pancake
plněná paprika f	pl-nye-na *puh*-pri-kuh	capsicum stuffed with minced meat & rice, in tomato sauce
Pražská šunka f	*pruzh*-ska *shun*-kuh	Prague ham – ham pickled in brine & spices & smoked over a fire
přírodní řízek m	przhee-rod-nyee rzhee-zek	pork or veal schnitzel without breadcrumbs
rizoto n	ri-zo-to	a mixture of pork, onions, peas & rice
ruské vejce n pl	rus-kair *vey*-tse	hard-boiled eggs & ham, topped with mayonnaise & caviar
rybí polévka f	ri-bee po-lairf-kuh	fish soup usually made with carp & some carrots, potatoes & peas
smažený květák s bramborem m	smuh-zhe-nee kvye-tak s bruhm-bo-rem	cauliflower florets fried in breadcrumbs & served with boiled potatoes & tartar sauce
svíčková na smetaně f	sveech-ko-va nuh sme-ta-nye	roast beef & dumplings in carrot cream sauce, topped with lemon, cranberries & whipped cream
tvarohový koláč m	tvuh-ro-ho-vee ko-lach	pastry with cottage cheese & raisins

emergencies

basics

Help!	*Pomoc!*	*po*·mots
Stop!	*Zastav!*	*zuhs*·tuhf
Go away!	*Běžte pryč!*	*byezh*·te prich
Thief!	*Zloděj!*	*zlo*·dyey
Fire!	*Hoří!*	*ho*·rzhee
Watch out!	*Pozor!*	*po*·zor
Call ...!	*Zavolejte ...!*	*zuh*·vo·ley·te ...
a doctor	*lékaře*	*lair*·kuh·rzhe
an ambulance	*sanitku*	*suh*·nit·ku
the police	*policii*	*po*·li·tsi·yi

It's an emergency.
To je naléhavý případ.
to ye *nuh*·lair·huh·vee *przhee*·puhd

Could you help me, please?
Můžete prosím pomoci?
moo·zhe·te *pro*·seem *po*·mo·tsi

Can I use the phone?
Mohu si zatelefonovat?
mo·hu si *zuh*·te·le·fo·no·vuht

I'm lost.
Zabloudil/Zabloudila jsem. m/f
zuh·bloh·dyil/*zuh*·bloh·dyi·luh ysem

Where are the toilets?
Kde jsou toalety?
gde ysoh *to*·uh·le·ti

police

Where's the police station?
Kde je policejní stanice?
gde ye *po*·li·tsey·nyee *stuh*·nyi·tse

I want to report an offence.
Chci nahlásit trestný čin.
khtsi *nuh*·hla·sit *trest*·nee chin

I have insurance.
Jsem pojištěný/pojištěná. m/f
ysem *po*·yish·tye·nee/*po*·yish·tye·na

I've been ...	... mě.	... mye
assaulted	*Přepadli*	*przhe*·puhd·li
raped	*Znásilnili*	*zna*·sil·nyi·li
robbed	*Okradli*	*o*·kruhd·li

I've lost my ...	Ztratil/Ztratila jsem ... m/f	ztruh·tyil/ztruh·tyi·luh ysem ...
My ... was/were stolen.	Ukradli mě ...	u·kruhd·li mye ...
backpack	batoh	buh·tawh
credit card	kreditní kartu	kre·dit·nyee kuhr·tu
bag	zavazadlo	zuh·vuh·zuhd·lo
handbag	kabelku	kuh·bel·ku
jewellery	šperky	shper·ki
money	peníze	pe·nyee·ze
passport	pas	puhs
travellers cheques	cestovní šeky	tses·tov·nyee she·ki
wallet	peněženku	pe·nye·zhen·ku
I want to contact my ...	Potřebuji se obrátit na ...	pot·rzhe·bu·yi se o·bra·tyit nuh ...
consulate	můj konzulát	mooy kon·zu·lat
embassy	mé velvyslanectví	mair vel·vi·sluh·nets·tvee

health

medical needs

Where's the nearest ...?	Kde je nejbližší ...?	gde ye ney·blizh·shee ...
dentist	zubař	zu·buhrzh
doctor	lékař	lair·kuhrzh
hospital	nemocnice	ne·mots·nyi·tse
(night) pharmacist	(non-stop) lékárník	(non·stop) lair·kar·nyeek

I need a doctor (who speaks English).
Potřebuji (anglickomluvícího) doktora. — pot·rzhe·bu·yi (uhn·glits·kom·lu·vee·tsee·ho) dok·to·ruh

Could I see a female doctor?
Mohla bych být vyšetřená lékařkou? — mo·hluh bikh beet vi·shet·rzhe·na lair·kuhrzh·koh

I've run out of my medication.
Došly mi léky. — dosh·li mi lair·ki

symptoms, conditions & allergies

I'm sick.	Jsem nemocný/ nemocná. m/f	ysem ne·mots·nee/ ne·mots·na
It hurts here.	Tady to bolí.	tuh·di to bo·lee
I have (a) ...	Mám ...	mam ...

asthma	astma n	uhst·muh
bronchitis	zánět průdušek m	za·nyet proo·du·shek
constipation	zácpa f	zats·puh
cough n	kašel m	kuh·shel
diarrhoea	průjem m	proo·yem
fever	horečka f	ho·rech·kuh
headache	bolesti hlavy f	bo·les·tyi hluh·vi
heart condition	srdeční porucha f	sr·dech·nyee po·ru·khuh
nausea	nevolnost f	ne·vol·nost
pain n	bolest f	bo·lest
sore throat	bolest v krku f	bo·lest f kr·ku
toothache	bolení zubu n	bo·le·nyee zu·bu

I'm allergic to ...	Jsem alergický/ alergická na ... m/f	ysem uh·ler·gits·kee/ uh·ler·gits·ka nuh ...
antibiotics	antibiotika	uhn·ti·bi·o·ti·kuh
anti-inflammatories	protizánětlivé léky	pro·tyi·za·nyet·li·vair lair·ki
aspirin	aspirin	uhs·pi·rin
bees	včely	fche·li
codeine	kodein	ko·deyn
penicillin	penicilin	pe·ni·tsi·lin

antiseptic	antiseptický prostředek m	uhn·ti·sep·tits·kee prost·rzhe·dek
bandage	obvaz m	ob·vuhz
condoms	prezervativy m pl	pre·zer·vuh·ti·vi
contraceptives	antikoncepce f	uhn·ti·kon·tsep·tse
diarrhoea medicine	lék na průjem m	lairk nuh proo·yem
insect repellent	prostředek na hubení hmyzu m	pros·trzhe·dek nuh hu·be·nyee hmi·zu
laxatives	projímadla m pl	pro·yee·muhd·la
painkillers	prášky proti bolesti m pl	prash·ki pro·tyi bo·les·tyi
rehydration salts	iontový nápoj m	yon·to·vee na·poy
sleeping tablets	prášky na spaní m pl	prash·ki nuh spuh·nyee

english–czech dictionary

Czech nouns in this dictionary have their gender indicated by ⓜ (masculine), ⓕ (feminine) or ⓝ (neuter). If it's a plural noun, you'll also see see pl. Adjectives are given in the masculine form only. Words are also marked as a (adjective), v (verb), sg (singular), pl (plural), inf (informal) or pol (polite) where necessary.

A

A

accident nehoda ⓕ ne-ho-duh
accommodation ubytování ⓝ u-bi-to-va-nyee
adaptor adaptor ⓜ uh-duhp-tor
address adresa ⓕ uh-dre-suh
after po po
air-conditioned klimatizovaný kli-muh-ti-zo-vuh-nee
airplane letadlo ⓝ le-tuhd-lo
airport letiště ⓝ le-tyish-tye
alcohol alkohol ⓜ uhl-ko-hol
all a všichni vshikh-nyi
allergy alergie ⓕ uh-ler-gi-ye
ambulance ambulance ⓕ uhm-bu-luhn-tse
and a uh
ankle kotník ⓜ kot-nyeek
arm paže ⓕ puh-zhe
ashtray popelník ⓜ po-pel-nyeek
ATM bankomat ⓜ buhn-ko-muht

B

baby nemluvně ⓝ nem-luv-nye
back (body) záda ⓕ za-duh
backpack batoh ⓜ buh-tawh
bad špatný shpuht-nee
bag taška ⓕ tuhsh-kuh
baggage claim výdej zavazadel ⓜ vee-dey zuh-vuh-zuh-del
bank banka ⓕ buhn-kuh
bar bar ⓜ buhr
bathroom koupelna ⓕ koh-pel-nuh
battery baterie ⓕ buh-te-ri-ye
beautiful krásný kras-nee
bed postel ⓕ pos-tel
beer pivo ⓝ pi-vo
before před przhed
behind za zuh
bicycle kolo ⓝ ko-lo
big velký vel-kee
bill účet ⓜ oo-chet
black černý cher-nee

blanket deka ⓕ de-kuh
blood group krevní skupina ⓕ krev-nyee sku-pi-nuh
blue modrý mod-ree
book (make a reservation) v objednat ob-yed-nuht
bottle láhev ⓕ la-hef
bottle opener otvírák na láhve ⓜ ot-vee-rak nuh lah-ve
boy chlapec ⓜ khluh-pets
brakes (car) brzdy ⓕ pl brz-di
breakfast snídaně ⓕ snee-duh-nye
broken (faulty) zlomený zlo-me-nee
bus autobus ⓜ ow-to-bus
business obchod ⓜ op-khod
buy koupit koh-pit

C

café kavárna ⓕ kuh-var-nuh
camera fotoaparát ⓜ fo-to-uh-puh-rat
camp site autokempink ⓜ ow-to-kem-pink
cancel zrušit zru-shit
can opener otvírák na konzervy ⓜ ot-vee-rak nuh kon-zer-vi
car auto ⓝ ow-to
cash hotovost ⓕ ho-to-vost
cash (a cheque) v inkasovat šek in-kuh-so-vuht shek
cell phone mobil ⓜ mo-bil
centre střed ⓜ strzhed
change (money) v vyměnit vi-mye-nyit
cheap levný lev-nee
check (bill) účet ⓜ oo-chet
check-in recepce ⓕ re-tsep-tse
chest hruď ⓕ hrud'
child dítě ⓝ dyee-tye
cigarette cigareta ⓕ tsi-guh-re-tuh
city město ⓝ myes-to
clean a čistý chis-tee
closed zavřený zuh-vrzhe-nee
coffee káva ⓕ ka-vuh
coins mince ⓕ min-tse
cold a chladný khluhd-nee
collect call hovor na účet volaného ⓜ ho-vor nuh oo-chet vo-luh-nair-ho

come *přijít* *przhi-yeet*
computer *počítač* ⓜ *po-chee-tuhch*
condom *prezervativ* ⓜ *pre-zer-vuh-tif*
contact lenses *kontaktní čočky* ① pl
  kon-tuhkt-nyee choch-ki
cook v *vařit* *vuh-rzhit*
cost *cena* ① *tse-nuh*
credit card *kreditní karta* ①
  kre-dit-nyee kuhr-tuh
cup *šálek* ⓜ *sha-lek*
currency exchange *směnárna* ① *smye-nar-nuh*
customs (immigration) *celnice* ① *tsel-ni-tse*
Czech a *český* *ches-kee*
Czech (language) *čeština* ① *chesh-tyi-nuh*
Czech Republic *Česká republika* ①
  ches-ka re-pu-bli-kuh

D

dangerous *nebezpečný* *ne-bez-pech-nee*
date (time) *schůzka* ① *skhooz-kuh*
day *den* ⓜ *den*
delay *zpoždění* ⓝ *zpozh-dye-nyee*
dentist *zubař/zubařka* ⓜ/① *zu-buhrzh/zu-buhrzh-kuh*
depart *odjet* *od-yet*
diaper *plénka* ① *plairn-kuh*
dictionary *slovník* ⓜ *slov-nyeek*
dinner *večeře* ⓜ *ve-che-rzhe*
direct *přímý* *przhee-mee*
dirty *špinavý* *shpi-nuh-vee*
disabled *invalidní* *in-vuh-lid-nyee*
discount *sleva* ① *sle-vuh*
doctor *doktor/doktorka* ⓜ/① *dok-tor/dok-tor-kuh*
double bed *manželská postel* ① *muhn-zhels-ka pos-tel*
double room *dvoulůžkový pokoj* ⓜ
  dvoh-loozh-ko-vee po-koy
drink *nápoj* ⓜ *na-poy*
drive v *řídit* *rzhee-dyit*
drivers licence *řidičský průkaz* ⓜ
  rzhi-dyich-skee proo-kuhz
drugs (illicit) *drogy* ① pl *dro-gi*
dummy (pacifier) *dudlík* ⓜ *dud-leek*

E

ear *ucho* ⓝ *u-kho*
east *východ* ⓜ *vee-khod*
eat *jíst* *yeest*
economy class *turistická třída* ① *tu-ris-tits-ka trzhee-duh*
electricity *elektřina* ① *e-lek-trzhi-nuh*
elevator *výtah* ⓜ *vee-tuh*
email *email* ⓜ *ee-meyl*

embassy *velvyslanectví* ⓝ *vel-vi-sluh-nets-tvee*
emergency *pohotovost* ① *po-ho-to-vost*
English (language) *angličtina* ① *uhn-glich-tyi-nuh*
entrance *vstup* ⓜ *vstup*
evening *večer* ⓜ *ve-cher*
exchange rate *směnný kurs* ⓜ *smye-nee kurz*
exit *východ* ⓜ *vee-khod*
expensive *drahý* *druh-hee*
express mail *expresní zásilka* ① *eks-pres-nyee za-sil-kuh*
eye *oko* ⓝ *o-ko*

F

far *daleko* *duh-le-ko*
fast *rychlý* *rikh-lee*
father *otec* ⓜ *o-tets*
film (camera) *film* ⓜ *film*
finger *prst* ⓜ *prst*
first-aid kit *lékárnička* ① *lair-kar-nyich-kuh*
first class *první třída* ① *prv-nyee trzhee-duh*
fish *ryba* ① *ri-buh*
food *jídlo* ⓝ *yeed-lo*
foot *chodidlo* ⓝ *kho-dyid-lo*
fork *vidlička* ① *vid-lich-kuh*
free (of charge) *bezplatný* *bez-pluht-nee*
friend *přítel/přítelkyně* ⓜ/①
  przhee-tel/przhee-tel-ki-nye
fruit *ovoce* ⓝ *o-vo-tse*
full *plný* *pl-nee*
funny *legrační* *le-gruhch-nyee*

G

gift *dar* ⓜ *duhr*
girl *dívka* ① *dyeef-kuh*
glass (drinking) *sklenička* ① *skle-nyich-kuh*
glasses *brýle* ① pl *bree-le*
go *jít* *yeet*
good *dobrý* *do-bree*
green *zelený* *ze-le-nee*
guide *průvodce* ⓜ *proo-vod-tse*

H

half *polovina* ① *po-lo-vi-nuh*
hand *ruka* ① *ru-kuh*
handbag *kabelka* ① *kuh-bel-kuh*
happy *šťastný* *shtyast-nee*
have *mít* *meet*
he *on* *on*
head *hlava* ① *hluh-vuh*
heart *srdce* ⓝ *srd-tse*

heat *horko* ⓝ *hor*-ko
heavy *těžký* *tyezh*-kee
help v *pomoci* po-mo-tsi
here *tady* *tuh*-di
high *vysoký* *vi*-so-kee
highway *dálnice* ⓕ *dal*-nyi-tse
hike v *trampovat* *truhm*-po-vuht
holiday *svátek* ⓜ *sva*-tek
homosexual *homosexuál* ⓜ *ho*-mo-sek-su-al
hospital *nemocnice* ⓕ *ne*-mots-nyi-tse
hot *horký* *hor*-kee
hotel *hotel* ⓜ *ho*-tel
hungry *hladový* *hluh*-do-vee
husband *manžel* ⓜ *muhn*-zhel

I

I *já* ya
identification (card) *osobní doklad* ⓝ *o*-sob-nyee *dok*-luhd
ill *nemocný* *ne*-mots-nee
important *důležitý* *doo*-le-zhi-tee
included *včetně* *fchet*-nye
injury *zranění* ⓝ *zruh*-nye-nyee
insurance *pojištění* ⓝ *po*-yish-tye-nyee
Internet *internet* ⓜ *in*-ter-net
interpreter *tlumočník/tlumočnice* ⓜ/ⓕ *tlu*-moch-nyeek/*tlu*-moch-nyi-tse

J

jewellery *šperky* ⓜ pl *shper*-ki
job *zaměstnání* ⓝ *zuh*-myest-na-nyee

K

key *klíč* ⓜ kleech
kilogram *kilogram* ⓜ *ki*-lo-gruhm
kitchen *kuchyň* ⓕ *ku*-khin'
knife *nůž* ⓜ noozh

L

laundry (place) *prádelna* ⓕ *pra*-del-nuh
lawyer *advokát/advokátka* ⓜ/ⓕ *uhd*-vo-kat/*uhd*-vo-kat-kuh
left (direction) *levý* *le*-vee
left-luggage *úschovna zavazadel* ⓕ *oos*-khov-nuh *zuh*-vuh-zuh-del
leg *noha* ⓕ *no*-huh

lesbian *lesbička* ⓕ *les*-bich-kuh
less *menší* *men*-shee
letter (mail) *dopis* ⓜ *do*-pis
lift (elevator) *výtah* ⓜ *vee*-tah
light *světlo* ⓝ *svyet*-lo
like v *mít rád* meet rad
lock *zámek* ⓜ *za*-mek
long *dlouhý* *dloh*-hee
lost *ztracený* *ztruh*-tse-nee
lost-property office *ztráty a nálezy* ⓕ *ztra*-ti uh *na*-le-zi
love v *milovat* *mi*-lo-vuht
luggage *zavazadlo* ⓝ *zuh*-vuh-zuhd-lo
lunch *oběd* ⓜ *o*-byed

M

mail *pošta* ⓕ *posh*-tuh
man *muž* ⓜ muzh
map (of country) *mapa* ⓕ *muh*-puh
map (of town) *plán* ⓜ plan
market *trh* ⓜ trh
matches *zápalky* ⓕ pl *za*-puhl-ki
meat *maso* ⓝ *muh*-so
medicine *lék* ⓝ lairk
menu *jídelní lístek* ⓜ *yee*-del-nyee *lees*-tek
message *zpráva* ⓕ *zpra*-vuh
milk *mléko* ⓝ *mlair*-ko
minute *minuta* ⓕ *mi*-nu-tuh
mobile phone *mobil* ⓜ *mo*-bil
money *peníze* ⓜ pl *pe*-nyee-ze
month *měsíc* ⓜ *mye*-seets
morning *ráno* ⓝ *ra*-no
mother *matka* ⓕ *muht*-kuh
motorcycle *motorka* ⓕ *mo*-tor-kuh
motorway *dálnice* ⓕ *dal*-nyi-tse
mouth *ústa* ⓕ *oos*-tuh
music *hudba* ⓕ *hud*-buh

N

name *jméno* ⓝ *ymair*-no
napkin *ubrousek* ⓜ *u*-broh-sek
nappy *plenka* ⓕ *plen*-kuh
near *blízko* *bleez*-ko
neck *krk* ⓜ krk
new *nový* *no*-vee
news *zprávy* ⓕ pl *zpra*-vi
newspaper *noviny* ⓕ pl *no*-vi-ni
night *noc* ⓕ nots
no *ne* ne

noisy *hlučný hluch*-nee
nonsmoking *nekuřácký ne*-ku-rzhats-kee
north *sever* ⓜ *se*-ver
nose *nos* ⓜ nos
now *teď* ted'
number *číslo* ⓝ *chees*-lo

O

oil (engine) *olej* ⓜ *o*-ley
old *starý stuh*-ree
one-way ticket *jednoduchá jízdenka* ⓕ *yed*-no-du-kha *yeez*-den-kuh
open a *otevřený o*-tev-rzhe-nee
outside *venku ven*-ku

P

package *balík* ⓜ *buh*-leek
paper *papír* ⓜ *puh*-peer
park (car) ∨ *parkovat puhr*-ko-vuht
passport *pas* ⓜ puhs
pay *platit pluh*-tyit
pen *propiska* ⓕ *pro*-pis-kuh
pharmacy *lékárna* ⓕ *lair*-kar-nuh
phonecard *telefonní karta* ⓕ *te*-le-fo-nyee *kuhr*-tuh
photo *fotka* ⓕ *fot*-kuh
plate *talíř* ⓝ *tuh*-leerzh
police *policie* ⓕ *po*-li-tsi-ye
postcard *pohled* ⓜ *po*-hled
post office *pošta* ⓕ *posh*-tuh
pregnant *těhotná tye*-hot-na
price *cena* ⓕ *tse*-nuh

Q

quiet *tichý tyi*-khee

R

rain *déšť* ⓜ dairsht'
razor *břitva* ⓕ *brzhit*-vuh
receipt *stvrzenka* ⓕ *stvr*-zen-kuh
red *červený cher*-ve-nee
refund *vrácení peněz* ⓝ *vruh*-tse-nyee pe-nyez
registered mail *doporučená zásilka* ⓕ *do*-po-ru-che-na za-sil-kuh
rent ∨ *pronajmout pro*-nai-moht

repair ∨ *opravit o*-pruh-vit
reservation *rezervace* ⓕ *re*-zer-vuh-tse
restaurant *restaurace* ⓕ *res*-tow-ruh-tse
return ∨ *vrátit se vra*-tyit se
return ticket *zpáteční jízdenka* ⓕ *zpa*-tech-nyee *yeez*-den-kuh
right (direction) *pravý pruh*-vee
road *silnice* ⓕ *sil*-nyi-tse
room *pokoj* ⓜ *po*-koy

S

safe a *bezpečný bez*-pech-nee
sanitary napkins *dámské vložky* ⓕ pl *dams*-kair vlozh-ki
seat *místo* ⓝ *mees*-to
send *poslat pos*-luht
service station *benzínová pumpa* ⓕ *ben*-zee-no-va *pum*-puh
sex *pohlaví* ⓝ *po*-hluh-vee
shampoo *šampon* ⓜ *shuhm*-pon
share (a dorm) *spoluobývat spo*-lu-o-bee-vuht
shaving cream *pěna na holení* ⓕ *pye*-nuh nuh ho-le-nyee
she *ona o*-nuh
sheet (bed) *prostěradlo* ⓝ *pros*-tye-ruhd-lo
shirt *košile* ⓝ *ko*-shi-le
shoes *boty* ⓕ pl *bo*-ti
shop *obchod* ⓜ *op*-khod
short *krátký krat*-kee
shower *sprcha* ⓕ *spr*-khuh
single room *jednolůžkový pokoj* ⓜ *yed*-no-loozh-ko-vee *po*-koy
skin *kůže* ⓕ *koo*-zhe
skirt *sukně* ⓕ *suk*-nye
sleep ∨ *spát* spat
slowly *pomalu po*-muh-lu
small *malý muh*-lee
smoke (cigarettes) ∨ *kouřit koh*-rzhit
soap *mýdlo* ⓝ *meed*-lo
some *několik nye*-ko-lik
soon *brzy br*-zi
souvenir shop *obchod se suvenýry* ⓜ *op*-khod se su-ve-nee-ri
speak *říci rzhee*-tsi
spoon *lžíce* ⓕ *lzhee*-tse
stamp *známka* ⓕ *znam*-kuh
station (train) *nádraží* ⓝ *na*-druh-zhee
stomach *žaludek* ⓜ *zhuh*-lu-dek

stop v *zastavit* zuhs-tuh-vit
stop (bus) *zastávka* ① zuhs-taf-kuh
street *ulice* ① u-li-tse
student *student/studentka* ⑩/①
    stu-dent/stu-dent-kuh
sun *slunce* ⑩ slun-tse
sunscreen *opalovací krém* ⑩ o-puh-lo-vuh-tsee krairm
swim v *plavat* pluh-vuht

T

tampons *tampon* ⑩ tuhm-pon
taxi *taxík* ⑩ tuhk-seek
teaspoon *lžička* ① lzhich-kuh
teeth *zuby* ⑩ pl zu-bi
telephone *telefon* te-le-fon
television *televize* ① te-le-vi-ze
temperature (weather) *teplota* ① te-plo-tuh
tent *stan* ⑩ stuhn
that (one) *tamten* tuhm-ten
they *oni* o-nyi
thirsty *žíznivý* zheez-nyi-vee
this (one) *tenhle* ten-hle
throat *hrdlo* ① hrd-lo
ticket *vstupenka* ① fstu-pen-kuh
time *čas* ⑩ chuhs
tired *unavený* u-nuh-ve-nee
tissues *kosmetické kapesníčky* ⑩ pl
    kos-me-tits-kair kuh-pes-neech-ki
today *dnes* dnes
toilet *toaleta* ① to-uh-le-tuh
tomorrow *zítra* zeet-ruh
tonight *dnes večer* dnes ve-cher
toothbrush *zubní kartáček* ⑩ zub-nyee kuhr-ta-chek
toothpaste *zubní pasta* ① zub-nyee puhs-tuh
torch (flashlight) *baterka* ① buh-ter-kuh
tour *okružní jízda* ① o-kruzh-nyee yeez-duh
tourist office *turistická informační kancelář* ①
    tu-ris-tits-ka in-for-muhch-nyee kuhn-tse-larzh
towel *ručník* ⑩ ruch-nyeek
train *vlak* ⑩ vluhk
translate *přeložit* przhe-lo-zhit
travel agency *cestovní kancelář* ①
    tses-tov-nyee kuhn-tse-larzh
travellers cheque *cestovní šek* ⑩ tses-tov-nyee shek
trousers *kalhoty* ① pl kuhl-ho-ti
twin beds *dvoupostel* ① dvoh-pos-tel
tyre *pneumatika* ① pne-u-muh-ti-kuh

U

underwear *spodní prádlo* ⑪ spod-nyee prad-lo
urgent *naléhavý* nuh-lair-huh-vee

V

vacant *volný* vol-nee
vacation (from school) *prázdniny* ① prazd-nyi-ni
vacation (from work) *dovolená* ① do-vo-le-na
vegetable *zelenina* ① ze-le-nyi-nuh
vegetarian a *vegetariánský* ve-ge-tuh-ri-yans-kee

W

waiter/waitress *číšník/číšnice* ⑩/①
    cheesh-nyeek/cheesh-nyi-tse
wallet *peněženka* ① pe-nye-zhen-ka
walk v *jít* yeet
warm a *teplý* tep-lee
wash (something) *umýt* u-meet
watch *hodinky* ① pl ho-dyin-ki
water *voda* ① vo-duh
we *my* mi
weekend *víkend* ⑩ vee-kend
west *západ* ⑩ za-puhd
wheelchair *invalidní vozík* ⑩ in-vuh-lid-nyee vo-zeek
when *kdy* gdi
where *kde* gde
white *bílý* bee-lee
who *kdo* gdo
why *proč* proch
wife *manželka* ① muhn-zhel-kuh
window *okno* ① ok-no
wine *víno* ⑩ vee-no
with s s
without *bez* bez
woman *žena* ① zhe-nuh
write *psát* p-sat

Y

yellow *žlutý* zhlu-tee
yes *ano* uh-no
yesterday *včera* fche-ruh
you sg inf *ty* ti
you sg pol&pl *vy* vi

Hungarian

A a o	*Á á* a	*B b* bey	*C c* tsey	*Cs cs* chey	*D d* dey	*Dz dz* dzey	*Dzs dzs* jey
E e e	*É é* ey	*F f* ef	*G g* gey	*Gy gy* dyey	*H h* ha	*I i* i	*Í í* ee
J j yey	*K k* ka	*L l* el	*Ly ly* ey	*M m* em	*N n* en	*Ny ny* en'	*O o* aw
Ó ó āw	*Ö ö* eu	*Ő ő* ëü	*P p* pey	*Q q* ku	*R r* er	*S s* esh	*Sz sz* es
T t tey	*Ty ty* tyey	*U u* u	*Ú ú* ū	*Ü ü* ew	*Ű ű* ēw	*V v* vey	*W w* *du*-plo-vey
X x iks	*Y y* *ip*-sil-awn	*Z z* zey	*Zs zs* zhey				

hungarian

MAGYAR

introduction

Hungarian (*magyar mo*-dyor) is a unique language. Though distantly related to Finnish, it has no significant similarities to any other language in the world. If you have some background in European languages you'll be surprised at just how different Hungarian is. English actually has more in common with Russian and Sinhala (from Sri Lanka) than it does with Hungarian – even though words like *goulash*, *paprika* and *vampire* came to English from this language.

So how did such an unusual language end up in the heart of the European continent? The answer lies somewhere beyond the Ural mountains in western Siberia, where the nomadic ancestors of today's Hungarian speakers began a slow migration west about 2000 years ago. At some point in the journey the group began to split. One group turned towards Finland, while the other continued towards the Carpathian Basin, arriving in the late 9th century. Calling themselves Magyars (derived from the Finno-Ugric words for 'speak' and 'man') they cultivated and developed the occupied lands. By AD 1000 the Kingdom of Hungary was officially established. Along the way Hungarian acquired words from languages like Latin, Persian, Turkish and Bulgarian, yet overall changed remarkably little.

With more than 14.5 million speakers worldwide, Hungarian is nowadays the official language of Hungary and a minority language in the parts of Eastern Europe which belonged to the Austro-Hungarian Empire before WWI – Slovakia, Croatia, the northern Serbian province of Vojvodina and parts of Austria, Romania and the Ukraine.

Hungarian is a language rich in grammar and expression. These characteristics can be both alluring and intimidating. Word order in Hungarian is fairly free, and it has been argued that this stimulates creative or experimental thinking. Some believe that the flexibility of the tongue, combined with Hungary's linguistic isolation, has encouraged the culture's strong tradition of poetry and literature. For the same reason, however, the language is resistant to translation and much of the nation's literary heritage is still unavailable to English speakers. Another theory holds that Hungary's extraordinary number of great scientists is also attributable to the language's versatile nature. Still, Hungarian needn't be intimidating and you won't need to look very far to discover the beauty of the language. You may even find yourself unlocking the poet or scientist within!

pronunciation

The Hungarian language may seem daunting with its long words and many accent marks, but it's surprisingly easy to pronounce. Like English, Hungarian isn't always written the way it's pronounced, but just stick to the coloured phonetic guides that accompany each phrase or word and you can't go wrong.

vowel sounds

Hungarian vowels sounds are similar to those found in the English words listed in the table below. The symbol ˉ over a vowel, like ā, means you say it as a long vowel sound.

symbol	english equivalent	hungarian example	transliteration
a	father	*hátizsák*	*ha*-ti-zhak
aw	**law** (but short)	*kor*	kawr
e	bet	*zsebkés*	*zheb*-keysh
ee	see	*cím*	tseem
eu	her	*zöld*	zeuld
ew	ee pronounced with rounded lips	*csütörtök*	*chew*-teur-teuk
ey	hey	*én*	eyn
i	bit	*rizs*	rizh
o	pot	*gazda*	*goz*-do
oy	toy	*megfojt,* *komoly*	*meg*-foyt, *kaw*-moy
u	put	*utas*	*u*-tosh

word stress

Accent marks over vowels don't influence word stress, which always falls on the first syllable of the word. The stressed syllables in our coloured pronunciation guides are always in italics.

consonant sounds

2

Always pronounce y like the 'y' in 'yes'. We've also used the ' symbol to show this y sound when it's attached to n, d, and t and at the end of a syllable. You'll also see double consonants like bb, dd or tt — draw them out a little longer than you would in English.

symbol	english equivalent	hungarian example	transliteration
b	bed	*bajusz*	*bo*·yus
ch	cheat	*család*	*cho*·lad
d	dog	*dervis*	*der*·vish
dy	during	*magyar*	*mo*·dyor
f	fat	*farok*	*fo*·rawk
g	go	*gallér, igen*	*gol*·leyr, *i*·gen
h	hat	*hát*	hat
j	joke	*dzsem, hogy*	jem, hawj
k	kit	*kacsa*	*ko*·cho
l	lot	*lakat*	*lo*·kot
m	man	*most*	mawsht
n	not	*nem*	nem
p	pet	*pamut*	*po*·mut
r	run (rolled)	*piros*	*pi*·rawsh
s	sun	*kolbász*	*kawl*·bas
sh	shot	*tojást*	*taw*·yasht
t	top	*tag*	tog
ty	tutor	*kártya*	*kar*·tyo
ts	hats	*koncert*	*kawn*·tsert
v	very	*vajon*	*vo*·yawn
y	yes	*hajó, melyik*	*ho*·yāw, *me*·yik
z	zero	*zab*	zob
zh	pleasure	*zsemle*	*zhem*·le
'	a slight y sound	*poggyász, hány*	*pawd'*·dyas, han'

basics

language difficulties

Do you speak English?
Beszél/Beszélsz angolul? pol/inf · be·seyl/be·seyls on·gaw·lul

Do you understand?
Érti/Érted? pol/inf · eyr·ti/eyr·ted

I (don't) understand.
(Nem) Értem. · (nem) eyr·tem

What does (lángos) mean?
Mit jelent az, hogy (lángos)? · mit ye·lent oz hawj (lan·gawsh)

How do you ...?	*Hogyan ...?*	haw·dyon ...
pronounce this	*mondja ki ezt*	mawnd·yo ki ezt
write (útlevél)	*írja azt, hogy (útlevél)*	eer·yo ozt hawj (út·le·veyl)

Could you please ...?	*..., kérem.*	... key·rem
repeat that	*Megismételné ezt*	meg·ish·mey·tel·ney ezt
speak more slowly	*Tudna lassabban beszélni*	tud·no losh·shob·bon be·seyl·ni
write it down	*Leírná*	le·eer·na

numbers

0	*nulla*	nul·lo	16	*tizenhat*	ti·zen·hot
1	*egy*	ej	17	*tizenhét*	ti·zen·heyt
2	*kettő*	ket·tēū	18	*tizennyolc*	ti·zen·nyawlts
3	*három*	ha·rawm	19	*tizenkilenc*	ti·zen·ki·lents
4	*négy*	neyj	20	*húsz*	hūs
5	*öt*	eut	21	*huszonegy*	hu·sawn·ej
6	*hat*	hot	22	*huszonkettő*	hu·sawn·ket·tēū
7	*hét*	heyt	30	*harminc*	hor·mints
8	*nyolc*	nyawlts	40	*negyven*	nej·ven
9	*kilenc*	ki·lents	50	*ötven*	eut·ven
10	*tíz*	teez	60	*hatvan*	hot·von
11	*tizenegy*	ti·zen·ej	70	*hetven*	het·ven
12	*tizenkettő*	ti·zen·ket·tēū	80	*nyolcvan*	nyawlts·von
13	*tizenhárom*	ti·zen·ha·rawm	90	*kilencven*	ki·lents·ven
14	*tizennégy*	ti·zen·neyj	100	*száz*	saz
15	*tizenöt*	ti·zen·eut	1000	*ezer*	e·zer

time & dates

What time is it?	*Hány óra?*	han' āw·ra
It's one o'clock.	*(Egy) óra van.*	(ej) āw·ra von
It's (10) o'clock.	*(Tíz) óra van.*	(teez) āw·ra von
Quarter past (10).	*Negyed (tizenegy).*	ne·dyed (ti·zen·ej)
Half past (10).	*Fél (tizenegy).*	feyl (ti·zen·ej)
Quarter to (11).	*Háromnegyed (tizenegy).*	ha·rawm·ne·dyed (ti·zen·ej)
At what time ...?	*Hány órakor ...?*	han' āw·ro·kawr ...
At ...	*... kor.*	...kawr
am (morning)	*délelőtt*	deyl·e·lēütt
pm (afternoon)	*délután*	deyl·u·tan
pm (evening)	*este*	esh·te
Monday	*hétfő*	heyt·fēū
Tuesday	*kedd*	kedd
Wednesday	*szerda*	ser·do
Thursday	*csütörtök*	chew·teur·teuk
Friday	*péntek*	peyn·tek
Saturday	*szombat*	sawm·bot
Sunday	*vasárnap*	vo·shar·nop

January	*január*	*yo*·nu·ar
February	*február*	*feb*·ru·ar
March	*március*	*mar*·tsi·ush
April	*április*	*ap*·ri·lish
May	*május*	*ma*·yush
June	*június*	*yū*·ni·ush
July	*július*	*yū*·li·ush
August	*augusztus*	*o*·u·gus·tush
September	*szeptember*	*sep*·tem·ber
October	*október*	*awk*·tāw·ber
November	*november*	*naw*·vem·ber
December	*december*	*de*·tsem·ber

What date is it today?
Hányadika van ma?   *ha*·nyo·di·ko von mo

It's (18 October).
(Október tizennyolcadika) van.   (*awk*·tāw·ber *ti*·zen·nyawl·tso·di·ko) von

since (May)	*(május) óta*	(*ma*·yush) *āw*·to
until (June)	*(június)ig*	(*yū*·ni·ush)·ig
yesterday	*tegnap*	*teg*·nop
last night	*tegnap éjjel*	*hawl*·nop *ey*·yel
today	*ma*	mo
tonight	*ma este*	mo *esh*·te
tomorrow	*holnap*	*hawl*·nop
last/next ...	*a múlt/a jövő ...*	o mült/o *yeu*·vēū ...
week	*héten*	*hey*·ten
month	*hónapban*	*hāw*·nop·bon
year	*évben*	*eyv*·ben
yesterday/tomorrow ...	*tegnap/holnap ...*	*teg*·nop/*hawl*·nop ...
morning	*reggel*	*reg*·gel
afternoon	*délután*	*deyl*·u·tan
evening	*este*	*esh*·te

weather

What's the weather like?	*Milyen az idő?*	*mi*·yen oz *i*·dēū
It's ...		
cloudy	*Az idő felhős.*	oz *i*·dēū *fel*·hēūsh
cold	*Az idő hideg.*	oz *i*·dēū *hi*·deg
hot	*Az idő nagyon meleg.*	oz *i*·dēū *no*·dyawn *me*·leg
raining	*Esik az eső.*	*e*·shik oz *e*·shēū
snowing	*Esik a hó.*	*e*·shik o hāw
sunny	*Az idő napos.*	oz *i*·dēū *no*·pawsh
warm	*Az idő meleg.*	oz *i*·dēū *me*·leg
windy	*Az idő szeles.*	oz *i*·dēū *se*·lesh
spring	*tavasz*	*to*·vos
summer	*nyár*	nyar
autumn	*ősz*	ēūs
winter	*tél*	teyl

border crossing

I'm ...	*... vagyok.*	*... vo*·dyawk
in transit	*Átutazóban*	*at*·u·to·zāw·bon
on business	*Üzleti úton*	*ewz*·le·ti *ū*·tawn
on holiday	*Szabadságon*	*so*·bod·sha·gawn
I'm here for ...	*... vagyok itt.*	*... vo*·dyawk itt
(10) days	*(Tíz) napig*	(teez) *no*·pig
(two) months	*(Két) hónapig*	(keyt) *hāw*·no·pig
(three) weeks	*(Három) hétig*	(*ha*·rawm) *hey*·tig

I'm going to (Szeged).
(Szeged)re megyek. (*se*·ged)·re *me*·dyek

I'm staying at (the Gellért Hotel).
A (Gellért)ben fogok lakni. o (*gel*·leyrt)·ben *faw*·gawk *lok*·ni

I have nothing to declare.
Nincs elvámolnivalóm. ninch *el*·va·mawl·ni·vo·lāwm

I have something to declare.
Van valami elvámolnivalóm. von *vo*·lo·mi *el*·va·mawl·ni·vo·lāwm

That's (not) mine.
Az (nem) az enyém. oz (nem) oz *e*·nyeym

transport

tickets & luggage

Where can I buy a ticket?
Hol kapok jegyet? — hawl *ko*·pawk *ye*·dyet

Do I need to book a seat?
Kell helyjegyet váltanom? — kell *he*·ye·dyet *val*·ta·nawm

One ... ticket to (Eger), please.
Egy ... jegy (Eger)be. — ej ... yej (*e*·ger)·be
- **one-way** *csak oda* — chok *aw*·do
- **return** *oda-vissza* — *aw*·do·*vis*·so

I'd like to ... my ticket, please.
Szeretném ... a jegyemet. — se·ret·neym ... o ye·dye·met
- **cancel** *törölni* — *teu*·reul·ni
- **change** *megváltoztatni* — *meg*·val·tawz·tot·ni
- **collect** *átvenni* — *at*·ven·ni
- **confirm** *megerősíteni* — *meg*·e·rēū·shee·te·ni

I'd like a ... seat, please.
... helyet szeretnék. — ... *he*·yet se·ret·neyk
- **nonsmoking** *Nemdohányzó* — *nem*·daw·han'·zāw
- **smoking** *Dohányzó* — *daw*·han'·zāw

How much is it?
Mennyibe kerül? — men'·nyi·be *ke*·rewl

Is there air conditioning?
Van légkondicionálás? — von *leyg*·kawn·di·tsi·aw·na·lash

Is there a toilet?
Van vécé? — von *vey*·tsey

How long does the trip take?
Mennyi ideig tart az út? — men'·nyi *i*·de·ig tort oz üt

Is it a direct route?
Ez közvetlen járat? — ez *keuz*·vet·len *ya*·rot

My luggage has been ...
A poggyászom ... — o *pawd'*·dya·sawm ...
- **damaged** *megsérült* — *meg*·shey·rewlt
- **lost** *elveszett* — *el*·ve·sett

My luggage has been stolen.
 Ellopták a poggyászomat.   el·lawp·tak o pawd′·dya·saw·mot

Where can I find a luggage locker?
 Hol találok egy poggyász-   hawl to·la·lawk ej pawd′·dyas·
 megőrző automatát?   meg·ēūr·zēū o·u·taw·mo·tat

getting around

Where does flight (BA15) arrive?
 Hova érkezik a (BA tizenötös)   haw·vo eyr·ke·zik a (bey o ti·zen·eu·teush)
 számú járat?   sa·mū ya·rot

Where does flight (BA26) depart?
 Honnan indul a (BA huszonhatos)   hawn·non in·dul a (bey o hu·sawn·ho·tawsh)
 számú járat?   sa·mū ya·rot

Where's (the) ...?	*Hol van ...?*	hawl von ...
arrivals hall	*az érkezési csarnok*	oz eyr·ke·zey·shi chor·nawk
departures hall	*az indulási csarnok*	oz in·du·la·shi chor·nawk
duty-free shop	*a vámmentes üzlet*	o vam·men·tesh ewz·let
gate (five)	*az (ötös) kapu*	oz (eu·teush) ko·pu

Which ... goes	*Melyik ... megy*	me·yik ... mej
to (Budapest)?	*(Budapest)re?*	(bu·do·pesht)·re
boat	*hajó*	ho·yāw
bus	*busz*	bus
plane	*repülőgép*	re·pew·lēū·geyp
train	*vonat*	vaw·not

What time's the	*Mikor megy ... (busz)?*	mi·kawr mej ... (bus)
... (bus)?		
first	*az első*	oz el·shēū
last	*az utolsó*	oz u·tawl·shāw
next	*a következő*	o keu·vet·ke·zēū

At what time does it arrive/leave?
 Mikor érkezik/indul?   mi·kawr eyr·kez·ik/in·dul

How long will it be delayed?
 Mennyit késik?   men′·nyit key·shik

What station/stop is this?
 Ez milyen állomás/megálló?   ez mi·yen al·law·mash/meg·al·lāw

What's the next station/stop?
Mi a következő állomás/megálló?   mi o *keu*·vet·ke·zēū *al*·law·mash/*meg*·al·lāw

Does it stop at (Visegrád)?
Megáll (Visegrád)on?   *meg*·all (*vi*·she·grad)·on

Please tell me when we get to (Eger).
| *Kérem, szóljon, amikor* | *key*·rem *sāwl*·yawn *o*·mi·kawr |
| *(Eger)be érünk.* | (e·ger)·be *ey*·rewnk |

How long do we stop here?
Mennyi ideig állunk itt?   *men*'·nyi *i*·de·ig *al*·lunk itt

Is this seat available?
Szabad ez a hely?   *so*·bod ez o *he*·y

That's my seat.
Az az én helyem.   oz oz eyn *he*·yem

I'd like a taxi ...	*Szeretnék egy taxit ...*	*se*·ret·neyk ej *tok*·sit ...
at (9am)	*(reggel kilenc)re*	(*reg*·gel *ki*·lents)·re
now	*most*	mawsht
tomorrow	*holnapra*	*hawl*·nop·ro

Is this taxi available?
Szabad ez a taxi?   *so*·bod ez o *tok*·si

How much is it to ...?
Mennyibe kerül ...ba?   *men*'·nyi·be *ke*·rewl ...·bo

Please put the meter on.
Kérem, kapcsolja be az órát.   *key*·rem *kop*·chawl·yo be oz *āw*·rat

Please take me to (this address).
Kérem, vigyen el (erre a címre).   *kay*·rem *vi*·dyen el (*er*·re o *tseem*·re)

Please ...	*Kérem, ...*	*key*·rem ...
slow down	*lassítson*	*losh*·sheet·shawn
stop here	*álljon meg itt*	*all*·yawn meg itt
here	*várjon itt*	*var*·yawn itt

car, motorbike & bicycle hire

I'd like to hire a ...	*Szeretnék egy ... bérelni.*	*se*·ret·neyk ej ... *bey*·rel·ni
bicycle	*biciklit*	*bi*·tsik·lit
car	*autót*	*o*·u·tāwt
motorbike	*motort*	*maw*·tawrt

with a driver	soförrel	shaw·feūr·rel
with air conditioning	lég-kondicionálóval	leyg·kawn·di·tsi·aw·na·lāw·vol
with antifreeze	fagyállóval	fod'·al·lāw·vol
with snow chains	hólánccal	hāw·lant'·tsol

How much	Mennyibe kerül	men'·nyi·be ke·rewl
for ... hire?	a kölcsönzés ...?	o keul·cheun·zeysh ...
hourly	óránként	āw·ran·keynt
daily	egy napra	ej nop·ro
weekly	egy hétre	ej heyt·re

air	levegő	le·ve·gēū
oil	olaj	aw·lo·y
petrol	benzin	ben·zin
tyres	gumi	gu·mi

I need a mechanic.
Szükségem van egy
autószerelőre.
sewk·shey·gem von ej
o·u·tāw·se·re·lēū·re

I've run out of petrol.
Kifogyott a benzinem.
ki·faw·dyawtt o ben·zi·nem

I have a flat tyre.
Defektem van.
de·fek·tem von

directions

Where's the ...?	Hol van a ...?	hawl von o ...
bank	bank	bonk
city centre	városközpont	va·rawsh·keuz·pawnt
hotel	szálloda	sal·law·do
market	piac	pi·ots
police station	rendőrség	rend·ēūr·sheyg
post office	postahivatal	pawsh·to·hi·vo·tol
public toilet	nyilvános vécé	nyil·va·nawsh vey·tsey
tourist office	turistairoda	tu·rish·to·i·raw·do

Is this the road to (Sopron)?
Ez az út vezet (Sopron)ba?
ez oz üt ve·zet (shawp·rawn)·bo

Can you show me (on the map)?
Meg tudja mutatni nekem
(a térképen)?
meg tud·yo mu·tot·ni ne·kem
(o teyr·key·pen)

What's the address?
Mi a cím? mi o tseem

How far is it?
Milyen messze van? *mi*·yen *mes*·se von

How do I get there?
Hogyan jutok oda? haw·dyon *yu*·tawk *aw*·do

Turn ...	*Forduljon ...*	*fawr*·dul·yawn ...
at the corner	*a saroknál*	o *sho*·rawk·nal
at the traffic lights	*a közlekedési lámpánál*	o *keuz*·le·ke·dey·shi *lam*·pa·nal
left/right	*balra/jobbra*	*bol*·ro/*yawbb*·ro
It's ...	*... van.*	... von
behind ...	*... mögött*	... *meu*·geutt
far away	*Messze*	*mes*·se
here	*Itt*	itt
in front of ...	*... előtt*	... e·*lēütt*
left	*Balra*	*bol*·ro
near ...	*... közelében*	... *keu*·ze·ley·ben
next to ...	*... mellett*	... *mel*·lett
on the corner	*A sarkon*	o *shor*·kawn
opposite ...	*... val szemben*	... vol *sem*·ben
right	*Jobbra*	*yawbb*·ro
straight ahead	*Egyenesen előttünk*	e·dye·ne·shen e·*lēüt*·tewnk
there	*Ott*	ott
by bus	*busszal*	*bus*·sol
by taxi	*taxival*	*tok*·si·vol
by train	*vonattal*	*vaw*·not·tol
on foot	*gyalog*	*dyo*·lawg
north	*észak*	*ey*·sok
south	*dél*	deyl
east	*kelet*	*ke*·let
west	*nyugat*	*nyu*·got

signs

Bejárat/Kijárat	*be·*ya·rot/*ki·*ya·rot	Entrance/Exit
Nyitva/Zárva	*nyit·*vo/*zar·*vo	Open/Closed
Van Üres Szoba	von *ew·*resh *saw·*bo	Rooms Available
Minden Szoba Foglalt	*min·*den *saw·*bo *fawg·*lolt	No Vacancies
Információ	*in·*fawr·ma·tsi·āw	Information
Rendőrség	*rend·*ēūr·sheyg	Police Station
Tilos	*ti·*lawsh	Prohibited
Mosdó	*mawsh·*dāw	Toilets
Férfiak	*feyr·*fi·ok	Men
Nők	nēūk	Women
Meleg/Hideg	*me·*leg/*hi·*deg	Hot/Cold

accommodation

finding accommodation

Where's a ...?	*Hol van egy ...?*	hawl von ej ...
camping ground	*kemping*	*kem·*ping
guesthouse	*panzió*	*pon·*zi·āw
hotel	*szálloda*	*sal·*law·do
youth hostel	*ifjúsági szálló*	*if·*yū·sha·gi *sal·*lāw
Can you recommend somewhere ...?	*Tud ajánlani egy ... helyet?*	tud *o·*yan·lo·ni ej ... *he·*yet
cheap	*olcsó*	*awl·*chāw
good	*jó*	yāw
nearby	*közeli*	*keu·*ze·li
I'd like to book a room, please.	*Szeretnék egy szobát foglalni.*	*se·*ret·neyk ej *saw·*bāt *fawg·*lol·ni
I have a reservation.	*Van foglalásom.*	von *fawg·*lo·la·shawm
My name's ...	*A nevem ...*	o *ne·*vem ...
Do you have a ... room?	*Van Önnek kiadó egy ... szobája?*	von *eun·*nek *ki·*o·dāw ed' ... *saw·*ba·yo
single	*egyágyas*	*ej·*a·dyosh
double	*dupla ágyas*	*dup·*lo·a·dyosh
twin	*kétágyas*	*keyt·*a·dyosh

accommodation – HUNGARIAN

183

How much is it per ...?	*Mennyibe kerül egy ...?*	men'·nyi·be ke·rewl ej ...
night	*éjszakára*	ey·so·ka·ro
person	*főre*	fēū·re

Can I pay by ...?	*Fizethetek ...?*	fi·zet·he·tek ...
credit card	*hitelkártyával*	hi·tel·kar·tya·vol
travellers cheque	*utazási csekkel*	u·to·za·shi chek·kel

I'd like to stay for (three) nights.
(Három) éjszakára. — (ha·rawm) ey·so·ka·ro

From (July 2) to (July 6).
(Július kettő)től (július hat)ig. — (yū·li·ush ket·tēū)·tēūl (yū·li·ush hot)·ig

Can I see it?
Megnézhetem? — meg·neyz·he·tem

Am I allowed to camp here?
Táborozhatok itt? — ta·baw·rawz·ho·tawk itt

Where can I find the camping ground?
Hol találom a kempinget? — hawl to·la·lawm o kem·pin·get

requests & queries

When/Where is breakfast served?
Mikor/Hol van a reggeli? — mi·kawr/hawl von o reg·ge·li

Please wake me at (seven).
Kérem, ébresszen fel (hét)kor. — key·rem eyb·res·sen fel (heyt)·kawr

Could I have my key, please?
Megkaphatnám a kulcsomat, kérem? — meg·kop·hot·nam o kul·chaw·mot key·rem

Can I get another (blanket)?
Kaphatok egy másik (takaró)t? — kop·ho·tawk ej ma·shik (to·ko·rāw)t

Is there a/an ...?	*Van Önöknél ...?*	von eu·neuk·neyl ...
elevator	*lift*	lift
safe	*széf*	seyf

The room is too ...	*Túl ...*	tül ...
expensive	*drága*	dra·go
noisy	*zajos*	zo·yawsh
small	*kicsi*	ki·chi

The ... doesn't work.	A ... nem működik.	o ... nem *mēw*·keu·dik
air conditioning	légkondicionáló	*leyg*·kawn·di·tsi·aw·na·lāw
fan	ventilátor	*ven*·ti·la·tawr
toilet	vécé	*vey*·tsey

This ... isn't clean.	Ez a ... nem tiszta.	ez o ... nem *tis*·to
sheet	lepedő	*le*·pe·dēū
towel	törülköző	*teu*·rewl·keu·zēū

checking out

What time is checkout?
Mikor kell kijelentkezni? — mi·kawr kell *ki*·ye·lent·kez·ni

Can I leave my luggage here?
Itt hagyhatom a csomagjaimat? — itt *hoj*·ho·tawm o *chaw*·mog·yo·i·mot

Could I have my ..., please?	Visszakaphatnám ..., kérem?	*vis*·so·kop·hot·nam ... *key*·rem
deposit	a letétemet	o *le*·tey·te·met
passport	az útlevelemet	oz *üt*·le·ve·le·met
valuables	az értékeimet	oz *eyr*·tey·ke·i·met

communications & banking

the internet

Where's the local Internet café?
Hol van a legközelebbi internet kávézó? — hawl von o *leg*·keu·ze·leb·bi *in*·ter·net ka·vey·zāw

How much is it per hour?
Mennyibe kerül óránként? — men'·nyi·be ke·rewl *āw*·ran·keynt

I'd like to check my email.
Szeretném megnézni az e-mailjeimet. — se·ret·neym *meg*·neyz·ni oz *ee*·meyl·ye·i·met

I'd like to ...	Szeretnék ...	se·ret·neyk ...
get Internet access	rámenni az internetre	*ra*·men·ni oz *in*·ter·net·re
use a printer	használni egy nyomtatót	*hos*·nal·ni ej *nyawm*·to·tāwt
use a scanner	használni egy szkennert	*hos*·nal·ni ej *sken*·nert

mobile/cell phone

I'd like a ...	Szeretnék egy ...	se·ret·neyk ej ...
mobile/cell phone	mobiltelefont	maw·bil·te·le·fawnt
for hire	bérelni	bey·rel·ni
SIM card	SIM-kártyát	sim·kar·tyat
for your network	ennek a hálózatnak	en·nek o ha·lāw·zot·nok
What are the rates?	Milyen díjak vannak?	mi·yen dee·yok von·nok

telephone

What's your phone number?
Mi a telefonszáma/ mi o te·le·fawn·sa·ma/
telefonszámod? pol/inf te·le·fawn·sa·mawd

The number is ...
A szám ... o sam ...

Where's the nearest public phone?
Hol a legközelebbi hawl o leg·keu·ze·leb·bi
nyilvános telefon? nyil·va·nawsh te·le·fawn

I'd like to buy a phonecard.
Szeretnék telefonkártyát venni. se·ret·neyk te·le·fawn·kar·tyat ven·ni

I want to make a reverse-charge call.
'R' beszélgetést szeretnék kérni. er·be·seyl·ge·teysht se·ret·neyk keyr·ni

I want to ...	Szeretnék ...	se·ret·neyk ...
call (Singapore)	(Szingapúr)ba	(sin·go·pūr)·bo
	telefonálni	te·le·faw·nal·ni
make a local call	helyi telefon-	he·yi te·le·fawn-
	beszélgetést	be·seyl·ge·teysht
	folytatni	faw·y·tot·ni

How much	Mennyibe	men'·nyi·be
does ... cost?	kerül ...?	ke·rewl ...
a (three)-minute	egy (három)perces	ej (ha·rawm)·per·tsesh
call	beszélgetés	be·seyl·ge·teysh
each extra minute	minden további perc	min·den taw·vab·bi perts

(30) forints per (30) seconds.
(Harminc) másodpercenként (hor·mints) ma·shawd·per·tsen·keynt
(harminc) forint. (hor·mints) faw·rint

post office

I want to send a ...	... szeretnék küldeni.	... se·ret·neyk kewl·de·ni
fax	Faxot	fok·sawt
letter	Levelet	le·ve·let
parcel	Csomagot	chaw·mo·gawt
postcard	Képeslapot	key·pesh·lo·pawt

I want to buy a/an ...	... szeretnék venni.	... se·ret·neyk ven·ni
envelope	Borítékot	baw·ree·tey·kawt
stamp	Bélyeget	bey·ye·get

Please send it to (Australia) by ...	Kérem, küldje ... (Ausztráliá)ba.	key·rem kewld·ye ... (o·ust·ra·li·a)·bo
airmail	légipostán	ley·gi·pawsh·tan
express mail	expresszel	eks·press·zel
registered mail	ajánlottan	o·yan·law·tton
surface mail	simán	shi·man

Is there any mail for me?	Van levelem?	von le·ve·lem

bank

Where's a/an ...?	Hol van egy ...?	hawl von ej ...
ATM	bankautomata	bonk·o·u·taw·mo·to
foreign exchange office	valutaváltó ügynökség	vo·lu·to·val·tāw ewj·neuk·sheyg

I'd like to ...	Szeretnék ...	se·ret·neyk ...
Where can I ...?	Hol tudok ...?	hawl tu·dawk ...
arrange a transfer	pénzt átutalni	peynzt at·u·tol·ni
cash a cheque	beváltani egy csekket	be·val·to·ni ej chek·ket
change a travellers cheque	beváltani egy utazási csekket	be·val·to·ni ej u·to·za·shi chek·ket
change money	pénzt váltani	peynzt val·to·ni
get a cash advance	készpénzelőleget felvenni	keys·peynz·e·lēū·le·get fel·ven·ni
withdraw money	pénzt kivenni	peynzt ki·ven·ni

What's the ...?	Mennyi ...?	men'·nyi ...
charge for that	a díj	o dee·y
exchange rate	a valutaárfolyam	o vo·lu·to·ar·faw·yom

It's (100) euros.	(Száz) euró.	(saz) e·u·raw
It's (500) forints.	(Ötszáz) forint.	(eut·saz) faw·rint
It's free.	Ingyen van.	in·dyen von

What time does the bank open?
Mikor nyit a bank?   mi·kawr nyit o bonk

Has my money arrived yet?
Megérkezett már a pénzem?   meg·eyr·ke·zett mar o peyn·zem

sightseeing

getting in

What time does it open/close?
Mikor nyit/zár?   mi·kawr nyit/zar

What's the admission charge?
Mennyibe kerül a belépőjegy? men'·nyi·be ke·rewl o be·ley·pēū·yej

Is there a discount for students/children?
Van kedvezmény diákok/   von ked·vez·meyn' di·a·kawk/
gyerekek számára?   dye·re·kek sa·ma·ro

I'd like a ...	Szeretnék egy ...	se·ret·neyk ej ...
catalogue	katalógust	ko·to·lāw·gusht
guide	idegenvezetőt	i·de·gen·ve·ze·tēüt
local map	itteni térképet	it·te·ni teyr·key·pet

I'd like to see ...	Szeretnék látni ...	se·ret·neyk lat·ni ...
What's that?	Az mi?	oz mi
Can I take a photo?	Fényképezhetek?	feyn'·key·pez·he·tek

tours

When's the next ...?	Mikor van a következő ...?	mi·kawr von o keu·vet·ke·zēū ...
day trip	egynapos kirándulás	ej·no·pawsh ki·ran·du·lash
tour	túra	tū·ro

188

sightseeing

castle	*vár*	var
cathedral	*székesegyház*	sey·kesh·ej·haz
church	*templom*	temp·lawm
main square	*fő tér*	feū ter
monastery	*kolostor*	kaw·lawsh·tawr
monument	*emlékmű*	em·leyk·mēw
museum	*múzeum*	mū·ze·um
old city	*óváros*	āw·va·rawsh
palace	*palota*	po·law·to
ruins	*romok*	raw·mawk
stadium	*stadion*	shto·di·awn
statues	*szobrok*	saw·brawk

Is ... included?	*Benne van az árban ...?*	ben·ne von oz ar·bon ...
accommodation	*a szállás*	o sal·lash
the admission charge	*a belépőjegy*	o be·ley·pēū·yej
food	*az ennivaló*	oz en·ni·vo·lāw
transport	*a közlekedés*	o keuz·le·ke·deysh

How long is the tour?
Mennyi ideig tart a túra?   men'·nyi i·de·ig tort o tū·ra

What time should we be back?
Mikorra érünk vissza?   mi·kawr·ro ey·rewnk vis·so

shopping

enquiries

Where's a ...?	*Hol van egy ...?*	hawl von ej ...
bank	*bank*	bonk
bookshop	*könyvesbolt*	keun'·vesh·bawlt
camera shop	*fényképezőgép-bolt*	feyn'·key·pe·zēū·geyp·bawlt
department store	*áruház*	a·ru·haz
grocery store	*élelmiszerbolt*	ey·lel·mi·ser·bawlt
market	*piac*	pi·ots
newsagency	*újságárus*	ū·y·shag·a·rush
supermarket	*élelmiszeráruház*	ey·lel·mi·ser·a·ru·haz

Where can I buy (a padlock)?
Hol tudok venni (egy lakatot)?   hawl *tu*·dawk *ven*·ni (ej *lo*·ko·tawt)

I'm looking for . . .
Keresem a . . .   *ke*·re·shem o . . .

Can I look at it?
Megnézhetem?   meg·neyz·he·tem

Do you have any others?
Van másmilyen is?   von *mash*·mi·yen ish

Does it have a guarantee?
Van rajta garancia?   von *ro*·y·to *go*·ron·tsi·o

Can I have it sent overseas?
El lehet küldetni külföldre?   el *le*·het kewl·det·ni *kewl*·feuld·re

Can I have my . . . repaired?
Megjavíttathatnám itt . . . ?   meg·yo·veet·tot·hot·nam itt . . .

It's faulty.
Hibás.   hi·bash

I'd like . . ., please.   . . ., *kérem.*   . . . key·rem
    a bag   *Kaphatnék egy zacskót*   *kop*·hot·neyk ej *zoch*·kāwt
    a refund   *Vissza szeretném*   *vis*·so se·ret·neym
       kapni a pénzemet   *kop*·ni o *peyn*·ze·met
    to return this   *Szeretném*   *se*·ret·neym
       visszaadni ezt   *vis*·so·od·ni ezt

paying

How much is it?
Mennyibe kerül?   men'·nyi·be ke·rewl

Could you write down the price?
Le tudná írni az árat?   le *tud*·na *eer*·ni oz *a*·rot

That's too expensive.
Ez túl drága.   ez tül *dra*·go

Do you have something cheaper?
Van valami olcsóbb?   von *vo*·lo·mi *awl*·chāwbb

I'll give you (500 forints).
Adok Önnek (ötszáz forintot).   o·dawk *eun*·nek (eut·saz *faw*·rin·tawt)

There's a mistake in the bill.
Valami nem stimmel a számlával.   *vo*·lo·mi nem *shtim*·mel o *sam*·la·vol

Do you accept ...?	Elfogadnak ...?	el·faw·god·nok ...
credit cards	hitelkártyát	hi·tel·kar·tyat
debit cards	bankkártyát	bonk·kar·tyat
travellers cheques	utazási csekket	u·to·za·shi chek·ket

I'd like ..., please.	..., kérem.	... key·rem
a receipt	Kaphatnék egy nyugtát	kop·hot·neyk ej nyug·tat
my change	Szeretném megkapni	se·ret·neym meg·kop·ni
	a visszajáró pénzt	o vis·so·ya·rāw peynzt

clothes & shoes

Can I try it on?	Felpróbálhatom?	fel·prāw·bal·ho·tawm
My size is (40).	A méretem	o mey·re·tem
	(negyvenes).	(nej·ve·nesh)
It doesn't fit.	Nem jó.	nem yāw

small	kicsi	ki·chi
medium	közepes	keu·ze·pesh
large	nagy	noj

books & music

I'd like a ...	Szeretnék egy ...	se·ret·neyk ej ...
newspaper	(angol)	(on·gawl)
(in English)	újságot	üy·sha·gawt
pen	tollat	tawl·lot

Is there an English-language bookshop?
Van valahol egy angol   von vo·lo·hawl ej on·gawl
nyelvű könyvesbolt?   nyel·vēw keun'·vesh·bawlt

I'm looking for something by (Zsuzsa Koncz).
(Koncz Zsuzsá)tól   (konts zhu·zha)·tāwl
keresek valamit.   ke·re·shek vo·lo·mit

Can I listen to this?
Meghallgathatom ezt?   meg·holl·got·ho·tawm ezt

photography

Can you transfer photos from my camera to CD?
Át tudják vinni a képeket
a fényképezőgépemről CD-re?
at *tud*·yak *vin*·ni o *key*·pe·ket
o feyn'·key·pe·zēū·gey·pem·rēūl *tsey*·dey·re

Can you develop this film?
Elő tudják hívni ezt a filmet?
e·lēū *tud*·yak *heev*·ni ezt o *fil*·met

Can you load my film?
Bele tudják tenni a filmet
a gépembe?
be·le *tud*·yak *ten*·ni o *fil*·met
o *gey*·pem·be

I need a ... film for this camera.	... *filmet szeretnék.*	... *fil*·met se·ret·neyk
B&W	*Fekete-fehér*	fe·ke·te·*fe*·heyr
colour	*Színes*	*see*·nesh
slide	*Dia*	*di*·o
(200) speed	*(Kétszáz)as* *fényérzékenységű*	*(keyt*·saz)·osh feyn'·*eyr*·zey·ken'·shey·gēw

When will it be ready? *Mikor lesz kész?* *mi*·kawr les keys

meeting people

greetings, goodbyes & introductions

Hello.	*Szervusz/Szervusztok.* sg/pl	*ser*·vus/*ser*·vus·tawk
Hi.	*Szia/Sziasztok.* sg/pl	*si*·o/*si*·os·tawk
Good night.	*Jó éjszakát.*	yāw *ey*·y·so·kat
Goodbye.	*Viszlát.*	*vis*·lat
Bye.	*Szia/Sziasztok.* sg/pl	*si*·o/*si*·os·tawk
Mr	*Úr*	ūr
Mrs	*Asszony*	*os*·sawn'
Miss	*Kisasszony*	*kish*·os·sawn'
How are you?	*Hogy van/vagy?* pol/inf	hawj von/voj
Fine. And you?	*Jól. És Ön/te?* pol/inf	yāwl eysh eun/te
What's your name?	*Mi a neve/neved?* pol/inf	mi o *ne*·ve/*ne*·ved
My name is ...	*A nevem ...*	o *ne*·vem ...
I'm pleased to meet you.	*Örvendek.*	*eur*·ven·dek

This is my ...	Ez ...	ez ...
boyfriend	a barátom	o bo·ra·tawm
brother (older)	a bátyám	o ba·tyam
brother (younger)	az öcsém	oz eu·cheym
daughter	a lányom	o la·nyawm
father	az apám	oz o·pam
friend	a barátom/barátném m/f	o bo·ra·tawm/bo·rat·nēūm
girlfriend	a barátném	o bo·rat·nēūm
husband	a férjem	o feyr·yem
mother	az anyám	oz o·nyam
partner (intimate)	a barátom/barátném m/f	o bo·ra·tawm/bo·rat·nēūm
sister (older)	a nővérem	o nēū·vey·rem
sister (younger)	a húgom	o hū·gawm
son	a fiam	o fi·om
wife	a feleségem	o fe·le·shey·gem

Here's my ...	Itt van ...	itt von ...
address	a címem	o tsee·mem
email address	az e-mail címem	oz ee·meyl tsee·mem
fax number	a faxszámom	o foks·sa·mawm
phone number	a telefonszámom	o te·le·fawn·sa·mawm

What's your ...?	Mi ...?	mi ...
address	a címe	o tsee·me
email address	az e-mail címe	oz ee·meyl tsee·me
fax number	a faxszáma	o foks·sa·ma
phone number	a telefonszáma	o te·le·fawn·sa·ma

occupations

What's your occupation?	Mi a foglalkozása/ foglalkozásod? pol/inf	mi o fawg·lol·kaw·za·sho/ fawg·lol·kaw·za·shawd
I'm a/an ...	... vagyok.	... vo·dyawk
artist	Művész	mēw·veys
businessperson	Üzletember m	ewz·let·em·ber
	Üzletasszony f	ewz·let·os·sawn'
farmer	Gazda	goz·do
office worker	Irodai dolgozó	i·raw·do·i dawl·gaw·zāw
scientist	Természettudós	ter·mey·set·tu·dāwsh
student	Diák	di·ak
tradesperson	Kereskedő	ke·resh·ke·dēū

background

Where are you from?	Ön honnan jön? pol	eun *hawn*-non yeun
	Te honnan jössz? inf	te *hawn*-non yeuss
I'm from ...	Én ... jövök.	eyn ... *yeu*-veuk
Australia	Ausztráliából	o-ust-ra-li-a-bāwl
Canada	Kanadából	ko-no-da-bāwl
England	Angliából	ong-li-a-bāwl
New Zealand	Új-Zélandból	ū-y-zey-lond-bāwl
the USA	USAból	u-sho-bāwl
Are you married? m	Nős?	nēush
Are you married? f	Férjnél van?	feyr-y-neyl von
I'm ...	... vagyok.	... vo-dyawk
married	Nős/Férjnél m/f	nēush/feyr-y-neyl
single	Egyedülálló	e-dye-dewl-al-lāw

age

How old are you?	Hány éves? pol	han' *ey*-vesh
	Hány éves vagy? inf	han' *ey*-vesh voj
How old are your children?	Hány évesek a gyerekei/gyerekeid? pol/inf	han' *ey*-ve-shek o dye-re-ke-i/dye-re-ke-id
I'm ... years old.	... éves vagyok.	... *ey*-vesh vo-dyawk
He/She is ... years old.	... éves.	... *ey*-vesh

feelings

Are you ...?	... vagy?	... voj
happy	Boldog	bawl-dawg
hungry	Éhes	ey-hesh
sad	Szomorú	saw-maw-rū
thirsty	Szomjas	sawm-yosh
I'm ...	... vagyok.	... vo-dyawk
I'm not ...	Nem vagyok ...	nem vo-dyawk ...
happy	boldog	bawl-dawg
hungry	éhes	ey-hesh
sad	szomorú	saw-maw-rū
thirsty	szomjas	sawm-yosh

Are you cold?	Fázik/Fázol? pol/inf	fa-zik/fa-zawl
I'm (not) cold.	(Nem) Fázom.	(nem) fa-zawm
Are you hot?	Melege/Meleged van? pol/inf	me-le-ge/me-le-ged von
I'm hot.	Melegem van.	me-le-gem von
I'm not hot.	Nincs melegem.	ninch me-le-gem

entertainment

going out

Where can I find ...?	Hol találok ...?	hawl to-la-lawk ...
clubs	klubokat	klu-baw-kot
gay venues	meleg	me-leg
	szórakozóhelyeket	sāw-ro-kaw-zāw-he-ye-ket
pubs	pubokat	po-baw-kot
I feel like going	Szeretnék	se-ret-neyk
to a/the ...	elmenni egy ...	el-men-ni ej ...
concert	koncertre	kawn-tsert-re
movies	moziba	maw-zi-bo
party	partira	por-ti-ro
restaurant	étterembe	eyt-te-rem-be
theatre	színházba	seen-haz-bo

interests

Do you like ...?	Szereted ...?	se-re-ted ...
I (don't) like ...	(Nem) Szeretem ...	(nem) se-re-tem ...
art	a művészetet	o mēw-vey-se-tet
movies	a filmeket	o fil-me-ket
sport	a sportot	o shpawr-tawt
Do you like ...?	Szeretsz ...?	se-rets ...
I (don't) like ...	(Nem) Szeretek ...	(nem) se-re-tek ...
cooking	főzni	fēūz-ni
nightclubs	diszkóba járni	dis-kāw-bo yar-ni
reading	olvasni	awl-vosh-ni
shopping	vásárolni	va-sha-rawl-ni
travelling	utazni	u-toz-ni

Do you ...?		
dance	*Táncolsz?*	*tan·*tsawls
go to concerts	*Jársz koncertre?*	yars *kawn·*tsert·re
listen to music	*Hallgatsz zenét?*	*holl·*gots ze·neyt

food & drink

finding a place to eat

Can you recommend a ...?	*Tud/Tudsz ajánlani egy ...?* pol/inf	tud/tuds *o·*yan·lo·ni ej ...
bar	*bárt*	bart
café	*kávézót*	*ka·*vey·zāwt
restaurant	*éttermet*	*eyt·*ter·met
I'd like ...	*Szeretnék ...*	se·ret·neyk ...
a table for (five)	*egy asztalt (öt) személyre*	ej *os·*tolt (eut) *se·*mey·re

ordering food

breakfast	*reggeli*	*reg·*ge·li
lunch	*ebéd*	*e·*beyd
dinner	*vacsora*	*vo·*chaw·ro
snack	*snack*	snekk
today's special	*napi ajánlat*	*no·*pi *oy·*an·lot

How long is the wait?
Mennyi ideig kell várni?   *men'·*nyi *i·*de·ig kell *vaar·*ni

What would you recommend?
Mit ajánlana?   mit *o·*yan·lo·no

I'd like (the) ...	*... szeretném.*	... se·ret·neym
bill	*A számlát*	o *sam·*lat
drink list	*Az itallapot*	oz *i·*tol·lo·pawt
menu	*Az étlapot*	oz *eyt·*lo·pawt
that dish	*Azt az ételt*	ozt oz *ey·*telt

drinks

(cup of) coffee ...	(csésze) kávé ...	(chey·se) ka·vey ...
(cup of) tea ...	(csésze) tea ...	(chey·se) te·o ...
with milk	tejjel	ey·yel
without sugar	cukor nélkül	tsu·kawr neyl·kewl
... mineral water	... ásványvíz	... ash·van'·veez
sparkling	szénsavas	seyn·sho·vosh
still	szénsavmentes	seyn·shov·men·tesh
orange juice	narancslé	no·ronch·ley
soft drink	üdítőital	ew·dee·tēū·i·tal
(boiled) water	(forralt) víz	(fawr·rolt) veez

in the bar

I'll have ...	... kérek.	... key·rek
I'll buy you a drink.	Fizetek neked egy italt.	fi·ze·tek ne·ked ej i·tolt
What would you like?	Mit kérsz?	mit keyrs
Cheers! (to one person)	Egészségedre!	e·geys·shey·ged·re
Cheers! (to more than one person)	Egészségetekre!	e·geys·shey·ge·tek·re
brandy	brandy	bren·di
champagne	pezsgő	pezh·gēū
cocktail	koktél	kawk·teyl
a bottle/glass of (beer)	egy üveg/pohár (sör)	ej ew·veg/paw·har (sheur)
a shot of (whisky)	egy kupica (whisky)	ej ku·pi·tso (vis·ki)
a bottle/glass of ... wine	egy üveg/pohár ... bor	ej ew·veg/paw·har ... bawr
red	vörös	veu·reush
sparkling	pezsgő	pezh·gēū
white	fehér	fe·heyr

What's the local speciality?
Mi az itteni specialitás?   mi oz it·te·ni shpe·tsi·o·li·tash

What's that?
Az mi?   oz mi

How much is (a kilo of cheese)?
Mennyibe kerül (egy kiló sajt)?   men'·nyi·be ke·rewl (ej ki·lāw shoyt)

I'd like ...	Kérek ...	key·rek ...
200 grams	húsz dekát	hūs de·kat
a kilo	egy kilót	ej ki·lāwt
a piece	egy darabot	ej do·ro·bawt
a slice	egy szeletet	ej se·le·tet

Less.	Kevésbé.	ke·veysh·bey
Enough.	Elég.	e·leyg
More.	Több.	teubb

special diets & allergies

Is there a vegetarian restaurant near here?
Van a közelben   von o keu·zel·ben
vegetáriánus étterem?   ve·ge·ta·ri·a·nush eyt·te·rem

Do you have vegetarian food?
Vannak Önöknél   von·nok eu·neuk·neyl
vegetáriánus ételek?   ve·ge·ta·ri·a·nush ey·te·lek

Could you prepare	Tudna készíteni	tud·no key·see·te·ni
a meal without ...?	egy ételt ... nélkül?	ej ey·telt ... neyl·kewl
butter	vaj	vo·y
eggs	tojás	taw·yash
meat stock	húsleveskocka	hūsh·le·vesh·kawts·ko

I'm allergic to ...	Allergiás vagyok a ...	ol·ler·gi·ash vo·dyawk o ...
dairy produce	tejtermékekre	te·y·ter·mey·kek·re
gluten	sikérre	shi·keyr·re
MSG	monoszódium	maw·naw·sāw·di·um
	glutamátra	glu·to·mat·ro
nuts	diófélékre	di·āw·fey·leyk·re
seafood	tenger gyümölcseire	ten·ger yew·meul·che·i·re

menu decoder

bableves csülökkel	bob·le·vesh chew·leuk·kel	bean soup with smoked pork
csúsztatott palacsinta	chüs·to·tawtt po·lo·chin·to	pancakes in a stack sprinkled with chocolate
dobostorta	daw·bawsh·tawr·to	sponge cake with chocolate cream, with a glazed sponge layer on top
gombaleves	gom·bo·le·vesh	mushroom & onion soup seasoned with paprika
grenadírmas	gre·no·deer·morsh	potatoes with sweet paprika, onion & pasta, served with sour gherkins
gulyásleves	gu·yash·le·vesh	beef soup with vegetables & pasta
halászlé vegyes halból	ho·las·ley ve·dyesh hol·bāwl	fish soup with onion, tomato & a dose of paprika
hortobágyi ürügulyás	hawr·taw·ba·dyi ew·rew·gu·yash	mutton stew
kacsapecsenye	ko·cho·pe·che·nye	roasted duck with apples, quinces & marjoram
korhelyleves	kawr·he·y·le·vesh	stew of smoked ham, sauerkraut & sliced sausage
kürtőskalács	kewr·tēüsh·ko·lach	dough wrapped around a roller, coated with honey & almonds or walnuts & roasted on a spit
lángos	lan·gawsh	deep-fried potato cakes topped with cabbage, ham, cheese or sour cream
lecsó	le·chāw	stewed tomatoes, peppers, onions & paprika
lekváros szelet	lek·va·rawsh se·let	sponge cake layered with strawberry jam

májgaluska	*ma·y·go·lush·ko*	*fried egg dumplings made from chicken, veal or pork livers*
mákos tészta	*ma·kawsh teys·to*	*sweet pasta with poppy seeds*
meggyes rétes	*mej·dyesh rey·tesh*	*cherry & walnut strudel*
meggyleves	*mejj·le·vesh*	*chilled soup with cherries, sour cream & red wine*
palóc leves	*po·lāwts le·vesh*	*soup made from cubed leg of mutton or beef & vegetables*
paprikás	*pop·ri·kash*	*veal, chicken or rabbit stew*
pörkölt	*peur·keult*	*diced meat stew with a paprika gravy*
sonkás kocka	*shawn·kash kots·ko*	*chopped ham mixed with sour cream & pasta, then baked*
sonkával töltött gomba	*shawn·ka·vol teul·teutt gawm·bo*	*mushrooms stuffed with smoked ham in cheese sauce & grilled*
székely gulyás	*sey·ke·y gu·yash*	*stew of sautéed pork, bacon, sauerkraut & sour cream*
szilvás gombóc	*sil·vash gawm·bāwts*	*boiled potato-based dumplings filled with pitted plums*
tokány	*taw·kan'*	*meat stewed in white wine, tomato paste & seasonings*
töltött káposzta	*teul·teutt ka·paws·to*	*cabbage leaves stuffed with rice & ground pork*
töltött paprika	*teul·teutt pop·ri·ko*	*capsicums stuffed with rice & ground pork*
tűzdelt fácán	*tēwz·delt fa·tsan*	*pheasant larded with smoked bacon & roasted in red wine gravy*
vargabéles	*vor·go·bey·lesh*	*layered pasta & dough topped with a custard-like mixture*
zöldbabfőzelék	*zeuld·bob·fēū·ze·leyk*	*cooked green beans with sour cream & seasonings*

emergencies

basics

Help!	Segítség!	she·geet·sheyg
Stop!	Álljon meg!	all·yawn meg
Go away!	Menjen innen!	men·yen in·nen
Thief!	Tolvaj!	tawl·voy
Fire!	Tűz!	tēwz
Watch out!	Vigyázzon!	vi·dyaz·zawn
Call a doctor!	Hívjon orvost!	heev·yawn awr·vawsht
Call an ambulance!	Hívja a mentőket!	heev·yo o men·tēū·ket
Call the police!	Hívja a rendőrséget!	heev·yo o rend·ēūr·shey·get

It's an emergency!
Sürgős esetről van szó.   shewr·gēūsh e·shet·rēūl von sāw

Could you help me, please?
Tudna segíteni?   tud·no she·gee·te·ni

Can I use your phone?
Használhatom a telefonját?   hos·nal·ho·tawm o te·le·fawn·yat

I'm lost.
Eltévedtem.   el·tey·ved·tem

Where are the toilets?
Hol a vécé?   hawl o vey·tsey

police

Where's the police station?
Hol a rendőrség?   hawl o rend·ēūr·sheyg

I want to report an offence.
Bűncselekményt szeretnék   bēwn·che·lek·meynyt se·ret·neyk
bejelenteni.   be·ye·len·te·ni

I have insurance.
Van biztosításom.   von biz·taw·shee·ta·shawm

I've been ...

assaulted	Megtámadtak.	meg·ta·mod·tok
raped	Megerőszakoltak.	meg·e·rēū·so·kawl·tok
robbed	Kiraboltak.	ki·ro·bawl·tok

I've lost my ...	Elvesztettem ...	el·ves·tet·tem ...
My ... was/were stolen.	Ellopták ...	el·lawp·tak ...
backpack	a hátizsákomat	o ha·ti·zha·kaw·mot
bags	a csomagjaimat	o chaw·mog·yo·i·mot
credit card	a hitelkártyámat	o hi·tel·kar·tya·mot
handbag	a kézitáskámat	o key·zi·tash·ka·mot
jewellery	az ékszereimet	oz eyk·se·re·i·met
money	a pénzemet	o peyn·ze·met
passport	az útlevelemet	oz üt·le·ve·le·met
travellers cheques	az utazási csekkjeimet	oz u·to·za·shi chekk·ye·i·met
wallet	a tárcámat	o tar·tsa·mot

I want to contact my embassy/consulate.

Kapcsolatba akarok lépni
a követségemmel/
konzulátusommal.

kop·chaw·lot·bo o·ko·rawk leyp·ni
o keu·vet·shey·gem·mel/
kawn·zu·la·tu·shawm·mol

health

medical needs

Where's the nearest ...?	Hol a legközelebbi ...?	hawl o leg·keu·ze·leb·bi ...
dentist	fogorvos	fawg·awr·vawsh
doctor	orvos	awr·vawsh
hospital	kórház	kāwr·haz
(night) pharmacist	(éjszaka nyitvatartó) gyógyszertár	(ey·so·ko nyit·vo·tor·tāw) dyāwj·ser·tar

I need a doctor (who speaks English).

(Angolul beszélő) Orvosra
van szükségem.

(on·gaw·lul be·sey·lēū) awr·vawsh·ro
von sewk·shey·gem

Could I see a female doctor?

Beszélhetnék egy orvosnővel?

be·seyl·het·neyk ej awr·vawsh·nēū·vel

I've run out of my medication.

Elfogyott az orvosságom.

el·faw·dyawtt oz awr·vawsh·sha·gawm

symptoms, conditions & allergies

I'm sick.	Rosszul vagyok.	raws·sul vo·dyawk
It hurts here.	Itt fáj.	itt fa·y

I have a ...		
cough	Köhögök.	keu·heu·geuk
headache	Fáj a fejem.	fa·y o fe·yem
sore throat	Fáj a torkom.	fa·y o tawr·kawm
toothache	Fáj a fogam.	fa·y o faw·gom

I have (a) ...	... van.	... von
asthma	Asztmám	ost·mam
bronchitis	Hörghurutom	heurg·hu·rut·awm
constipation	Székrekedésem	seyk·re·ke·dey·shem
diarrhoea	Hasmenésem	hosh·me·ney·shem
fever	Lázam	la·zom
heart condition	Szívbetegségem	seev·be·teg·sheyg·em
nausea	Hányingerem	han'·in·ge·rem
pain	Fájdalmam	fay·dol·mom

I'm allergic to ...	Allergiás vagyok ...	ol·ler·gi·ash vo·dyawk ...
antibiotics	az antibiotikumokra	oz on·ti·bi·aw·ti·ku·mawk·ro
anti-inflammatories	a gyulladásgátlókra	o dyul·lo·dash·gat·lawk·ro
aspirin	az aszpirinre	oz os·pi·rin·re
bees	a méhekre	o mey·hek·re
codeine	a kodeinre	o ko·de·in·re
penicillin	a penicillinre	o pe·ni·tsil·lin·re

antiseptic n	fertőzésgátló	fer·tēū·zeysh·gat·law
bandage	kötés	keu·teysh
condoms	óvszer	āwv·ser
contraceptives	fogamzásgátló	faw·gom·zash·gat·law
diarrhoea medicine	hasmenés gyógyszer	hosh·men·eysh dyāwd'·ser
insect repellent	rovarirtó	raw·vor·ir·tāw
laxatives	hashajtó	hosh·ho·y·tāw
painkillers	fájdalomcsillapító	fa·y·do·lawm·chil·lo·pee·tāw
rehydration salts	folyadékpótló sók	faw·yo·deyk·pāwt·law shāwk
sleeping tablets	altató	ol·to·tāw

english–hungarian dictionary

In this dictionary, words are marked as n (noun), a (adjective), v (verb), sg (singular), pl (plural), inf (informal) or pol (polite) where necessary.

A

accident *baleset* bol-e-shet
accommodation *szállás* sal-lash
adaptor *adapter* o-dop-ter
address n *cím* tseem
after *után* u-tan
air-conditioned *légkondicionált* leyg-kawn-di-tsi-aw-nalt
airplane *repülőgép* re-pew-lēū-geyp
airport *repülőtér* re-pew-lēū-teyr
alcohol *alkohol* ol-kaw-hawl
all *minden* min-den
allergy *allergia* ol-ler-gi-o
ambulance *mentő* men-tēū
and *és* eysh
ankle *boka* baw-ko
arm *kar* kor
ashtray *hamutartó* ho-mu-tor-tāw
ATM *bankautomata* bonk-o-u-taw-mo-to

B

baby *baba* bo-bo
back (body) *hát* hat
backpack *hátizsák* ha-ti-zhak
bad *rossz* rawss
bag *táska* tash-ko
baggage claim *poggyászkiadó* pawd'-dyas-ki-o-dāw
bank *bank* bonk
bar *bár* bar
bathroom *fürdőszoba* fewr-dēū-saw-bo
battery *elem* e-lem
beautiful *szép* seyp
bed *ágy* aj
beer *sör* sheur
before *előtt* e-lēütt
behind *mögött* meu-geutt
bicycle *bicikli* bi-tsik-li
big *nagy* noj
bill *számla* sam-lo
black *fekete* fe-ke-te

blanket *takaró* to-ko-rāw
blood group *vércsoport* veyr-chaw-pawrt
blue *kék* keyk
boat (big) *hajó* ho-yāw
boat (small) *csónak* chāw-nok
book (make a reservation) v *lefoglal* le-fawg-lol
bottle *üveg* ew-veg
bottle opener *sörnyitó* sheur-nyi-tāw
boy *fiú* fi-ū
brake (car) *fék* feyk
breakfast *reggeli* reg-ge-li
broken (faulty) *hibás* hi-bash
bus *busz* bus
business *üzlet* ewz-let
buy *vesz* ves

C

café *kávézó* ka-vey-zāw
camera *fényképezőgép* feyn'-key-pe-zēū-geyp
camp site *táborhely* ta-bawr-he-y
cancel *töröl* teu-reul
can opener *konzervnyitó* kawn-zerv-nyi-tāw
car *autó* o-u-tāw
cash n *készpénz* keys-peynz
cash (a cheque) v *bevált csekket* be-valt chek-ket
cell phone *mobil telefon* mo-bil te-le-fawn
centre n *központ* keuz-pawnt
change (money) v *pénzt vált* peynzt valt
cheap *olcsó* awl-chāw
check (bill) *számla* sam-lo
check-in n *bejelentkezés* be-ye-lent-ke-zeysh
chest *mellkas* mell-kosh
child *gyerek* dye-rek
cigarette *cigaretta* tsi-go-ret-to
city *város* va-rawsh
clean a *tiszta* tis-to
closed *zárva* zar-vo
coffee *kávé* ka-vey
coins *pénzérmék* peynz-eyr-meyk
cold a *hideg* hi-deg
collect call *'R' beszélgetés* er-be-seyl-ge-teysh
come *jön* yeun

computer *számítógép* sa-mee-täw-geyp
condom *óvszer* awv-ser
contact lenses *kontaktlencse* kawn-tokt-len-che
cook v *főz* feüz
cost n *ár* ar
credit card *hitelkártya* hi-tel-kar-tyo
cup *csésze* chey-se
currency exchange *valutaátváltás* vo-lu-to-at-val-tash
customs (immigration) *vám* vam

D

dangerous *veszélyes* ve-sey-yesh
date (time) *dátum* da-tum
day *nap* nop
delay n *késés* key-sheysh
dentist *fogorvos* fawg-awr-vawsh
depart *elutazik* el-u-to-zik
diaper *pelenka* pe-len-ko
dictionary *szótár* saw-tar
dinner *vacsora* vo-chaw-ro
direct *közvetlen* keuz-vet-len
dirty *piszkos* pis-kawsh
disabled *mozgássérült* mawz-gash-shey-rewlt
discount n *árengedmény* ar-en-ged-meyn'
doctor *orvos* awr-vawsh
double bed *dupla ágy* dup-lo aj
double room *duplaágyas szoba* dup-lo-a-dyosh saw-bo
drink v *ital* i-tol
drive v *vezet* ve-zet
drivers licence *jogosítvány* yaw-gaw-sheet-van'
drug (illicit) *kábítószerek* ka-bee-täw-se-rek
dummy (pacifier) *cumi* tsu-mi

E

ear *fül* fewl
east *kelet* ke-let
eat *eszik* e-sik
economy class *turistaosztály* tu-rish-to-aws-ta-y
electricity *villany* vil-lon'
elevator *lift* lift
email *e-mail* ee-meyl
embassy *nagykövetség* noj-keu-vet-sheyg
emergency *vészhelyzet* veys-he-y-zet
English (language) *angol* on-gawl
entrance *bejárat* be-ya-rot
evening *este* esh-te
exchange rate *átváltási árfolyam* at-val-ta-shi ar-faw-yom

exit n *kijárat* ki-ya-rot
expensive *drága* dra-go
express mail *expressz posta* eks-press pawsh-to
eye *szem* sem

F

far *messze* mes-se
fast *gyors* dyawrsh
father *apa* o-po
film (camera) *film* film
finger *ujj* u-y
first-aid kit *elsősegély-láda* el-shëü-she-gey-la-do
first class *első osztály* el-shëü aws-ta-y
fish n *hal* hol
food *ennivaló* en-ni-vo-läw
foot *lábfej* lab-fe-y
fork *villa* vil-lo
free (of charge) *ingyenes* in-dye-nesh
friend (female) *barátnő* bo-rat-nëü
friend (male) *barát* bo-rat
fruit *gyümölcs* dyew-meulch
full *tele* te-le
funny *mulatságos* mu-lot-sha-gawsh

G

gift *ajándék* o-yan-deyk
girl *lány* lan'
glass (drinking) *üveg* ew-veg
glasses *szemüveg* sem-ew-veg
go *megy* mej
good *jó* yäw
green *zöld* zeuld
guide n *idegenvezető* i-de-gen-ve-ze-tëü

H

half n *fél* feyl
hand *kéz* keyz
handbag *kézitáska* key-zi-tash-ko
happy *boldog* bawl-dawg
have *van neki* von ne-ki
he *ő* ëü
head *fej* fe-y
heart *szív* seev
heat n *forróság* fawr-räw-shag
heavy *nehéz* ne-heyz
help v *segít* she-geet
here *itt* itt

high *magas* mo-gosh
highway *országút* awr-sag-út
hike v *kirándul* ki-ran-dul
holiday *szabadság* so-bod-shag
homosexual n *homoszexuális* haw-maw-sek-su-a-lish
hospital *kórház* káwr-haz
hot *forró* fawr-ráw
hotel *szálloda* sal-law-do
Hungarian (language) *magyar* mo-dyor
Hungary *Magyarország* mo-dyor-awr-sag
hungry *éhes* ey-hesh
husband *férj* feyr-y

I

I *én* eyn
identification (card) *személyi igazolvány* se-mey-yi i-go-zawl-van'
ill *beteg* be-teg
important *fontos* fawn-tawsh
included *beleértve* be-le-eyrt-ve
injury *sérülés* shey-rew-leysh
insurance *biztosítás* biz-taw-shee-tash
Internet *Internet* in-ter-net
interpreter *tolmács* tawl-mach

J

jewellery *ékszerek* eyk-se-rek
job *állás* al-lash

K

key *kulcs* kulch
kilogram *kilogramm* ki-láw-gromm
kitchen *konyha* kawn'-ho
knife *kés* keysh

L

laundry (place) *mosoda* maw-shaw-do
lawyer *jogász* yaw-gas
left (direction) *balra* bol-ro
left-luggage office *csomagmegőrző*
 chaw-mog-meg-eür-zeü
leg *láb* lab
lesbian n *leszbikus* les-bi-kush
less *kevésbé* ke-veysh-bey
letter (mail) *levél* le-veyl
lift (elevator) *lift* lift

light n *fény* feyn'
like v *szeret* se-ret
lock n *zár* zar
long *hosszú* haws-sü
lost *elveszett* el-ve-sett
lost-property office *talált tárgyak hivatala*
 to-lalt tar-dyok hi-vo-to-lo
love v *szeret* se-ret
luggage *poggyász* pawd'-dyas
lunch *ebéd* e-beyd

M

mail n *posta* pawsh-to
man *férfi* feyr-fi
map *térkép* teyr-keyp
market *piac* pi-ots
matches *gyufa* dyu-fo
meat *hús* hüsh
medicine *orvosság* awr-vawsh-shag
menu *étlap* eyt-lop
message *üzenet* ew-ze-net
milk *tej* te-y
minute *perc* perts
mobile phone *mobil telefon* maw-bil te-le-fawn
money *pénz* peynz
month *hónap* háw-nop
morning *reggel* reg-gel
mother *anya* o-nyo
motorcycle *motorbicikli* maw-tawr-bi-tsik-li
motorway *autópálya* o-u-táw-pa-yo
mouth *száj* sa-y
music *zene* ze-ne

N

name *keresztnév* ke-rest-neyv
napkin *szalvéta* sol-vey-to
nappy *pelenka* pe-len-ko
near *közelében* keu-ze-ley-ben
neck *nyak* nyok
new *új* ü-y
news *hírek* hee-rek
newspaper *újság* ü-y-shag
night *éjszaka* ey-so-ko
no *nem* nem
noisy *zajos* zo-yawsh
nonsmoking *nemdohányzó* nem-daw-han'-záw
north *észak* ey-sok
nose *orr* awrr
now *most* mawsht
number *szám* sam

19

O

oil (engine) *olaj* aw-lo-y
old (person/thing) *öreg/régi* eu-reg/rey-gi
one-way ticket *csak oda jegy* chok aw-do yej
open a *nyitva* nyit-vo
outside *kint* kint

P

package *csomag* chaw-mog
paper *papír* po-peer
park (a car) v *parkol* por-kawl
passport *útlevél* üt-le-veyl
pay *fizet* fi-zet
pen *golyóstoll* gaw-yàwsh-tawll
petrol *benzin* ben-zin
pharmacy *gyógyszertár* dyàwj-ser-tar
phonecard *telefonkártya* te-le-fawn-kar-tyo
photo *fénykép* feyn'-keyp
plate *tányér* ta-nyeyr
police *rendőrség* rend-eür-sheyg
postcard *levelezőlap* le-ve-le-zēü-lop
post office *postahivatal* pawsh-to-hi-vo-tol
pregnant *terhes* ter-hesh
price *ár* ar

Q

quiet *csendes* chen-desh

R

rain n *eső* e-shēü
razor *borotva* baw-rawt-vo
receipt n *nyugta* nyug-to
red *piros* pi-rawsh
refund n *visszatérítés* vis-so-tey-ree-teysh
registered mail *ajánlott levél* o-yan-lawtt le-veyl
rent v *bérel* bey-rel
repair v *megjavít* meg-yo-veet
reservation *foglalás* fawg-lo-lash
restaurant *étterem* eyt-te-rem
return v *visszatér* vis-so-teyr
return ticket *oda-vissza jegy* aw-do-vis-so yej
right (direction) *jobbra* yawbb-ro
road *út* üt
room *szoba* saw-bo

S

safe a *biztonságos* biz-tawn-sha-gawsh
sanitary napkin *egészségügyi törlőkendő* e-geys-sheyg-ew-dyi teur-lēü-ken-dēü
seat *ülés* ew-leysh
send *küld* kewld
service station *benzinkút* ben-zin-küt
sex *szex* seks
shampoo *sampon* shom-pawn
share (a dorm) *ben/ban lakik* -ben/-ban lo-kik
shaving cream *borotvakrém* baw-rawt-vo-kreym
she *ő* ēü
sheet (bed) *lepedő* le-pe-dēü
shirt *ing* ing
shoes *cipők* tsi-pēük
shop n *üzlet* ewz-let
short *alacsony* o-lo-chawn'
shower *zuhany* zu-hon'
single room *egyágyas szoba* ej-a-dyosh saw-bo
skin *bőr* bēür
skirt *szoknya* sawk-nyo
sleep v *alszik* ol-sik
slowly *lassan* losh-shon
small *kicsi* ki-chi
smoke (cigarettes) v *dohányzik* daw-han'-zik
soap *szappan* sop-pon
some *néhány* ney-han'
soon *hamarosan* ho-mo-raw-shon
south *dél* deyl
souvenir shop *ajándékbolt* o-yan-deyk-bawlt
speak *beszél* be-seyl
spoon *kanál* ko-nal
stamp n *bélyeg* bey-yeg
stand-by ticket *készenléti jegy* key-sen-ley-ti yej
station (train) *állomás* al-law-mash
stomach *gyomor* dyaw-mawr
stop v *abbahagy* ob-bo-hoj
stop (bus) n *megálló* meg-al-läw
street *utca* ut-tso
student *diák* di-ak
sun *nap* nop
sunscreen *napolaj* nop-aw-lo-y
swim v *úszik* ü-sik

T

tampons *tampon* tom-pawn
taxi *taxi* tok-si
teaspoon *teáskanál* te-ash-ko-nal
teeth *fogak* faw-gok
telephone n *telefon* te-le-fawn

television *televízió* te-le-vee-zi-āw
temperature (weather) *hőmérséklet* hēū-meyr-sheyk-let
tent *sátor* sha-tawr
that (one) *az* oz
they *ők* ēūk
thirsty *szomjas* sawm-yosh
this (one) *ez* ez
throat *torok* taw-rawk
ticket *jegy* yej
time *idő* i-dēū
tired *fáradt* fa-rott
tissues *szövetek* seu-ve-tek
today *ma* mo
toilet *vécé* vey-tsey
tomorrow *holnap* hawl-nop
tonight *ma este* mo esh-te
toothbrush *fogkefe* fawg-ke-fe
toothpaste *fogkrém* fawg-kreym
torch (flashlight) *zseblámpa* zheb-lam-po
tour n *túra* tū-ro
tourist office *turistairoda* tu-rish-to-i-raw-do
towel *törülköző* teu-rewl-keu-zēū
train *vonat* vaw-not
translate *fordít* fawr-deet
travel agency *utazási iroda* u-to-za-shi i-raw-do
travellers cheque *utazási csekk* u-to-za-shi chekk
trousers *nadrág* nod-rag
twin beds *két ágy* keyt aj
tyre *autógumi* o-u-tāw-gu-mi

U

underwear *alsónemű* ol-shāw-ne-mēw
urgent *sürgős* shewr-gēūsh

V

vacant *üres* ew-resh
vacation *vakáció* vo-ka-tsi-āw

vegetable n *zöldség* zeuld-sheyg
vegetarian a *vegetáriánus* ve-ge-ta-ri-a-nush
visa *vízum* vee-zum

W

waiter *pincér* pin-tseyr
walk v *sétál* shey-tal
wallet *tárca* tar-tsa-mot
warm a *meleg* me-leg
wash (something) *megmos* meg-mawsh
watch n *óra* āw-ro
water *víz* veez
we *mi* mi
weekend *hétvége* heyt-vey-ge
west *nyugat* nyu-got
wheelchair *rokkantkocsi* rawk-kont-kaw-chi
when *mikor* mi-kawr
where *hol* hawl
white *fehér* fe-heyr
who *ki* ki
why *miért* mi-eyrt
wife *feleség* fe-le-sheyg
window *ablak* ob-lok
wine *bor* bawr
with *-val/-vel* -vol/-vel
without *nélkül* neyl-kewl
woman *nő* nēū
write *ír* eer

Y

yellow *sárga* shar-go
yes *igen* i-gen
yesterday *tegnap* teg-nop
you sg inf *te* te
you pl inf *ti* ti
you sg pol *Ön* eun
you pl pol *Önök* eu-neuk

Macedonian

macedonian alphabet

А а a	Б б buh	В в vuh	Г г guh	Д д duh	Ѓ ѓ gyuh
Е е e	Ж ж zhuh	З з zuh	Ѕ ѕ dzuh	И и i	Ј ј yuh
К к kuh	Л л luh	Љ љ lyuh	М м muh	Н н nuh	Њ њ nyuh
О о o	П п puh	Р р ruh	С с suh	Т т tuh	Ќ ќ kyuh
У у u	Ф ф fuh	Х х huh	Ц ц tsuh	Ч ч chuh	Џ џ juh
Ш ш shuh					

МАКЕДОНСКИ

macedonian

introduction

Macedonian (македонски ma·ke·don·ski), the language spoken in the Balkan peninsula to the north of Greece, shares only the name with the ancient language usually thought of in relation to the empire of Alexander the Great. The present-day Macedonian is a South Slavic language (with Bulgarian and Serbian its closest relatives) and the official language of Macedonia, the former Yugoslav republic which became an independent state in 1992. For the speakers of Macedonian – about 2 million people living in Macedonia and the neighbouring countries, as well as the diaspora – it has extreme significance as a confirmation of their national identity.

From the arrival of the Slavs to the Balkans in the 6th century until the Turkish conquest in the 15th century, the present-day Macedonia was passed back and forth between Byzantium and the medieval Bulgarian and Serbian kingdoms, and the heavy interaction between the three Slavic languages explains many of their common features. Most notably, Macedonian and Bulgarian differ from the other Slavic languages in the absence of noun cases. During the five centuries of Turkish rule in the Ottoman Empire, Turkish linguistic influence on Macedonian (mostly in the vocabulary) was rivalled only by Greek, as the liturgic language of the Greek Orthodox Church. Stronger exposure to Serbian within the Yugoslav state for most of the 20th century is reflected in the vocabulary (particularly slang) of Macedonian today.

The history of the Macedonian literary language is centred around Old Church Slavonic and the Cyrillic alphabet. The Byzantine Orthodox missionaries, St Cyril and Methodius, themselves from Salonica in Aegean Macedonia and speakers of a Slavic dialect of the region, invented the Glagolitic alphabet in the 9th century. They translated Greek religious literature into Old Church Slavonic, the language of the earliest written records from which the modern South Slavic literary languages all evolved. The Cyrillic alphabet was later developed by the disciples of the two missionaries, using the Greek and Glagolitic characters. The Macedonian Cyrillic alphabet in its present form is phonetic and very similar to the Serbian alphabet, with only a few different letters.

The creation of a modern literary standard started in the latter half of the 19th century and ended with the official codification in 1945 of a standard based on the west-central dialects. This form is the most distinct from Bulgarian and Serbian, whose boundaries with Macedonian can often be blurry.

pronunciation

vowel sounds

The Macedonian vowel system is very straightforward – it consists of the five basic vowels.

symbol	english equivalent	macedonian example	transliteration
a	father	здраво	*zdra*·vo
e	bet	вера	*ve*·ra
i	hit	син	sin
o	pot	добро	*dob*·ro
u	put	југ	yug

word stress

In the Macedonian literary standard the stress usually falls on the third syllable from the end in words with three syllables or more. If the word has only two syllables, the first is usually stressed. There are exceptions to this rule, such as with many new borrowings and other words of foreign origin – eg литература li·te·ra·*tu*·ra, not li·te·*ra*·tu·ra (literature). Just follow our coloured pronunciation guide, in which the stressed syllable is indicated in italics.

consonant sounds

The consonant sounds in Macedonian mostly have equivalents in English. You might need a little practice with the 'soft' ѓ gy and ќ ky sounds. Don't be intimidated by the consonant clusters as in црква tsrk·va (church) or брзо br·zo (fast) – try putting a slight 'uh' sound before the r, which serves as a semi-vowel.

symbol	english equivalent	macedonian example	transliteration
b	**b**ed	билет	*bi*·let
ch	**ch**eat	чист	chist
d	**d**og	мед	med
dz	a**dds**	sид	dzid
f	**f**at	кафе	*ka*·fe
g	**g**o	гуми	*gu*·mi
gy	leg**u**me	госпоѓа	*gos*·po·**gya**
h	**h**at	храм	hram
j	**j**oke	џамија	*ja*·mi·ya
k	**k**it	компир	*kom*·pir
ky	c**u**re	ноќ	noky
l	**l**ot	леб	leb
ly	mi**lli**on	љубов	*lyu*·bov
m	**m**an	месо	*me*·so
n	**n**ot	бензин	*ben*·zin
ny	ca**ny**on	бања	*ba*·nya
p	**p**et	писмо	*pis*·mo
r	**r**un	стар	star
s	**s**un	сега	*se*·ga
sh	**sh**ot	туш	tush
t	**t**op	исток	*is*·tok
ts	ha**ts**	деца	*de*·tsa
v	**v**ery	север	*se*·ver
y	**y**es	јас	yas
z	**z**ero	пазар	*pa*·zar
zh	plea**s**ure	плажа	*pla*·zha

pronunciation – MACEDONIAN

basics

language difficulties

Do you speak English?
Зборувате ли англиски?
zbo·*ru*·va·te li *an*·glis·ki

Do you understand?
Разбирате ли?
raz·*bi*·ra·te li

I (don't) understand.
Јас (не) разбирам.
yas (ne) *raz*·bi·ram

What does (добро) mean?
Што значи (добро)?
shto *zna*·chi (*dob*·ro)

How do you ...? | **Како се ...?** | *ka*·ko se ...
pronounce this | изговара ова | iz·*go*·va·ra *o*·va
write (утре) | пишува (утре) | *pi*·shu·va (*ut*·re)

Could you please ...? | ..., ве молам. | ... ve *mo*·lam
repeat that | Повторете го тоа | pov·to·*re*·te go *to*·a
speak more slowly | Зборувајте полека | zbo·*ru*·vay·te *po*·le·ka
write it down | Напишете го тоа | na·pi·*she*·te go *to*·a

essentials

Yes.	Да.	da
No.	Не.	ne
Please.	Молам.	*mo*·lam
Thank you (very much).	Благодарам. pol	bla·*go*·da·ram
Thanks a lot.	Фала многу. inf	*fa*·la *mno*·gu
You're welcome.	Нема зошто.	*ne*·ma *zosh*·to
Excuse me.	Извинете.	iz·*vi*·ne·te
Sorry.	Простете.	*pros*·te·te

numbers

0	нула	*nu*·la	15	петнаесет	pet·*na*·e·set
1	еден/една m/f	*e*·den/*ed*·na	16	шеснаесет	shes·*na*·e·set
	едно n	*ed*·no	17	седумнаесет	se·dum·*na*·e·set
2	два m	dva	18	осумнаесет	o·sum·*na*·e·set
	две f&n	dve	19	деветнаесет	de·vet·*na*·e·set
3	три	tri	20	дваесет	*dva*·e·set
4	четири	*che*·ti·ri	21	дваесет и еден	*dva*·e·set i *e*·den
5	пет	pet	22	дваесет и два	*dva*·e·set i dva
6	шест	shest	30	триесет	*tri*·e·set
7	седум	*se*·dum	40	четириесет	che·ti·*ri*·e·set
8	осум	*o*·sum	50	педесет	*pe*·de·set
9	девет	*de*·vet	60	шеесет	*she*·e·set
10	десет	*de*·set	70	седумдесет	se·*dum*·de·set
11	единаесет	e·di·*na*·e·set	80	осумдесет	o·*sum*·de·set
12	дванаесет	dva·*na*·e·set	90	деведесет	de·*ve*·de·set
13	тринаесет	tri·*na*·e·set	100	сто	sto
14	четиринаесет	che·ti·ri·*na*·e·set	1000	илјада	*il*·ya·da

time & dates

What time is it?	Колку е часот?	*kol*·ku e *cha*·sot
It's one o'clock.	Часот е еден.	*cha*·sot e *e*·den
It's (two) o'clock.	Часот е (два).	*cha*·sot e (dva)
Quarter past (one).	(Еден) и петнаесет.	(*e*·den) i pet·*na*·e·set
Half past (one).	(Еден) и пол.	(*e*·den) i pol
Quarter to (eight).	Петнаесет до (осум).	pet·*na*·e·set do (*o*·sum)
At what time ...?	Во колку часот ...?	vo *kol*·ku *cha*·sot ...
At ...	Во ...	vo ...
am	претпладне	*pret*·plad·ne
pm	попладне	*po*·plad·ne
Monday	понеделник	po·*ne*·del·nik
Tuesday	вторник	*vtor*·nik
Wednesday	среда	*sre*·da
Thursday	четврток	chet·*vr*·tok
Friday	петок	*pe*·tok
Saturday	сабота	*sa*·bo·ta
Sunday	недела	*ne*·de·la

January	јануари	ya·nu·*a*·ri
February	февруари	fev·ru·*a*·ri
March	март	mart
April	април	*ap*·ril
May	мај	may
June	јуни	*yu*·ni
July	јули	*yu*·li
August	август	*av*·gust
September	септември	sep·*tem*·vri
October	октомври	ok·*tom*·vri
November	ноември	no·*em*·vri
December	декември	de·*kem*·vri

What date is it today?
Кој датум е денес? — koy *da*·tum e *de*·nes

It's (15 December).
Денес е (петнаесетти декември). — *de*·nes e (pet·na·e·set·ti de·*kem*·vri)

| since (May) | од (мај) | od (may) |
| until (June) | до (јуни) | do (*yu*·ni) |

last ...		
night	синоќа	*si*·no·kya
week	минатата недела	mi·*na*·ta·ta ne·de·la
month	минатиот месец	mi·*na*·ti·ot me·sets
year	минатата година	mi·*na*·ta·ta go·di·na

next ...		
week	следната недела	*sled*·na·ta ne·de·la
month	следниот месец	*sled*·ni·ot me·sets
year	следната година	*sled*·na·ta go·di·na

yesterday/tomorrow ...	вчера/утре ...	*vche*·ra/*ut*·re ...
morning	наутро	na·*ut*·ro
afternoon	попладне	*pop*·lad·ne
evening	вечер	*ve*·cher

weather

What's the weather like?	Какво е времето?	*kak·*vo e *vre·*me·to
It' snowing.	Паѓа снег.	*pa·*gya sneg
It's ...	Времето е ...	*vre·*me·to e ...
cloudy	облачно	*ob·*lach·no
cold	студено	*stu·*de·no
hot	жешко	*zhesh·*ko
raining	врнежливо	vr·*nezh·*li·vo
sunny	сончево	*son·*che·vo
warm	топло	*top·*lo
windy	ветровито	vet·*ro·*vi·to
spring	пролет f	*pro·*let
summer	лето n	*le·*to
autumn	есен m	*e·*sen
winter	зима f	*zi·*ma

border crossing

I'm here ...	Јас сум овде ...	yas sum *ov·*de ...
in transit	транзит	*tran·*zit
on business	службено	*sluzh·*be·no
on holiday	на одмор	na *od·*mor
I'm here for ...	Јас овде останувам ...	yas *ov·*de os·*ta·*nu·vam ...
(10) days	(десет) дена	(*de·*set) *de·*na
(two) months	(два) месеца	(dva) *me·*se·tsa
(three) weeks	(три) недели	(tri) *ne·*de·li

I'm going to (Ohrid).
Јас одам во (Охрид). yas *o·*dam vo (*oh·*rid)

I'm staying at the (Hotel Park).
Јас престојувам во (хотел 'Парк'). yas pres·*to·*yu·vam vo (*ho·*tel park)

I have nothing to declare.
Јас немам да пријавам ништо. yas *ne·*mam da *pri·*ya·vam *nish·*to

I have something to declare.
Јас имам нешто да пријавам. yas *i·*mam *nesh·*to da *pri·*ya·vam

That's (not) mine.
Тоа (не) е мое. *to·*a (ne) e *mo·*e

transport

tickets & luggage

Where can I buy a ticket?
Каде можам да купам билет?   *ka*-de *mo*-zham da *ku*-pam *bi*-let

Do I need to book a seat?
Ми треба ли резервација?   mi *tre*-ba li re-zer-*va*-tsi-ya

One ... ticket (to Ohrid), please.	Еден ... (за Охрид), ве молам.	*e*-den ... (za *oh*-rid) ve *mo*-lam
one-way	билет во еден правец	*bi*-let vo *e*-den *pra*-vets
return	повратен билет	*pov*-ra-ten *bi*-let
I'd like to ... my ticket, please.	Сакам да го ... мојот билет, ве молам.	*sa*-kam da go ... *mo*-yot *bi*-let ve *mo*-lam
cancel	откажам	*ot*-ka-zham
change	променам	*pro*-me-nam
collect	земам	*ze*-mam
confirm	потврдам	*pot*-vr-dam
I'd like a ... seat, please.	Сакам едно седиште за ..., ве молам.	*sa*-kam *ed*-no *se*-dish-te za ... ve *mo*-lam
nonsmoking	непушачи	ne-*pu*-sha-chi
smoking	пушачи	*pu*-sha-chi

How much is it?
Колку чини тоа?   *kol*-ku *chi*-ni *to*-a

Is there air conditioning?
Дали има клима уред?   *da*-li *i*-ma *kli*-ma *u*-red

Is there a toilet?
Дали има тоалет?   *da*-li *i*-ma to-a-*let*

How long does the trip take?
Колку време се патува?   *kol*-ku *vre*-me se *pa*-tu-va

Is it a direct route? (train/bus)
Дали е овој воз/автобус директен?   *da*-li e *o*-voy voz/*av*-to-bus di-*rek*-ten

I'd like a luggage locker.
Сакам шкаф за багаж.   *sa*-kam shkaf za *ba*-gazh

My luggage has been ...	Мојот багаж е ...	mo·yot ba·gazh e ...
damaged	оштетен	osh·te·ten
lost	загубен	za·gu·ben
stolen	украден	uk·ra·den

getting around

Where does flight (912) arrive/depart?

Каде слетува/полетува авионот со лет (912)?	ka·de sle·tu·va/po·le·tu·va a·vi·o·not so let (de·vet e·den dva)

Where's (the) ...?	Каде е ...?	ka·de e ...
arrivals hall	чекалната за пристигнување	che·kal·na·ta za pris·tig·nu·va·nye
departures hall	чекалната за заминување	che·kal·na·ta za za·mi·nu·va·nye
duty-free shop	дјутифри продавницата	dyu·ti·fri pro·dav·ni·tsa·ta
gate (12)	излезот (дванаесет)	iz·le·zot (dva·na·e·set)

Is this the ... to (Bitola)?	Дали овој ... оди за (Битола)?	da·li o·voy ... o·di za (bi·to·la)
boat	брод	brod
bus	автобус	av·to·bus
plane	авион	a·vi·on
train	воз	voz

What time's the ... bus?	Кога поаѓа ... автобус?	ko·ga po·a·gya ... av·to·bus
first	првиот	pr·vi·ot
last	последниот	pos·led·ni·ot
next	следниот	sled·ni·ot

At what time does it arrive/leave?

Кога пристигнува/поаѓа?	ko·ga pris·tig·nu·va/po·a·gya

How long will it be delayed?

Колку време ќе доцни?	kol·ku vre·me kye dots·ni

What station/stop is this?

Која е оваа станица?	ko·ya e o·va·a sta·ni·tsa

What's the next station/stop?

Која е следната станица?	ko·ya e sled·na·ta sta·ni·tsa

Does it stop at (Prilep)?
Дали застанува во (Прилеп)? *da·*li zas·*ta·*nu·va vo (*pri·*lep)

Please tell me when we get to (Skopje).
Ве молам кажете ми кога
ќе стигнеме во (Скопје). *ve mo·*lam ka·*zhe·*te mi *ko·*ga kye *stig·*ne·me vo (*skop·*ye)

How long do we stop here?
Колку долго ќе стоиме овде? *kol·*ku *dol·*go kye *sto·*i·me *ov·*de

Is this seat available?
Дали е ова седиште слободно? *da·*li e *o·*va se·*dish·*te *slo·*bod·no

That's my seat.
Тоа е мое седиште. *to·*a e *mo·*e se·*dish·*te

I'd like a taxi ...	Сакам такси ...	*sa·*kam *tak·*si ...
at (9am)	во (девет претпладне)	vo (*de·*vet *pret·*plad·ne)
now	сега	*se·*ga
tomorrow	утре	*ut·*re

Is this taxi available?
Дали е ова такси слободно? *da·*li e *o·*va *tak·*si *slo·*bod·no

How much is it to ...?
Колку ќе чини до ...? *kol·*ku kye *chi·*ni do ...

Please put the meter on.
Ве молам вклучете го
таксиметарот. *ve mo·*lam vklu·*che·*te go *tak·*si·*me·*ta·rot

Please take me to (this address).
Ве молам одвезете ме до
(оваа адреса). *ve mo·*lam od·ve·*ze·*te me do (*o·*va·a *a·*dre·sa)

Please ...	Ве молам ...	*ve mo·*lam ...
slow down	возете побавно	*vo·*ze·te *po·*bav·no
stop here	застанете овде	zas·*ta·*ne·te *ov·*de
wait here	причекајте овде	pri·*che·*kay·te *ov·*de

car, motorbike & bicycle hire

I'd like to hire a ...	Сакам да изнајмам ...	*sa·*kam da *iz·*nay·mam ...
bicycle	точак	*to·*chak
car	кола	*ko·*la
motorbike	моторцикл	mo·tor·*tsikl*

with ...	со ...	so ...
a driver	возач	*vo*·zach
air conditioning	клима уред	*kli*·ma *u*·red
antifreeze	антифриз	*an*·ti·friz
snow chains	синџири за снег	*sin*·ji·ri za sneg

How much for ... hire?	Колку чини ...?	*kol*·ku *chi*·ni ...
hourly	на час	na chas
daily	дневно	*dnev*·no
weekly	неделно	*ne*·del·no

air	воздух m	*voz*·duh
oil	масло n	*mas*·lo
petrol	бензин m	*ben*·zin
tyres	гуми f pl	*gu*·mi

I need a mechanic.
Ми треба механичар.　　　　　　　　　mi *tre*·ba me·*ha*·ni·char

I've run out of petrol.
Останав без бензин.　　　　　　　　　　*os*·ta·nav bez *ben*·zin

I have a flat tyre.
Имам издишена гума.　　　　　　　　　*i*·mam iz·*di*·she·na *gu*·ma

directions

Where's the ...?	Каде е ...?	*ka*·de e ...
bank	банката	*ban*·ka·ta
city centre	центарот на градот	*tsen*·ta·rot na *gra*·dot
hotel	хотелот	*ho*·te·lot
market	пазарот	*pa*·za·rot
police station	полициската	po·li·*tsis*·ka·ta
	станица	*sta*·ni·tsa
post office	поштата	*posh*·ta·ta
public toilet	јавниот тоалет	*yav*·ni·ot to·a·*let*
tourist office	туристичкото биро	tu·ris·*tich*·ko·to bi·*ro*

Is this the road to (Bitola)?
Дали овој пат води до (Битола)?　　　*da*·li o·voy pat *vo*·di do (*bi*·to·la)

Can you show me (on the map)?
Можете ли да ми покажете　　　　　　*mo*·zhe·te li da mi po·*ka*·zhe·te
(на картава)?　　　　　　　　　　　　(na *kar*·ta·va)

What's the address?
Која е адресата?   *ko·ya e ad·re·sa·ta*

How far is it?
Колку е тоа далеку?   *kol·ku e to·a da·le·ku*

How do I get there?
Како да стигнам до таму?   *ka·ko da stig·nam do ta·mu*

Turn ...	Свртете ...	*svr·te·te ...*
at the corner	на аголот	*na a·go·lot*
at the traffic lights	на семафорите	*na se·ma·fo·ri·te*
left/right	лево/десно	*le·vo/des·no*

It's ...	Тоа е ...	*to·a e ...*
behind ...	зад ...	*zad ...*
far away	далеку	*da·le·ku*
here	овде	*ov·de*
in front of ...	пред ...	*pred ...*
left	лево	*le·vo*
near (to ...)	блиску (до ...)	*blis·ku (do ...)*
next to ...	веднаш до ...	*ved·nash do ...*
on the corner	на аголот	*na a·go·lot*
opposite ...	спроти ...	*spro·ti ...*
right	десно	*des·no*
straight ahead	право напред	*pra·vo nap·red*
there	таму	*ta·mu*

by bus	со автобус	so *av·to·bus*
by taxi	со такси	so *tak·si*
by train	со воз	so voz
on foot	пешки	*pesh·ki*
north	север	*se·ver*
south	југ	yug
east	исток	*is·tok*
west	запад	*za·pad*

signs

Влез/Излез	vlez/iz·lez	Entrance/Exit
Отворено/Затворено	ot·vo·re·no/zat·vo·re·no	Open/Closed
Соби за издавање	so·bi za iz·da·va·nye	Rooms Available
Нема место	ne·ma mes·to	No Vacancies
Информации	in·for·ma·tsi·i	Information
Полициска станица	po·li·tsis·ka sta·ni·tsa	Police Station
Забрането	za·bra·ne·to	Prohibited
Тоалети	to·a·le·ti	Toilets
Машки	mash·ki	Men
Женски	zhen·ski	Women
Топло/Ладно	top·lo/lad·no	Hot/Cold

accommodation

finding accommodation

Where's a ...?	**Каде има ...?**	ka·de i·ma ...
camping ground	камп	kamp
guesthouse	приватно сместување	pri·vat·no smes·tu·va·nye
hotel	хотел	ho·tel
youth hostel	младинско	mla·din·sko
	преноќиште	pre·no·kyish·te
Can you	**Можете ли да ми**	mo·zhe·te li da mi
recommend	**препорачате**	pre·po·ra·cha·te
somewhere ...?	**нешто ...?**	nesh·to ...
cheap	поевтино	po·ev·ti·no
good	добро	dob·ro
nearby	близу	bli·zu

I'd like to book a room, please.

Сакам да резервирам соба,
ве молам.

sa·kam da re·zer·vi·ram so·ba
ve mo·lam

I have a reservation.

Јас имам резервација.

yas i·mam re·zer·va·tsi·ya

My name's ...

Јас се викам ...

yas se vi·kam ...

accommodation – MACEDONIAN

Do you have a ... room?	Дали имате...?	*da*·li *i*·ma·te ...
single	еднокреветна соба	ed·no·*kre*·vet·na *so*·ba
double	соба со брачен кревет	*so*·ba so *bra*·chen *kre*·vet
twin	двокреветна соба	dvo·*kre*·vet·na *so*·ba

How much is it per ...?	Која е цената за ...?	*ko*·ya e *tse*·na·ta za ...
night	ноќ	noky
person	еден	*e*·den

Can I pay ...?	Примате ли ...?	*pri*·ma·te li ...
by credit card	кредитни картички	*kre*·dit·ni *kar*·tich·ki
with a travellers cheque	патнички чекови	*pat*·nich·ki *che*·ko·vi

I'd like to stay for (two) nights.
Сакам да останам (две) ноќи.   *sa*·kam da *os*·ta·nam (dve) *no*·kyi

From (2 July) to (6 July).
Од (втори јули) до (шести јули).   od (*vto*·ri *yu*·li) do (*shes*·ti *yu*·li)

Can I see it?
Може ли да ја видам?   *mo*·zhe li da ya *vi*·dam

Am I allowed to camp here?
Може ли да кампувам овде?   *mo*·zhe li da *kam*·pu·vam *ov*·de

Is there a camp site nearby?
Дали во близината има камп?   *da*·li vo bli·*zi*·na·ta *i*·ma kamp

requests & queries

When's breakfast served?
Кога е појадокот?   *ko*·ga e po·*ya*·do·kot

Where's breakfast served?
Каде се појадува?   *ka*·de se po·*ya*·du·va

Please wake me at (seven).
Ве молам разбудете ме во (седум).   ve *mo*·lam raz·*bu*·de·te me vo (*se*·dum)

Could I have my key, please?
Може ли да го добијам клучот, ве молам?   *mo*·zhe li da go *do*·bi·yam *klu*·chot ve *mo*·lam

Is there a/an ...?	Дали има ...?	*da*·li *i*·ma ...
elevator	лифт	lift
safe	сеф	sef

The room is too ...	Собата е премногу ...	*so*·ba·ta e *prem*·no·gu ...
expensive	скапа	*ska*·pa
noisy	бучна	*buch*·na
small	мала	*ma*·la

The ... doesn't work.	Не работи ...	ne *ra*·bo·ti ...
air conditioning	клима уредот	*kli*·ma *u*·re·dot
fan	фенот	*fe*·not
toilet	тоалетот	to·a·*le*·tot

This ... isn't clean.	Овој ... не е чист.	*o*·voy ... ne e chist
sheet	чаршаф	*char*·shaf
towel	пешкир	*pesh*·kir

This pillow isn't clean.
Оваа перница не е чиста.   *o*·va·a *per*·ni·tsa ne e *chis*·ta

Can I get another (blanket)?
Може ли да добијам уште   *mo*·zhe li da *do*·bi·yam *ush*·te
едно (ќебе)?   *ed*·no (*kye*·be)

checking out

What time is checkout?
Во колку часот треба да се   vo *kol*·ku *cha*·sot *tre*·ba da se
одјавам?   *od*·ya·vam

Can I leave my luggage here?
Може ли да го оставам мојот   *mo*·zhe li da go *os*·ta·vam *mo*·yot
багаж овде?   *ba*·gazh *ov*·de

Could I have my valuables, please?
Може ли да ги добијам моите   *mo*·zhe li da gi *do*·bi·yam *mo*·i·te
вредни предмети, ве молам?   *vred*·ni *pred*·me·ti ve *mo*·lam

Could I have	Може ли да го добијам	*mo*·zhe li da go *do*·bi·yam
my ..., please?	мојот..., ве молам?	*mo*·yot ... ve *mo*·lam
deposit	депозит	de·*po*·zit
passport	пасош	*pa*·sosh

communications & banking

the internet

Where's the local Internet café?
Каде има тука интернет кафе?   *ka*·de *i*·ma *tu*·ka *in*·ter·net ka·*fe*

How much is it per hour?
Колку чини на час?   *kol*·ku *chi*·ni na chas

I'd like to ...	Сакам да ...	*sa*·kam da ...
check my email	си ја проверам	si ya *pro*·ve·ram
	електронската	e·lek·*tron*·ska·ta
	пошта	*posh*·ta
get Internet access	добијам пристап	*do*·bi·yam *pris*·tap
	на интернет	na *in*·ter·net
use a printer	користам печатар	ko·*ris*·tam *pe*·cha·tar
use a scanner	користам скенер	ko·*ris*·tam *ske*·ner

mobile/cell phone

I'd like to buy ...	Сакам да купам ...	*sa*·kam da *ku*·pam ...
a mobile/cell phone	мобилен телефон	*mo*·bi·len *te*·le·fon
SIM card for your network	СИМ картичка за	sim *kar*·tich·ka za
	вашата мрежа	*va*·sha·ta *mre*·zha

What are the rates?
Кои се цените?   *ko*·i se *tse*·ni·te

telephone

What's your phone number?
Кој е вашиот телефонски број?   koy e *va*·shi·ot te·le·*fon*·ski broy

The number is ...
Бројот е ...   *bro*·yot e ...

Where's the nearest public phone?
Каде е најблиската јавна
говорница?   *ka*·de e nay·*blis*·ka·ta *yav*·na *go*·vor·ni·tsa

I'd like to buy a phonecard.
Сакам да купам телефонска
картичка.   *sa*·kam da *ku*·pam te·le·*fon*·ska *kar*·tich·ka

I want to ...	Сакам да ...	sa·kam da ...
call (Singapore)	се јавам во (Сингапур)	se ya·vam vo (sin·ga·pur)
make a local call	телефонирам локално	te·le·fo·ni·ram lo·kal·no
reverse the charges	телефонирам на нивна сметка	te·le·fo·ni·ram na niv·na smet·ka

How much does ... cost?	Колку чини ...?	kol·ku chi·ni ...
a (three)-minute call	разговор од (три) минути	raz·go·vor od (tri) mi·nu·ti
each extra minute	секоја наредна минута	se·ko·ya na·red·na mi·nu·ta

(Ten) denars per minute.
(Десет) денари за минута. (de·set) de·na·ri za mi·nu·ta

post office

I want to send a ...	Сакам да испратам ...	sa·kam da is·pra·tam ...
letter	писмо	pis·mo
parcel	пакет	pa·ket
postcard	разгледница	raz·gled·ni·tsa

I want to buy ...	Сакам да купам ...	sa·kam da ku·pam ...
an envelope	плик	plik
stamps	поштенски марки	posh·ten·ski mar·ki

Please send it (to Australia) by ...	Ве молам испратете го (во Австралија) ...	ve mo·lam is·pra·te·te go (vo av·stra·li·ya) ...
airmail	авионски	a·vi·on·ski
express mail	експресно	eks·pres·no
registered mail	препорачано	pre·po·ra·cha·no
surface mail	обично	o·bich·no

Is there any mail for me?
Дали има пошта за мене? da·li i·ma posh·ta za me·ne

bank

Where's a/an ...?	Каде има ...?	ka·de i·ma ...
ATM	банкомат	ban·ko·mat
foreign exchange office	менувачница	me·nu·vach·ni·tsa

I'd like to ...	Сакам да ...	*sa*·kam da ...
Where can I ...?	Каде можам да ...?	*ka*·de mo·*zham* da ...
arrange a transfer	направам трансфер	na·*pra*·vam *trans*·fer
cash a cheque	разменам чек	raz·*me*·nam chek
change a travellers cheque	разменам патнички чекови	raz·*me*·nam *pat*·nich·ki *che*·ko·vi
change money	разменам пари	raz·*me*·nam *pa*·ri
get a cash advance	добијам кредит	do·bi·yam *kre*·dit
withdraw money	извадам пари	*iz*·va·dam *pa*·ri

What's the ...?	Колку ...?	*kol*·ku ...
charge for that	се наплаќа за тоа	se na·*pla*·kya za *to*·a
commission	е провизијата	e pro·vi·*zi*·ya·ta
exchange rate	е курсот	e *kur*·sot

| It's (12) denars. | (Дванаесет) денари. | (dva·*na*·e·set) *de*·na·ri |
| It's free. | Бесплатно е. | *bes*·plat·no e |

What time does the bank open?
Кога се отвора банката?
ko·ga se *ot*·vo·ra *ban*·ka·ta

Has my money arrived yet?
Дали пристигнаа моите пари?
da·li pris·*tig*·na·a *mo*·i·te *pa*·ri

sightseeing

getting in

What time does it open/close?
Кога се отвора/затвора?
ko·ga se *ot*·vo·ra/zat·vo·ra

What's the admission charge?
Колку чини влезница?
kol·ku *chi*·ni *vlez*·ni·tsa

Is there a discount for students/children?
Има ли попуст за студенти/деца?
i·ma li *po*·pust za stu·*den*·ti/*de*·tsa

I'd like a ...	Сакам ...	*sa*·kam ...
catalogue	каталог	*ka*·ta·log
guide	водич	*vo*·dich
local map	локална карта	*lo*·kal·na *kar*·ta

I'd like to see ...
Сакам да видам...
sa-kam da *vi*-dam ...

What's that?
Што е ова?
shto e *o*-va

Can I take a photo?
Може ли да сликам?
mo-zhe li da *sli*-kam

tours

When's the next ...?	Кога е следната ...?	*ko*-ga e *sled*-na-ta ...
day trip	целодневна тура	tse-*lo*-dnev-na *tu*-ra
tour	тура	*tu*-ra
Is ... included?	Дали е ...?	*da*-li e ...
accommodation	вклучено	*vklu*-che-no
	сместувањето	smes-tu-*va*-nye-to
the admission	вклучена цената	*vklu*-che-na *tse*-na-ta
charge	на влезниците	na vlez-*ni*-tsi-te
food	вклучена храна	*vklu*-che-na *hra*-na
transport	вклучен превоз	*vklu*-chen *pre*-voz

How long is the tour?
Колку долго трае турата?
kol-ku *dol*-go *tra*-e *tu*-ra-ta

What time should we be back?
Во колку часот ќе се вратиме?
vo *kol*-ku *cha*-sot kye se *vra*-ti-me

sightseeing – MACEDONIAN

sightseeing

castle	тврдина f	*tvr*-di-na
church	црква f	*tsrk*-va
main square	главен плоштад m	*gla*-ven *plosh*-tad
monastery	манастир m	*ma*-nas-tir
monument	споменик m	*spo*-me-nik
mosque	џамија f	*ja*-mi-ya
museum	музеј m	*mu*-zey
old city	стар град m	star grad
palace	палата f	pa-*la*-ta
ruins	урнатини f pl	ur-*na*-ti-ni
stadium	стадион m	sta-di-*on*
statue	статуа f	*sta*-tu-a

229

shopping

enquiries

Where's a ...?	Каде има ...?	*ka·*de *i·*ma ...
bank	банка	*ban·*ka
bookshop	книжарница	kni·*zhar·*ni·tsa
camera shop	продавница за	pro·*dav·*ni·tsa za
	фотоапарати	*fo·*to·a·pa·*ra·*ti
department store	стоковна куќа	*sto·*kov·na *ku·*kya
grocery store	бакалница	ba·*kal·*ni·tsa
market	пазар	*pa·*zar
newsagency	киоск за весници	*ki·*osk za *ves·*ni·tsi
supermarket	супермаркет	*su·*per·mar·ket

Where can I buy (a padlock)?
Каде можам да купам (катинар)?   *ka·*de *mo·*zham da *ku·*pam (*ka·*ti·nar)

I'm looking for ...
Барам ...   *ba·*ram ...

Can I look at it?
Може ли да ја видам?   *mo·*zhe li da ya *vi·*dam

Do you have any others?
Имате ли други?   *i·*ma·te li *dru·*gi

Does it have a guarantee?
Дали има гаранција?   *da·*li *i·*ma ga·*ran·*tsi·ya

Can I have it sent abroad?
Може ли да ми го испратите   *mo·*zhe li da mi go is·*pra·*ti·te
во странство?   vo *strans·*tvo

Can I have my ... repaired?
Може ли да ми го поправите ...?   *mo·*ze li da mi go pop·*ra·*vi·te ...

It's faulty.
Расипан е.   *ra·*si·pan e

I'd like ..., please.	Јас би сакал ...,	yas bi *sa·*kal ...
	ве молам.	ve *mo·*lam
a bag	торба	*tor·*ba
a refund	да ми ги вратите	da mi gi *vra·*ti·te
	парите	*pa·*ri·te
to return this	да го вратам ова	da go *vra·*tam *o·*va

paying

How much is it?
Колку чини тоа?   *kol*·ku *chi*·ni *to*·a

Can you write down the price?
Можете ли да ми ја напишете   *mo*·zhe·te li da mi ya na·*pi*·she·te
цената?   *tse*·na·ta

That's too expensive.
Тоа е многу скапо.   *to*·a e *mno*·gu *ska*·po

What's your lowest price?
Која е вашата најниска цена?   *ko*·ya e *va*·sha·ta *nai*·nis·ka *tse*·na

I'll give you (five) denars.
Јас ќе ви дадам (пет) денари.   yas kye vi *da*·dam (pet) *de*·na·ri

There's a mistake in the bill.
Има грешка во сметката.   *i*·ma *gresh*·ka vo *smet*·ka·ta

Do you accept …?   Примате ли …?   *pri*·ma·te li …
   credit cards   кредитни картички   *kre*·dit·ni *kar*·tich·ki
   debit cards   дебитни картички   *de*·bit·ni *kar*·tich·ki
   travellers cheques   патнички чекови   *pat*·nich·ki *che*·ko·vi

I'd like …, please.   Сакам …, ве молам.   *sa*·kam … ve *mo*·lam
   a receipt   признаница   priz·*na*·ni·tsa
   my change   кусур   *ku*·sur

clothes & shoes

Can I try it on?
Може ли да го пробам тоа?   *mo*·zhe li da go *pro*·bam *to*·a

My size is (42).
Јас носам (четириесет и два).   yas *no*·sam (che·ti·*ri*·e·set i dva)

It doesn't fit.
Не ми е точно.   ne mi e *toch*·no

small	мал	mal
medium	среден	sre·den
large	голем	go·lem

books & music

I'd like a ...	Сакам ...	sa·kam ...
newspaper	весник	ves·nik
(in English)	(на англиски)	(na an·glis·ki)
pen	пенкало	pen·ka·lo

Is there an English-language bookshop?
Дали има англиска книжарница? da·li i·ma an·glis·ka kni·zhar·ni·tsa

I'm looking for something by (Simon Trpcheski/Blazhe Koneski).
Барам нешто од (Симон ba·ram nesh·to od (si·mon
Трпчески/Блаже Конески). trp·ches·ki/bla·zhe ko·nes·ki)

Can I listen to this?
Може ли да го слушнам ова? mo·zhe li da go slush·nam o·va

photography

Can you ...?	Можете ли ...?	mo·zhe·te li ...
burn a CD from	да преснимите од ЦД	da pres·ni·mi·te od tse·de
my memory card	од мојата картичка	od mo·ya·ta kar·tich·ka
	со меморија	so me·mo·ri·ya
develop this	да го развиете овој	da go raz·vi·e·te o·voy
film	филм	film
load my film	да го ставите филмот	da go sta·vi·te fil·mot
	во апаратот	vo a·pa·ra·tot

I need a/an ... film	Сакам ... за овој	sa·kam ... za o·voy
for this camera.	фотоапарат.	fo·to·a·pa·rat
APS	АПС филм	a·pe·es film
B&W	црно-бел филм	tsr·no·bel film
colour	филм во боја	film vo bo·ya
slide	слајд филм	slayd film
(200) speed	филм со брзина	film so br·zi·na
	(двеста)	(dves·ta)

When will it be ready?	Кога ќе биде готов?	ko·ga kye bi·de go·tov

meeting people

greetings, goodbyes & introductions

Hello/Hi.	Здраво/Чао.	*zdra*·vo/*cha*·o
Good night.	Добра нок.	*dob*·ra noky
Goodbye/Bye.	До гледање/Чао.	do *gle*·da·nye/*cha*·o
See you later.	Се гледаме.	se *gle*·da·me
Mr	Господин	*gos*·po·din
Mrs	Госпоѓа	*gos*·po·gya
Miss	Госпоѓица	gos·*po*·gyi·tsa
How are you?	Како сте/си? pol/inf	*ka*·ko ste/si
Fine. And you?	Добро. А вие/ти? pol/inf	*dob*·ro a *vi*·e/ti
What's your name?	Како се викате/	*ka*·ko se *vi*·ka·te/
	викаш? pol/inf	*vi*·kash
My name is ...	Jac се викам ...	yas se *vi*·kam ...
I'm pleased to	Драго ми е што	*dra*·go mi e shto
meet you.	се запознавме.	se za·*poz*·nav·me
This is my ...	Ова е ...	*o*·va e ...
boyfriend	моето момче	*mo*·e·to *mom*·che
brother	мојот брат	*mo*·yot brat
daughter	мојата ќерка	mo·*ya*·ta *kyer*·ka
father	мојот татко	mo·yot *tat*·ko
friend	мојот пријател m	*mo*·yot pri·*ya*·tel
	мојата пријателка f	mo·*ya*·ta pri·*ya*·tel·ka
girlfriend	мојата девојка	mo·*ya*·ta *de*·voy·ka
husband	мојот сопруг	*mo*·yot *sop*·rug
mother	мојата мајка	mo·*ya*·ta *may*·ka
partner (intimate)	мојот партнер m&f	*mo*·yot *part*·ner
sister	мојата сестра	mo·*ya*·ta *ses*·tra
son	мојот син	*mo*·yot sin
wife	мојата сопруга	mo·*ya*·ta *so*·pru·ga
Here's my ...	Ова е мојата ...	*o*·va e mo·*ya*·ta ...
What's your ...?	Која е вашата ...?	*ko*·ya e *va*·sha·ta ...
address	адреса	*ad*·re·sa
email address	имеил адреса	*i*·me·il *ad*·re·sa

Here's my ...	Ова е мојот ...	o·va e mo·yot ...
What's your ...?	Кој е вашиот ...?	koy e va·shi·ot ...
fax number	број на факс	broy na faks
phone number	телефонски број	te·le·fon·ski broy

occupations

What's your occupation?	Што работите?	shto ra·bo·ti·te
I'm a/an ...	Јас сум ...	yas sum ...
artist	уметник m&f	u·met·nik
farmer	фармер m&f	far·mer
office worker	службеник m	sluzh·be·nik
	службеничка f	sluzh·be·nich·ka
scientist	научник m&f	na·uch·nik
tradesperson	трговец m&f	tr·go·vets

background

Where are you from?	Од каде сте?	od ka·de ste
I'm from ...	Јас сум од ...	yas sum od ...
Australia	Австралија	av·stra·li·ya
Canada	Канада	ka·na·da
England	Англија	an·gli·ya
New Zealand	Нов Зеланд	nov ze·land
the USA	Америка	a·me·ri·ka
Are you married?	Дали сте женет/	da·li ste zhe·net/
	мажена? m/f	ma·zhe·na
I'm married.	Јас сум женет/	yas sum zhe·net/
	мажена. m/f	ma·zhe·na
I'm single.	Јас сум неженет/	yas sum ne·zhe·net/
	немажена. m/f	ne·ma·zhe·na

age

How old ...?	Колку години ...?	kol·ku go·di·ni ...
are you	имате/имаш pol/inf	i·ma·te/i·mash
is your daughter	има вашата ќерка	i·ma va·sha·ta kyer·ka
is your son	има вашиот син	i·ma va·shi·ot sin

| I'm ... years old. | Јас имам ... години. | yas i·mam ... go·di·ni |
| He/She is ... years old. | Тој/Таа има ... години. | toy/ta·a i·ma ... go·di·ni |

feelings

I'm (not) ...	Јас (не) сум ...	yas (ne) sum ...
Are you ...?	Дали си ...?	da·li si ...
happy	среќен/среќна m/f	sre·kyen/srekj·na
hungry	гладен/гладна m/f	gla·den/glad·na
sad	тажен/тажна m/f	ta·zhen/tazh·na
thirsty	жеден/жедна m/f	zhe·den/zhed·na

I'm ...	Мене ми е ...	me·ne mi e ...
I'm not ...	Не ми е ...	ne mi e ...
Are you ...?	Дали ти е ...?	da·li ti e ...
cold	студено	stu·de·no
hot	топло	top·lo

entertainment

going out

Where can I find ...?	Каде можам да најдам ...?	ka·de mo·zham da nay·dam ...
clubs	клубови	klu·bo·vi
gay venues	собиралишта на хомосексуалци	so·bi·ra·lish·ta na ho·mo·sek·su·al·tsi
pubs	пабови	pa·bo·vi

I feel like going to a/the ...	Ми се оди ...	mi se o·di ...
concert	на концерт	na kon·tsert
movies	на кино	na ki·no
party	на забава	na za·ba·va
restaurant	во ресторан	vo res·to·ran
theatre	на театар	na te·a·tar

interests

Do you like ...?	Дали сакате ...?	*da*·li sa·*ka*·te ...
I (don't) like ...	Jac (не) сакам ...	yas (ne) *sa*·kam ...
art	уметност	*u*·met·nost
cooking	готвење	*got*·ve·nye
movies	филмови	*fil*·mo·vi
reading	читање	*chi*·ta·nye
shopping	купување	*ku*·pu·va·nye
sport	спорт	sport
travelling	патување	*pa*·tu·va·nye
Do you like to ...?	Дали сакате да ...?	*da*·li sa·*ka*·te da ...
dance	танцувате	tan·*tsu*·va·te
go to concerts	одите на концерти	*o*·di·te na *kon*·tsert
listen to music	слушате музика	*slu*·sha·te *mu*·zi·ka

food & drink

finding a place to eat

Can you recommend a ...?	Можете ли да ми препорачате ...?	*mo*·zhe·te li da mi pre·po·*ra*·cha·te ...
bar	некој бар	*ne*·koy bar
café	некое кафе	*ne*·ko·e ka·*fe*
restaurant	некој ресторан	*ne*·koy res·to·*ran*
I'd like ..., please.	Сакам ..., ве молам.	*sa*·kam ... ve *mo*·lam
a table for (four)	маса за (четворица)	*ma*·sa za (chet·*vo*·ri·tsa)
the (non)smoking section	на место за (не)пушачи	na *mes*·to za (ne·)*pu*·sha·chi

ordering food

breakfast	појадок m	*po*·ya·dok
lunch	ручек m	*ru*·chek
dinner	вечера f	*ve*·che·ra
snack	закуска f	*za*·kus·ka
today's special	специјалитет на денот m	spe·tsi·ya·li·*tet* na *de*·not

What would you recommend?
Што препорачувате вие?   shto pre·po·ra·*chu*·va·te *vi*·e

I'd like (the) …, please.   Ве молам …   ve *mo*·lam …
    bill   сметката   *smet*·ka·ta
    drink list   листа со пијалаци   *lis*·ta so pi·*ya*·la·tsi
    menu   мени   me·*ni*
    that dish   ова јадење   *o*·va ya·de·nye

drinks

(cup of) coffee …	(шолја) кафе …	(*sho*·lya) *ka*·fe …
(cup of) tea …	(шолја) чај …	(*sho*·lya) chay …
with milk	со млеко	so *mle*·ko
without sugar	без шеќер	bez *she*·kyer
(orange) juice	сок (од поморанџа) m	sok (od po·mo·*ran*·ja)
soft drink	безалкохолен пијалак m	bez·al·*ko*·ho·len *pi*·ya·lak
… water	… вода	… *vo*·da
boiled	превриена	pre·*vri*·e·na
mineral	минерална	mi·ne·*ral*·na

in the bar

I'll have …   Јас ќе земам …   yas kye *ze*·mam …
I'll buy you a drink.   Јас ќе ви/ти купам   yas kye vi/ti *ku*·pam
    пијалак. pol/inf   *pi*·ya·lak
What would you like?   Што сакате вие/ти? pol/inf   shto *sa*·ka·te *vi*·e/ti
Cheers!   На здравје!   na *zdrav*·ye

brandy	ракија f	*ra*·ki·ya
cocktail	коктел m	kok·*tel*
cognac	коњак m	*ko*·nyak
a bottle/glass of beer	шише/чаша пиво	*shi*·she/*cha*·sha *pi*·vo
a shot of (whisky)	чашка (виски)	*chash*·ka (*vis*·ki)
a bottle/glass	шише/чаша	*shi*·she/*cha*·sha
of … wine	… вино	… *vi*·no
red	црвено	*tsr*·ve·no
sparkling	пенливо	*pen*·li·vo
white	бело	*be*·lo

self-catering

What's the local speciality?
Што е локален специјалитет?   *shto e* lo·ka·len spe·tsi·ya·li·*tet*

What's that?
Што е тоа?   *shto e* to·a

How much is (a kilo of cheese)?
Колку чини (кило сирење)?   *kol*·ku *chi*·ni (*ki*·lo *si*·re·nye)

I'd like ...	Сакам ...	sa·kam ...
(100) grams	(сто) грама	(sto) *gra*·ma
(two) kilos	(две) кила	(dve) *ki*·la
(three) pieces	(три) парчиња	(tri) par·chi·nya
(six) slices	(шест) парчиња	(shest) par·chi·nya

Less.	Помалку.	po·mal·ku
Enough.	Доволно.	do·vol·no
More.	Повеќе.	po·ve·kye

special diets & allergies

Is there a vegetarian restaurant near here?
Дали овде близу има   *da*·li *ov*·de *bli*·zu *i*·ma
вегетаријански ресторан?   ve·ge·ta·ri·yan·ski res·to·*ran*

Do you have vegetarian food?
Дали имате вегетаријанска храна?   *da*·li *i*·ma·te ve·ge·ta·ri·yan·ska *hra*·na

Could you prepare a meal without ...?	Може ли да подготвите јадење без ...?	mo·zhe li da pod·got·vi·te ya·de·nye bez ...
butter	путер	pu·ter
eggs	јајца	yay·tsa
meat stock	производи од месо	pro·iz·vo·di od me·so

I'm allergic to ...	Јас сум алергичен/ алергична на ... m/f	yas sum a·ler·gi·chen/ a·ler·gich·na na ...
dairy produce	млечни производи	mlech·ni pro·iz·vo·di
gluten	глутен	glu·ten
MSG	МСГ	muh suh guh
nuts	ореви, бадеми, лешници	o·re·vi ba·de·mi lesh·ni·tsi
seafood	морска храна	mor·ska hra·na

menu decoder

ајвар m	*ay·var*	spicy mixture of grilled, ground & fried red peppers (sometimes with eggplant and/or carrots added)
алва f	*al·va*	sesame seeds crushed in honey
баклава f	*bak·la·va*	flaky pastry with nuts, soaked in syrup
бурек m	*bu·rek*	flaky pastry with layers of cheese, spinach, potato or minced meat & onion
ѓувеч m	*gyu·vech*	stew made of meat (usually chicken), rice, peppers, carrots & onion, baked in the oven
зелник m	*zel·nik*	thin, flaky pastry filled with leek, spinach, cabbage or potatoes, with cheese & eggs added
качамак m	*ka·cha·mak*	a paste-like entrée, made of ground maize cooked in salt water & served with feta cheese & fried bacon
мусака f	*mu·sa·ka*	alternate layers of minced meat & potato or eggplant
пастрмајлија f	*pas·tr·may·li·ya*	similar to a pizza, with meat (usually pork) & eggs
пилав m	*pi·lav*	meat cut into small pieces & mixed with seasoned rice before being cooked in the oven
пилешка супа f	*pi·lesh·ka su·pa*	chicken soup
пинџур m	*pin·jur*	a mixture of baked, ground or crushed & stir-fried green peppers, tomatoes, eggplant & garlic
пита/баница f	*pi·ta/ba·ni·tsa*	flaky pastry filled with spinach & cheese, eggs, or pumpkin

плескавица f	ples·*ka*·vi·tsa	burger of minced pork, beef or lamb
подварок m	pod·va·rok	finely shredded sour cabbage cooked in the oven with slices of meat
полнети пиперки f pl	pol·ne·ti pi·per·ki	peppers stuffed with minced beef or pork & rice
рибја чорба f	rib·ya chor·ba	fish soup
сарма f	sar·ma	minced meat rolled in sour cabbage leaves
селско месо n	sel·sko me·so	fried meat, meatballs, smoked meat, mushrooms, tomatoes & onions, cooked in a clay pot in the oven
сирење n	si·re·nye	white cheese
скара f	ska·ra	barbecue (chicken, lamb or pork)
слатко n	slat·ko	fruit (either cherries, grapes, plums etc) cooked in sugar to get a thick mixture, kept in small jars & served with water
сутлијаш m	sut·li·yash	rice pudding garnished with almonds & cinnamon
тавче гравче n	tav·che grav·che	boiled beans cooked in a clay pot in the oven
таратор m	ta·ra·tor	cold appetiser made of yogurt, cucumbers & garlic
телешка чорба f	te·lesh·ka chor·ba	veal soup
турли тава f	tur·li ta·va	stew of meat (pork, veal & mutton) & vegetables, cooked in the oven
ќофтиња n pl	kyof·ti·nya	meatballs
шампити f pl	sham·pi·ti	whisked egg whites with sugar placed in a thick layer on baked pastry
шопска салата f	shop·ska sa·*la*·ta	salad of peppers, cucumbers, tomatoes, onions & feta cheese

emergencies

basics

Help!	Помош!	po·mosh
Stop!	Застани!	za·sta·ni
Go away!	Одете си!	o·de·te si
Thief!	Крадец!	kra·dets
Fire!	Пожар!	po·zhar
Watch out!	Внимавајте!	vni·ma·vay·te
It's an emergency!	Итно е!	it·no e
I'm lost.	Се загубив.	se za·gu·biv
Where are the toilets?	Каде се тоалетите?	ka·de se to·a·le·ti·te

Call ...!	Викнете ...!	vik·ne·te ...
a doctor	лекар	le·kar
an ambulance	брза помош	br·za po·mosh
the police	полиција	po·li·tsi·ya

Could you help me, please?
Може ли да ми помогнете,
ве молам?
mo·zhe li da mi po·mog·ne·te ve mo·lam

I have to use the telephone.
Треба да телефонирам.
tre·ba da te·le·fo·ni·ram

police

Where's the police station?
Каде е полициската станица?
ka·de e po·li·tsis·ka·ta sta·ni·tsa

I want to report an offence.
Сакам да пријавам престап.
sa·kam da pri·ya·vam pres·tap

I have insurance.
Имам осигурување.
i·mam o·si·gu·ru·va·nye

I've been ...	Бев ...	bev ...
assaulted	нападнат m	na·pad·nat
	нападната f	na·pad·na·ta
raped	силуван/силувана m/f	si·lu·van/si·lu·va·na
robbed	опљачкан m	op·lyach·kan
	опљачкана f	op·lyach·ka·na

I've lost my ...	Го загубив мојот ...	go za·gu·biv mo·yot ...
My ...was stolen.	Мојот ... беше украден.	mo·yot ... be·she uk·ra·den
jewellery	накит	na·kit
passport	пасош	pa·sosh
wallet	паричник	pa·rich·nik

I've lost my ...	Ја загубив мојата ...	ya za·gu·biv mo·ya·ta ...
My ...was stolen.	Мојата ... беше украдена.	mo·ya·ta ... be·she uk·ra·de·na
credit card	кредитна картичка	kre·dit·na kar·tich·ka
handbag	чанта	chan·ta

I've lost my ...	Ги загубив моите ...	gi za·gu·biv mo·i·te ...
My ...were stolen.	Моите ... беа украдени.	mo·i·te ... be·a uk·ra·de·ni
bags	торби	tor·bi
travellers cheques	патнички чекови	pat·nich·ki che·ko·vi

I want to contact my ...	Сакам да се јавам во ...	sa·kam da se ya·vam vo ...
consulate	мојот конзулат	mo·yot kon·zu·lat
embassy	мојата амбасада	mo·ya·ta am·ba·sa·da

health

medical needs

Where's the nearest ...?	Каде има најблиску ...?	ka·de i·ma nay·blis·ku ...
dentist	заболекар	za·bo·le·kar
doctor	лекар	le·kar
hospital	болница	bol·ni·tsa
(night) pharmacist	(дежурна) аптека	(de·zhur·na) ap·te·ka

I need a doctor (who speaks English).
Ми треба доктор (што зборува англиски). — mi tre·ba dok·tor (shto zbo·ru·va an·glis·ki)

Could I see a female doctor?
Може ли да одам кај докторка? — mo·zhe li da o·dam kay dok·tor·ka

I've run out of my medication.
Останав без лекови. — os·ta·nav bez le·ko·vi

symptoms, conditions & allergies

| I'm sick. | Јас сум болен/болна. m/f | yas sum bo·len/bol·na |
| It hurts here. | Овде ме боли. | ov·de me bo·li |

I have (a) …	Имам …	i·mam …
asthma	астма	ast·ma
bronchitis	бронхитис	bron·hi·tis
constipation	констипација	kon·sti·pa·tsi·ya
cough	кашлица	kash·li·tsa
diarrhoea	пролив	pro·liv
fever	треска	tres·ka
headache	главоболка	gla·vo·bol·ka
heart condition	тешкотии со срцето	tesh·ko·ti·i so sr·tse·to
nausea	лошење	lo·she·nye
pain	болка	bol·ka
sore throat	воспаление на грлото	vos·pa·le·ni·e na gr·lo·to
toothache	заболка	za·bo·bol·ka

I'm allergic to …	Јас сум алергичен/ алергична на … m/f	yas sum a·ler·gi·chen/ a·ler·gich·na na …
antibiotics	антибиотици	an·ti·bi·o·ti·tsi
anti-inflammatories	анти-инфламатори	an·ti·in·fla·ma·to·ri
aspirin	аспирин	as·pi·rin
bees	пчели	pche·li
codeine	кодеин	ko·de·in
penicillin	пенцилин	pe·ni·tsi·lin

antiseptic	антисептик m	an·ti·sep·tik
bandage	завој m	za·voy
condoms	кондоми m pl	kon·do·mi
contraceptives	средства за контрацепција n pl	sreds·tva za kon·tra·tsep·tsi·ya
diarrhoea medicine	лекови против пролив m pl	le·ko·vi pro·tiv pro·liv
insect repellent	средство против инсекти n	sreds·tvo pro·tiv in·sek·ti
laxatives	лаксативи m pl	lak·sa·ti·vi
painkillers	средства против болки n pl	sreds·tva pro·tiv bol·ki
rehydration salts	соли за рехидрирање f pl	so·li za re·hid·ri·ra·nye
sleeping tablets	таблети за спиење f pl	tab·le·ti za spi·e·nye

english–macedonian dictionary

Macedonian nouns in this dictionary have their gender indicated by ⓜ (masculine), ⓕ (feminine) or ⓝ (neuter). If it's a plural noun, you'll also see pl. Adjectives are given in the masculine form only. Words are also marked as a (adjective), v (verb), sg (singular), pl (plural), inf (informal) or pol (polite) where necessary.

A

accident несреќа ⓕ *nes-re-*kya
accommodation сместување ⓝ smes-*tu-*va-nye
adaptor адаптер ⓜ a-*dap-*ter
address адреса ⓕ *a-*dre-sa
after потоа po-*to-*a
air-conditioned климатизиран kli-ma-ti-*zi-*ran
airplane авион ⓜ a-*vi-*on
airport аеродром ⓜ a-e-ro-*drom
alcohol алкохол ⓜ *al-*ko-hol
all сите *si-*te
allergy алергија ⓕ a-*ler-*gi-ya
ambulance брза помош ⓕ *br-*za *po-*mosh
and и i
ankle зглоб ⓜ zglob
arm рака ⓕ *ra-*ka
ashtray пепелник ⓜ *pe-*pel-nik
ATM банкомат ⓜ ban-ko-*mat

B

baby бебе ⓝ *be-*be
back (body) грб ⓜ grb
backpack ранец ⓜ *ra-*nets
bad лош losh
bag торба ⓕ *tor-*ba
baggage claim подигање на багаж ⓝ po-*di-*ga-nye na *ba-*gazh
bank банка ⓕ *ban-*ka
bar бар ⓜ bar
bathroom бања ⓕ *ba-*nya
battery батерија ⓕ ba-*te-*ri-ya
beautiful убав *u-*bav
bed кревет ⓜ *kre-*vet
beer пиво ⓝ *pi-*vo
before пред pred
behind зад zad
bicycle точак ⓜ *to-*chak
big голем *go-*lem
bill сметка ⓕ *smet-*ka
black црн tsrn
blanket ќебе ⓝ *kye-*be

blood group крвна група ⓕ *krv-*na *gru-*pa
blue син sin
boat брод ⓜ brod
book (make a reservation) v резервира re-zer-*vi-*ra
bottle шише ⓝ *shi-*she
bottle opener отворач за шишиња ⓜ *o-*tvo-rach za *shi-*shi-nya
boy момче ⓝ *mom-*che
brakes (car) кочници ⓕ pl *koch-*ni-tsi
breakfast појадок ⓜ *po-*ya-dok
broken (faulty) расипан *ra-*si-pan
bus автобус ⓜ *av-*to-bus
business бизнис ⓜ *biz-*nis
buy купува *ku-*pu-va

C

café кафуле ⓝ *ka-*fu-le
camera фото апарат ⓜ *fo-*to a-pa-*rat
camp site камп ⓜ kamp
cancel откажува ot-*ka-*zhu-va
can opener отворач за конзерви ⓜ *ot-*vo-rach za kon-*zer-*vi
car автомобил ⓜ av-to-mo-*bil
(pay) cash (плаќа) во готово (*pla-*kya) vo *go-*to-vo
cash (a cheque) v менува (чек) *me-*nu-va (chek)
cell phone мобилен телефон ⓜ *mo-*bi-len te-le-*fon
centre центар ⓜ *tsen-*tar
change (money) v разменува (пари) raz-*me-*nu-va (*pa-*ri)
cheap евтин *ev-*tin
check (bill) сметка ⓕ *smet-*ka
check-in пријавување ⓝ pri-ya-*vu-*va-nye
chest гради ⓕ pl *gra-*di
child дете ⓝ *de-*te
cigarette цигара ⓕ *tsi-*ga-ra
city град ⓜ grad
clean a чист chist
closed затворен zat-*vo-*ren
coffee кафе ⓝ *ka-*fe
coins метални пари ⓕ pl *me-*tal-ni *pa-*ri
cold a студен *stu-*den
collect call разговор платен од примачот ⓜ *raz-*go-vor *pla-*ten od *pri-*ma-chot

come доаѓа *do-a-gya*
computer компјутер ⑩ *komp-yu-ter*
condom кондом ⑩ *kon-dom*
contact lenses контактни леќи ① pl
   kon-takt-ni le-kyi
cook v готви *got-vi*
cost цена ① *tse-na*
credit card кредитна картичка ①
   kre-dit-na kar-tich-ka
cup шолја ① *sho-lya*
currency exchange курс на валути ⑩ *kurs na va-lu-ti*
customs (immigration) царинарница ①
   tsa-ri-nar-ni-tsa

D

dangerous опасен *o-pa-sen*
date (time) датум ⑩ *da-tum*
day ден *den*
delay n доцнење ⑩ *dots-ne-nye*
dentist забар ⑩ *za-bar*
depart заминува *za-mi-nu-va*
diaper пелена ① *pe-le-na*
dictionary речник ⑩ *rech-nik*
dinner вечера ① *ve-che-ra*
direct директен *di-rek-ten*
dirty нечист *ne-chist*
disabled (person) инвалид ⑩ *in-va-lid*
discount попуст ⑩ *po-pust*
doctor доктор ⑩ *dok-tor*
double bed брачен кревет ⑩ *bra-chen kre-vet*
double room двокреветна соба ①
   dvo-kre-vet-na so-ba
drink пијалак ⑩ *pi-ya-lak*
drive v вози *vo-zi*
drivers licence возачка дозвола ①
   vo-zach-ka doz-vo-la
drug (illicit) дрога ① *dro-ga*
dummy (pacifier) цуцла ① *tsuts-la*

E

ear уво ⑩ *u-vo*
east исток ⑩ *is-tok*
eat јаде *ya-de*
economy class економска класа ①
   e-ko-nom-ska kla-sa
electricity електрична струја ① *e-lek-trich-na stru-ya*
elevator лифт ⑩ *lift*
email имеил ⑩ *i-me-il*
embassy амбасада ① *am-ba-sa-da*
emergency итна ситуација ① *it-na si-tu-a-tsi-ya*

English (language) англиски ⑩ *an-glis-ki*
entrance влез ⑩ *vlez*
evening вечер ① *ve-cher*
exchange rate курс ⑩ *kurs*
exit излез ⑩ *iz-lez*
expensive скап *skap*
express mail брза пошта ① *br-za posh-ta*
eye око ① *o-ko*

F

far далеку *da-le-ku*
fast брз *brz*
father татко ⑩ *tat-ko*
film (camera) филм ⑩ *film*
finger прст *prst*
first-aid kit кутија за прва помош ①
   ku-ti-ya za pr-va po-mosh
first class прва класа ① *pr-va kla-sa*
fish риба ① *ri-ba*
food храна ① *hra-na*
foot нога ① *no-ga*
fork виљушка ① *vi-lyush-ka*
free (of charge) бесплатен *bes-pla-ten*
friend пријател/пријателка ⑩/①
   pri-ya-tel/pri-ya-tel-ka
fruit овошје ① *o-vosh-ye*
full полн *poln*
funny смешен *sme-shen*

G

gift подарок ⑩ *po-da-rok*
girl девојка ① *de-voy-ka*
glass (drinking) чаша ① *cha-sha*
glasses очила ① pl *o-chi-la*
go оди *o-di*
good добар *do-bar*
green зелен *ze-len*
guide водич ⑩ *vo-dich*

H

half половина ① *po-lo-vi-na*
hand рака ① *ra-ka*
handbag женска чанта ① *zhen-ska chan-ta*
happy среќен *sre-kyen*
have има *i-ma*
he тој *toy*
head глава ① *gla-va*
heart срце ① *sr-tse*
heat топлина ① *to-pli-na*

heavy тежок *te*-zhok
help v помага po-*ma*-ga
here овде *ov*-de
high висок *vi*-sok
highway автопат *av*-to-pat
hike v планинари pla-*ni*-na-ri
holiday годишен одмор ⓜ *go*-di-shen *od*-mor
homosexual хомосексуалец ⓜ ho-mo-sek-su-*a*-lets
hospital болница ⓕ *bol*-ni-tsa
hot жежок *zhe*-zhok
hotel хотел *ho*-tel
hungry гладен *gla*-den
husband сопруг ⓜ *sop*-rug

I

I jac yas
identification (card) лична карта ⓕ *lich*-na *kar*-ta
ill болен *bo*-len
important важен *va*-zhen
included вклучен *vklu*-chen
injury повреда ⓕ *po*-vre-da
insurance осигурување ⓝ o-si-gu-*ru*-va-nye
Internet интернет ⓜ *in*-ter-net
interpreter толкувач ⓜ *tol*-ku-vach

J

jewellery накит ⓜ *na*-kit
job работа ⓕ *ra*-bo-ta

K

key клуч ⓜ kluch
kilogram килограм ⓜ *ki*-lo-gram
kitchen кујна ⓕ *kuy*-na
knife нож ⓜ nozh

L

laundry (place) перална ⓕ pe-*ral*-na
lawyer адвокат ⓜ ad-vo-*kat*
left (direction) лево *le*-vo
left-luggage office место за чување багаж ⓝ
  mes-to za chu-*va*-nye ba-*gazh*
leg нога ⓕ *no*-ga
lesbian лезбејка ⓕ lez-*bey*-ka
less помалку po-*mal*-ku
letter (mail) писмо ⓝ *pis*-mo
lift (elevator) лифт ⓜ lift
light светлина ⓕ *svet*-li-na

like v сака *sa*-ka
lock катанец ⓜ *ka*-ta-nets
long долг dolg
lost загубен za-*gu*-ben
lost-property office биро за загубени работи ⓝ
  bi-ro za za-*gu*-be-ni *ra*-bo-ti
love v љуби *lyu*-bi
luggage багаж ⓜ *ba*-gazh
lunch ручек ⓜ *ru*-chek

M

Macedonia Македонија ⓕ ma-ke-*do*-ni-ya
Macedonian (language) македонски ⓜ
  ma-*ke*-don-ski
Macedonian a македонски ma-*ke*-don-ski
mail пошта ⓕ *posh*-ta
man маж ⓜ mazh
map мапа ⓕ *ma*-pa
market пазар ⓜ *pa*-zar
matches кибрит ⓜ *kib*-rit
meat месо ⓝ *me*-so
medicine лек ⓜ lek
menu мени ⓝ me-*ni*
message порака ⓕ *po*-ra-ka
milk млеко ⓝ *mle*-ko
minute минута ⓕ *mi*-nu-ta
mobile phone мобилен телефон ⓜ
  mo-bi-len te-le-*fon*
money пари ⓜ pl *pa*-ri
month месец ⓜ *me*-sets
morning утро ⓝ *ut*-ro
mother мајка ⓕ *may*-ka
motorcycle мотор ⓜ *mo*-tor
motorway автопат ⓜ *av*-to-pat
mouth уста ⓕ *us*-ta
music музика ⓕ *mu*-zi-ka

N

name име ⓝ *i*-me
napkin салфета ⓕ sal-*fe*-ta
nappy пелена ⓕ pe-*le*-na
near блиску *blis*-ku
neck врат ⓜ vrat
new нов nov
news вести ⓕ pl *ves*-ti
newspaper весник ⓜ *ves*-nik
night ноќ ⓕ noky
no ne не
noisy бучен *bu*-chen
nonsmoking за непушачи za ne-*pu*-sha-chi

north север ⓜ *se*-ver
nose нос ⓜ nos
now сега *se*-ga
number број ⓜ broy

O

oil (engine) масло ⓝ *mas*-lo
old стар ⓜ star
one-way ticket билет во еден правец ⓜ
   bi-let vo *e*-den *pra*-vets
open a отворен *ot*-vo-ren
outside надвор *nad*-vor

P

package пакет ⓜ *pa*-ket
paper хартија ① *har*-ti-ya
park (car) v паркира par-*ki*-ra
passport пасош ⓜ *pa*-sosh
pay плаќа *pla*-kya
pen пенкало ⓝ *pen*-ka-lo
petrol бензин ⓜ *ben*-zin
pharmacy аптека ① *ap*-te-ka
phonecard телефонска картичка ①
   te-le-*fon*-ska kar-*tich*-ka
photo фотографија ① fo-to-*gra*-fi-ya
plate чинија ① *chi*-ni-ya
police полиција ① po-*li*-tsi-ya
postcard поштенска картичка ①
   posh-ten-ska kar-*tich*-ka
post office пошта ① *posh*-ta
pregnant бремена ① *bre*-me-na
price цена ① *tse*-na

Q

quiet тивок *ti*-vok

R

rain дожд ⓜ dozhd
razor жилет ① *zhi*-let
receipt белешка ① *be*-lesh-ka
red црвен *tsr*-ven
refund враќање на пари ⓝ *vra*-kya-nye na *pa*-ri
registered mail препорачано писмо ⓜ
   pre-po-*ra*-cha-no *pis*-mo
rent v изнајмува iz-*nay*-mu-va
repair v поправа *pop*-ra-va
reservation резервација ① re-zer-*va*-tsi-ya

restaurant ресторан ⓜ res-to-*ran*
return v враќа *vra*-kya
return ticket повратен билет ⓜ *po*-vra-ten *bi*-let
right (direction) десно *des*-no
road пат ⓜ pat
room соба ① *so*-ba

S

safe a безбеден *bez*-be-den
sanitary napkin хигиенска влошка ①
   hi-gi-*en*-ska *vlosh*-ka
seat седиште ⓝ *se*-dish-te
send испраќа *is*-pra-kya
service station бензинска пумпа ①
   ben-zin-ska *pum*-pa
sex секс ⓜ seks
shampoo шампон ⓜ sham-*pon*
share (a dorm) дели *de*-li
shaving cream крем за бричење ⓜ
   krem za *bri*-che-nye
she таа *ta*-a
sheet (bed) чаршаф ⓜ *char*-shaf
shirt кошула ① *ko*-shu-la
shoes чевли ⓜ pl *chev*-li
shop продавница ① pro-*dav*-ni-tsa
short кус kus
shower туш ⓜ tush
single room еднокреветна соба ①
   ed-no-*kre*-vet-na *so*-ba
skin кожа ① *ko*-zha
skirt здолниште ⓝ *zdol*-nish-te
sleep v спие *spi*-e
slowly полека *po*-le-ka
small мал mal
smoke (cigarettes) v пуши *pu*-shi
soap сапун ⓜ *sa*-pun
some неколку *ne*-kol-ku
soon наскоро *nas*-ko-ro
south југ ⓜ yug
souvenir shop продавница за сувенири ①
   pro-*dav*-ni-tsa za su-ve-*ni*-ri
speak зборува *zbo*-ru-va
spoon лажица ① *la*-zhi-tsa
stamp марка ① *mar*-ka
stand-by ticket стендбај билет ⓜ *stend*-bay *bi*-let
station (train) (железничка) станица ①
   (zhe-*lez*-nich-ka) *sta*-ni-tsa
stomach стомак ⓜ *sto*-mak
stop v запира za-*pi*-ra
(bus) stop (автобуска) станица ①
   (av-to-*bus*-ka) *sta*-ni-tsa
street улица ① *u*-li-tsa

student студент/студентка ⓜ/ⓕ
stu-dent/stu-dent-ka
sun сонце ⓝ *son-tse*
sunscreen лосион за сончање ⓜ
lo-si-on za son-cha-nye
swim v плива *pli-va*

T

tampons тампони ⓜ pl *tam-po-ni*
taxi такси ⓝ *tak-si*
teaspoon лажиче ⓝ *la-zhi-che*
teeth заби ⓜ pl *za-bi*
telephone телефон ⓜ te-le-*fon*
television телевизија ⓕ te-le-*vi-zi-ya*
temperature (weather) температура ⓕ
tem-pe-ra-*tu-ra*
tent шатор ⓜ *sha-tor*
that (one) она *o-na*
they тие *ti-e*
thirsty жеден *zhe-den*
this (one) ова *o-va*
throat грло ⓝ *gr-lo*
ticket билет ⓜ *bi-let*
time време ⓝ *vre-me*
tired уморен *u-mo-ren*
tissues книжни марамчиња ⓝ pl
knizh-ni ma-ram-chi-nya
today денес *de-nes*
toilet тоалет ⓜ to-a-*let*
tomorrow утре *ut-re*
tonight вечерва ve-cher-va
toothbrush четка за заби ⓕ *chet-ka za za-bi*
toothpaste паста за заби ⓕ *pas-ta za za-bi*
torch (flashlight) џепна ламба ⓕ *jep-na lam-ba*
tour патување ⓝ pa-tu-va-nye
tourist office туристичко биро ⓝ tu-*ris-tich-ko bi-ro*
towel пешкир ⓜ *pesh-kir*
train воз ⓜ voz
translate преведува pre-ve-*du-va*
travel agency туристичка агенција ⓕ
tu-*ris-tich-ka a-gen-tsi-ya*
travellers cheque патнички чек ⓜ *pat-nich-ki chek*
trousers панталони ⓜ pl pan-ta-*lo-ni*
twin beds двоен кревет ⓜ *dvo-en kre-vet*
tyre гума ⓕ *gu-ma*

U

underwear долна облека ⓕ *dol-na ob-le-ka*
urgent итен *i-ten*

V

vacant слободен *slo-bo-den*
vacation годишен одмор ⓜ *go-di-shen od-mor*
vegetable зеленчук ⓜ *ze-len-chuk*
vegetarian a вегетаријански ve-ge-ta-*ri-yan-ski*
visa виза ⓕ *vi-za*

W

waiter келнер ⓜ *kel-ner*
walk v пешачи pe-*sha-chi*
wallet паричник ⓜ *pa-rich-nik*
warm a топол *to-pol*
wash (something) мие *mi-e*
watch часовник ⓜ *cha-sov-nik*
water вода ⓕ *vo-da*
we ние *ni-e*
weekend викенд ⓜ *vi-kend*
west запад ⓜ *za-pad*
wheelchair инвалидска количка ⓕ
in-va-*lid-ska ko-lich-ka*
when кога *ko-ga*
where каде *ka-de*
white бел bel
who кој koy
why зошто *zosh-to*
wife сопруга ⓕ *so-pru-ga*
window прозорец ⓜ *pro-zo-rets*
wine вино ⓝ *vi-no*
with со so
without без bez
woman жена ⓕ *zhe-na*
write пишува *pi-shu-va*

Y

yellow жолт zholt
yes да da
yesterday вчера *vche-ra*
you sg inf ти ti
you sg pol & pl вие *vi-e*

Polish

polish alphabet

A a a	*Ą ą* om/on	*B b* be	*C c* tse	*Ć ć* che	*D d* de
E e e	*Ę ę* em/en	*F f* ef	*G g* gye	*H h* kha	*I i* ee
J j yot	*K k* ka	*L l* el	*Ł ł* ew	*M m* em	*N n* en
Ń ń en'	*O o* o	*Ó ó* oo	*P p* pe	*R r* er	*S s* es
Ś ś esh	*T t* te	*U u* oo	*W w* woo	*Y y* i	*Z z* zet
Ź ź zhet	*Ż ż* zhyet				

■ polish

POLSKI

introduction

Ask most English speakers what they know about Polish (*polski pol*-skee), the language which donated the words *horde, mazurka* and *vodka* to English, and they will most likely dismiss it as an unpronounceable language. Who could pronounce an apparently vowel-less word like *szczyt* shchit (peak), for example? To be put off by this unfairly gained reputation, however, would be to miss out on a rich and rewarding language. The mother tongue of Copernicus, Chopin, Marie Curie and Pope John Paul II has a fascinating and turbulent past and symbolises the resilience of the Polish people in the face of domination and adversity.

The Polish tribes who occupied the basins of the Oder and Vistula rivers in the 6th century spoke a range of West Slavic dialects, which over time evolved into Polish. The closest living relatives of Polish are Czech and Slovak which also belong to the wider West Slavic family of languages. The language reached the apex of its influence during the era of the Polish Lithuanian Commonwealth (1569–1795). The Commonwealth covered a swath of territory from what are now Poland and Lithuania through Belarus, Ukraine and Latvia and part of Western Russia. Polish became a lingua franca throughout much of Central and Eastern Europe at this time due to the political, cultural, scientific and military might of this power.

When Poland was wiped off the map of Europe from 1795 to 1918 after three successive partitions in the second half of the 18th century (when it was carved up between Russia, Austria and Prussia), the language suffered attempts at both Germanisation and Russification. Later, after WWII, Poland became a satellite state of the Soviet Union and the language came under the renewed influence of Russian. Polish showed impressive resistance in the face of this oppression. The language not only survived these onslaughts but enriched itself by borrowing many words from both Russian and German. The works of Poland's greatest literary figures who wrote in exile – the Romantic poet Adam Mickiewicz and, during Communist rule, the Nobel Prize winner Czesław Miłosz – are testament to this fact.

Today, Poland is linguistically one of the most homogenous countries in Europe – over 95% of the population speaks Polish as their first language. There are significant Polish-speaking minorities in the western border areas of Ukraine, Belarus and in southern Lithuania, with smaller populations in other neighbouring countries.

pronunciation

vowel sounds

Polish vowels are generally prounounced short, giving them a 'clipped' quality.

symbol	english equivalent	polish example	transliteration
a	run	*tak*	tak
ai	aisle	*tutaj*	*too*-tai
e	bet	*bez*	bes
ee	see	*wino*	*vee*-no
ey	hey	*kolejka*	ko-*ley*-ka
i	bit	*czy*	chi
o	pot	*woda*	*vo*-da
oo	zoo	*zakupy, mój*	za-*koo*-pi, mooy
ow	how	*migdał*	*meeg*-dow
oy	toy	*ojciec*	*oy*-chets

Polish also has nasal vowels, pronounced as though you're trying to force the air out of your nose rather than your mouth. Nasal vowels are indicated in written Polish by the letters ą and ę. Depending upon the letters that follow these vowels, they're pronounced with either an 'm' or an 'n' sound following the vowel.

symbol	english equivalent	polish example	transliteration
em	like the 'e' in 'get' plus nasal consonant sound	*wstęp*	fstemp
en		*mięso*	*myen*-so
om	like the 'o' in 'not' plus nasal consonant sound	*kąpiel*	*kom*-pyel
on		*wąsy*	*von*-si

word stress

In Polish, stress almost always falls on the second-last syllable. In our coloured pronunciation guides, the stressed syllable is italicised.

consonant sounds

Most Polish consonant sounds are also found in English, with the exception of the kh sound (pronounced as in the Scottish word *loch*) and the rolled r sound.

symbol	english equivalent	polish example	transliteration
b	bed	*babka*	*bap*·ka
ch	cheat	*cień, czas, ćma*	chen', chas, chma
d	dog	*drobne*	*drob*·ne
f	fat	*fala*	*fa*·la
g	go	*garnek*	*gar*·nek
j	joke	*dzieci*	*je*·chee
k	kit	*kac*	kats
kh	loch	*chata, hałas*	*kha*·ta, *kha*·was
l	lot	*lato*	*la*·to
m	man	*malarz*	*ma*·lash
n	not	*nagle*	*na*·gle
p	pet	*palec*	*pa*·lets
r	run (rolled)	*róg*	roog
s	sun	*samolot*	*sa*·mo·lot
sh	shot	*siedem, śnieg, szlak*	*shye*·dem, shnyek, shlak
t	top	*targ*	tark
v	very	*widok*	*vee*·dok
w	win	*złoto*	*zwo*·to
y	yes	*zajęty*	za·*yen*·ti
z	zero	*zachód*	*za*·khoot
zh	pleasure	*zima, żart, rzeźba*	*zhee*·ma, zhart, *zhezh*·ba
'	a slight y sound	*kwiecień*	*kfye*·chen'

basics

language difficulties

Do you speak English?
*Czy pan/pani mówi
po angielsku?* m/f pol

chi pan/*pa*-nee *moo*-vee
po an-*gyel*-skoo

Do you understand?
Czy pan/pani rozumie? m/f pol

chi pan/*pa*-nee ro-*zoo*-mye

I (don't) understand.
(Nie) Rozumiem.

(nye) ro-*zoo*-myem

What does (*nieczynne*) mean?
Co to znaczy (nieczynne)?

tso to *zna*-chi (nye-*chi*-ne)

How do you ...? *Jak się ...?* yak shye ...
  pronounce this *to wymawia* to vi-*mav*-ya
  write (*pierogi*) *pisze (pierogi)* *pee*-she (pye-*ro*-gee)

Could you please ...? *Proszę ...* *pro*-she ...
  repeat that *to powtórzyć* to pov-*too*-zhich
  speak more *mówić trochę* *moo*-veech *tro*-khe
    slowly *wolniej* *vol*-nyey
  write it down *to napisać* to na-*pee*-sach

essentials

Yes.	*Tak.*	tak
No.	*Nie.*	nye
Please.	*Proszę.*	*pro*-she
Thank you (very much).	*Dziękuję (bardzo).*	jyen-*koo*-ye (*bar*-dzo)
You're welcome.	*Proszę.*	*pro*-she
Excuse me.	*Przepraszam.*	pshe-*pra*-sham
Sorry.	*Przepraszam.*	pshe-*pra*-sham

numbers

0	zero	ze·ro		15	piętnaście	pyent·nash·chye
1	jeden m	ye·den		16	szesnaście	shes·nash·chye
	jedna f	yed·na		17	siedemnaście	shye·dem·nash·chye
	jedno n	yed·no		18	osiemnaście	o·shem·nash·chye
2	dwa m	dva		19	dziewiętnaście	jye·vyet·nash·chye
	dwie f	dvye		20	dwadzieścia	dva·jyesh·chya
	dwoje n	dvo·ye		21	dwadzieścia	dva·jyesh·chya
3	trzy	tshi			jeden	ye·den
4	cztery	chte·ri		22	dwadzieścia	dva·jyesh·chya
5	pięć	pyench			dwa	dva
6	sześć	sheshch		30	trzydzieści	tshi·jyesh·chee
7	siedem	shye·dem		40	czterdzieści	chter·jyesh·chee
8	osiem	o·shyem		50	pięćdziesiąt	pyen·jye·shont
9	dziewięć	jye·vyench		60	sześćdziesiąt	shesh·jye·shont
10	dziesięć	jye·shench		70	siedemdziesiąt	shye·dem·jye·shont
11	jedenaście	ye·de·nash·chye		80	osiemdziesiąt	o·shem·jye·shont
12	dwanaście	dva·nash·chye		90	dziewięćdziesiąt	jye·vyen·jye·shont
13	trzynaście	tshi·nash·chye		100	sto	sto
14	czternaście	chter·nash·chye		1000	tysiąc	ti·shonts

time & dates

What time is it?	Która jest godzina?	ktoo·ra yest go·jee·na
It's one o'clock.	Pierwsza.	pyerf·sha
It's (10) o'clock.	Jest (dziesiąta).	yest (jye·shon·ta)
Quarter past (10).	Piętnaście po (dziesiątej).	pyent·nash·chye po (jye·shon·tey)
Half past (10).	Wpół do (jedenastej).	fpoow do (ye·de·nas·tey)
Quarter to (11).	Za piętnaście (jedenasta).	za pyent·nash·chye (ye·de·nas·ta)
At what time ...?	O której godzinie ...?	o ktoo·rey go·jee·nye ...
At ...	O ...	o ...
in the morning	rano	ra·no
in the afternoon	po południu	po po·wood·nyoo
in the evening (6pm–10pm)	wieczorem	vye·cho·rem
at night (11pm–3am)	w nocy	v no·tsi

Monday	*poniedziałek*	po-nye-*jya*-wek
Tuesday	*wtorek*	*fto*-rek
Wednesday	*środa*	*shro*-da
Thursday	*czwartek*	*chfar*-tek
Friday	*piątek*	*pyon*-tek
Saturday	*sobota*	so-*bo*-ta
Sunday	*niedziela*	nye-*jye*-la

January	*styczeń*	*sti*-chen'
February	*luty*	*loo*-ti
March	*marzec*	*ma*-zhets
April	*kwiecień*	*kfye*-chen'
May	*maj*	mai
June	*czerwiec*	*cher*-vyets
July	*lipiec*	*lee*-pyets
August	*sierpień*	*shyer*-pyen'
September	*wrzesień*	*vzhe*-shyen'
October	*październik*	pazh-*jyer*-neek
November	*listopad*	lees-*to*-pat
December	*grudzień*	*groo*-jyen'

What date is it today?	*Którego jest dzisiaj?*	ktoo-*re*-go yest *jee*-shai
It's (18 October).	*Jest (osiemnastego października).*	yest (o-shem-nas-*te*-go pazh-jyer-*nee*-ka)
last night	*wczoraj wieczorem*	fcho-rai vye-*cho*-rem

last/next ...	*w zeszłym/przyszłym ...*	v zesh-wim/pshish-wim ...
week	*tygodniu*	ti-*god*-nyoo
month	*miesiącu*	mye-*shon*-tsoo
year	*roku*	*ro*-koo

yesterday/	*wczoraj/*	*fcho*-rai/
tomorrow ...	*jutro ...*	*yoo*-tro ...
morning	*rano*	*ra*-no
afternoon	*po południu*	po po-*wood*-nyoo
evening	*wieczorem*	vye-*cho*-rem

weather

What's the weather like?	*Jaka jest pogoda?*	ya·ka yest po·go·da
It's ...		
cloudy	*Jest pochmurnie.*	yest pokh·moor·nye
cold	*Jest zimno.*	yest zheem·no
hot	*Jest gorąco.*	yest go·ron·tso
raining	*Pada deszcz.*	pa·da deshch
snowing	*Pada śnieg.*	pa·da shnyeg
sunny	*Jest słonecznie.*	yest swo·nech·nye
warm	*Jest ciepło.*	yest chyep·wo
windy	*Jest wietrznie.*	yest vyetzh·nye
spring	*wiosna* f	vyos·na
summer	*lato* n	la·to
autumn	*jesień* f	ye·shyen'
winter	*zima* f	zhee·ma

border crossing

I'm ...	*Jestem ...*	yes·tem ...
in transit	*w tranzycie*	v tran·zi·chye
on business	*służbowo*	swoozh·bo·vo
on holiday	*na wakacjach*	na va·kats·yakh
I'm here for ...	*Będę tu przez ...*	ben·de too pshes ...
(10) days	*(dziesięć) dni*	(jye·shench) dnee
(three) weeks	*(trzy) tygodnie*	(tshi) ti·god·nye
(two) months	*(dwa) miesiące*	(dva) mye·shon·tse

I'm going to (Kraków).
Jadę do (Krakowa). ya·de do (kra·ko·va)

I'm staying at the (Pod Różą Hotel).
Zatrzymuję się w (hotelu 'pod Różą'). za·tshi·moo·ye shye v (ho·te·loo pod roo·zhom)

I have nothing to declare.
Nie mam nic do zgłoszenia. nye mam neets do zgwo·she·nya

I have something to declare.
Mam coś do zgłoszenia. mam tsosh do zgwo·she·nya

That's (not) mine.
To (nie) jest moje. to (nye) yest mo·ye

transport

tickets & luggage

Where can I buy a ticket?
Gdzie mogę kupić bilet?　　　gjye *mo*-ge *koo*-peech *bee*-let

Do I need to book a seat?
Czy muszę rezerwować?　　　chi *moo*-she re-zer-*vo*-vach

One ... ticket	*Proszę bilet ...*	*pro*-she *bee*-let ...
(to Katowice), please.	*(do Katowic).*	do (ka-*to*-veets)
one-way	*w jedną stronę*	v *yed*-nom *stro*-ne
return	*powrotny*	po-*vro*-tni

I'd like to ...	*Chcę ... mój bilet.*	khtse ... mooy *bee*-let
my ticket, please.		
cancel	*odwołać*	od-*vo*-wach
change	*zmienić*	*zmye*-neech
collect	*odebrać*	o-*de*-brach
confirm	*potwierdzić*	po-*tvyer*-jyeech

How much is it?
Ile kosztuje?　　　*ee*-le kosh-*too*-ye

Is there air conditioning?
Czy jest tam klimatyzacja?　　　chi yest tam klee-ma-ti-*za*-tsya

Is there a toilet?
Czy jest tam toaleta?　　　chi yest tam to-a-*le*-ta

How long does the trip take?
Ile trwa podróż?　　　*ee*-le trfa *po*-droosh

Is it a direct route?
Czy to jest bezpośrednie połączenie?　　　chi to yest bes-po-*shred*-nye po-won-*che*-nye

Where can I find a luggage locker?
Gdzie jest schowek na bagaż?　　　gjye yest *skho*-vek na *ba*-gazh

My luggage	Mój bagaż	mooy ba·gazh
has been ...	został ...	zos·tow ...
damaged	uszkodzony	oosh·ko·dzo·ni
lost	zagubiony	za·goo·byo·ni
stolen	skradziony	skra·jyo·ni

getting around

Where does flight (LO125) arrive/depart?
Skąd przylatuje/odlatuje   skont pshi·la·*too*·ye/od·la·*too*·ye
lot (LO125)?   lot (el o sto dva·*jyesh*·chya pyench)

Where's (the) ...?	Gdzie jest ...?	gjye yest ...
arrivals hall	hala przylotów	kha·la pshi·lo·toof
departures hall	hala odlotów	kha·la od·lo·toof
duty-free shop	sklep wolnocłowy	sklep vol·no·tswo·vi
gate (five)	wejście	veysh·chye
	(numer pięć)	(noo·mer pyench)

Is this the ...	Czy to jest ...	chi to yest ...
to (Wrocław)?	do (Wrocławia)?	do (vrots·wa·vya)
bus	autobus	ow·to·boos
plane	samolot	sa·mo·lot
train	pociąg	po·chonk

When's the ... bus?	Kiedy jest ... autobus?	kye·di yest ... ow·to·boos
first	pierwszy	pyerf·shi
last	ostatni	os·tat·nee
next	następny	nas·temp·ni

At what time does it arrive/leave?
O której godzinie przyjeżdża/   o *ktoo*·rey go·*jee*·nye pshi·*yezh*·ja/
odjeżdża?   ot·*yezh*·ja

How long will it be delayed?
Jakie będzie opóźnienie?   *ya*·kye *ben*·jye o·poozh·*nye*·nye

What's the next station?
Jaka jest następna stacja?   *ya*·ka yest nas·*temp*·na *sta*·tsya

What's the next stop?
Jaki jest następny przystanek?   *ya*·kee yest nas·*tem*·pni pshi·*sta*·nek

Does it stop at (Kalisz)?
Czy on się zatrzymuje w (Kaliszu)?   chi on shye za·tshi·*moo*·ye f (ka·*lee*·shoo)

Please tell me when we get to (Krynica).
Proszę mi powiedzieć gdy   *pro*·she mee po·*vye*·jyech gdi
dojedziemy do (Krynicy).   do·ye·*jye*·mi do (kri·*nee*·tsi)

How long do we stop here?
Na jak długo się tu zatrzymamy?   na yak *dwoo*·go shye too za·tshi·*ma*·mi

Is this seat available?
Czy to miejsce jest wolne?   chi to *myeys*·tse yest *vol*·ne

That's my seat.
To jest moje miejsce.   to yest *mo*·ye *myeys*·tse

I'd like a taxi ...	*Chcę zamówić*	khtse za·*moo*·veech
	taksówę na ...	tak·*soof*·ke na ...
now	*teraz*	*te*·ras
tomorrow	*jutro*	*yoo*·tro
at (9am)	*(dziewiątą rano)*	(jye·*vyon*·tom *ra*·no)

Is this taxi available?
Czy ta taksówka jest wolna?   chi ta tak·*soof*·ka yest *vol*·na

How much is it to (Szczecin)?
Ile kosztuje do (Szczecina)?   *ee*·le kosh·*too*·ye (do shche·*chee*·na)

Please put the meter on.
Proszę włączyć taksometr.   *pro*·she *vwon*·chich tak·*so*·metr

Please take me to (this address).
Proszę mnie zawieźć pod (ten adres).   *pro*·she mnye za·*vyeshch* pod (ten *ad*·res)

Please ...	*Proszę ...*	*pro*·she ...
slow down	*zwolnić*	*zvol*·neech
stop here	*się tu zatrzymać*	shye too za·*tshi*·mach
wait here	*tu zaczekać*	too za·*che*·kach

car, motorbike & bicycle hire

I'd like to hire a ...	*Chcę wypożyczyć ...*	khtse vi·po·*zhi*·chich ...
bicycle	*rower*	*ro*·ver
car	*samochód*	sa·*mo*·khoot
motorbike	*motocykl*	mo·*to*·tsikl

with ...	z ...	z ...
air conditioning	*klimatyzacją*	klee·ma·ti·*za*·tsyom
a driver	*kierowcą*	kye·*rof*·tsom
antifreeze	*płynem nie*	*pwi*·nem nye
	zamarzającym	za·mar·za·*yon*·tsim
snow chains	*łańcuchami*	wan'·tsoo·*kha*·mee
	śnieżnymi	shnezh·*ni*·mee
How much for	*Ile kosztuje*	ee·le kosh·*too*·ye
... hire?	*wypożyczenie na ... ?*	vi·po·zhi·*che*·nye na ...
hourly	*godzinę*	go·*jee*·ne
daily	*dzień*	jyen'
weekly	*tydzień*	ti·jyen'
air	*powietrze* n	po·*vye*·tshe
oil	*olej* m	*o*·ley
petrol	*benzyna* f	ben·*zi*·na
tyre	*opona* f	o·*po*·na

I need a mechanic.
Potrzebuję mechanika.   po·tshe·*boo*·ye me·kha·*nee*·ka

I've run out of petrol.
Zabrakło mi benzyny.   za·*bra*·kwo mee ben·*zi*·ni

I have a flat tyre.
Złapałem/Złapałam gumę. m/f   zwa·*pa*·wem/zwa·*pa*·wam *goo*·me

directions

Where's the ...?	*Gdzie jest ...?*	gjye yest ...
bank	*bank*	bank
city centre	*centrum miasta*	*tsen*·troom *myas*·ta
hotel	*hotel*	*ho*·tel
market	*targ*	tark
police station	*komisariat*	ko·mee·*sar*·yat
	policji	po·*leets*·yee
post office	*urząd pocztowy*	*oo*·zhond poch·*to*·vi
public toilet	*toaleta publiczna*	to·a·*le*·ta poo·*bleech*·na
tourist office	*biuro turystyczne*	*byoo*·ro too·ris·*tich*·ne

Is this the road to (Malbork)?
Czy to jest droga do (Malborka)?   chi to yest *dro*·ga do (mal·*bor*·ka)

Can you show me (on the map)?
Czy może pan/pani — chi *mo*·zhe pan/*pa*·nee
mi pokazać (na mapie)? m/f — mee po·*ka*·zach (na *ma*·pye)

What's the address?
Jaki jest adres? — *ya*·kee yest *ad*·res

How far is it?
Jak daleko to jest? — yak da·*le*·ko to yest

How do I get there?
Jak tam mogę się dostać? — yak tam *mo*·ge shye *dos*·tach

Turn ...	*Proszę skręcić ...*	*pro*·she skren·cheech ...
at the corner	*na rogu*	na *ro*·goo
at the traffic lights	*na światłach*	na *shfyat*·wakh
left/right	*w lewo/prawo*	v *le*·vo/*pra*·vo

It's ...	*To jest ...*	to yest ...
behind ...	*za ...*	za ...
far away	*daleko*	da·*le*·ko
here	*tu*	too
in front of ...	*przed ...*	pshet ...
left	*po lewej*	po *le*·vey
near	*blisko*	*blees*·ko
next to ...	*obok ...*	*o*·bok ...
on the corner	*na rogu*	na *ro*·goo
opposite ...	*naprzeciwko ...*	nap·she·*cheef*·ko ...
right	*po prawej*	po *pra*·vey
straight ahead	*na wprost*	na *fprost*
there	*tam*	tam

by bus	*autobusem*	ow·to·*boo*·sem
by taxi	*taksówką*	tak·*soof*·kom
by train	*pociągiem*	po·*chon*·gyem
on foot	*pieszo*	*pye*·sho

north	*północ*	*poow*·nots
south	*południe*	po·*wood*·nye
east	*wschód*	fskhoot
west	*zachód*	*za*·khoot

Wjazd/Wyjazd	vyazd/*vi*-yazd	**Entrance/Exit**
Otwarte/Zamknięte	ot-*far*-te/zamk-*nyen*-te	**Open/Closed**
Wolne pokoje	*vol*-ne po-*ko*-ye	**Rooms Available**
Brak wolnych miejsc	brak *vol*-nikh myeysts	**No Vacancies**
Informacja	een-for-*ma*-tsya	**Information**
Komisariat policji	ko-mee-*sar*-yat po-*lee*-tsyee	**Police Station**
Zabroniony	za-bro-*nyo*-ni	**Prohibited**
Toalety	to-a-*le*-ti	**Toilets**
Męskie	*mens*-kye	**Men**
Damskie	*dams*-kye	**Women**
Zimna/Gorąca	*zheem*-na/go-*ron*-tsa	**Hot/Cold**

accommodation

finding accommodation

Where's a ...?	*Gdzie jest ...?*	*gjye yest ...*
camping ground	*kamping*	*kam*-peeng
guesthouse	*pokoje gościnne*	po-*ko*-ye gosh-*chee*-ne
hotel	*hotel*	*ho*-tel
youth hostel	*schronisko*	skhro-*nees*-ko
	młodzieżowe	mwo-jye-*zho*-ve
Can you recommend	*Czy może pan/pani*	chi *mo*-zhe pan/*pa*-nee
somewhere ...?	*polecić coś ...?* m/f	po-*le*-cheech tsosh ...
cheap	*taniego*	ta-*nye*-go
good	*dobrego*	do-*bre*-go
nearby	*coś w pobliżu*	tsosh f po-*blee*-zhoo

I'd like to book a room, please.
Chcę zarezerwować pokój. khtse za-re-zer-*vo*-vach po-kooy

I have a reservation.
Mam rezerwację. mam re-zer-*va*-tsye

My name's ...
Nazywam się ... na-*zi*-vam shye ...

Do you have a ... room?	Czy jest pokój ...?	chi yest po·kooy ...
single	jednoosobowy	yed·no·o·so·bo·vi
double	z podwójnym	z pod·vooy·nim
	łóżkiem	woozh·kyem
twin	z dwoma łóżkami	z dvo·ma wozh·ka·mee

How much is it per ...?	Ile kosztuje za ...?	ee·le kosh·too·ye za ...
night	noc	nots
person	osobę	o·so·be

Can I pay ...?	Czy mogę zapłacić ...?	chi mo·ge za·pwa·cheech ...
by credit card	kartą kredytową	kar·tom kre·di·to·vom
with a travellers cheque	czekami podróżnymi	che·ka·mee po·droozh·ni·mee

For (three) nights/weeks.
Na (trzy) noce/tygodnie.   na (tshi) no·tse/ti·god·nye

From (2 July) to (6 July).
Od (drugiego lipca) do (szóstego lipca).   od (droo·gye·go leep·tsa) do (shoos·te·go leep·tsa)

Can I see it?
Czy mogę go zobaczyć?   chi mo·ge go zo·ba·chich

Am I allowed to I camp here?
Czy mogę się tutaj rozbić?   chi mo·ge shye too·tai roz·beech

Where can I find the camping ground?
Gdzie jest pole kampingowe?   gjye yest po·le kam·peen·go·ve

requests & queries

When's breakfast served?
O której jest śniadanie?   o ktoo·rey yest shnya·da·nye

Where's breakfast served?
Gdzie jest śniadanie?   gjye yest shnya·da·nye

Please wake me at (seven).
Proszę obudzić mnie o (siódmej).   pro·she o·boo·jeech mnye o (shyood·mey)

Could I have my key, please?
Czy mogę prosić o klucz?   chi mo·ge pro·sheech o klooch

Can I get another (blanket)?
Czy mogę prosić o jeszcze jeden (koc)?   chi mo·ge pro·sheech o yesh·che ye·den (kots)

Is there an elevator/a safe?
Czy jest winda/sejf? — chi yest *veen*-da/seyf

This (towel) isn't clean.
Ten (ręcznik) nie jest czysty. — ten (*rench*-neek) nye yest *chis*-ti

It's too ... — *Jest zbyt ...* — yest zbit ...
- expensive — *drogi* — *dro*-gee
- noisy — *głośny* — *gwosh*-ni
- small — *mały* — *ma*-wi

The ... doesn't work. — *... nie działa.* — ... nye *jya*-wa
- air conditioner — *Klimatyzator* — klee-ma-ti-*za*-tor
- fan — *Wentylator* — ven-ti-*la*-tor
- toilet — *Ubikacja* — oo-bee-*kats*-ya

checking out

What time is checkout?
O której godzinie — o *ktoo*-rey go-*jye*-nye
muszę się wymeldować? — *moo*-she shye vi-mel-*do*-vach

Can I leave my luggage here?
Czy mogę tu zostawić — chi *mo*-ge too zo-*sta*-veech
moje bagaże? — *mo*-ye ba-*ga*-zhe

Could I have
my ..., please? — *Czy mogę prosić* — chi *mo*-ge *pro*-sheech
o mój/moje ...? sg/pl — o mooy/*mo*-ye ...
- deposit — *depozyt* sg — de-*po*-zit
- passport — *paszport* sg — *pash*-port
- valuables — *kosztowności* pl — kosh-tov-*nosh*-chee

communications & banking

the internet

Where's the local Internet café?
Gdzie jest kawiarnia internetowa? — gjye yest ka-*vyar*-nya een-ter-ne-*to*-va

How much is it per hour?
Ile kosztuje za godzinę? — *ee*-le kosh-*too*-ye za go-*jee*-ne

I'd like to ...	Chciałem/Chciałam ... m/f	khchow·em/khchow·am ...
check my email	sprawdzić mój email	sprav·jeech mooy ee·mayl
get Internet	podłączyć się	pod·won·chich shye
access	do internetu	do een·ter·ne·too
use a printer	użyć drukarki	oo·zhich droo·kar·kee
use a scanner	użyć skaner	oo·zhich ska·ner

mobile/cell phone

I'd like a ...	Chciałem/Chciałam ... m/f	khchow·em/khchow·am ...
mobile/cell	wypożyczyć	vi·po·zhi·chich
phone for hire	telefon komórkowy	te·le·fon ko·moor·ko·vi
SIM card for	kartę SIM	kar·te seem
your network	na waszą sieć	na va·shom shyech
What are the rates?	Jakie są stawki za rozmowy?	ya·kye som staf·kee za roz·mo·vi

telephone

What's your phone number?
Jaki jest pana/pani
numer telefonu? m/f pol

ya·kee yest pa·na/pa·nee
noo·mer te·le·fo·noo

The number is ...
Numer jest ...

noo·mer yest ...

Where's the nearest public phone?
Gdzie jest najbliższy telefon?

gjye yest nai·bleezh·shi te·le·fon

I'd like to buy a chip phonecard.
Chciałem/Chciałam kupić
czipową kartę telefoniczną. m/f

khchow·em/khchow·am koo·peech
chee·po·vom kar·te te·le·fo·neech·nom

I want to ...	Chciałem/Chciałam ... m/f	khchow·em/khchow·am ...
call (Singapore)	zadzwonić do (Singapuru)	zad·zvo·neech do (seen·ga·poo·roo)
make a local	zadzwonić pod	zad·zvo·neech pod
call	lokalny numer	lo·kal·ni noo·mer
reverse the	zamówić	za·moo·veech
charges	rozmowę na koszt odbiorcy	roz·mo·ve na kosht od·byor·tsi

How much does ... cost?	Ile kosztuje ...?	*ee·le kosh·too·ye ...*
a (three)-minute call	*rozmowa (trzy) minutowa*	roz·*mo*·va (tshi) mee·noo·*to*·va
each extra minute	*każda dodatkowa minuta*	*kazh*·da do·dat·*ko*·va mee·*noo*·ta

(Two złotys) per (30) seconds.	(*Dwa złote*) *za* (*trzydzieści*) *sekund.*	(dva *zwo*·te) za (tshi·*jyesh*·chee) se·koond

post office

I want to send a ...	*Chciałem/Chciałam wysłać ...* m/f	khchow·em/khchow·am vis·wach ...
fax	*faks*	faks
letter	*list*	leest
parcel	*paczkę*	*pach*·ke
postcard	*pocztówkę*	poch·*toof*·ke

I want to buy a/an ...	*Chciałem/Chciałam kupić ...* m/f	khchow·em/khchow·am koo·peech ...
envelope	*kopertę*	ko·*per*·te
stamp	*znaczek*	*zna*·chek

Please send it (to Australia) by ...	*Proszę wysłać to ... (do Australii).*	pro·she vis·wach to ... (do aus·*tra*·lyee)
airmail	*pocztą lotniczą*	poch·tom lot·*nee*·chom
express mail	*pocztą ekspresową*	poch·tom eks·pre·*so*·vom
registered mail	*pocztą poleconą*	poch·tom po·le·*tso*·nom
surface mail	*pocztą lądową*	poch·tom lon·*do*·vom

Is there any mail for me?	*Czy jest dla mnie jakaś korespondencja?*	chi yest dla mnye *ya*·kash ko·res·pon·*den*·tsya

bank

Where's a/an ...?	*Gdzie jest ...?*	gjye yest ...
ATM	*bankomat*	ban·*ko*·mat
foreign exchange office	*kantor walut*	*kan*·tor *va*·loot

I'd like to ...	Chciałem/Chciałam ... m/f	khchow·em/khchow·am ...
Where can I ...?	Gdzie mogę ...?	gjye mo·ge ...
cash a cheque	wymienić czek	vi·mye·neech chek
	na gotówkę	na go·toof·ke
change a travellers cheque	wymienić czek podróżny	vi·mye·neech chek po·droozh·ni
change money	wymienić pieniądze	vi·mye·neech pye·nyon·dze
get a cash advance	dostać zaliczkę na moją kartę kredytową	dos·tach za·leech·ke na mo·yom kar·te kre·di·to·vom
withdraw money	wypłacić pieniądze	vi·pwa·cheech pye·nyon·dze

What's the ...?	Jaki/Jaka jest ...? m/f	ya·kee/ya·ka yest ...
charge for that	prowizja f	pro·veez·ya
exchange rate	kurs wymiany m	koors vi·mya·ni

It's (12) złotys.
To kosztuje (dwanaście) złotych.   to kosh·too·ye (dva·nash·chye) zwo·tikh

It's free.
Jest bezpłatny.   yest bes·pwat·ni

What time does the bank open?
W jakich godzinach jest bank otwarty?   v ya·keekh go·jee·nakh yest bank ot·far·ti

Has my money arrived yet?
Czy doszły już moje pieniądze?   chi dosh·wi yoosh mo·ye pye·nyon·dze

sightseeing

getting in

What time does it open/close?
O której godzinie jest otwarte/zamknięte?   o ktoo·rey go·jee·nye yest ot·far·te/zam·knyen·te

What's the admission charge?
Ile kosztuje wstęp?   ee·le kosh·too·ye fstemp

Is there a discount for students/children?
*Czy jest zniżka dla
studentów/dzieci?*
chi yest *zneezh*·ka dla
stoo·*den*·toof/*jye*·chee

I'd like to see ...
Chciałem/Chciałam obejrzeć ... m/f
khchow·em/*khchow*·am o·*bey*·zhech ...

What's that?
Co to jest?
tso to yest

Can I take a photo?
Czy mogę zrobić zdjęcie?
chi *mo*·ge *zro*·beech *zdyen*·chye

I'd like a ...   *Chciałem/Chciałam ...* m/f   *khchow*·em/*khchow*·am ...
  catalogue   *broszurę*   bro·*shoo*·re
  guide   *przewodnik*   pshe·*vod*·neek
  local map   *mapę okolic*   *ma*·pe o·*ko*·leets

tours

When's the next ...?   *Kiedy jest następna ...?*   *kye*·di yest nas·*temp*·na ...
  day trip   *wycieczka*   vi·*chyech*·ka
     jednodniowa   yed·no·*dnyo*·va
  tour   *tura*   *too*·ra

Is ... included?   *Czy ... wliczone/a?* n&pl/f   chi ... vlee·*cho*·ne/na
  accommodation   *noclegi są* pl   nots·*le*·gee som
  the admission charge   *opłata za wstęp jest* f   o·*pwa*·ta za fstemp yest
  food   *wyżywienie jest* n   vi·zhi·*vye*·nye yest

Is transport included?
Czy transport jest wliczony?
chi *trans*·port yest vlee·*cho*·ne

How long is the tour?
Jak długo trwa wycieczka?
yak *dwoo*·go trfa vi·*chyech*·ka

What time should we be back?
*O której godzinie
powinniśmy wrócić?*
o *ktoo*·rey go·*jee*·nye
po·vee·*neesh*·mi *vroo*·cheech

sightseeing

castle	*zamek* m	*za*-mek
cathedral	*katedra* f	ka-*te*-dra
church	*kościół* m	*kosh*-chyoow'
main square	*rynek główny* m	*ri*-nek *gwoov*-ni
monastery	*klasztor* m	*klash*-tor
monument	*pomnik* m	*pom*-neek
museum	*muzeum* n	moo-*ze*-oom
old city	*stare miasto* n	*sta*-re *myas*-to
palace	*pałac* m	*pa*-wats
ruins	*ruiny* f pl	roo-*ee*-ni
stadium	*stadion* m	*sta*-dyon
statue	*pomnik* m	*pom*-neek

shopping

enquiries

Where's a ...?	*Gdzie jest ...?*	gjye yest ...
bank	*bank*	bank
bookshop	*księgarnia*	kshyen-*gar*-nya
camera shop	*sklep fotograficzny*	sklep fo-to-gra-*feech*-ni
department store	*dom towarowy*	dom to-va-*ro*-vi
grocery store	*sklep spożywczy*	sklep spo-*zhiv*-chi
market	*targ*	tark
newsagency	*kiosk*	kyosk
supermarket	*supermarket*	soo-per-*mar*-ket

Where can I buy (a padlock)?
Gdzie mogę kupić (kłódkę)?   gjye *mo*-ge *koo*-peech (*kwoot*-ke)

I'm looking for ...
Szukam ...   *shoo*-kam

Can I look at it?
Czy mogę to zobaczyć?   chi *mo*-ge to zo-*ba*-chich

Do you have any others?
Czy są jakieś inne?   chi som *ya*-kyesh *ee*-ne

Does it have a guarantee?
Czy to ma gwarancję?   chi to ma gva-*ran*-tsye

Can I have it sent overseas?
Czy mogę to wysłać za granicę?   chi *mo*·ge to *vis*·wach za gra·*nee*·tse

Can I have my ... repaired?
Czy mogę tu oddać ... do naprawy?   chi *mo*·ge too *ot*·dach ... do na·*pra*·vi

It's faulty.
To jest wadliwe.   to yest vad·*lee*·ve

I'd like to return this, please.
Chciałem/Chciałam to zwrócić. m/f   khchow·em/khchow·am to zvroo·cheech

I'd like a ..., please.   *Proszę o ...*   pro·she o ...
   bag   *torbę*   *tor*·be
   refund   *zwrot pieniędzy*   zvrot pye·*nyen*·dzi

paying

How much is it?
Ile to kosztuje?   ee·le to kosh·*too*·ye

Can you write down the price?
Proszę napisać cenę.   pro·she na·*pee*·sach *tse*·ne

That's too expensive.
To jest za drogie.   to yest za *dro*·gye

What's your final price?
Jaka jest pana/pani   *ya*·ka yest *pa*·na/*pa*·nee
ostateczna cena? m/f   os·ta·*tech*·na *tse*·na

I'll give you (10 złotys).
Dam panu/pani (dziesięć złotych). m/f   dam *pa*·noo/*pa*·nee (*jye*·shench *zwo*·tikh)

There's a mistake in the bill.
Na czeku jest pomyłka.   na *che*·koo yest po·*miw*·ka

Do you accept ...?   *Czy mogę zapłacić ...?*   chi *mo*·ge za·*pwa*·cheech ...
   credit cards   *kartą kredytową*   *kar*·tom kre·di·*to*·vom
   debit cards   *kartą debetową*   *kar*·tom de·be·*to*·vom
   travellers   *czekami*   che·*ka*·mee
   cheques   *podróżnymi*   pod·roozh·*ni*·mee

I'd like ..., please.   *Proszę o ...*   pro·she o ...
   a receipt   *rachunek*   ra·*khoo*·nek
   my change   *moją resztę*   *mo*·yom *resh*·te

clothes & shoes

Can I try it on?	*Czy mogę przymierzyć?*	chi *mo*·ge pshi·*mye*·zhich
My size is (40).	*Noszę rozmiar*	*no*·she *roz*·myar
	(czterdzieści).	(chter·*jyesh*·chee)
It doesn't fit.	*Nie pasuje.*	nye pa·*soo*·ye
large/medium/small	*L/M/S*	*el*·ke/*em*·ke/*es*·ke

books & music

I'd like a ...	*Chciałem/Chciałam ...* m/f	*khchow*·em/*khchow*·am ...
newspaper	*gazetę (w języku*	ga·*ze*·te (v yen·*zi*·koo
(in English)	*angielskim)*	an·*gyel*·skeem)
pen	*długopis*	dwoo·*go*·pees

Is there an English-language bookshop?
Czy jest tu księgarnia angielska? chi yest too kshyen·*gar*·nya an·*gyel*·ska

I'm looking for something by (Górecki).
Szukam czegoś (Góreckiego). *shoo*·kam che·*gosh* (goo·rets·*kye*·go)

Can I listen to this?
Czy mogę tego posłuchać? chi *mo*·ge *te*·go pos·*woo*·khach

photography

Can you ...?	*Czy może pan/pani ...?* m/f	chi *mo*·zhe pan/*pa*·nee ...
develop this film	*wywołać ten film*	vi·*vo*·wach ten film
load my film	*założyć film*	za·*wo*·zhich film
transfer photos	*skopiować zdjęcia*	sko·*pyo*·vach zdyen·chya
from my camera	*z mojego aparatu*	z mo·ye·go a·pa·*ra*·too
to CD	*na płytę kompaktową*	na *pwi*·te kom·pak·*to*·vom

I need a/an ... film	*Potrzebuję film ...*	po·tshe·*boo*·ye film ...
for this camera.	*do tego aparatu.*	do *te*·go a·pa·*ra*·too
APS	*APS*	a pe es
B&W	*panchromatyczny*	pan·khro·ma·*tich*·ni
colour	*kolorowy*	ko·lo·*ro*·vi
slide	*do slajdów*	do *slai*·doof
(200) speed	*(dwieście) ASA*	(dvyesh·chye) *a*·sa

When will it be ready? *Na kiedy będzie gotowe?* na *kye*·di *ben*·jye go·*to*·ve

meeting people

greetings, goodbyes & introductions

Hello/Hi.	*Cześć.*	cheshch
Good night.	*Dobranoc.*	do·*bra*·nots
Goodbye.	*Do widzenia.*	do vee·*dze*·nya
Bye.	*Pa.*	pa
See you later.	*Do zobaczenia.*	do zo·ba·*che*·nya
Mr/Mrs/Miss	*Pan/Pani/Panna*	pan/*pa*·nee/*pa*·na
How are you?	*Jak pan/pani*	yak pan/*pa*·nee
	się miewa? m/f pol	shye *mye*·va
	Jak się masz? inf	yak shye mash
Fine. And you?	*Dobrze. A pan/pani?* m/f pol	*dob*·zhe a pan/*pa*·nee
	Dobrze. A ty? inf	*dob*·zhe a ti
What's your name?	*Jak się pan/pani*	yak shye pan/*pa*·nee
	nazywa? m/f pol	na·*zi*·va
	Jakie się nazywasz? inf	yak shye na·*zi*·vash
My name is …	*Nazywam się …*	na·*zi*·vam shye …
I'm pleased to	*Miło mi pana/panią*	*mee*·wo mee *pa*·na/*pa*·nyom
meet you.	*poznać.* m/f pol	*po*·znach
	Miło mi ciebie poznać. inf	*mee*·wo mee *chye*·bye *po*·znach
This is my …	*To jest mój/moja …* m/f	to yest mooy/*mo*·ya …
boyfriend	*chłopak*	*khwo*·pak
brother	*brat*	brat
daughter	*córka*	*tsoor*·ka
father	*ojciec*	*oy*·chyets
friend	*przyjaciel* m	pzhi·*ya*·chyel
	przyjaciółka f	pzhi·*ya*·chyoow·ka
girlfriend	*dziewczyna*	jyev·*chi*·na
husband	*mąż*	monzh
mother	*matka*	*mat*·ka
partner (intimate)	*partner/partnerka* m/f	*part*·ner/*part*·*ner*·ka
sister	*siostra*	*shyos*·tra
son	*syn*	sin
wife	*żona*	*zho*·na

Here's my ...	*Tu jest mój ...*	too yest mooy ...
What's your ...?	*Jaki jest pana/*	ya-kee yest pa-na/
	pani ...? m/f pol	pa-nee ...
(email) address	*adres (emailowy)*	ad-res (e-mai-lo-vi)
fax number	*numer faksu*	noo-mer fak-soo
phone number	*numer telefonu*	noo-mer te-le-fo-noo

occupations

What's your occupation?	*Jaki jest pana/pani zawód?* m/f pol	ya-kee yest pa-na/pa-nee za-vood
I'm a/an ...	*Jestem ...*	yes-tem ...
artist	*artystą/artystką* m/f	ar-tis-tom/ar-tist-kom
farmer	*rolnikiem* m&f	rol-nee-kyem
manual worker	*pracownikiem fizycznym* m&f	pra-tsov-nee-kyem fee-zich-nim
office worker	*pracownikiem biurowym* m&f	pra-tsov-nee-kyem byoo-ro-vim
scientist	*naukowcem* m&f	now-kov-tsem
tradesperson	*rzemieślnikiem* m&f	zhe-mye-shlnee-kyem

background

Where are you from?	*Skąd pan/pani jest?* m/f pol	skont pan/pa-nee yest
I'm from ...	*Jestem z ...*	yes-tem z ...
Australia	*Australii*	ow-stra-lyee
Canada	*Kanady*	ka-na-di
England	*Anglii*	ang-lee
New Zealand	*Nowej Zelandii*	no-vey ze-lan-dyee
the USA	*USA*	oo es a

Are you married? (to a man)
Czy jest pan żonaty? pol — chi yest pan zho-na-ti

Are you married? (to a woman)
Czy jest pani zamężna? pol — chi yest pa-nee za-menzh-na

I'm married.
Jestem żonaty/zamężna. m/f — yes-tem zho-na-ti/za-menzh-na

I'm single.
Jestem nieżonaty/niezamężna. m/f — nye-zho-na-ti/nye-za-menzh-na

age

How old is your ...?	Ile lat ma pana/ pani ...? m/f pol	ee·le lat ma pa·na/ pa·nee ...
daughter	córka	tsoor·ka
son	syn	sin
How old are you?	Ile pan/pani ma lat? m/f pol	ee·le pan/pa·nee ma lat
	Ile masz lat? inf	ee·le mash lat
I'm ... years old.	Mam ... lat.	mam ... lat
He/She is ... years old.	On/Ona ma ... lat.	on/o·na ma ... lat

feelings

I'm (not) ...	(Nie) Jestem ...	(nye) yes·tem ...
Are you ...?	Czy jest pan/pani ...? m/f pol	chi yest pan/pa·nee ...
cold	zmarznięty/a m/f	zmar·znyen·ti/a
happy	szczęśliwy/a m/f	shchen·shlee·vi/a
hungry	głodny/a m/f	gwod·ni/a
sad	smutny/a m/f	smoot·ni/a
thirsty	spragniony/a m/f	sprag·nyo·ni/a

entertainment

going out

Where can I find ...?	Gdzie mogę znaleźć ...?	gjye mo·ge zna·lezhch ...
clubs	kluby nocne	kloo·bi nots·ne
gay venues	kluby dla gejów	kloo·bi dla ge·yoof
pubs	puby	pa·bi
I feel like going to a/the ...	Mam ochotę pójść ...	mam o·kho·te pooyshch ...
concert	na koncert	na kon·tsert
movies	na film	na feelm
party	na imprezę	na eem·pre·ze
restaurant	do restauracji	do res·tow·ra·tsyee
theatre	na sztukę	na shtoo·ke

interests

Do you like ...?	*Czy lubisz ...?* inf	chi *loo*·beesh ...
I like ...	*Lubię ...*	*loo*·bye ...
cooking	*gotować*	go·*to*·vach
movies	*oglądać filmy*	o·*glon*·dach *feel*·mi
reading	*czytać*	*chi*·tach
sport	*sport*	sport
travelling	*podróżować*	po·droo·*zho*·vach
Do you like art?	*Czy lubisz sztukę?* inf	chi *loo*·beesh *shtoo*·ke
I like art.	*Lubię sztukę.*	*loo*·bye *shtoo*·ke
Do you ...?	*Czy ...?* inf	chi ...
dance	*tańczysz*	*tan'*·chish
go to concerts	*chodzisz na koncerty*	*kho*·jeesh na *kon*·tser·ti
listen to music	*słuchasz muzyki*	*swoo*·khash moo·*zi*·kee

food & drink

finding a place to eat

Can you recommend a ...?	*Czy może pan/pani polecić ...?* m/f	chi *mo*·zhe pan/*pa*·nee po·*le*·cheech ...
bar	*bar*	bar
café	*kawiarnię*	ka·*vyar*·nye
restaurant	*restaurację*	res·tow·*rats*·ye
I'd like ..., please.	*Proszę ...*	*pro*·she ...
a table for (five)	*o stolik na (pięć) osób*	o *sto*·leek na (pyench) o·soob

ordering food

breakfast	*śniadanie* n	shnya·*da*·nye
lunch	*obiad* m	*o*·byad
dinner	*kolacja* f	ko·*la*·tsya
snack	*przekąska* f	pshe·*kons*·ka

What would you recommend?

Co by pan polecił? m		tso bi pan po·*le*·cheew
Co by pani poleciła? f		tso bi *pa*·nee po·le·*chee*·wa

I'd like (the) ..., please.	Proszę ...	*pro*·she ...
bill	o rachunek	o ra·*khoo*·nek
drink list	o spis napojów	o spees na·*po*·yoof
menu	o jadłospis	o ya·*dwo*·spees
that dish	to danie	to *da*·nye

drinks

(cup of) coffee ...	(filiżanka) kawy ...	(fee·lee·*zhan*·ka) *ka*·vi ...
(cup of) tea ...	(filiżanka) herbaty ...	(fee·lee·*zhan*·ka) her·*ba*·ti ...
with milk	z mlekiem	z *mle*·kyem
without sugar	bez cukru	bez *tsoo*·kroo
(orange) juice	sok (pomarańczowy) m	sok (po·ma·ran'·*cho*·vi)
soft drink	napój m	*na*·pooy
... water	woda ...	*vo*·da ...
hot	gorąca	go·*ron*·tsa
mineral	mineralna	mee·ne·*ral*·na

in the bar

I'll have ...	Proszę ...	*pro*·she ...
I'll buy you a drink.	Kupię ci drinka. inf	*koo*·pye chee *dreen*·ka
What would you like?	Co zamówić dla ciebie? inf	tso za·*moo*·veech dla *chye*·bye
Cheers!	Na zdrowie!	na *zdro*·vye
brandy	brandy m	*bren*·di
champagne	szampan m	*sham*·pan
a shot of (vodka)	kieliszek (wódki)	kye·*lee*·shek (*vood*·kee)
a bottle/glass of beer	butelka/szklanka piwa	boo·*tel*·ka/*shklan*·ka *pee*·va
a bottle/glass	butelka/kieliszek	boo·*tel*·ka/kye·*lee*·shek
of ... wine	wina ...	*vee*·na ...
red	czerwonego	cher·vo·*ne*·go
sparkling	musującego	moo·soo·*yon*·tse·go
white	białego	bya·*we*·go

self-catering

What's the local speciality?
*Co jest miejscową
specjalnością?*
tso yest myeys·*tso*·vom
spe·tsyal·*nosh*·chyom

What's that?
Co to jest?
tso to yest

How much (is a kilo of cheese)?
Ile kosztuje (kilogram sera)?
ee·le kosh·*too*·ye (kee·*lo*·gram *se*·ra)

I'd like ...	*Proszę ...*	*pro·*she ...
200 grams	*dwadzieścia deko*	dva·*jyesh*·chya de·ko
(two) kilos	*(dwa) kilo*	(dva) *kee*·lo
(three) pieces	*(trzy) kawałki*	(tshi) ka·*vow*·kee
(six) slices	*(sześć) plasterków*	(sheshch) plas·*ter*·koof

Less.	*Mniej.*	mney
Enough.	*Wystarczy.*	vis·*tar*·chi
More.	*Więcej.*	vyen·tsey

special diets & allergies

Is there a vegetarian restaurant near here?
*Czy jest tu gdzieś restauracja
wegetariańska?*
chi yest too gjyesh res·tow·*ra*·tsya
ve·ge·ta·*ryan'*·ska

Do you have vegetarian food?
Czy jest żywność wegetariańska?
chi yest *zhiv*·noshch ve·ge·tar·*yan'*·ska

Could you prepare a meal without ...?	*Czy można przygotować jedzenie bez ...?*	chi *mo*·zhna pshi·go·*to*·vach ye·*dze*·nye bes ...
butter	*masła*	*mas*·wa
eggs	*jajek*	*yai*·ek
meat stock	*wywaru mięsnego*	vi·*va*·roo myens·*ne*·go

I'm allergic to ...	*Mam uczulenie na ...*	mam oo·choo·*le*·nye na ...
dairy produce	*produkty mleczne*	pro·*dook*·ti *mlech*·ne
gluten	*gluten*	*gloo*·ten
MSG	*glutaminian sodu*	gloo·ta·*mee*·nyan *so*·doo
nuts	*orzechy*	o·*zhe*·khi
seafood	*owoce morza*	o·*vo*·tse *mo*·zha

POLSKI – food & drink

278

menu decoder

barszcz biały m	barshch *bya*·wi	*thick sourish wheat & potato-starch soup with marjoram*
barszcz czerwony m	barshch cher·*vo*·ni	*beetroot soup with dumplings, hard-boiled egg slices or beans*
bigos m	*bee*·gos	*sauerkraut, cabbage & meat stew, simmered with mushrooms & prunes & flavoured with red wine*
bliny m pl	*blee*·ni	*small thick pancakes made from wheat or buckwheat flour & yeast*
budyń m	*boo*·din'	*milk-based cream dessert in a range of flavours (eg strawberry, vanilla or chocolate)*
chłodnik m	*khwod*·neek	*baby beetroot soup with yogurt & fresh vegetables, served cold*
ćwikła f	*chfeek*·wa	*boiled & grated beetroot with horseradish, served with roast or smoked meat & sausages*
drożdżówka f	drozh·*joof*·ka	*brioche (sweet yeast bun)*
flaczki m pl	*flach*·kee	*seasoned tripe & vegetables cooked in bouillon*
galareta f	ga·la·*re*·ta	*appetiser of meat or fish encased in aspic • sweet flavoured jelly*
gofry m pl	*go*·fri	*thick rectangular waffles served with toppings such as whipped cream, chocolate or jam*
golonka f	go·*lon*·ka	*boiled pigs' hocks served with sauerkraut or puréed yellow peas*
gołąbki m pl	go·*womb*·kee	*cabbage leaves stuffed with minced beef & rice*
grahamka f	gra·*kham*·ka	*small wholemeal roll*
grochówka f	gro·*khoof*·ka	*lentil soup*

jabłecznik m	*ya·bwech·neek*	*apple strudel*
kapuśniak m	*ka·poosh·nyak*	*sauerkraut soup*
kisiel m	*kee·shyel*	*jelly-type dessert made with potato starch*
klopsiki m pl	*klop·shee·kee*	*meatballs made with ground beef, pork and/or veal*
knedle m pl	*kned·le*	*dumplings stuffed with plums, cherries or apples*
kopytka n pl	*ko·pit·ka*	*potato dumplings similar to gnocchi*
łosoś wędzony m	*wo·sosh ven·dzo·ni*	*smoked salmon*
makowiec m	*ma·ko·vyets*	*poppy-seed strudel*
melba f	*mel·ba*	*ice cream, fruit & whipped cream*
mizeria f	*mee·zer·ya*	*sliced cucumber in sour cream*
naleśniki m pl	*na·lesh·nee·kee*	*crèpes • pancakes*
nóżki w galarecie n pl	*noosh·kee v ga·la·re·chye*	*jellied pigs' knuckles*
pierogi m pl	*pye·ro·gee*	*ravioli-like dumplings made from noodle dough, usually stuffed with mincemeat, sauerkraut, mushroom, cheese & potato*
rosół z makaronem m	*ro·soow z ma·ka·ro·nem*	*bouillon with noodles*
sałatka jarzynowa f	*sa·wat·ka ya·zhi·no·va*	*salad made with potato, vegetables & mayonnaise*
sernik m	*ser·neek*	*cheesecake*
szaszłyk m	*shash·wik*	*shish kebab*
śledź w śmietanie m	*shlej v shmye·ta·nye*	*herring in sour cream*
tatar m	*ta·tar*	*minced sirloin served raw with onion, raw egg yolk & chopped dill cucumber*
zapiekanka f	*za·pye·kan·ka*	*half a bread roll filled with cheese & mushrooms, baked & served hot*

emergencies

basics

Help!	Na pomoc!	na *po*·mots
Stop!	Stój!	stooy
Go away!	Odejdź!	o·deyj
Thief!	Złodziej!	zwo·jyey
Fire!	Pożar!	*po*·zhar
Watch out!	Uważaj!	oo·*va*·zhai

Call ...!	Zadzwoń po ...!	*zad*·zvon' po ...
a doctor	lekarza	le·*ka*·zha
an ambulance	karetkę	ka·*ret*·ke
the police	policję	po·*lee*·tsye

It's an emergency.
To nagły wypadek.   to *nag*·wi vi·*pa*·dek

Could you help me, please?
Czy może pan/pani mi pomóc? m/f   chi *mo*·zhe pan/*pa*·nee mee *po*·moots

Can I use the telephone?
Czy mogę użyć telefon?   chi *mo*·ge oo·zhich te·*le*·fon

I'm lost.
Zgubiłem/Zgubiłam się. m/f   zgoo·*bee*·wem/zgoo·*bee*·wam shye

Where are the toilets?
Gdzie są toalety?   gjye som to·a·*le*·ti

police

Where's the police station?
Gdzie jest posterunek policji?   gje yest pos·te·*roo*·nek po·*lee*·tsyee

I want to report an offence.
Chciałem/Chciałam zgłosić   khchow·em/khchow·am *zgwo*·sheech
przestępstwo. m/f   pshe·*stemps*·tfo

I have insurance.
Mam ubezpieczenie.   mam oo·bes·pye·*che*·nye

I've been ...	Zostałem/Zostałam ... m/f	zo·stow·em/zo·stow·am ...
assaulted	napadnięty/a m/f	na·pad·nyen·ti/a
raped	zgwałcony/a m/f	zgvow·tso·ni/a
robbed	okradziony/a m/f	o·kra·jyo·ni/a

I've lost my ...	Zgubiłem/ Zgubiłam ... m/f	zgoo·bee·wem/ zgoo·bee·wam ...
backpack	plecak	ple·tsak
bag	torbę	tor·be
credit card	kartę kredytową	kar·te kre·di·to·vom
handbag	torebkę	to·rep·ke
jewellery	biżuterię	bee·zhoo·ter·ye
money	pieniądze	pye·nyon·dze
passport	paszport	pash·port
wallet	portfel	port·fel

I want to contact my ...	Chcę się skontaktować z ...	khtse shye skon·tak·to·vach z ...
consulate	moim konsulatem	mo·yeem kon·soo·la·tem
embassy	moją ambasadą	mo·yom am·ba·sa·dom

health

medical needs

Where's the nearest ...?	Gdzie jest najbliższy/a ...? m/f	gjye yest nai·bleezh·shi/a ...
dentist	dentysta m	den·tis·ta
doctor	lekarz m	le·kash
hospital	szpital m	shpee·tal
(night) pharmacist	apteka (nocna) f	ap·te·ka (nots·na)

I need a doctor (who speaks English).
Szukam lekarza (który mówi po angielsku).
shoo·kam le·ka·zha (ktoo·ri moo·vee po an·gyel·skoo)

Could I see a female doctor?
Czy mogę się widzieć z lekarzem kobietą?
chi mo·ge shye vee·jyech z le·ka·zhem ko·bye·tom

I've run out of my medication.
Skończyły mi się lekarstwa.
skon·chi·wi mee shye le·kars·tfa

symptoms, conditions & allergies

I'm sick.	Jestem chory/a. m/f	yes·tem kho·ri/a
It hurts here.	Tutaj boli.	too·tai bo·lee
I have (a) ...	Mam ...	mam ...

asthma	astma f	ast·ma
constipation	zatwardzenie n	zat·far·dze·nye
cough	kaszel m	ka·shel
diarrhoea	rozwolnienie n	roz·vol·nye·nye
fever	gorączka f	go·ronch·ka
headache	ból głowy vi	bool gwo·vi
heart condition	stan serca m	stan ser·tsa
nausea	mdłości f pl	mdwosh·chee
pain	ból m	bool
sore throat	ból gardła m	bool gar·dwa
toothache	ból zęba m	bool zem·ba

I'm allergic to ...	Mam alergię na ...	mam a·ler·gye na ...
antibiotics	antybiotyki	an·ti·byo·ti·kee
anti-inflammatories	leki przeciwzapalne	le·kee pshe·cheef·za·pal·ne
aspirin	aspirynę	as·pee·ri·ne
bees	pszczoły	pshcho·wi
codeine	kodeinę	ko·de·ee·ne
penicillin	penicylinę	pe·nee·tsi·lee·ne

antiseptic	środki odkażające m pl	shrod·kee od·ka·zha·yon·tse
bandage	bandaż m	ban·dash
condoms	kondom m pl	kon·dom
contraceptives	środki antykoncepcyjne m pl	shrod·kee an·ti·kon·tsep·tsiy·ne
diarrhoea medicine	rozwolnienie	ros·vol·nye·nye
insect repellent	środek na owady m	shro·dek na o·va·di
laxatives	środek przeczyszczający m	shro·dek pshe·chish·cha·yon·tsi
painkillers	środki przeciwbólowe m pl	shrod·kee pshe·cheef·boo·lo·ve
rehydration salts	sole fizjologiczne f pl	so·le fee·zyo·lo·geech·ne
sleeping tablets	pigułki nasenne f pl	pee·goow·kee na·se·ne

english–polish dictionary

Polish nouns in this dictionary have their gender indicated by ⓜ (masculine), ⓕ (feminine) or ⓝ (neuter). If it's a plural noun, you'll also see pl. Adjectives are given in the masculine form only. Words are also marked as a (adjective), v (verb), sg (singular), pl (plural), inf (informal) or pol (polite) where necessary.

A

accident *wypadek* ⓜ vi-pa-dek
accommodation *nocleg* ⓜ nots-leg
adaptor *zasilacz* ⓕ za-shee-lach
address *adres* ⓜ a-dres
after *po* • *za* po • za
air conditioning *klimatyzacja* ⓕ klee-ma-ti-za-tsya
airplane *samolot* ⓝ sa-mo-lot
airport *lotnisko* ⓝ lot-nees-ko
alcohol *alkohol* ⓜ al-ko-khol
all *wszystko* fshist-ko
allergy *alergia* ⓕ a-ler-gya
ambulance *karetka pogotowia* ⓕ ka-ret-ka po-go-to-vya
and *i* ee
ankle *kostka* ⓕ kost-ka
arm *ręka* ⓕ ren-ka
ashtray *popielniczka* ⓕ po-pyel-neech-ka
ATM *bankomat* ⓜ ban-ko-mat

B

baby *niemowlę* ⓝ nye-mov-le
back (body) *plecy* pl ple-tsi
backpack *plecak* ⓜ ple-tsak
bad *zły* zwi
bag *torba* ⓕ tor-ba
baggage claim *odbiór bagażu* ⓜ od-byoor ba-ga-zhoo
bank *bank* ⓜ bank
bar *bar* ⓜ bar
bathroom *łazienka* ⓕ wa-zhyen-ka
battery *bateria* ⓕ ba-te-rya
beautiful *piękny* pyen-kni
bed *łóżko* ⓝ woozh-ko
beer *piwo* ⓝ pee-vo
before *przed* pshet
behind *za* za
bicycle *rower* ⓜ ro-ver
big *duży* doo-zhi
bill *rachunek* ⓜ ra-khoo-nek
black *czarny* char-ni
blanket *koc* ⓜ kots

blood group *grupa krwi* ⓕ groo-pa krfee
blue *niebieski* nye-byes-kee
boat *łódź* ⓕ wooj
book (make a reservation) v *rezerwować* re-zer-vo-vach
bottle *butelka* ⓕ boo-tel-ka
bottle opener *otwieracz do butelek* ⓜ ot-fye-rach do boo-te-lek
boy *chłopiec* ⓜ khwo-pyets
brakes (car) *hamulce* ⓕ pl ha-mool-tse
breakfast *śniadanie* ⓝ shnya-da-nye
broken (faulty) *połamany* po-wa-ma-ni
bus *autobus* ⓜ ow-to-boos
business *firma* ⓕ feer-ma
buy *kupować* koo-po-vach

C

café *kawiarnia* ⓕ ka-vyar-nya
camera *aparat* ⓜ a-pa-rat
camp site *kamping* ⓜ kam-peeng
cancel *unieważniać* oo-nye-vazh-nyach
can opener *otwieracz do konserw* ⓜ ot-fye-rach do kon-serf
car *samochód* ⓜ sa-mo-khoot
cash *gotówka* ⓕ go-toof-ka
cash (a cheque) v *zrealizować czek* zre-a-lee-zo-vach chek
cell phone *telefon komórkowy* ⓜ te-le-fon ko-moor-ko-vi
centre *środek* ⓜ shro-dek
change (money) v *rozmieniać* roz-mye-nyach
cheap *tani* ta-nee
check (bill) *sprawdzenie* ⓝ sprav-dze-nye
check-in *zameldowanie* ⓝ za-mel-do-va-nye
chest *klatka piersiowa* ⓕ klat-ka pyer-shyo-va
child *dziecko* ⓝ jye-tsko
cigarette *papieros* ⓜ pa-pye-ros
city *miasto* ⓝ myas-to
clean a *czysty* chi-sti
closed *zamknięty* zam-knyen-ti
coffee *kawa* ⓕ ka-va
coins *monety* ⓕ pl mo-ne-ti
cold a *zimny* zheem-ni

collect call *rozmowa opłacona przez odbierającego* ①
roz-*mo*-va o-*pwa*-*tso*-na pshes od-bye-ra-yon-*tse*-go
come (by vehicle) *przyjść* pshiyshch
come (on foot) *przychodzić* pshi-*kho*-jeech
computer *komputer* ⑩ kom-*poo*-ter
condom *kondom* ⑩ *kon*-dom
contact lenses *soczewki kontaktowe* ① pl
so-*chef*-ke kon-tak-*to*-ve
cook v *gotować* go-*to*-vach
cost *koszt* kosht
credit card *karta kredytowa* ① *kar*-ta kre-di-*to*-va
cup *filiżanka* ① fee-lee-*zhan*-ka
currency exchange *kantor* ⑩ *kan*-tor
customs (immigration) *urząd celny* ⑩
oo-zhont *tsel*-ni

D

dangerous *niebezpieczny* nye-bes-*pyech*-ni
date (time) *data* ① *da*-ta
day *dzień* ⑩ jyen'
delay *opóźnienie* ① o-poozh-*nye*-nye
dentist *dentysta* ⑩ den-*tis*-ta
depart *odjeżdżać* od-*yezh*-jach
diaper *pieluszka* ① pye-*loosh*-ka
dictionary *słownik* ⑩ *swov*-neek
dinner *kolacja* ① ko-*la*-tsya
direct *bezpośredni* bes-po-*shred*-nee
dirty *brudny* *brood*-ni
disabled *niepełnosprawny* nye-pew-no-*sprav*-ni
discount *zniżka* ① *zneesh*-ka
doctor *lekarz* ⑩ *le*-kash
double bed *łóżko małżeńskie* ⑩
woozh-ko mow-*zhen'*-skye
double room *pokój dwuosobowy* ⑩
po-kooy dvoo-o-so-*bo*-vi
drink *napój* ⑩ *na*-pooy
drive v *kierować* kye-ro-vach
drivers licence *prawo jazdy* ① *pra*-vo *yaz*-di
drugs (illicit) *narkotyki* ⑩ pl nar-ko-*ti*-kee
dummy (pacifier) *smoczek* ⑩ *smo*-chek

E

ear *ucho* ① *oo*-kho
east *wschód* ⑩ vskhood
eat *jeść* yeshch
economy class *klasa oszczędnościowa* ①
kla-sa osh-chend-nosh-*chyo*-va
electricity *elektryczność* ① e-lek-*trich*-noshch
elevator *winda* ① *veen*-da
email *email* ⑩ e-*mail*

embassy *ambasada* ① am-ba-*sa*-da
emergency *nagły przypadek* ⑩ *nag*-wi pshi-*pa*-dek
English (language) *angielski* an-*gyel*-skee
entrance *wejście* ① *veysh*-chye
evening *wieczór* ⑩ *vye*-choor
exchange rate *kurs wymiany* ⑩ koors vi-*mya*-ni
exit *wyjście* ① *viysh*-chye
expensive *drogi* *dro*-gee
express mail *list ekspresowy* ⑩ leest eks-pre-*so*-vi
eye *oko* ① *o*-ko

F

far *daleki* da-*le*-kee
fast *szybki* *shib*-kee
father *ojciec* ⑩ *oy*-chyets
film (camera) *film* ⑩ feelm
finger *palec* ⑩ *pa*-lets
first-aid kit *apteczka pierwszej pomocy* ①
ap-*tech*-ka pyerf-shey po-*mo*-tsi
first class *pierwsza klasa* ① *pyerf*-sha *kla*-sa
fish *ryba* ① *ri*-ba
food *żywność* ① *zhiv*-noshch
foot *stopa* ① *sto*-pa
fork *widelec* ⑩ vee-*de*-lets
free (of charge) *bezpłatny* bes-*pwat*-ni
friend *przyjaciel/przyjaciółka* ⑩ / ①
pshi-*ya*-chyel/pshi-ya-*choow*-ka
fruit *owoc* ⑩ *o*-vots
full *pełny* *pew*-ni
funny *zabawny* za-*bav*-ni

G

gift *prezent* ⑩ *pre*-zent
girl *dziewczyna* ① jyev-*chi*-na
glass (drinking) *szklanka* ① *shklan*-ka
glasses *okulary* pl o-koo-*la*-ri
go (by vehicle) *jechać* *ye*-khach
go (on foot) *iść* eeshch
good *dobry* *do*-bri
green *zielony* zhye-*lo*-ni
guide *przewodnik* ⑩ pshe-*vod*-neek

H

half *połówka* ① po-*woof*-ka
hand *ręka* ① *ren*-ka
handbag *torebka* ① to-*rep*-ka
happy *szczęśliwy* shchen-*shlee*-vi
have *mieć* myech
he *on* on

head *głowa* ① *gwo*-va
heart *serce* ⓝ *ser*-tse
heat *upał* ⓜ *oo*-pow
heavy *ciężki* ⓜ *chyensh*-kee
help v *pomagać* po-*ma*-gach
here *tutaj* too-tai
high *wysoki* vi-*so*-kee
highway *szosa* ① *sho*-sa
hike v *wędrować* ven-*dro*-vach
holiday *święto* ⓝ *shvyen*-to
homosexual n *homoseksualista* ⓜ
    ho-mo-sek-soo-a-*lees*-ta
hospital *szpital* ⓜ *shpee*-tal
hot *gorący* go-*ron*-tsi
hotel *hotel* ⓜ *ho*-tel
hungry *głodny* *gwo*-dni
husband *mąż* ⓜ monzh

I

I *ja* ya
identification (card) *dowód tożsamości* ⓜ
    do-vood tozh-sa-*mosh*-chee
ill *chory* kho-ri
important *ważny* vazh-ni
included *wliczony* vlee-*cho*-ni
injury *rana* ① *ra*-na
insurance *ubezpieczenie* ⓝ oo-bes-pye-*che*-nye
Internet *internet* ⓜ een-ter-net
interpreter *tłumacz/tłumaczka* ⓜ / ①
    twoo-mach/twoo-*mach*-ka

J

jewellery *biżuteria* ① bee-zhoo-*ter*-ya
job *praca* ① *pra*-tsa

K

key *klucz* ⓜ klooch
kilogram *kilogram* ⓜ kee-*lo*-gram
kitchen *kuchnia* ① kookh-nya
knife *nóż* ⓜ noosh

L

laundry (place) *pralnia* ① pral-nya
lawyer *prawnik* ⓜ prav-neek
left (direction) *lewy* ⓜ le-vi
left-luggage office *przechowalnia bagażu* ①
    pshe-kho-*val*-nya ba-*ga*-zhoo

leg *noga* ① *no*-ga
lesbian n *lesbijka* ① les-*beey*-ka
less *mniej* mnyey
letter (mail) *list* ⓜ leest
lift (elevator) *winda* ① veen-da
light *światło* ⓝ *shvyat*-wo
like v *lubić* loo-beech
lock *zamek* ⓜ za-mek
long *długi* dwoo-gee
lost *zgubiony* zgoo-*byo*-ni
lost-property office *biuro rzeczy znalezionych* ⓝ
    byoo-ro zhe-chi zna-le-*zhyo*-nikh
love v *kochać* ko-khach
luggage *bagaż* ① *ba*-gash
lunch *lunch* ⓜ lanch

M

mail (letters) *list* ⓜ leest
mail (postal system) *poczta* ① *poch*-ta
man *mężczyzna* ⓜ menzh-*chiz*-na
map (of country) *mapa* ① *ma*-pa
map (of town) *plan* ⓜ plan
market *rynek* ⓜ ri-nek
matches *zapałki* ① pl za-*pow*-kee
meat *mięso* ⓝ *myen*-so
medicine *lekarstwo* ⓝ le-*karst*-fo
menu *jadłospis* ⓜ ya-*dwo*-spees
message *wiadomość* ① vya-do-moshch
milk *mleko* ⓝ *mle*-ko
minute *minuta* ① mee-*noo*-ta
mobile phone *telefon komórkowy* ⓜ
    te-*le*-fon ko-moor-*ko*-vi
money *pieniądze* ⓜ pl pye-*nyon*-dze
month *miesiąc* ⓜ *mye*-shonts
morning *rano* ⓝ *ra*-no
mother *matka* ① *mat*-ka
motorcycle *motor* ⓜ mo-tor
motorway *autostrada* ① ow-to-*stra*-da
mouth *usta* pl *oos*-ta
music *muzyka* ① moo-*zi*-ka

N

name *imię* ⓝ *ee*-mye
napkin *serwetka* ① ser-*vet*-ka
nappy *pieluszka* ① pye-*loosh*-ka
near *bliski* blees-kee
neck *szyja* ① *shi*-ya
new *nowy* no-vi
news *wiadomości* ① pl vya-do-*mosh*-chee
newspaper *gazeta* ① ga-*ze*-ta
night *noc* ① nots

no *nie* nye
noisy *hałaśliwy* ha-wa-*shlee*-vi
nonsmoking *niepalący* nye-pa-*lon*-tsi
north *północ* ① *poow*-nots
nose *nos* ⑩ nos
now *teraz* *te*-ras
number *numer* ⑩ *noo*-mer

O

oil (engine) *olej* ⑩ *o*-ley
old *stary* *sta*-ri
one-way ticket *bilet w jedną stronę* ⑩
  bee-let v *yed*-nom *stro*-ne
open a *otwarty* ot-*far*-ti
outside *na zewnątrz* na *zev*-nontsh

P

package *paczka* ① *pach*-ka
paper *papier* ⑩ *pa*-pyer
park (car) v *parkować* par-*ko*-vach
passport *paszport* ⑩ *pash*-port
pay *płacić* *pwa*-cheech
pen *długopis* ⑩ dwoo-*go*-pees
petrol *benzyna* ① ben-*zi*-na
pharmacy *apteka* ① ap-*te*-ka
phonecard *karta telefoniczna* ① *kar*-ta te-le-fo-*neech*-na
photo *zdjęcie* ① *zdyen*-chye
plate *talerz* ⑩ *ta*-lesh
Poland *Polska* ① *pol*-ska
police *policja* ① po-*lee*-tsya
Polish (language) *polski* ⑩ *pol*-skee
postcard *pocztówka* ① poch-*toof*-ka
post office *urząd pocztowy* ⑩ *oo*-zhond poch-*to*-vi
pregnant *w ciąży* v *chyon*-zhi
price *cena* ① *tse*-na

Q

quiet *cichy* *chee*-khi

R

rain *deszcz* ⑩ deshch
razor *brzytwa* ① *bzhit*-fa
receipt *rachunek* ① ra-*khoo*-nek
red *czerwony* cher-*vo*-ni
refund *zwrot pieniędzy* ⑩ zvrot pye-*nyen*-dzi
registered mail *list polecony* ⑩ leest po-le-*tso*-ni
rent v *wynająć* vi-*na*-yonch

repair v *naprawić* na-*pra*-veech
reservation *rezerwacja* ① re-zer-*va*-tsya
restaurant *restauracja* ① res-tow-*ra*-tsya
return v *wracać* *vra*-tsach
return ticket *bilet powrotny* ⑩ *bee*-let po-*vro*-tni
right (direction) *prawoskrętny* pra-vo-*skrent*-ni
road *droga* ① *dro*-ga
room *pokój* ⑩ *po*-kooy

S

safe a *bezpieczny* bes-*pyech*-ni
sanitary napkin *podpaski higieniczne* ① pl
  pod-*pas*-kee hee-gye-*neech*-ne
seat *miejsce* ⑩ *myeys*-tse
send *wysyłać* vi-*si*-wach
service station *stacja obsługi* ① *sta*-tsya ob-*swoo*-gee
sex *seks* ⑩ seks
shampoo *szampon* ⑩ *sham*-pon
share (a dorm) v *mieszkać z kimś* *myesh*-kach z keemsh
shaving cream *krem do golenia* ⑩ krem do go-*le*-nya
she *ona* *o*-na
sheet (bed) *prześcieradło* ① pshesh-chye-*ra*-dwo
shirt *koszula* ① ko-*shoo*-la
shoes *buty* ① pl *boo*-ti
shop *sklep* ⑩ sklep
short *krótki* *kroot*-kee
shower *prysznic* ⑩ *prish*-neets
single room *pokój jednoosobowy* ⑩
  po-kooy ye-dno-o-so-*bo*-vi
skin *skóra* ① *skoo*-ra
skirt *spódnica* ① spood-*nee*-tsa
sleep v *spać* spach
slowly *powoli* po-*vo*-lee
small *mały* *ma*-wi
smoke (cigarettes) v *palić* *pa*-leech
soap *mydło* ① *mid*-wo
some *kilka* *keel*-ka
soon *wkrótce* fkroot-tse
south *południe* ① po-*wood*-nye
souvenir shop *sklep z pamiątkami* ⑩
  sklep z pa-*myont*-ka-mi
speak *mówić* *moo*-veech
spoon *łyżka* ① *wish*-ka
stamp *znaczek* ① *zna*-chek
stand-by ticket *bilet z listy rezerwowej* ⑩
  bee-let z *lees*-ti re-zer-*vo*-vey
station (train) *stacja* ① *sta*-tsya
stomach *żołądek* ⑩ zho-*won*-dek
stop v *przestać* *pshes*-tach
stop (bus) *przystanek* ⑩ pshis-*ta*-nek
street *ulica* ① oo-*lee*-tsa
student *student* ⑩ *stoo*-dent

sun *słońce* ⓝ *swon'*-tse
sunscreen *krem przeciwsłoneczny* ⓜ
  krem pshe-cheef-swo-*nech*-ni
swim v *pływać* pwi-vach

T

tampon *tampon* ⓜ *tam*-pon
taxi *taksówka* ⓕ tak-*soof*-ka
teaspoon *łyżeczka* ⓕ wi-*zhech*-ka
teeth *zęby* ⓜ pl *zem*-bi
telephone *telefon* ⓜ te-*le*-fon
television *telewizja* ⓕ te-le-*veez*-ya
temperature (weather) *temperatura* ⓕ
  tem-pe-ra-*too*-ra
tent *namiot* ⓜ *na*-myot
that (one) *który* ktoo-ri
they *oni* o-nee
thirsty *spragniony* sprag-*nyo*-ni
this (one) *ten* ⓜ ten
throat *gardło* *gard*-wo
ticket *bilet* ⓜ *bee*-let
time *czas* ⓜ chas
tired *zmęczony* zmen-*cho*-ni
tissues *chusteczki* ⓕ pl khoos-*tech*-kee
today *dzisiaj* jee-shyai
toilet *toaleta* ⓕ to-a-*le*-ta
tomorrow *jutro* yoo-tro
tonight *dzisiaj wieczorem* jee-shyai vye-*cho*-rem
toothbrush *szczotka do zębów* ⓕ *shchot*-ka do *zem*-boof
toothpaste *pasta do zębów* ⓕ *pas*-ta do *zem*-boof
torch (flashlight) *latarka* ⓕ la-*tar*-ka
tour *wycieczka* ⓕ vi-*chyech*-ka
tourist office *biuro turystyczne* ⓝ *byoo*-ro too-ris-*tich*-ne
towel *ręcznik* ⓜ *rench*-neek
train *pociąg* ⓜ po-chyonk
translate *przetłumaczyć* pshe-twoo-*ma*-chich
travel agency *biuro podróży* ⓝ *byoo*-ro po-*droo*-zhi
travellers cheques *czeki podróżne* ⓜ pl
  che-kee po-*droozh*-ne
trousers *spodnie* pl *spo*-dnye
twin beds *dwa łóżka* ⓝ pl dva *woosh*-ka
tyre *opona* ⓕ o-*po*-na

U

underwear *bielizna* ⓕ bye-*leez*-na
urgent *pilny* peel-ni

V

vacant *wolny* vol-ni
vacation *wakacje* pl va-*ka*-tsye
vegetable *warzywo* ⓝ va-*zhi*-vo
vegetarian a *wegetariański* ve-ge-tar-*yan'*-skee
visa *wiza* ⓕ *vee*-za

W

waiter *kelner* ⓜ *kel*-ner
walk v *spacerować* spa-tse-*ro*-vach
wallet *portfel* ⓜ *port*-fel
warm a *ciepły* chyep-wi
Warsaw *Warszawa* ⓕ var-*sha*-va
wash (something) *prać* prach
watch *zegarek* ⓜ ze-*ga*-rek
water *woda* ⓕ *vo*-da
we *my* mi
weekend *weekend* ⓜ *wee*-kend
west *zachód* ⓜ za-khood
wheelchair *wózek inwalidzki* ⓜ
  voo-zek een-va-*leets*-kee
when *kiedy* kye-di
where *gdzie* gjye
white *biały* bya-wi
who *kto* kto
why *dlaczego* dla-*che*-go
wife *żona* ⓕ *zho*-na
window *okno* ⓝ *ok*-no
wine *wino* ⓝ *vee*-no
with *z* z
without *bez* bes
woman *kobieta* ⓕ ko-*bye*-ta
write *pisać* *pee*-sach

Y

yellow *żółty* zhoow-ti
yes *tak* tak
yesterday *wczoraj* fcho-rai
you sg inf *ty* ti
you sg pol *pan/pani* ⓜ/ⓕ pan/*pa*-nee
you pl inf *wy* vi
you pl pol *panowie/panie* ⓜ/ⓕ pa-no-vye/*pa*-nye
you pl pol *państwo* ⓜ&ⓕ *pan'*-stfo*

Romanian

romanian alphabet

A a a	*Ă ă* uh	*Â â* ew	*B b* be	*C c* che
D d de	*E e* e	*F f* ef	*G g* je	*H h* hash
I i ee	*Î î* ew	*J j* zhe	*K k* ka	*L l* el
M m em	*N n* en	*O o* o	*P p* pe	*R r* er
S s es	*Ş ş* shew	*T t* te	*Ţ ţ* tsew	*U u* oo
V v ve	*X x* eeks	*Y y* ee grek	*Z z* zed	

LIMBA ROMÂNĂ

romanian

introduction

Romanian (*limba română* leem-ba ro-*mew*-nuh), 'a Latin island in a Slav sea', holds the intriguing status of being the only member of the Romance language family in Eastern Europe. As a descendant of Latin, it shares a common heritage with French, Italian, Spanish and Portuguese – but its evolution took a separate path, mainly due to its geographical isolation from Rome and the influence of Catholicism. The Slavic invasion of the Balkans and the historical circumstances which placed Romanians in the Orthodox cultural sphere added to Romanian's distinguishing characteristics. Greek, Turkish and Hungarian touches spiced up the mixture even more.

It's generally believed that the base for modern Romanian was the language of the Dacians, who in ancient times inhabited the Danubian lands near the Black Sea. After Dacia became a province of the Roman Empire in AD 106, its Romanisation was so thorough that most of vocabulary and grammar of Romanian today is of Latin origin. However, with the withdrawal of the Romans from the area by AD 275, their linguistic influence ceased, leaving behind in Romanian many aspects of Latin that no longer exist in other Romance languages (such as noun cases). The void was filled with the arrival of the Slavs in the Balkans in the 6th century. The interaction with Bulgarian and Serbian (reflected in many loanwords) was intensified from the 13th century, through the shared Byzantine culture and the influence of Old Church Slavonic, the liturgical language of the Orthodox Church until the 18th century.

The oldest written record in Romanian is a letter from 1521 to the mayor of Braşov, written in the Cyrillic alphabet. The Roman alphabet first came into use in the 17th century, along with Hungarian spelling conventions, but it only replaced the earlier script in the mid-19th century. It was gradually adapted to the sounds of Romanian with the creation of some additional letters and officially recognised in 1859. During the Soviet rule, a Russian version of the Cyrillic alphabet was used in Moldova, but the Roman alphabet was reintroduced in 1989.

Today, Romanian is the official language of Romania and Moldova (where it's called Moldovan – *limba moldovenească* leem-ba mol-do-ve-ne-*as*-kuh), with about 24 million speakers, including the Romanian-speaking minorities in Hungary, Serbia and Ukraine. Considering the Latin origin of much of the English vocabulary and the phonetic nature of the Romanian alphabet, communicating in Romanian with this phrasebook should be *floare la ureche* flo-*a*-re la oo-*re*-ke (lit: 'flower at your ear') – a piece of cake!

pronunciation

vowel sounds

Romanian vowels form vowel combinations with adjacent vowels. At the beginning of a word, *e* and *i* are pronounced as if there were a faint y sound preceding them. At the end of a word, a single *i* is usually almost silent (and represented in our pronunciation guides with an apostrophe), while *ii* is pronounced as ee.

symbol	english equivalent	romanian example	transliteration
a	father	*pat*	pat
ai	aisle	*mai*	mai
e	bet	*sete*	*se*·te
ee	see	*bine*	*bee*·ne
ew	ee pronounced with rounded lips	*frîne*	*frew*·ne
i	bit	*ochi*	*o*·ki
o	pot	*opt*	opt
oh	oh	*cadou*	ka·*doh*
oo	zoo	*bun*	boon
ow	how	*restaurant*	res·*tow*·rant
oy	toy	*noi*	noy
uh	ago	*casă*	*ka*·suh
'	very short, unstressed i	*cinci*	cheench'

word stress

There's no general rule for stress in Romanian. It falls on different syllables in different words, and just has to be learned. You'll be fine if you just follow our coloured pronunciation guides, in which the stressed syllable is always in italics.

consonant sounds

Romanian consonant sounds all have equivalents in English. Note that the sounds w and y generally act as semi-vowels.

symbol	english equivalent	romanian example	transliteration
b	**bed**	*bilet*	bee-*let*
ch	**cheat**	*rece*	re-*che*
d	**dog**	*verde*	ver-de
f	**fat**	*frate*	fra-te
g	**go**	*negru*	ne-groo
h	**hat**	*hartă*	har-tuh
j	**joke**	*gest*	jest
k	**kit**	*cald*	kald
l	**lot**	*lapte*	lap-te
m	**man**	*maro*	ma-ro
n	**not**	*inel*	ee-nel
p	**pet**	*opus*	o-poos
r	**run**	*aprozar*	a-pro-zar
s	**sun**	*săpun*	suh-poon
sh	**shot**	*şah*	shah
t	**top**	*trist*	treest
ts	**hats**	*soţ*	sots
v	**very**	*vin*	veen
w	**win**	*două*	do-wuh
y	**yes**	*iată*	yaa-tuh
z	**zero**	*zero*	ze-ro
zh	**pleasure**	*dejun*	de-zhoon

basics

language difficulties

Do you speak English?
Vorbiţi engleza? — vor·*beets*' en·*gle*·za

Do you understand?
Înţelegeţi? — ewn·tse·*le*·gets'

I (don't) understand.
Eu (nu) înţeleg. — ye·oo (noo) ewn·tse·*leg*

What does (azi) mean?
Ce înseamnă (azi)? — che ewn·se·*am*·nuh (*a*·zi)

How do you ...? — *Cum ...?* — koom ...
  pronounce this — *se pronunţă asta* — se pro·*noon*·tsuh *as*·ta
  write (*mulţumesc*) — *se scrie (mulţumesc)* — se *skree*·ye (mool·tsoo·*mesk*)

Could you please ...? — *Aţi putea ...?* — uhts' poo·te·*a* ...
  repeat that — *repeta* — re·pe·*ta*
  speak more slowly — *vorbi mai rar* — vor·*bee* mai rar
  write it down — *scrie* — *skree*·ye

essentials

Yes.	*Da.*	da
No.	*Nu.*	noo
Please.	*Vă rog.*	vuh rog
Thank you (very much).	*Mulţumesc.*	mool·tsoo·*mesk*
You're welcome.	*Cu plăcere.*	koo pluh·*che*·re
Excuse me.	*Scuzaţi-mă.*	skoo·*za*·tsee·muh
Sorry.	*Îmi pare rău.*	ewm' *pa*·re ruh·oo

numbers

0	zero	ze·ro	17	şapte- sprezece	shap·te· spre·ze·che
1	unu	oo·noo	18	optsprezece	opt·spre·ze·che
2	doi	doy	19	nouă- sprezece	no·wuh· spre·ze·che
3	trei	trey	20	douăzeci	do·wuh·ze·chi
4	patru	pa·troo	21	douăzeci şi unu	do·wuh·ze·chi shee oo·noo
5	cinci	cheench'	22	douăzeci şi doi	do·wuh·ze·chi shee doy
6	şase	sha·se	30	treizeci	trey·ze·chi
7	şapte	shap·te	40	patruzeci	pa·troo·ze·chi
8	opt	opt	50	cincizeci	cheench·ze·chi
9	nouă	no·wuh	60	şaizeci	shai·ze·chi
10	zece	ze·che	70	şaptezeci	shap·te·ze·chi
11	unsprezece	oon·spre·ze·che	80	optzeci	opt·ze·chi
12	doisprezece	doy·spre·ze·che	90	nouăzeci	no·wuh·ze·chi
13	treisprezece	trey·spre·ze·che	100	o sută	o soo·tuh
14	paisprezece	pai·spre·ze·che	1000	o mie	o mee·e
15	cinci- sprezece	cheench'· spre·ze·che			
16	şai- sprezece	shai· spre·ze·che			

time & dates

What time is it?	Cât e ceasul?	kewt ye che·a·sool
It's one o'clock.	E ora unu.	ye o·ra oo·noo
It's (two) o'clock.	E ora (două).	ye o·ra (do·wuh)
Quarter past (one).	(Unu) şi un sfert.	(oo·noo) shee oon sfert
Half past (one).	(Unu) şi jumătate.	(oo·noo) shee zhoo·muh·ta·te
Quarter to (eight).	(Opt) fără un sfert.	(opt) fuh·ruh oon sfert
At what time ...?	La ce oră ...?	la che o·ruh ...
At ...	La ora ...	la o·ra ...
am	dimineaţa	dee·mee·ne·a·tsa
pm (afternoon)	după masa	doo·puh ma·sa
pm (evening)	seara	se·a·ra

Monday	*luni*	*loo*-ni
Tuesday	*marţi*	*muhr*-tsi
Wednesday	*miercuri*	*myer*-koo-ri
Thursday	*joi*	zhoy
Friday	*vineri*	*vee*-ne-ri
Saturday	*sâmbătă*	*sewm*-buh-tuh
Sunday	*duminică*	doo-*mee*-nee-kuh

January	*ianuarie*	ya-*nwa*-rye
February	*februarie*	fe-*brwa*-rye
March	*martie*	*mar*-tye
April	*aprilie*	a-*pree*-lye
May	*mai*	mai
June	*iunie*	*yoo*-nye
July	*iulie*	*yoo*-lye
August	*august*	*ow*-goost
September	*septembrie*	sep-*tem*-brye
October	*octombrie*	ok-*tom*-brye
November	*noiembrie*	no-*yem*-brye
December	*decembrie*	de-*chem*-brye

What date is it today?
    Ce dată este astăzi?   che *da*-tuh *yes*-te as-*tuh*-zi

It's (15 December).
    E (cincisprezece decembrie).   ye (*cheench*-spre-ze-che de-*chem*-brye)

since (May)	*din (mai)*	deen (mai)
until (June)	*până în (iunie)*	*pew*-nuh ewn (*yoo*-nye)

last ...	... *trecut/trecută* m/f	... tre-*koot*/tre-*koo*-tuh
next ...	... *viitor/viitoare* m/f	... vee-ee-*tor*/vee-ee-to-*a*-re
night	*noaptea* f	*no*-ap-te-a
week	*săptămâna* f	suhp-tuh-*mew*-na
month	*luna* f	*loo*-na
year	*anul* m	*a*-nool

yesterday/tomorrow ...	*ieri/mâine* ...	*ye*-ri/mew-*ee*-ne ...
morning	*dimineaţă*	dee-mee-ne-*a*-tsuh
afternoon	*după amiază*	*doo*-puh a-*mya*-zuh
evening	*seară*	se-*a*-ruh

weather

What's the weather like?	*Cum e afară?*	koom ye a·*fa*·ruh
It's...	*E ...*	ye ...
cloudy	*înnorat*	ew·no·*rat*
cold	*frig*	freeg
hot	*foarte cald*	fo·*ar*·te kald
sunny	*soare*	so·*a*·re
warm	*cald*	kald
It's snowing.	*Ninge.*	*neen*·je
It's raining.	*Plouă.*	*plo*·wuh
It's windy.	*Bate vântul.*	*ba*·te vewn·tool
spring	*primăvară* f	pree·muh·*va*·ruh
summer	*vară* f	*va*·ruh
autumn	*toamnă* f	to·*am*·nuh
winter	*iarnă* f	*yar*·nuh

border crossing

I'm here ...	*Sunt aici ...*	soont a·*eech* ...
on business	*cu afaceri*	koo a·*fa*·che·ri
on holiday	*în vacanţă*	ewn va·*kan*·tsuh
I'm here for ...	*Sunt aici pentru ...*	soont a·*eech* pen·troo ...
(10) days	*(zece) zile*	(*ze*·che) *zee*·le
(two) months	*(două) luni*	(*do*·wuh) *loo*·ni
(three) weeks	*(trei) săptămâni*	(trey) suhp·tuh·*mew*·ni

I'm going to (Braşov).
Mă duc la (Braşov).
muh dook la (bra·*shov*)

I'm staying at the (Park Hotel).
Stau la (Hotel Park).
stow la (ho·*tel* park)

I have nothing to declare.
Nu am nimic de declarat.
noo am nee·*meek* de de·kla·*rat*

I have something to declare.
Am ceva de declarat.
am che·*va* de de·kla·*rat*

That's (not) mine.
Acesta (nu) e al meu.
a·*ches*·ta (noo) ye al *me*·oo

transport

tickets & luggage

Where can I buy a ticket?
Unde pot cumpăra un bilet?   *oon*-de pot koom-puh-*ra* oon bee-*let*

Do I need to book a seat?
Trebuie să rezerv locul?   tre-boo-ye suh re-*zerv* lo-*kool*

One ... ticket	*Un bilet ...*	oon bee-*let* ...
(to Cluj), please.	*(până la Cluj), vă rog.*	(pew-nuh la kloozh) vuh rog
one-way	*dus*	doos
return	*dus-întors*	doos ewn-*tors*

I'd like to ...	*Aş dori să-mi ...*	ash do-*ree* suhm' ...
my ticket, please.	*biletul, vă rog.*	bee-*le*-tool vuh rog
cancel	*anulez*	a-noo-*lez*
change	*schimb*	skeemb
collect	*jau*	yow
confirm	*confirm*	kon-*feerm*

I'd like a ... seat,	*Aş dori un loc la ...,*	ash do-*ree* oon lok la ...
please.	*vă rog.*	vuh rog
nonsmoking	*nefumători*	ne-foo-muh-*to*-ri
smoking	*fumători*	foo-muh-*to*-ri

How much is it?
Cât costă?   kewt *kos*-tuh

Is there air conditioning?
Are aer condiţionat?   *a*-re *a*-er kon-dee-tsyo-*nat*

Is there a toilet?
Are toaletă?   *a*-re to-a-*le*-tuh

How long does the trip take?
Cât durează călătoria?   kewt doo-re-*a*-zuh kuh-luh-to-*ree*-a

Is it a direct route?
E o rută directă?   ye o *roo*-tuh dee-*rek*-tuh

I'd like a luggage locker.
Aş dori un dulap de încuiat bagajul.   ash do-*ree* oon doo-*lap* de ewn-koo-*yat* ba-*ga*-zhool

My luggage has been ...	*Bagajul meu a fost ...*	ba·*ga*·zhool *me*·oo a fost ...
damaged	*deteriorat*	de·te·*ryo*·rat
lost	*pierdut*	pyer·*doot*
stolen	*furat*	foo·*rat*

getting around

Where does flight (7) arrive/depart?

Unde soseşte/pleacă   *oon*·de so·*sesh*·te/ple·*a*·kuh
cursa (7)?   *koor*·sa (*shap*·te)

Where's (the) ...?	*Unde este ...?*	*oon*·de *yes*·te ...
arrivals hall	*sala pentru sosiri*	*sa*·la *pen*·troo so·*see*·ri
departures hall	*sala pentru plecări*	*sa*·la *pen*·troo ple·*kuh*·ri
duty-free shop	*magazinul*	ma·ga·*zee*·nool
	duty-free	*dyoo*·tee·free
gate (12)	*poarta de îmbarcare*	po·*ar*·ta de ewm·bar·*ka*·re
	(doisprezece)	(*doy*·spre·ze·che)

Is this the ... to (Cluj)?	*Acesta e ... de (Cluj)?*	a·*ches*·ta ye ... de (kloozh)
boat	*vaporul*	va·*po*·rool
bus	*autobuzul*	ow·to·*boo*·zool
plane	*avionul*	a·*vyo*·nool
train	*trenul*	*tre*·nool

What time's the ... bus?	*Când este ... autobuz?*	kewnd *yes*·te ... ow·to·*booz*
first	*primul*	*pree*·mool
last	*ultimul*	*ool*·tee·mool
next	*următorul*	oor·muh·*to*·rool

At what time does it arrive/leave?

La ce oră soseşte/pleacă?   la che *o*·ruh so·*sesh*·te/ple·*a*·kuh

How long will it be delayed?

Cât întârzie?   kewt ewn·*tewr*·zye

What station/stop is this?

Ce gară/staţie e aceasta?   che *ga*·ruh/*sta*·tsye ye a·che·*as*·ta

What's the next station/stop?

Care este următoarea   *ca*·re *yes*·te oor·muh·to·*a*·re·a
gară/staţie?   *ga*·ruh/*sta*·tsye

Does it stop at (Galaţi)?		
Opreşte la (Galaţi)?		o-*presh*-te la (ga-*la*-tsi)
Please tell me when we get to (Iaşi).		
Vă rog, când ajungem la (Iaşi)?		vuh rog kewnd a-*zhoon*-jem la (*ya*-shi)
How long do we stop here?		
Cât stăm aici?		kewt stuhm a-*eech*
Is this seat available?		
E liber locul?		ye *lee*-ber lo-*kool*
That's my seat.		
Acesta e locul meu.		a-*ches*-ta ye lo-*kool* me-oo
I'd like a taxi …	*Aş dori un taxi …*	ash do-*ree* oon tak-*see* …
at (9am)	*la ora (nouă*	la o-ra (*no*-wuh
	dimineaţa)	dee-mee-*ne*-a-tsa)
now	*acum*	a-*koom*
tomorrow	*mâine*	mew-ee-ne
Is this taxi available?		
E liber taxiul?		ye *lee*-ber tak-*see*-ool
How much is it to …?		
Cât costă până la …?		kewt kos-tuh *pew*-nuh la …
Please put the meter on.		
Vă rog, daţi drumul la aparat.		vuh rog dats' *droo*-mool la a-pa-*rat*
Please take me to (this address).		
Vă rog, duceţi-mă la (această adresă).		vuh rog doo-*chets*'-muh la (a-che-*as*-tuh a-*dre*-suh)
Please …	*Vă rog, …*	vuh rog …
slow down	*încetiniţi*	ewn-che-tee-*neets*'
stop here	*opriţi aici*	o-*preets*' a-*eech*
wait here	*aşteptaţi aici*	ash-tep-*tats*' a-*eech*

car, motorbike & bicycle hire

I'd like to hire a …	*Aş dori să*	ash do-*ree* suh
	închiriez o …	ewn-kee-*ryez* o …
bicycle	*bicicletă*	bee-chee-*kle*-tuh
car	*maşină*	ma-*shee*-nuh
motorbike	*motocicletă*	mo-to-chee-*kle*-tuh

with ...	cu ...	koo ...
a driver	*şofer*	sho·*fer*
air conditioning	*aer condiţionat*	*a*·er kon·dee·tsyo·*nat*
antifreeze	*antigel*	an·tee·*jel*
snow chains	*lanţuri pentru zăpadă*	lan·*tsoo*·ri *pen*·troo zuh·*pa*·duh

How much for ... hire?	Cât costă chiria pe ...?	kewt *kos*·tuh kee·*ree*·a pe ...
hourly	*oră*	*o*·ruh
daily	*zi*	zee
weekly	*săptămână*	suhp·tuh·*mew*·nuh

air	*aer* n	*a*·er
oil	*ulei* n	oo·*ley*
petrol	*benzină* f	ben·*zee*·nuh
tyres	*cauciucuri* n pl	kow·*choo*·koo·ri

I need a mechanic.
Am nevoie de un mecanic. am ne·*vo*·ye de oon me·*ka*·neek

I've run out of petrol.
Am rămas fără benzină. am ruh·*mas fuh*·ruh ben·*zee*·nuh

I have a flat tyre.
Am un cauciuc dezumflat. am oon kow·*chook* de·zoom·*flat*

directions

Where's the ...?	Unde este ...?	*oon*·de *yes*·te ...
bank	*banca*	*ban*·ka
city centre	*centrul oraşului*	*chen*·trool o·*ra*·shoo·looy
hotel	*hotelul*	ho·*te*·lool
market	*piaţa*	*pya*·tsa
police station	*secţia de poliţie*	*sek*·tsya de po·*lee*·tsye
post office	*poşta*	*posh*·ta
public toilet	*toaleta publică*	to·a·*le*·ta *poo*·blee·kuh
tourist office	*biroul de informaţii turistice*	bee·*ro*·ool de een·for·*ma*·tsee too·*rees*·tee·che

Is this the road to (Arad)?
Acesta e drumul spre (Arad)?
a·*ches*·ta ye *droo*·mool spre (a·*rad*)

Can you show me (on the map)?
Puteți să-mi arătați (pe hartă)?
poo·*te*·tsi *suh*·mi a·ruh·*tats'* (pe *har*·tuh)

What's the address?
Care este adresa?
ka·re *yes*·te a·*dre*·sa

How far is it?
Cît e de departe?
kewt ye de de·*par*·te

How do I get there?
Cum ajung acolo?
koom a·*zhoong* a·*ko*·lo

Turn ...	*Virați la ...*	vee·*rats'* la ...
at the corner	*colț*	kolts
at the traffic lights	*semafor*	se·ma·*for*
left/right	*stînga/dreapta*	stewn·*ga*/dre·*ap*·ta

It's ...	*Este ...*	*yes*·te ...
behind ...	*în spatele ...*	ewn *spa*·te·le ...
far away	*departe*	de·*par*·te
here	*aici*	a·*eech*
in front of ...	*în fața ...*	ewn *fa*·tsa ...
left	*la stânga*	la stewn·*ga*
near (to ...)	*aproape (de ...)*	a·pro·*a*·pe (de ...)
next to ...	*lângă ...*	*lewn*·guh ...
on the corner	*pe colț*	pe kolts
opposite ...	*vis-à-vis de ...*	vee·za·*vee* de ...
right	*la dreapta*	la dre·*ap*·ta
straight ahead	*tot înainte*	tot ew·na·*een*·te
there	*acolo*	a·*ko*·lo

by bus	*cu autobuzul*	koo ow·to·*boo*·zool
by taxi	*cu taxiul*	koo tak·*see*·ool
by train	*cu trenul*	koo *tre*·nool
on foot	*pe jos*	pe zhos

north	*nord*	nord
south	*sud*	sood
east	*est*	est
west	*vest*	vest

Intrare	een-*tra*-re	**Entrance**
Ieşire	ye-*shee*-re	**Exit**
Deschis	des-*kees*	**Open**
Închis	ewn-*kees*	**Closed**
Camere libere	ka-me-re *lee*-be-re	**Rooms Available**
Ocupat	o-koo-*pat*	**No Vacancies**
Informaţii	een-for-*ma*-tsee	**Information**
Secţie de poliţie	sek-tsye de po-*lee*-tsye	**Police Station**
Interzis	een-ter-*zees*	**Prohibited**
Toalete	to-a-*le*-te	**Toilets**
Bărbaţi	buhr-*ba*-tsi	**Men**
Femei	fe-*mey*	**Women**
Cald/Rece	kald/*re*-che	**Hot/Cold**

accommodation

finding accommodation

Where's a ...?	*Unde se află ...?*	*oon*-de se *a*-fluh ...
camping ground	*un teren de camping*	oon te-*ren* de *kem*-peeng
guesthouse	*o pensiune*	o pen-*syoo*-ne
hotel	*un hotel*	oon ho-*tel*
youth hostel	*un hostel*	oon *hos*-tel

Can you recommend somewhere ...?	*Puteţi recomanda ceva ...?*	poo-*te*-tsi re-ko-man-*da* che-*va* ...
cheap	*ieftin*	*yef*-teen
good	*bun*	boon
nearby	*în apropiere*	ewn a-pro-*pye*-re

I'd like to book a room, please.
Aş dori să rezerv o cameră, vă rog.   ash do-*ree* suh re-*zerv* o *ka*-me-ruh vuh rog

I have a reservation.
Am o rezervaţie.   am o re-zer-*va*-tsye

My name's ...
Numele meu este ...   *noo*-me-le *me*-oo *yes*-te ...

Do you have a ... room?	Aveţi o cameră ...?	a-vets' o ka-me-ruh ...
single	de o persoană	de o per-so-a-nuh
double	dublă	doo-bluh
twin	dublă cu două paturi separate	doo-bluh koo do-wuh pa-too-ri se-pa-ra-te
How much is it per ...?	Cît costă ...?	kewt kos-tuh ...
night	pe noapte	pe no-ap-te
person	de persoană	de per-so-a-nuh
Can I pay ...?	Pot plăti ...?	pot pluh-tee ...
by credit card	cu carte de credit	koo kar-te de kre-deet
with a travellers cheque	cu un cec de călătorie	koo on chek de kuh-luh-to-ree-e

I'd like to stay for (two) nights.
Aş dori să stau (două) nopţi.   ash doo-ree suh stow (do-wuh) nop-tsi

From (2 July) to (6 July).
Din (doi iulie) până în   deen (doy yoo-lye) pew-nuh ewn
(şase iulie).   (sha-se yoo-lye)

Can I see it?
Pot să văd?   pot suh vuhd

Am I allowed to camp here?
Pot să-mi pun cortul aici?   pot suhm' poon kor-tool a-eech

Is there a camp site nearby?
Există un loc de camping   eg-zees-tuh oon lok de kem-peeng
prin apropiere?   preen a-pro-pye-re

requests & queries

When/Where is breakfast served?
Când/Unde se serveşte   kewnd/oon-de se ser-vesh-te
micul dejun?   mee-kool de-zhoon

Please wake me at (seven).
Vă rog treziţi-mă la (şapte).   vuh rog tre-zee-tsee-muh la (shap-te)

304

Could I have my key, please?
Puteți să-mi dați o cheie? — poo-*tets*'suhm' dats' o *ke*-ye

Can I get another (blanket)?
Puteți să-mi dați încă (o pătură)? — poo-*tets*'suhm' dats' *ewn*-kuh (o *puh*-too-ruh)

Is there a/an ...? — *Există ...?* — eg-*zees*-tuh ...
  elevator — *lift* — leeft
  safe — *seif* — seyf

The room is too ... — *Camera e prea ...* — *ka*-me-ra ye pre-*a* ...
  expensive — *scumpă* — *skoom*-puh
  noisy — *gălăgioasă* — guh-luhj-yo-*a*-suh
  small — *mică* — *mee*-kuh

The ... doesn't work. — *Nu funcționează ...* — noo foonk-tsyo-ne-*a*-zuh ...
  air conditioning — *aerul condiționat* — *a*-e-rool kon-dee-tsyo-*nat*
  fan — *ventilatorul* — ven-tee-la-*to*-rool
  toilet — *toaleta* — to-a-*le*-ta

This ... isn't clean. — *Acest ... nu este curat.* — a-*chest* ... noo yes-te koo-*rat*
  sheet — *cearceaf* — che-ar-che-*af*
  towel — *prosop* — pro-*sop*

This pillow isn't clean.
Această pernă nu este curată. — a-che-*as*-tuh *per*-nuh noo yes-te koo-*ra*-tuh

checking out

What time is checkout?
La ce oră trebuie eliberată camera? — la che *o*-ruh *tre*-boo-ye e-lee-be-*ra*-tuh *ka*-me-ra

Can I leave my luggage here?
Pot să-mi las bagajul aici? — pot suhm' las ba-*ga*-zhool a-*eech*

Could I have my ..., please? — *Vă rog, îmi puteți înapoia ...?* — vuh rog ewm' poo-*tets*' ew-na-po-*ya* ...
  deposit — *aconto-ul* — a-*kon*-to-ool
  passport — *pașaportul* — pa-sha-*por*-tool
  valuables — *obiectele de valoare* — o-*byek*-te-le de va-lo-*a*-re

communications & banking

the internet

Where's the local Internet café?
Unde se află un internet
café în apropiere?
oon·de se *a*·fluh oon een·ter·*net*
ka·*fe* ewn a·pro·*pye*·re

How much is it per hour?
Cât costă pe oră?
kewt *kos*·tuh pe *o*·ruh

I'd like to ...	*Aş dori ...*	ash do·*ree* ...
check my email	*să-mi verific*	suhm' ve·*ree*·feek
	e-mailul	*ee*·meyl·ool
get Internet access	*să accesez*	suh ak·che·*sez*
	internetul	een·ter·*ne*·tool
use a printer	*să folosesc o*	suh fo·lo·*sesk* o
	imprimantă	eem·pree·*man*·tuh
use a scanner	*să folosesc un scanner*	suh fo·lo·*sesk* oon *ske*·ner

mobile/cell phone

I'd like a ...	*Aş dori ...*	ash do·*ree* ...
mobile/cell phone	*să închiriez*	suh ewn·kee·*ryez*
for hire	*un telefon mobil*	oon te·le·*fon* mo·*beel*
SIM card for your	*un SIM card pentru*	oon seem kard *pen*·troo
network	*reţeaua locală*	re·tse·*a*·wà lo·*ka*·luh

What are the rates?
Care este tariful?
ka·re *yes*·te ta·*ree*·fool

telephone

What's your phone number?
Ce număr de telefon aveţi?
che *noo*·muhr de te·le·*fon* a·*vets'*

Where's the nearest public phone?
Unde se află cel mai apropiat
telefon public?
oon·de se *a*·fluh chel mai a·pro·*pyat*
te·le·*fon* *poo*·bleek

I'd like to buy a phonecard.
Aş dori să cumpăr o cartelă
de telefon.
ash do·*ree* suh *koom*·puhr o kar·*te*·luh
de te·le·*fon*

I want to ...	Aş dori ...	ash do-ree ...
call (Singapore)	să telefonez la (Singapore)	suh te-le-fo-nez la (seen-ga-po-re)
make a local call	să dau un telefon local	suh dow oon te-le-fon lo-kal
reverse the charges	o convorbire cu taxă inversă	o kon-vor-bee-re koo tak-suh een-ver-suh

How much does ... cost?	Cât costă ...?	kewt kos-tuh ...
a (three)-minute call	o convorbire de (trei) minute	o kon-vor-bee-re de (trey) mee-noo-te
each extra minute	fiecare minut suplimentar	fye-ka-re mee-noot soo-plee-men-tar

(10) lei per minute. — (Zece) lei pe minut. — (ze-che) ley pe mee-noot

post office

I want to send a ...	Aş dori să trimit ...	ash do-ree suh tree-meet ...
letter	o scrisoare	o skree-so-a-re
parcel	un colet	oon ko-let
postcard	o carte poştală	o kar-te posh-ta-luh

I want to buy a/an ...	Aş dori să cumpăr un ...	ash do-ree suh koom-puhr oon ...
envelope	plic	pleek
stamp	timbru	teem-broo

Please send it (to Australia) by ...	Vă rog, expediaţi-l (în Australia) ...	vuh rog ek-spe-dya-tseel (ewn ows-tra-lya) ...
airmail	cu avionul	koo a-vyo-nool
express mail	expres	eks-pres
registered mail	recomandat	re-ko-man-dat
surface mail	cu vaporul	koo va-po-rool

Is there any mail for me? — Am primit scrisori? — am pree-meet skree-so-ri

bank

Where's a/an ...?	Unde se află un ...?	oon-de se a-fluh oon ...
ATM	bancomat	ban-ko-mat
foreign exchange office	birou de schimb valutar	bee-roh de skeemb va-loo-tar

I'd like to ...	Aş dori să ...	ash do-ree suh ...
Where can I ...?	Unde aş putea ...?	oon-de ash poo-te-a ...
arrange a transfer	efectua un transfer	e-fek-twa oon trans-fer
cash a cheque	încasa un cec	ewn-ka-sa oon chek
change a travellers cheque	schimba un cec de călătorie	skeem-ba oon chek de kuh-luh-to-ree-e
change money	schimba bani	skeem-ba ba-ni
get a cash advance	obţine un imprumut financiar	ob-tsee-ne oon ewm-proo-moot fee-nan-chyar
withdraw money	retrage bani	re-tra-je ba-ni
What's the ...?	Care este ...?	ka-re yes-te ...
charge for that	taxa pentru	tak-sa pen-troo
commission	comision	ko-mee-syon
exchange rate	rata de schimb	ra-ta de skeemb
It's ...	Este ...	yes-te ...
(12) euros	(doisprezece) euro	(doy-spre-ze-che) e-oo-ro
(20) lei	(douăzeci) lei	(do-wuh-ze-chi) ley
free	gratis	gra-tees

What time does the bank open?
La ce oră se deschide banca? — la che o-ruh se des-kee-de ban-ka

Has my money arrived yet?
Mi-au sosit banii? — myow so-seet ba-nee

sightseeing

getting in

What time does it open/close?
La ce oră se deschide/închide? — la che o-ruh se des-kee-de/ewn-kee-de

What's the admission charge?
Cât costă intrarea? — kewt kos-tuh een-tra-re-a

Is there a discount for students/children?
Există reducere pentru studenţi/copii? — eg-zees-tuh re-doo-che-re pen-troo stoo-den-tsi/ko-pee

I'd like a ...	Aş dori ...	ash do-*ree* ...
catalogue	un catalog	oon ka-ta-*log*
guide	un ghid	oon geed
local map	o hartă a	o *har*-tuh a
	localităţii	lo-ka-lee-*tuh*-tsee

I'd like to see ...	Aş dori să văd ...	ash do-*ree* suh vuhd ...
What's that?	Ce-i asta?	chey *as*-ta
Can I take a photo?	Pot să fac o fotografie?	pot suh fak o fo-to-gra-*fye*

tours

When's the next ...?	Când este ...?	kewnd *yes*-te ...
day trip	următoarea	oor-muh-to-*a*-re-a
	excursie de zi	eks-*koor*-sye de zee
tour	următorul tur	oor-muh-*to*-rool toor

Is ... included?	Sunt incluse ...?	soont een-*kloo*-se ...
accommodation	cazarea	ka-*za*-re-a
the admission charge	taxa de intrare	*tak*-sa de een-*tra*-re
food	mâncarea	mewn-*ka*-re-a
transport	transportul	trans-*por*-tool

How long is the tour?
Cît durează turul?   kewt doo-re-*a*-zuh *too*-rool

What time should we be back?
La ce oră e întoarcerea?   la che *o*-ruh ye ewn-to-*ar*-che-re-a

sightseeing		
castle	castel n	kas-*tel*
cathedral	catedrală f	ka-te-*dra*-luh
church	biserică f	bee-*se*-ree-kuh
main square	piaţa centrală f	*pya*-tsa chen-*tra*-luh
monastery	mănăstire f	muh-nuhs-*tee*-re
monument	monument n	mo-noo-*ment*
museum	muzeu n	moo-*ze*-oo
old city	oraşul vechi n	o-*ra*-shool *ve*-ki
palace	palat n	pa-*lat*
ruins	ruine f pl	roo-*ee*-ne
statue	statuie f	sta-*too*-ye

shopping

enquiries

Where's a ... ?	Unde se află ...?	oon·de se a·fluh ...
bank	o bancă	o ban·kuh
bookshop	o librărie	o lee·bruh·ree·e
camera shop	un magazin foto	oon ma·ga·zeen fo·to
grocery store	un magazin	oon ma·ga·zeen
	alimentar	a·lee·men·tar
department store	un magazin	oon ma·ga·zeen
	universal	oo·nee·ver·sal
market	o piaţă	o pya·tsuh
newsagency	un stand de ziare	oon stand de zee·a·re
supermarket	un supermarket	oon soo·per·mar·ket

Where can I buy (a padlock)?
Unde pot cumpăra (un lacăt)?　　　oon·de pot koom·puh·ra (oon la·kuht)

I'm looking for ...
Caut ...　　　kowt ...

Can I look at it?
Pot să mă uit?　　　pot suh muh ooyt

Do you have any others?
Mai aveţi şi altele?　　　mai a·vets' shee al·te·le

Does it have a guarantee?
E cu garanţie?　　　ye koo ga·ran·tsee·e

Can I have it sent overseas?
Îl puteţi expedia peste hotare?　　　ewl poo·tets' eks·pe·dya pes·te ho·ta·re

Can I have my ... repaired?
Îmi puteţi repara ...?　　　ewm' poo·tets' re·pa·ra ...

It's faulty.
E defect.　　　ye de·fekt

I'd like ..., please.	Vă rog, aş dori ...	vuh rog ash do·ree ...
a bag	o geantă	o je·an·tuh
a refund	o rambursare	o ram·boor·sa·re
to return this	să returnez asta	suh re·toor·nez as·ta

LIMBA ROMÂNĂ – shopping

paying

How much is it?
Cât costă?
kewt *kos*·tuh

Can you write down the price?
Puteți scrie prețul?
poo·*tets'* skree·e *pre*·tsool

That's too expensive.
E prea scump.
ye pre·*a* skoomp

What's your lowest price?
Care e prețul cel mai redus?
ka·re ye *pre*·tsool chel mai re·*doos*

I'll give you (five) euros.
Vă dau (cinci) euro.
vuh dow (cheench') e·oo·ro

I'll give you (50) lei.
Vă dau (cincizeci) lei.
vuh dow (cheench·ze·chi) ley

There's a mistake in the bill.
Chitanța conține o greșeală.
kee·*tan*·tsa kon·*tsee*·ne o gre·she·*a*·luh

Do you accept ...?	*Acceptați ...?*	ak·chep·*tats'* ...
credit cards	*cărți de credit*	*kuhr*·tsi de *kre*·deet
debit cards	*cărți de debit*	*kuhr*·tsi de *de*·beet
travellers cheques	*cecuri de*	*che*·koo·ri de
	călătorie	kuh·luh·to·*ree*·e

I'd like ..., please.	*Vă rog, dați-mi ...*	vuh rog *da*·tsee·mi ...
a receipt	*chitanța*	kee·*tan*·tsa
my change	*restul*	*res*·tool

clothes & shoes

Can I try it on?
Pot să probez?
pot suh pro·*bez*

My size is (40).
Port numărul (patruzeci).
port noo·muh·rool (*pa*·troo·ze·chi)

It doesn't fit.
Nu mi se potrivește.
noo mee se po·tree·*vesh*·te

small	*mic*	meek
medium	*mijlociu*	meezh·lo·*chyoo*
large	*mare*	*ma*·re

books & music

I'd like a . . .	Aş dori . . .	ash do·ree . . .
newspaper	un ziar	oon zee·ar
(in English)	(în engleză)	(ewn en·gle·zuh)
pen	un pix	oon peeks

Is there an English-language bookshop?

Există o librărie cu cărţi   eg·zees·tuh o lee·bruh·ree·e koo kuhr·tsi
în limba engleză?   ewn leem·ba en·gle·zuh

I'm looking for something by (Enescu/Caragiale).

Caut ceva de (Enescu/Caragiale).   kowt che·va de (e·nes·koo/ka·raj·ya·le)

Can I listen to this?

Pot asculta asta?   pot as·kool·ta as·ta

photography

Can you . . . ?	Îmi puteţi . . . ?	ewm' poo·tets' . . .
burn a CD from	imprima un	eem·pree·ma oon
my memory card	CD după	see·dee doo·puh
	cardul de memorie	kar·dool de me·mo·ree·e
develop this film	developa acest film	de·ve·lo·pa a·chest feelm
load my film	încărca filmul	ewn·kuhr·ka feel·mool
	în aparat	ewn a·pa·rat

I need a/an . . . film	Am nevoie de un film . . .	am ne·vo·ye de oon feelm . . .
for this camera.	pentru acest aparat.	pen·troo a·chest a·pa·rat
APS	APS	a·pe·se
B&W	alb-negru	alb·ne·groo
colour	color	ko·lor
slide	diapozitiv	dee·a·po·zee·teev
(200) speed	de (două sute) ASA	de (do·wuh soo·te) a·sa

When will it be ready?	Când va fi gata?	kewnd va fee ga·ta

meeting people

greetings, goodbyes & introductions

Hello/Hi.	Bună ziua/Bună.	boo-nuh zee-wa/boo-nuh
Good night.	Noapte bună.	no-ap-te boo-nuh
Goodbye/Bye.	La revedere/Pa.	la re-ve-de-re/pa
Mr/Mrs	Domnul/Doamna	dom-nool/do-am-na
Miss	Domnişoara	dom-nee-sho-a-ra
How are you?	Ce mai faceţi?	che mai fa-chets'
Fine. And you?	Bine.	bee-ne
	Dumneavoastră?	doom-ne-a-vo-as-truh
What's your name?	Cum vă numiţi?	koom vuh noo-meets'
My name is ...	Numele meu este ...	noo-me-le me-oo yes-te ...
I'm pleased to	Încântat/	ewn-kewn-tat/
meet you.	Încântată	ewn-kewn-ta-tuh
	de cunoştinţă. m/f	de koo-nosh-teen-tsuh
This is my ...	Vă prezint ...	vuh pre-zeent ...
boyfriend	prietenul meu	pree-e-te-nool me-oo
brother	fratele meu	fra-te-le me-oo
daughter	fiica mea	fee-ee-ka me-a
father	tatăl meu	ta-tuhl me-oo
friend	un prieten m	oon pree-e-ten
	o prietenă f	o pree-e-te-nuh
girlfriend	prietena mea	pree-e-te-na me-a
husband	soţul meu	so-tsool me-oo
mother	mama mea	ma-ma me-a
partner (intimate)	partenerul meu m	par-te-ne-rool me-oo
	partenera mea f	par-te-ne-ra me-a
sister	sora mea	so-ra me-a
son	fiul meu	fee-ool me-oo
wife	soţia mea	so-tsee-a me-a
Here's my ...	Acesta/Aceasta este	a-ches-ta/a-che-as-ta yes-te
	... meu/mea. m/f	... me-oo/me-a
What's your ...?	Care e ...?	ka-re ye ...
(email) address	adresa ta (de e-mail)	a-dre-sa ta (de ee-meyl)
phone number	numărul tău	noo-muh-rool tuh-oo
	de telefon	de te-le-fon

occupations

What's your occupation?	*Ce meserie aveţi?*	che me·se·ree·e a·vets'
I'm a/an ...	*Sunt ...*	soont ...
artist	*artist* m&f	ar·teest
businessperson	*om de afaceri* m&f	om de a·fa·che·ri
farmer	*fermier* m&f	fer·myer
office worker	*funcţionar* m	foonk·tsyo·nar
	funcţionară f	foonk·tsyo·na·ruh
scientist	*om de ştiinţă* m&f	om de shteen·tsuh
student	*student/studentă* m/f	stoo·dent/stoo·den·tuh
tradesperson	*comerciant* m&f	ko·mer·chyant

background

Where are you from?	*De unde sunteţi?*	de oon·de soon·tets'
I'm from ...	*Sunt din ...*	soont deen ...
Australia	*Australia*	ows·tra·lya
Canada	*Canada*	ka·na·da
England	*Anglia*	ang·lya
New Zealand	*Noua Zeelandă*	no·wa ze·e·lan·duh
the USA	*Statele Unite*	sta·te·le oo·nee·te
Are you married?	*Sunteţi căsătorit/ căsătorită?* m/f	soon·tets' kuh·suh·to·reet/ kuh·suh·to·ree·tuh
I'm ...	*Sunt ...*	soont ...
married	*căsătorit* m	kuh·suh·to·reet
	căsătorită f	kuh·suh·to·ree·tuh
single	*necăsătorit* m	ne·kuh·suh·to·reet
	necăsătorită f	ne·kuh·suh·to·ree·tuh

age

How old ...?	*Ce vârstă ...?*	che vewr·stuh ...
are you	*aveţi*	a·vets'
is your daughter	*are fiica*	a·re fee·ee·ka
	dumneavoastră	doom·ne·a·vo·as·truh
is your son	*are fiul*	a·re fee·ool
	dumneavoastră	doom·ne·a·vo·as·truh

I'm ... years old.
    Am ... ani.   am ... *a*·ni

He/She is ... years old.
    El/Ea are ... ani.   yel/ya *a*·re ... *a*·ni

feelings

I'm (not) ...	*(Nu) Îmi este ...*	(noo) ew·mi *yes*·te ...
Are you ...?	*Vă este ...?*	vuh *yes*·te ...
cold	*frig*	freeg
hot	*cald*	kald
hungry	*foame*	fo·*a*·me
thirsty	*sete*	se·te

I'm (not) ...	*(Nu) Sunt ...*	(noo) soont ...
Are you ...?	*Sunteți ...?*	*soon*·tets' ...
happy	*fericit* m	fe·ree·*cheet*
	fericită f	fe·ree·*chee*·tuh
OK	*bine* m&f	*bee*·ne
sad	*trist/tristă* m/f	treest/*trees*·tuh
tired	*obosit/obosită* m/f	o·bo·*seet*/o·bo·*see*·tuh

entertainment

going out

Where can I find ...?	*Unde pot găsi ...?*	*oon*·de pot guh·*see* ...
clubs	*cluburi*	*kloo*·boo·ri
gay venues	*cluburi gay*	*kloo*·boo·ri gey
pubs	*localuri*	lo·*ka*·loo·ri

I feel like going to a/the ...	*Aș merge la ...*	ash *mer*·je la ...
concert	*un concert*	oon kon·*chert*
movies	*un film*	oon feelm
party	*o petrecere*	o pe·*tre*·che·re
restaurant	*un restaurant*	oon res·tow·*rant*
theatre	*un teatru*	oon te·*a*·troo

interests

Do you like ...?	Vă place ...?	vuh pla·che ...
I (don't) like ...	Mie (nu) îmi place ...	mee·e (noo) ew·mi pla·che ...
art	arta	ar·ta
cooking	bucătăria	boo·kuh·tuh·ree·a
movies	cinema-ul	chee·ne·ma·ool
reading	lectura	lek·too·ra
shopping	la cumpărături	la koom·puh·ruh·too·ri
sport	sportul	spor·tool
travelling	să călătoresc	suh kuh·luh·to·resk
Do you like to ...?	Vă place ...?	vuh pla·che ...
dance	dansul	dan·sool
go to concerts	mersul la concerte	mer·sool la kon·cher·te
listen to music	să ascultați muzică	as·kool·tats' moo·zee·kuh

food & drink

finding a place to eat

Can you recommend a ...?	Îmi puteți recomanda ...?	ew·mi poo·tets' re·ko·man·da ...
bar	un bar	oon bar
café	o cafenea	o ka·fe·ne·a
restaurant	un restaurant	oon res·tow·rant
I'd like ..., please.	Vă rog, aş dori ...	vuh rog ash do·ree ...
a table for (four)	o masă de (patru) persoane	o ma·suh de (pa·troo) per·so·a·ne
the (non)smoking section	la (ne)fumători	la (ne·)foo·muh·to·ri

ordering food

breakfast	micul dejun n	mee·kool de·zhoon
lunch	dejun n	de·zhoon
dinner	cină f	chee·nuh
snack	gustare f	goos·ta·re

What would you recommend?
Ce recomandaţi? che re·ko·man·*dats'*

I'd like (the) ..., please. *Vă rog, aş dori ...* vuh rog ash do·*ree* ...
  bill *nota de plată* *no*·ta de *pla*·tuh
  drink list *lista de băuturi* *lees*·ta de buh·oo·*too*·ri
  menu *meniul* me·*nee*·ool
  that dish *acel fel de mâncare* a·*chel* fel de mewn·*ka*·re

drinks

(cup of) coffee ...	*(o ceaşcă de) cafea ...*	(o che·*ash*·kuh de) ka·fe·*a* ...
(cup of) tea ...	*(o cană de) ceai ...*	(o *ka*·nuh de) che·*ai* ...
with milk	*cu lapte*	koo *lap*·te
without sugar	*fără zahăr*	*fuh*·ruh za·*huhr*
(orange) juice	*suc (de portocale)* n	sook (de por·to·*ka*·le)
soft drink	*băutură*	buh·oo·*too*·ruh
	nealcoolică f	ne·al·ko·o·lee·kuh
(boiled/mineral)	*apă (fiartă/*	*a*·puh (fyar·tuh/
water	*minerală)* f	mee·ne·*ra*·luh)

in the bar

I'll have ...	*Aş dori ...*	ash do·*ree* ...
I'll buy you a drink.	*Vă ofer o băutură.*	vuh o·*fer* o buh·oo·*too*·ruh
What would you like?	*Ce v-ar plăcea?*	che var *pluh*·che·a
Cheers!	*Noroc!*	no·*rok*
brandy	*ţuică* f	*tsooy*·kuh
cocktail	*cocteil* n	kok·*teyl*
a shot of (whisky)	*un (whisky) mic*	oon (*wee*·skee) meek
a ... of beer	*... de bere*	... de *be*·re
bottle	*o sticlă*	o *stee*·kluh
glass	*un pahar*	oon pa·*har*
a bottle of ... wine	*o sticlă de vin ...*	o *stee*·kluh de veen ...
a glass of ... wine	*un pahar de vin ...*	*oon* pa·*har* de veen ...
red	*roşu*	*ro*·shoo
sparkling	*spumos*	spoo·*mos*
white	*alb*	alb

self-catering

What's the local speciality?
Care e specialitatea locală? ka·re ye spe·chya·lee·ta·te·a lo·ka·luh

What's that?
Ce-i aia? chey a·ya

How much is (a kilo of cheese)?
Cât costă (kilogramul de brânză)? kewt kos·tuh (kee·lo·gra·mool de brewn·zuh)

I'd like ...	Aş dori ...	ash do·ree ...
(100) grams	(o sută) de grame	(o soo·tuh) de gra·me
(two) kilos	(două) kile	(do·wuh) kee·le
(three) pieces	(trei) bucăţi	(trey) boo·kuh·tsi
(six) slices	(şase) felii	(sha·se) fe·lee

Less.	Mai puţin.	mai poo·tseen
Enough.	Destul.	des·tool
More.	Mai mult.	mai moolt

special diets & allergies

Is there a vegetarian restaurant near here?
Există pe aici un restaurant eg·zees·tuh pe a·eech oon res·tow·rant
vegetarian? ve·je·ta·ryan

Do you have vegetarian food?
Aveţi mâncare vegetariană? a·ve·tsi mewn·ka·re ve·je·ta·rya·nuh

Could you prepare	Puteţi servi ceva	poo·tets' ser·vee che·va
a meal without ...?	fără ...?	fuh·ruh ...
butter	unt	oont
eggs	ouă	o·wuh
meat stock	zeamă de carne	ze·a·muh de kar·ne

I'm allergic to ...	Am alergie la ...	am a·ler·jee·ye la ...
dairy produce	produse lactate	pro·doo·se lak·ta·te
gluten	gluten	gloo·ten
MSG	MSG (monosodiu	em·es·je (mo·no·so·dyoo
	glutamat)	gloo·ta·mat)
nuts	nuci şi alune	noo·chi shee a·loo·ne
seafood	peşte şi fructe	pesh·te shee frook·te
	de mare	de ma·re

menu decoder

ardei umpluţi m	ar-*dey* oom-*ploo*-tsi	*peppers stuffed with minced meat, rice & vegetables*
cabanos prăjit m	ka-ba-*nos* pruh-*zheet*	*fried sausages*
caşcaval pane n	kash-ka-*val* pa-*ne*	*breaded fried cheese*
cataif n	ka-ta-*eef*	*puff pastry & cream*
chifteluţe f pl	keef-te-*loo*-tse	*fried meatballs*
ciorbă de burtă f	*chyor*-buh de *boor*-tuh	*sour tripe soup*
ciorbă de legume f	*chyor*-buh de le-*goo*-me	*sour vegetable soup*
ciorbă de perişoare f	*chyor*-buh de pe-ree-sho-*a*-re	*sour soup with meatballs*
ciorbă de peşte f	*chyor*-buh de *pesh*-te	*sour fish soup*
ciorbă de potroace f	*chyor*-buh de po-tro-*a*-che	*very sour cabbage soup with chicken entrails*
ciorbă de văcuţă f	*chyor*-buh de vuh-*koo*-tsuh	*sour beef soup*
ciuperci f pl	chyoo-*per*-chi	*mushrooms*
cârnaţi m pl	kewr-*na*-tsi	*sausages*
clătite f pl	kluh-*tee*-te	*crepes*
crap prăjit m	krap pruh-*zheet*	*fried carp*
ficat la grătar m	fee-*kat* la gruh-*tar*	*grilled liver*
friptură de porc cu salată f	freep-*too*-ruh de pork koo sa-*la*-tuh	*roasted pork with vegetable salad*
galuste cu prune f pl	guh-*loosh*-te koo *proo*-ne	*plum-filled dumplings*
ghiveci n	gee-*ve*-chi	*vegetable casserole*
mititei/mici m pl	mee-tee-*tey*/mee-chi	*spicy skinless saussages*

musaca f	moo-sa-*ka*	oven-baked beef or pork mince with potatoes or eggplant
mușchi de miel/ porc/vacă m	*moosh*-ki de myel/ pork/*va*-kuh	filet of lamb/pork/beef
papanași m pl	pa-pa-*na*-shi	boiled or fried cheese dumplings
pastramă de porc f	pas-*tra*-muh de pork	pork pastrami
pate de ficat n	pa-*te* de fee-*kat*	liver pâté
pateuri cu brînză n pl	pa-*te*-oo-ri koo *brewn*-zuh	cheese pastries
piept de pui n	pyept de pooy	chicken fillet
piftie de porc f	peef-*tee*-e de pork	jellied pork
plăcintă f	pluh-*cheen*-tuh	pie
roșii umplute cu brînză f pl	ro-shee oom-*ploo*-te koo *brewn*-zuh	tomatoes stuffed with cheese
salată de vinete f	sa-*la*-tuh de *vee*-ne-te	eggplant dip
salată verde cu roșii f	sa-*la*-tuh *ver*-de koo ro-shee	lettuce & tomato salad
sarailie f	sa-ra-ee-*lee*-e	almond cake soaked in syrup
saramură de pește f	sa-ra-*moo*-ruh de *pesh*-te	grilled fish in brine
sarmale f pl	sar-*ma*-le	cabbage or vine leaves stuffed with pork & beef mince
supă de cartofi f	*soo*-puh de kar-*to*-fi	potato soup
supă de legume f	*soo*-puh de le-*goo*-me	vegetable soup
tocană f	to-*ka*-nuh	meat & onion stew
tuslama de burtă f	too-sla-*ma* de *boor*-tuh	tripe stew
varză à la Cluj f	*var*-zuh a la kloozh	oven-baked cabbage with minced meat & sour cream

emergencies

basics

English	Romanian	Pronunciation
Help!	Ajutor!	a·zhoo·tor
Stop!	Stop!	stop
Go away!	Pleacă!	ple·a·kuh
Thief!	Hoţii!	ho·tsee
Fire!	Foc!	fok
Watch out!	Atenţie!	a·ten·tsye
Call ...!	Chemaţi ...!	ke·mats' ...
a doctor	un doctor	oon dok·tor
an ambulance	o ambulanţă	o am·boo·lan·tsuh
the police	poliţia	po·lee·tsya

It's an emergency!
E un caz de urgenţă!
ye oon kaz de oor·jen·tsuh

Could you help me, please?
Ajutaţi-mă, vă rog!
a·zhoo·ta·tsee·muh vuh rog

I have to use the telephone.
Trebuie să dau un telefon.
tre·boo·ye suh dow oon te·le·fon

I'm lost.
M-am rătăcit.
mam ruh·tuh·cheet

Where are the toilets?
Unde este o toaletă?
oon·de yes·te o to·a·le·tuh

police

Where's the police station?
Unde e secţia de poliţie?
oon·de ye sek·tsya de po·lee·tsye

I want to report an offence.
Vreau să raportez o contravenţie.
vre·ow suh ra·por·tez o kon·tra·ven·tsye

I have insurance.
Am asigurare.
am a·see·goo·ra·re

English	Romanian	Pronunciation
I've been ...	Am fost ...	am fost ...
assaulted	atacat/atacată m/f	a·ta·kat/a·ta·ka·tuh
raped	violat/violată m/f	vee·o·lat/vee·o·la·tuh
robbed	jefuit/jefuită m/f	zhe·foo·eet/zhe·foo·ee·tuh

I've lost my ... My ... was/were stolen.	Mi-am pierdut ... Mi s-a/s-au furat ... sg/pl	myam pyer-doot ... mee sa/sow foo-rat ...
bags	valizele pl	va-lee-ze-le
credit card	cartea de credit sg	kar-te-a de kre-deet
handbag	geanta sg	je-an-ta
jewellery	bijuteriile pl	bee-zhoo-te-ree-ee-le
passport	paşaportul sg	pa-sha-por-tool
travellers cheques	cecurile de călătorie pl	che-koo-ree-le de kuh-luh-to-ree-e
wallet	portofelul sg	por-to-fe-lool

I want to contact my consulate/embassy.

Aş dori să contactez consulatul/ambasada.

ash do-ree suh kon-tak-tez kon-soo-la-tool/am-ba-sa-da

health

medical needs

Where's the nearest ...?	Unde se află cel mai apropiat ...?	oon-de se a-fluh chel mai a-pro-pyat ...
dentist	dentist	den-teest
doctor	doctor	dok-tor
hospital	spital	spee-tal

Where's the nearest (night) pharmacist?

Unde se află cea mai apropiată farmacie (cu program non-stop)?

oon-de se a-fluh che-a mai a-pro-pya-tuh far-ma-chee-e (koo pro-gram non stop)

I need a doctor (who speaks English).

Am nevoie de un doctor (care să vorbească engleza).

am ne-vo-ye de oon dok-tor (ka-re suh vor-be-as-kuh en-gle-za)

Could I see a female doctor?

Pot fi consultată de o doctoriţă?

pot fee kon-sool-ta-tuh de o dok-to-ree-tsuh

I've run out of my medication.

Mi s-a terminat doctoria prescrisă.

mee sa ter-mee-nat dok-to-ree-a pre-skree-suh

symptoms, conditions & allergies

I'm sick.	*Mă simt rău.*	muh seemt *ruh*·oo
It hurts here.	*Mă doare aici.*	muh do·*a*·re a·*eech*

I have (a) ...	*Sufăr de ...*	*soo*·fuhr de ...
asthma	*astm*	astm
bronchitis	*bronşită*	bron·*shee*·tuh
constipation	*constipaţie*	kon·stee·*pa*·tsye
cough	*tuse*	*too*·se
diarrhoea	*diaree*	dee·a·*re*·e
fever	*febră*	*fe*·bruh
headache	*durere de cap*	doo·*re*·re de kap
heart condition	*inimă*	ee·*nee*·muh
nausea	*greaţă*	gre·*a*·tsuh
pain	*dureri*	doo·*re*·ri
sore throat	*durere în gât*	doo·*re*·re ewn gewt
toothache	*durere de dinţi*	doo·*re*·re de *deen*·tsi

I'm allergic to ...	*Am alergie la ...*	am a·ler·*jee*·ye la ...
antibiotics	*antibiotice*	an·tee·*byo*·tee·che
anti-inflammatories	*anti-inflamatorii*	an·tee·een·fla·ma·*to*·ree
aspirin	*aspirină*	as·pee·*ree*·nuh
bees	*albine*	al·*bee*·ne
codeine	*codeină*	ko·de·ee·nuh
penicillin	*penicilină*	pe·nee·chee·*lee*·nuh

antiseptic	*antiseptic* n	an·tee·*sep*·teek
bandage	*bandaj* n	ban·*dazh*
condoms	*prezervative* n pl	pre·zer·va·*tee*·ve
contraceptives	*contraceptive* n pl	kon·tra·chep·*tee*·ve
diarrhoea medicine	*medicament*	me·dee·ka·*ment*
	împotriva	ewm·po·*tree*·va
	diareei n	dee·a·*re*·ey
insect repellent	*loţiune*	lo·*tsyoo*·ne
	împotriva	ewm·po·*tree*·va
	insectelor f	een·*sek*·te·lor
laxatives	*laxative* n pl	lak·sa·*tee*·ve
painkillers	*analgezice* n pl	a·nal·*je*·zee·che
rehydration salts	*săruri rehidratante* f pl	suh·*roo*·ri re·hee·dra·*tan*·te
sleeping tablets	*somnifere* n pl	som·nee·*fe*·re

english–romanian dictionary

Romanian nouns in this dictionary have their gender indicated by ⓜ (masculine), ⓕ (feminine) or ⓝ (neuter). If it's a plural noun, you'll also see pl. Note that neuter nouns take feminine adjectives in the plural and masculine adjectives in the singular. Words are also marked as a (adjective), v (verb), sg (singular), pl (plural), inf (informal) or pol (polite) where necessary.

A

accident *accident* ⓝ ak-chee-dent
accommodation *cazare* ⓕ ka-za-re
adaptor *adaptor* ⓝ a-dap-tor
address *adresă* ⓕ a-dre-suh
after *după* doo-puh
air-conditioned *cu aer condiţionat* koo a-er kon-dee-tsyo-nat
airplane *avion* ⓝ a-vyon
airport *aeroport* ⓝ a-e-ro-port
alcohol *alcool* ⓝ al-ko-ol
all *tot/toată* ⓜ/ⓕ tot/to-a-tă
allergy *alergie* ⓕ a-ler-jee-e
ambulance *ambulanţă* ⓕ am-boo-lan-tsuh
and *şi* shee
ankle *glezna* ⓕ glez-na
arm *braţ* ⓝ brats
ashtray *scrumieră* ⓕ skroo-mye-ruh
ATM *bancomat* ⓝ ban-ko-mat

B

baby *bebeluş* ⓜ be-be-loosh
back (body) *spatele* ⓝ spa-te-le
backpack *rucsac* ⓝ rook-sak
bad *rău/rea* ⓜ/ⓕ ruh-oo/re-a
bag *geantă* ⓕ je-an-tuh
baggage claim *bandă de bagaje* ⓕ ban-duh de ba-ga-zhe
bank *bancă* ⓕ ban-kuh
bar *bar* ⓝ bar
bathroom *baie* ⓕ ba-ye
battery *baterie* ⓕ ba-te-ree-e
beautiful *frumos/frumoasă* ⓜ/ⓕ froo-mos/froo-mo-a-suh
bed *pat* ⓝ pat
beer *bere* ⓕ be-re
before *înainte* ew-na-een-te
behind *înapoi* ew-na-poy
bicycle *bicicletă* ⓕ bee-chee-kle-tuh
big *mare* ⓜ&ⓕ ma-re
bill *plată* ⓕ pla-tuh
black *negru/neagră* ⓜ/ⓕ ne-groo/ne-a-gruh
blanket *pătură* ⓕ puh-too-ruh

blood group *grupa sanguină* ⓕ groo-pa san-gooy-nuh
blue *albastru/albastră* ⓜ/ⓕ al-bas-troo/al-bas-truh
boat *barcă* ⓕ bar-kuh
book (make a reservation) v *rezerva* re-zer-va
bottle *sticlă* ⓕ stee-kluh
bottle opener *tirbuşon* ⓝ teer-boo-shon
boy *băiat* ⓜ buh-yat
brakes (car) *frâne* ⓕ pl frew-ne
breakfast *micul dejun* ⓜ mee-kool de-zhoon
broken (faulty) *defect/defectă* ⓜ/ⓕ de-fekt/de-fek-tuh
bus *autobuz* ⓝ ow-to-booz
business *afacere* ⓕ a-fa-che-re
buy v *cumpăra* koom-puh-ra

C

café *cafenea* ⓕ ka-fe-ne-a
camera *aparat foto* ⓝ a-pa-rat fo-to
camp site *loc de camping* ⓝ lok de kem-peeng
cancel v *anula* a-noo-la
can opener *deschizător de conserve* ⓝ des-kee-zuh-tor de kon-ser-ve
car *maşină* ⓕ ma-shee-nuh
cash *bani cash* ⓜ pl ba-ni kesh
cash (a cheque) v *încasa (un cec)* ewn-ka-sa (oon check)
cell phone *celular* ⓝ che-loo-lar
centre *centru* ⓝ chen-troo
change (money) v *schimba (bani)* skeem-ba (ba-ni)
cheap *ieftin/ieftină* ⓜ/ⓕ yef-teen/yef-tee-nuh
check (bill) *nota de plată* ⓕ no-ta de pla-tuh
chest *cufăr* ⓝ koo-fuhr
child *copil* ⓝ ko-peel
cigarette *ţigaretă* ⓕ tsee-ga-re-tuh
city *oraş* ⓝ o-rash
clean *curat/curată* ⓜ/ⓕ koo-rat/koo-ra-tuh
closed *închis/închisă* ⓜ/ⓕ ewn-kees/ewn-kee-suh
coffee *cafea* ⓕ ka-fe-a
coins *monezi* ⓕ pl mo-ne-zi
cold a *rece* ⓜ&ⓕ re-che

collect call *telefon cu taxă inversă* ⓕ
te-le-fon koo *tak*-suh een-ver-suh
come *veni* ve-nee
computer *calculator* ⓝ kal-koo-*la*-tor
condom *prezervativ* ⓝ pre-zer-va-teev
contact lenses *lentile de contact* ⓕ pl
len-*tee*-le de kon-*takt*
cook v *găti* guh-*tee*
cost *cost* ⓝ kost
credit card *carte de credit* ⓕ *kar*-te de *kre*-deet
cup *cană* ⓕ *ka*-nuh
currency exchange *schimb valutar* ⓝ
skeemb va-loo-*tar*

D

dangerous *periculos/periculoasă* ⓜ/ⓕ
pe-ree-koo-*los*/pe-ree-koo-lo-*a*-suh
date (time) *data* ⓕ *da*-ta
day *ziua* ⓕ *zee*-wa
delay *întârziere* ⓕ ewn-tewr-*zye*-re
dentist *dentist* ⓝ den-*teest*
depart *pleca* ple-*ka*
diaper *scutec* ⓝ *skoo*-tek
dictionary *dicţionar* ⓝ deek-tsyo-*nar*
dinner *cină* ⓕ *chee*-nuh
direct *direct/directă* ⓜ/ⓕ dee-*rekt*/dee-*rek*-tuh
dirty *murdar/murdară* ⓜ/ⓕ *moor*-dar/*moor*-da-ruh
disabled *invalid/invalidă* ⓜ/ⓕ
een-va-*leed*/een-va-*lee*-duh
discount *reducere* ⓕ re-doo-*che*-re
doctor *doctor* ⓝ *dok*-tor
double bed *pat dublu* ⓝ pat *doo*-bloo
double room *cameră dublă* ⓕ *ka*-me-ruh *doo*-bluh
drink *băutură* ⓕ buh-oo-*too*-ruh
drive v *conduce* kon-*doo*-che
drivers licence *carnet de conducere* ⓝ
kar-*net* de kon-*doo*-che-re
drugs (illicit) *droguri* ⓝ pl *dro*-goo-ri
dummy (pacifier) *suzetă* ⓕ *soo*-ze-tuh

E

ear *ureche* ⓕ oo-*re*-ke
east *est* est
eat v *mânca* mewn-*ka*
economy class *clasa economy* ⓕ *kla*-sa e-ko-no-mee
electricity *electricitate* ⓕ e-lek-tree-chee-*ta*-te
elevator *lift* ⓝ leeft
email *e-mail* ⓝ *ee*-meyl
embassy *ambasadă* ⓕ am-ba-*sa*-duh
emergency *urgenţă* ⓕ oor-*jen*-tsuh
English (language) *engleza* ⓕ en-*gle*-za
entrance *intrare* ⓕ een-*tra*-re

evening *seară* ⓕ se-*a*-ruh
exchange rate *rata de schimb* ⓕ *ra*-ta de skeemb
exit *ieşire* ⓕ ye-shee-re
expensive *scump/scumpă* ⓜ/ⓕ skoomp/*skoom*-puh
express mail *poştă expres* ⓕ *posh*-tuh eks-*pres*
eye *ochi* ⓝ o-ki

F

far *departe* de-*par*-te
fast *repede* re-pe-de
father *tată* ⓜ *ta*-tuh
film (camera) *film* ⓝ feelm
finger *deget* ⓝ *de*-jet
first-aid kit *trusă de prim ajutor* ⓕ
troo-suh de preem a-zhoo-*tor*
first class *clasa întâi* ⓕ *kla*-sa ewn-*tew*-ee
fish *peşte* ⓝ *pesh*-te
food *mâncare* ⓕ mewn-*ka*-re
foot *picior* ⓝ pee-*chyor*
fork *furculiţă* ⓕ foor-koo-*lee*-tsuh
free (of charge) *gratis* *gra*-tees
friend *prieten/prietenă* ⓜ/ⓕ pree-e-ten/pree-e-te-nuh
fruit *fructe* ⓕ pl *frook*-te
full *plin/plină* ⓜ/ⓕ pleen/*plee*-nuh
funny *nostim/nostimă* ⓜ/ⓕ *nos*-teem/*nos*-tee-muh

G

gift *cadou* ⓝ ka-*doh*
girl *fată* ⓕ *fa*-tuh
glass (drinking) *pahar* ⓝ pa-*har*
glasses *ochelari* ⓝ pl o-ke-*la*-ri
go *merge* mer-je
good *bun/bună* ⓜ/ⓕ boon/*boo*-nuh
green *verde* ⓜ&ⓕ *ver*-de
guide *ghid* ⓝ geed

H

half *jumătate* ⓕ zhoo-muh-*ta*-te
hand *mână* ⓕ *mew*-nuh
handbag *poşetă* ⓕ po-*she*-tuh
happy *bucuros/bucuroasă* ⓜ/ⓕ
boo-koo-*ros*/boo-koo-ro-*a*-suh
have *avea* a-ve-*a*
he *el* yel
head *cap* ⓝ kap
heart *inimă* ⓕ *ee*-nee-muh
heat *căldură* ⓕ kuhl-*doo*-ruh
heavy *greu/grea* ⓜ/ⓕ *gre*-oo/gre-*a*
help v *ajuta* a-*zhoo*-ta
here *aici* a-*eech'*

high *înalt/înaltă* ⓜ/ⓕ ew-*nalt*/ew-*nal*-tuh
highway *şosea* ⓕ sho-se-*a*
hike ∨ *merge pe jos* *mer*-je pe zhos
holiday *vacanţă* ⓕ va-*kan*-tsuh
homosexual *homosexual* ⓝ ho-mo-sek-*swal*
hospital *spital* ⓝ spee-*tal*
hot *fierbinte* ⓜ/ⓕ fyer-*been*-te
hotel *hotel* ⓝ ho-*tel*
hungry *înfometat/înfometată* ⓜ/ⓕ
  ewn-fo-me-*tat*/ewn-fo-me-*ta*-tuh
husband *soţ* ⓜ sots

I

I *eu* ye-*oo*
identification (card) *buletin de identitate* ⓝ
  boo-le-*teen* de ee-den-tee-*ta*-te
ill *bolnav/bolnavă* ⓜ/ⓕ bol-*nav*/ bol-*na*-vuh
important *important/importantă* ⓜ/ⓕ
  eem-por-*tant*/eem-por-*tan*-tuh
included *inclus/inclusă* ⓜ/ⓕ een-*kloos*/een-*kloo*-suh
injury *rană* ⓕ *ra*-nuh
insurance *asigurare* ⓕ a-see-goo-*ra*-re
Internet *internet* ⓝ een-ter-*net*
interpreter *interpret* ⓜ een-ter-*pret*

J

jewellery *bijuterii* ⓕ pl bee-zhoo-te-*ree*
job *serviciu* ⓝ ser-*vee*-chyoo

K

key *cheie* ⓕ *ke*-ye
kilogram *kilogram* ⓝ kee-lo-*gram*
kitchen *bucătărie* ⓕ boo-kuh-tuh-*ree*-e
knife *cuţit* ⓝ koo-*tseet*

L

laundry (place) *spălătorie* ⓕ spuh-luh-to-*ree*-e
lawyer *avocat* ⓜ a-vo-*kat*
left (direction) *la stânga* la *stewn*-ga
left-luggage office *birou pentru păstrarea bagajelor*
  ⓝ bee-*roh* pen-troo puhs-*tra*-re-a ba-*ga*-zhe-lor
leg *picior* ⓝ pee-*chyor*
lesbian *lesbiană* ⓕ les-*bya*-nuh
less *mai puţin* mai poo-*tseen*
letter (mail) *scrisoare* ⓕ skree-so-*a*-re
lift (elevator) *lift* ⓝ leeft
light *lumină* ⓕ loo-*mee*-nuh

like ∨ *place* pla-che
lock *lacăt* ⓝ *la*-kuht
long *lung/lungă* ⓜ/ⓕ loong/*loon*-guh
lost *pierdut/pierdută* ⓜ/ⓕ pyer-*doot*/pyer-*doo*-tuh
lost-property office *birou bagaje pierdute* ⓝ
  bee-*roh* ba-ga-zhe pyer-*doo*-te
love ∨ *iubi* yoo-*bee*
luggage *bagaje* ⓝ pl ba-*ga*-zhe
lunch *dejun* ⓝ de-*zhoon*

M

mail *poştă* ⓕ *posh*-tuh
man *bărbat* ⓜ buhr-*bat*
map *hartă* ⓕ *har*-tuh
market *piaţă* ⓕ *pya*-tsuh
matches *chibrituri* ⓝ pl kee-*bree*-too-ri
meat *carne* ⓕ *kar*-ne
medicine *doctorie* ⓕ dok-to-*ree*-e
menu *meniu* ⓝ me-*nyoo*
message *mesaj* ⓝ me-*sazh*
milk *lapte* ⓝ *lap*-te
minute *minut* ⓝ mee-*noot*
mobile phone *telefon mobil* ⓝ te-le-*fon* mo-*beel*
Moldova *Moldova* mol-*do*-va
money *bani* ⓝ pl *ba*-ni
month *lună* ⓕ *loo*-nuh
morning *dimineaţă* ⓕ dee-mee-ne-*a*-tsuh
mother *mamă* ⓕ *ma*-muh
motorcycle *motocicletă* ⓕ mo-to-chee-*kle*-tuh
motorway *autostradă* ⓕ ow-to-*stra*-duh
mouth *gură* ⓕ *goo*-ruh
music *muzică* ⓕ *moo*-zee-kuh

N

name *nume* ⓝ *noo*-me
napkin *şerveţel* ⓝ *sher*-ve-tsel
nappy *scutec* ⓝ *skoo*-tek
near *aproape* a-pro-*a*-pe
neck *gâtul* ⓝ *gew*-tool
new *nou/nouă* ⓜ/ⓕ noh/no-*wuh*
news *ştiri* ⓕ pl *shtee*-ri
newspaper *ziar* ⓝ zee-*ar*
night *noapte* ⓕ no-*ap*-te
no *nu* noo
noisy *zgomotos/zgomotoasă* ⓜ/ⓕ
  zgo-mo-*tos*/zgo-mo-to-*a*-suh
nonsmoking section *la nefumători* la ne-foo-muh-*to*-ri
north *nord* nord
nose *nas* ⓝ nas
now *acum* a-*koom*
number *număr* ⓝ *noo*-muhr

O

oil (engine) *ulei de motor* ⓝ oo-ley de mo-*tor*
old *vechi/veche* ⓜ/ⓕ *ve*-ki/*ve*-ke
one-way ticket *bilet dus* ⓝ bee-*let* doos
open a *deschis/deschisă* ⓜ/ⓕ des-*kees*/des-*kee*-suh
outside *afară* a-*fa*-ruh

P

package *pachet* ⓝ pa-*ket*
paper *hârtie* ⓕ hewr-*tee*-e
park (car) v *parca* par-*ka*
passport *pașaport* ⓝ pa-sha-*port*
pay v *plăti* pluh-*tee*
petrol *benzină* ⓕ ben-*zee*-nuh
pharmacy *farmacie* ⓕ far-ma-*chee*-e
phonecard *cartelă de telefon* ⓕ kar-*te*-luh de te-le-*fon*
photo *fotografie* ⓕ fo-to-gra-*fee*-e
plate *farfurie* ⓕ far-foo-*ree*-e
police *poliție* ⓕ po-*lee*-tsye
postcard *carte poștală* ⓕ *kar*-te posh-*ta*-luh
post office *oficiu poștal* ⓝ o-*fee*-chyoo posh-*tal*
pregnant *însărcinată* ⓕ ewn-suhr-chee-*na*-tuh
price *preț* ⓝ prets

Q

quiet *liniștit/liniștită* ⓜ/ⓕ
   lee-neesh-*teet*/lee-neesh-*tee*-tuh

R

rain *ploaie* ⓕ plo-*a*-ye
razor *aparat de ras* ⓝ a-pa-*rat* de ras
receipt *chitanță* ⓕ kee-*tan*-tsuh
red *roșu/roșie* ⓜ/ⓕ *ro*-shoo/*ro*-shee-e
refund *rambursare* ⓕ ram-boor-*sa*-re
registered mail *poștă înregistrată* ⓕ
   posh-tuh ewn-re-jees-*tra*-tuh
rent v *închiria* ewn-kee-*rya*
repair v *repara* re-pa-*ra*
reservation *rezervație* ⓕ re-zer-*va*-tsye
restaurant *restaurant* ⓝ res-tow-*rant*
return v *se întoarce* se ewn-to-*ar*-che
return ticket *bilet dus-întors* ⓝ bee-*let* doos-ewn-*tors*
right (direction) *la dreapta* la dre-*ap*-ta
road *șosea* ⓕ sho-*se*-a
Romania *România* ro-mew-*nee*-a

Romanian (language) *limba română*
   leem-ba ro-*mew*-nuh
Romanian a *românesc/românească* ⓜ/ⓕ
   ro-mew-*nesk*/ro-mew-ne-*as*-kuh
room *cameră* ⓕ *ka*-me-ruh

S

safe a *protejat/protejată* ⓜ/ⓕ
   pro-te-*zhat*/pro-te-*zha*-tuh
sanitary napkin *absorbante* ⓝ ab-sor-*ban*-te
seat *loc* ⓝ lok
send v *trimite* tree-*mee*-te
service station *stație de benzină* ⓕ
   sta-tsye de ben-*zee*-nuh
sex *sex* ⓝ seks
shampoo *șampon* ⓝ sham-*pon*
share (a dorm) *împărți* ewm-*puhr*-tsee
shaving cream *cremă de ras* ⓕ *kre*-muh de ras
she *ea* ya
sheet (bed) *cearceaf* ⓝ che-ar-*che*-af
shirt *cămașă* ⓕ kuh-*ma*-shuh
shoes *pantofi* ⓜ pl pan-*to*-fi
shop *magazin* ⓝ ma-ga-*zeen*
short *scurt/scurtă* ⓜ/ⓕ skoort/*skoor*-tuh
shower *duș* ⓝ doosh
single room *cameră de o persoană* ⓕ
   ka-me-ruh de o per-so-*a*-nuh
skin *piele* ⓕ *pye*-le
skirt *fustă* ⓕ *foos*-tuh
sleep v *dormi* dor-*mee*
slowly *încet* ewn-*chet*
small *mic/mică* ⓜ/ⓕ meek/*mee*-kuh
smoke (cigarettes) v *fuma* foo-*ma*
soap *săpun* ⓝ suh-*poon*
some *niște* ⓜ&ⓕ *neesh*-te
soon *curând* koo-*rewnd*
south *sud* sood
souvenir shop *magazin de suveniruri* ⓝ
   ma-ga-*zeen* de soo-ve-nee-*roo*-ri
speak v *vorbi* vor-*bee*
spoon *lingură* ⓕ *leen*-goo-ruh
stamp *timbru* ⓝ *teem*-broo
stand-by ticket *bilet neconfirmat* ⓝ
   bee-*let* ne-kon-feer-*mat*
station (train) *gară* ⓕ *ga*-ruh
stomach *stomac* ⓝ sto-*mak*
stop v *opri* o-*pree*
stop (bus) *stație de autobuz* ⓕ
   sta-tsye de ow-to-*booz*
street *stradă* ⓕ *stra*-duh

student *student/studentă* m/f
stoo-*dent*/stoo-*den*-tuh
sun *soare* n so-*a*-re
sunscreen *loţiune contra soarelui* f
lo-*tsyoo*-ne kon-tra so-*a*-re-looy
swim v *înota* ew-no-*ta*

T

tampons *tampoane* pl tam-po-*a*-ne
taxi *taxi* n tak-*see*
teaspoon *linguriţă* f leen-goo-*ree*-tsa
teeth *dinţi* pl deen-tsi
telephone *telefon* n te-le-*fon*
television (set) *televizor* n te-le-vee-*zor*
temperature (weather) *temperatură* f
tem-pe-ra-*too*-ruh
tent *cort* f kort
that (one) *acela/aceea* m/f a-che-la/a-che-ya
they *ei/ele* yey/ye-le
thirsty *însetat/însetată* m/f ewn-se-*tat*/ewn-se-ta-tuh
this (one) *acesta/aceasta* m/f a-ches-ta/a-che-as-ta
throat *în gât* n ewn gewt
ticket *bilet* n bee-*let*
time *ora* f o-ra
tired *obosit/obosită* m/f o-bo-*seet*/o-bo-*see*-tuh
tissues *şerveţele* pl sher-ve-*tse*-le
today *azi* a-zi
toilet *toaletă* f to-a-*le*-tuh
tomorrow *mâine* mew-ee-ne
tonight *diseară* dee-se-*a*-ruh
toothbrush *periuţă de dinţi* f
pe-ree-*oo*-tsuh de deen-tsi
toothpaste *pastă de dinţi* f pas-tuh de deen-tsi
torch (flashlight) *lanternă* f lan-*ter*-nuh
tour *tur* n toor
tourist office *birou de informaţii turistice* f
bi-*roh* de in-for-*ma*-tsee too-*rees*-tee-che
towel *prosop* n pro-*sop*
train *tren* n tren
translate *traduce* tra-*doo*-che
travel agency *agenţie de voiaj* f
a-jen-*tsee*-e de vo-*yazh*
travellers cheque *cecuri de călătorie* n pl
che-koo-ri de kuh-luh-to-ree-e
trousers *pantaloni* m pan-ta-*lo*-ni
twin beds *cameră cu două paturi separate* f
ka-me-ruh koo do-wuh pa-too-ri se-pa-ra-te
tyre *cauciuc* n kow-*chook*

U

underwear *lenjerie de corp* f len-zhe-ree-e de korp
urgent *urgent/urgentă* m/f oor-*jent*/oor-*jen*-tuh

V

vacant *liber/liberă* m/f lee-ber/lee-be-ruh
vacation *vacanţă* f va-*kan*-tsuh
vegetable *legumă* f le-*goo*-muh
vegetarian a *vegetarian/vegetariana* m/f
ve-je-ta-ryan/ve-je-ta-rya-nuh
visa *viză* f *vee*-zuh

W

waiter *chelner* n *kel*-ner
walk v *merge pe jos* mer-je pe zhos
wallet *portofel* n por-to-*fel*
warm a *cald/caldă* m/f kald/kal-duh
wash (something) v *spăla* spuh-*la*
watch *ceas* n che-as
water *apă* f a-puh
we *noi* noy
weekend *weekend* n wee-*kend*
west *vest* vest
wheelchair *scaun cu rotile* n skown koo ro-*tee*-le
when *când* kewnd
where *unde* oon-de
white *alb/albă* m/f alb/*al*-buh
who *cine* chee-ne
why *de ce* de che
wife *nevastă* f ne-*vas*-tuh
window *fereastră* f fe-re-*as*-truh
wine *vin* f veen
with *cu* koo
without *fără* fuh-ruh
woman *femeie* f fe-me-ye
write v *scrie* skree-ye

Y

yellow *galben/galbenă* m/f gal-ben/gal-be-nuh
yes *da* da
yesterday *ieri* ye-ri
you sg inf *tu* too
you pl inf *voi* voy
you sg&pl pol *dumneavoastră* doom-ne-a-vo-as-truh

Russian

russian alphabet

А а a	Б б be	В в ve	Г г ge	Д д de
Е е ye	Ё ё yo	Ж ж zhe	З з ze	И и ee
Й й ee-*krat*-ka-ye	К к ka	Л л el	М м em	Н н en
О о o	П п pe	Р р er	С с es	Т т te
У у u	Ф ф ef	Х х kha	Ц ц tse	Ч ч che
Ш ш sha	Щ щ shcha	Ъ ъ *tvyor*-di znak	Ы ы ih	Ь ь *myakh*-ki znak
Э э e	Ю ю yu	Я я ya		

■ russian

ПУССКИЙ

introduction

Words such as *apparatchik*, *tsar* and *vodka* come from Russian (русский *rus*-kee) — the language which unites the largest nation in the world, the 'riddle wrapped in a mystery inside an enigma' spread over two continents and 11 time zones. The official language of the Russian Federation, Russian is also used as a second language in the former republics of the USSR and is widely spoken throughout Eastern Europe. With a total of more than 270 million speakers, it's the fifth most spoken language in the world.

Russian belongs to the East Slavic group of languages, together with Belarusian and Ukrainian. These languages were initially considered so similar that they were classified as one language – Old Russian. Russian was recognised as a distinct, modern language in the 10th century, when the Cyrillic alphabet was adopted along with Orthodox Christianity by way of Old Church Slavonic. This South Slavic language was used principally in religious literature, while written secular texts were much closer to the spoken East Slavic language. For centuries these two forms of Old Russian coexisted, and it was a third, 'middle' style which emerged in the 18th century as the basis of modern Russian. Pushkin, the nation's first great poet, was essentially writing in the Russian of today when he published *Eugene Onegin* in 1831. The alphabet was radically simplified at two major turning points in Russian history – as part of Peter the Great's reforms at the turn of the 17th century, and after the October Revolution in 1917.

For a language spoken across such a vast geographical area, Russian is surprisingly uniform, and the regional differences don't get in the way of communication. The language was standardised by the centralised education system in the USSR, which spread literacy and enforced 'literary' Russian. In practical terms, Russian is divided into the northern and the southern dialects; Moscow's dialect has some features of both. From the 16th century onward Muscovite Russian was the standard tongue, even after Peter the Great's court had moved to St Petersburg.

Some admirers of Russian literature have claimed that the русская душа *rus*-ka-ya du-*sha* (Russian soul) of Dostoevsky, Chekhov and Tolstoy simply can't be understood, or at least fully appreciated, in translation. All exaggeration aside, the Russian language boasts a rich vocabulary and highly colourful expressions. This linguistic flamboyance has thankfully resisted the influence of dour communist style and the 'socrealist' literature of the 20th century, as you'll soon find out on your travels!

pronunciation

Russian is often considered difficult to learn because of its script, but this is merely prejudice – some Cyrillic letters look and sound the same as their English peers, and the others aren't difficult to learn. Contrary to popular caricatures of the 'harsh' Russian accent, the language has a pleasant, soft sound characterised by several 'lisping' consonants. Most of the sounds in Russian are also found in English, and those that are unfamiliar aren't difficult to master. Use the coloured pronunciation guides to become familiar with them, and then read from the Cyrillic alphabet when you feel more confident.

There are remarkably few variations in modern Russian pronunciation and vocabulary. This phrasebook is written in standard Russian as it's spoken around Moscow, and you're sure to be understood by Russian speakers everywhere.

vowel sounds

symbol	english equivalent	russian example	transliteration
a	father	да	da
ai	aisle	май	mai
e	bet	это	e·ta
ee	see	мир	meer
ey	hey	бассейн	bas·yeyn
i	bit	мыло	mi·la
o	pot	дом	dom
oy	toy	сырой	si·roy
u	put	ужин	u·zheen

word stress

Russian stress is free (it can fall on any syllable) and mobile (it can change in different forms of the same word). Each word has only one stressed syllable, which you'll need to learn as you go. In the meantime, follow our pronunciation guides, which have the stressed syllable marked in italics.

consonant sounds

Most Russian consonants are similar to English sounds, so they won't cause you too much difficulty. The 'soft' sign ь and the 'hard' sign ъ don't have a sound of their own, but show in writing whether the consonant before them is pronounced 'soft' (with a slight y sound after it) or 'hard' (as it's written). In our pronunciation guides, the soft sign is represented with an apostrophe (') – as in бедность *byed*·nast' – but the hard sign isn't included as it's very rarely used.

symbol	english equivalent	russian example	transliteration
b	bed	брат	brat
ch	cheat	чай	chai
d	dog	вода	va·*da*
f	fat	кофе	*ko*·fee
g	go	город	*go*·rat
k	kit	сок	sok
kh	loch	смех	smyekh
l	lot	лифт	leeft
m	man	место	*mye*·sta
n	not	нога	na·*ga*
p	pet	письмо	pees·*mo*
r	run (rolled)	река	ree·*ka*
s	sun	снег	snyek
sh	shot	душа	du·*sha*
t	top	так	tak
ts	hats	отец	at·*yets*
v	very	врач	vrach
y	yes	мой	moy
z	zoo	звук	zvuk
zh	pleasure	жизнь	zhizn'
'	a slight y sound	власть	vlast'

basics

language difficulties

Do you speak English?
Вы говорите по-английски?
vi ga·va·*reet*·ye pa·an·*glee*·skee

Do you understand?
Вы понимаете?
vi pa·nee·*ma*·eet·ye

I (don't) understand.
Я (не) понимаю.
ya (nye) pa·nee·*ma*·yu

What does (пуп) mean?
Что обозначает слово (пуп)?
shto a·baz·na·*cha*·eet *slo*·va (pup)

How do you say ... in Russian?
Как будет ... по-русски?
kak *bu*·deet ... pa·*ru*·skee

How do you ...?	Как ...?	kak ...
pronounce this	это произносится	*e*·ta pra·eez·*no*·seet·sa
write (Путин)	пишется (Путин)	*pee*·shit·sa (*pu*·teen)

Could you please ...?	..., пожалуйста.	... pa·*zhal*·sta
repeat that	Повторите	paf·ta·*reet*·ye
speak more	Говорите	ga·va·*reet*·ye
slowly	помедленее	pa·meed·leen·*ye*·ye
write it down	Запишите	za·pee·*shit*·ye

numbers

0	ноль	nol'	15	пятнадцать	peet·nat·sat'	
1	один m	a·deen	16	шестнадцать	shist·nat·sat'	
	одна f	ad·na	17	семнадцать	seem·nat·sat'	
	одно n	ad·no	18	восемнадцать	va·seem·nat·sat'	
2	два m&n	dva	19	девятнадцать	dee·veet·nat·sat'	
	две f	dvye	20	двадцать	dvat·sat'	
3	три	tree	21	двадцать	dvat·sat'	
4	четыре	chee·ti·ree		один	a·deen	
5	пять	pyat'	22	двадцать два	dvat·sat' dva	
6	шесть	shest'	30	тридцать	treet·sat'	
7	семь	syem'	40	сорок	so·rak	
8	восемь	vo·seem'	50	пятьдесят	pee·dees·yat	
9	девять	dye·veet'	60	шестдесят	shis·dees·yat	
10	десять	dye·seet'	70	семьдесят	syem'·dee·seet	
11	одиннадцать	a·dee·nat·sat'	80	восемьдесят	vo·seem'·dee·seet	
12	двенадцать	dvee·nat·sat'	90	девяносто	dee·vee·no·sta	
13	тринадцать	tree·nat·sat'	100	сто	sto	
14	четырнадцать	chee·tir·nat·sat'	1000	тысяча	ti·see·cha	

time & dates

What time is it?	Который час?	ka·to·ri chas
It's one o'clock.	Час.	chas
It's (two/three/four) o'clock.	(Два/Три/Четыре) часа.	(dva/tree/chee·ti·ree) chee·sa
It's (10) o'clock.	(Десять) часов.	(dye·veet') chee·sof
Quarter past (10).	(Десять) пятнадцать.	(dye·seet') peet·nat·sat'
Half past (10).	(Десять) тридцать.	(dye·seet') treet·sat'
Twenty to (11).	(Десять) сорок. (lit: ten forty)	(dye·seet') so·rak
At what time ...?	В котором часу ...?	f ka·to·ram chee·su ...
At ...	В ... часов.	v ... chee·sof
in the morning	утра	ut·ra
in the afternoon	дня	dnya
in the evening	вечера	vye·chee·ra

Monday	понедельник	pa·nee·*dyel*'·neek
Tuesday	вторник	*ftor*·neek
Wednesday	среда	sree·*da*
Thursday	четверг	cheet·*vyerk*
Friday	пятница	*pyat*·neet·sa
Saturday	суббота	su·*bo*·ta
Sunday	воскресенье	vas·krees·*yen*'·ye
January	январь	yeen·*var*'
February	февраль	feev·*ral*'
March	март	mart
April	апрель	ap·*ryel*'
May	май	mai
June	июнь	ee·*yun*'
July	июль	ee·*yul*'
August	август	*av*·gust
September	сентябрь	seent·*yabr*'
October	октябрь	akt·*yabr*'
November	ноябрь	na·*yabr*'
December	декабрь	dee·*kabr*'

What date is it today?	Какое сегодня число?	ka·*ko*·ye see·*vod*·nya chees·*lo*
It's (1 May).	(Первое мая).	(*pyer*·va·ye *ma*·ya)

since (May)	с (мая)	s (*ma*·ya)
until (June)	до (июня)	da (ee·*yun*·ya)

last ...

night	вчера вечером	fchee·*ra vye*·chee·ram
week	на прошлой неделе	na *prosh*·ley need·*yel*·ye
month	в прошлом месяце	f *prosh*·lam *mye*·seet·se
year	в прошлом году	f *prosh*·lam ga·*du*

next ...

week	на следующей неделе	na *slye*·du·yu·shee need·*yel*·ye
month	в следующем месяце	f *slye*·du·yu·sheem *mye*·seet·se
year	в следующем году	f *slye*·du·yu·sheem ga·*doo*

yesterday/tomorrow ...

	вчера/завтра ...	fchee·*ra*/*zaf*·tra ...
morning	утром	*ut*·ram
afternoon	днём	dnyom
evening	вечером	*vye*·chee·ram

weather

What's the weather like?	Какая погода?	ka-*ka*-ya pa-*go*-da

It's ...

cloudy	Облачно.	*ob*-lach-na
cold	Холодно.	*kho*-lad-na
hot	Жарко.	*zhar*-ka
raining	Идёт дождь.	eed-*yot* dozhd'
snowing	Идёт снег.	eed-*yot* snyek
sunny	Солнечно.	*sol*-neech-na
warm	Тепло.	tee-*plo*
windy	Ветрено.	*vye*-tree-na

spring	весна f	vees-*na*
summer	лето n	*lye*-ta
autumn	осень f	*o*-seen'
winter	зима f	zee-*ma*

border crossing

I'm here ...

for study	учусь	u-*chus*'
on business	по бизнесу	pa *beez*-nee-su
on holiday	в отпуске	v *ot*-pus-kye

I'm here for ...   Я здесь ...   ya zdyes' ...

(10) days	(десять) дней	(*dye*-seet') dnyey
(three) weeks	(три) недели	(tree) need-*ye*-lee
(two) months	(два) месяца	(dva) *mye*-seet-sa

I'm going to (Akademgorodok).
Я еду в (Академгородок).   ya *ye*-du v (a-ka-deem-ga-ra-*dok*)

I'm staying at (the Kosmos).
Я останавливаюсь в (Космосе).   ya as-ta-*nav*-lee-va-yus' v (*kos*-mas-ye)

I have nothing to declare.
Мне нечего декларировать.   mnye *nye*-chee-va dee-kla-*ree*-ra-vat'

I have something to declare.
Мне нужно что-то задекларировать.   mnye *nuzh*-na *shto*-ta za-dee-kla-*ree*-ra-vat'

That's (not) mine.
Это (не) моё.   *e*-ta (nye) ma-*yo*

transport

tickets & luggage

Where can I buy a ticket?
Где можно купить билет?
gdye *mozh*·na ku·*peet'* beel·*yet*

Do I need to book a seat?
Мне нужно зарезервировать
место?
mnye *nuzh*·na za·re·zer·*vee*·ra·vat'
myes·ta

One ... ticket (to	Билет ...	beel·*yet* ...
Novgorod), please.	(на Новгород).	(na *nov*·ga·rat)
one-way	в один конец	v a·*deen* kan·*yets*
return	в оба конца	v *o*·ba kant·*sa*

I'd like to ...	Я бы хотел/хотела	ya bi khat·*yel*/khat·*ye*·la
my ticket, please.	... билет, пожалуйста. m/f	... beel·*yet* pa·*zhal*·sta
cancel	отменить	at·mee·*neet'*
change	поменять	pa·meen·*yat'*
collect	забрать	zab·*rat'*
confirm	подтвердить	pat·veer·*deet'*

I'd like a (non)smoking seat, please.
Я бы хотел/хотела место в
отделении для (не)курящих,
пожалуйста. m/f
ya bi khat·*yel*/khat·*ye*·la *mye*·sta v
a·deel·*ye*·nee·ee dlya (nee·)kur·*ya*·sheekh
pa·*zhal*·sta

How much is it?
Сколько стоит?
skol'·ka *sto*·eet

Is there air conditioning?
Есть кондиционер?
yest' kan·deet·si·an·*yer*

Is there a toilet?
Есть туалет?
yest' tu·al·*yet*

How long does the trip take?
Сколько времени
уйдёт на эту поездку?
skol'·ka *vrye*·mee·nee
uyd·*yot* na *e*·tu pa·*yest*·ku

Is it a direct route?
Это прямой рейс?
e·ta pree·*moy* ryeys

Where's the luggage locker?
Где камера-автомат?
gdye *ka*·mee·ra·af·ta·*mat*

My luggage	Мой багаж ...	moy ba·*gash* ...
has been ...		
damaged	повредили	pa·vree·*dee*·lee
lost	пропал	pra·*pal*
stolen	украли	u·*kra*·lee

getting around

Where does flight (M2) arrive?

Куда прибывает самолёт (M2)? — ku·*da* pree·bi·*va*·et sa·ma·*lyot* (em dva)

Where does flight (M2) depart?

Откуда отправляется самолёт (M2)? — at·*ku*·da at·prav·*lya*·eet·sa sa·ma·*lyot* (em dva)

Which gate for (Omsk)?

Какой выход на посадку до (Омска)? — ka·*koy* *vi*·khat na pa·*sat*·ku da (*om*·ska)

Where's (the) ...?	Где ...?	gdye ...
arrivals hall	зал прибытий	zal pree·*bi*·tee·ye
departures hall	зал отправлений	zal at·prav·*lye*·nee
duty-free shop	товары без пошлины	ta·*va*·ri byes *posh*·lee·ni
gate (three)	выход на посадку (три)	*vi*·khat na pa·*sat*·ku (tree)

Is this the ...	Этот ... идёт	*e*·tat ... eed·*yot*
to (Moscow)?	в (Москву)?	v (mask·*vu*)
boat	параход	pa·ra·*khot*
bus	автобус	af·*to*·bus
plane	самолёт	sa·mal·*yot*
train	поезд	*po*·yeest

What time's	Когда будет	kag·*da* bu·deet
the ... bus?	... автобус?	... af·*to*·bus
first	первый	*pyer*·vi
last	последний	pas·*lyed*·nee
next	следующий	*slye*·du·yu·shee

At what time does it arrive/leave?

Когда он прибывает/отправляется? — kag·*da* on pree·bi·*va*·et/ at·prav·*lya*·eet·sa

How long will it be delayed?

На сколько он опаздывает? — na *skol'*·ka on a·*paz*·di·va·yet

What station/stop is this?

Какая эта станция/остановка? — ka-*ka*-ya e-ta *stant*-si-ya/a-sta-*nof*-ka

What's the next station/stop?

Какая следующая — ka-*ka*-ya *slye*-du-yu-sha-ya
станция/остановка? — *stant*-si-ya/a-sta-*nof*-ka

Does it stop at (Solntsevo)?

Поезд останавливается — *po*-yeest a-sta-*nav*-lee-va-yeet-sa
в (Солнцево)? — v (*sont*-see-va)

Please tell me when we get to (Magadan).

Объявите, пожалуйста, когда — ab-yee-*veet*-ye pa-*zhal*-sta kag-*da*
мы подъедем к (Магадану). — mi pad-*ye*-deem k (ma-ga-da-*nu*)

How long do we stop here?

Сколько времени поезд — *skol*'-ka *vrye*-mee-nee *po*-eest
стоит на этой станции? — sta-*eet* na e-tay *stant*-see

Is this seat available?

Это место занято? — e-ta *mye*-sta *za*-nee-ta

That's my seat.

Это моё место. — e-ta ma-*yo mye*-sta

I'd like a taxi ...	Мне нужно такси ...	mnye *nuzh*-na tak-*see* ...
at (9am)	в (девять часов утра)	v (*dye*-veet' chee-*sof* u-*tra*)
now	сейчас	see-*chas*
tomorrow	завтра	*zaf*-tra

Is this taxi available?

Свободен? — sva-*bo*-deen

How much is it to ...?

Сколько стоит доехать до ...? — *skol*'-ka *sto*-eet da-*ye*-khat' da ...

Please put the meter on.

Включите счётчик, пожалуйста! — fklyu-*cheet*-ye *shot*-cheek pa-*zhal*-sta

Please take me to (this address).

До (этого адреса) не довезёте? — da (e-ta-va *a*-dree-sa) nye da-veez-*yot*-ye

Please ...	..., пожалуйста!	... pa-*zhal*-sta
slow down	Не так быстро	nee tak *bi*-stra
stop here	Остановитесь здесь	a-sta-na-*veet*-yes' zdyes'
wait here	Подождите здесь	pa-dazh-*deet*-ye zdyes'

car, motorbike & bicycle hire

I'd like to hire a …	Я бы хотел/хотела взять … на прокат. m/f	ya bi khat·*yel*/khat·*ye*·la vzyat' … na pra·*kat*
bicycle	велосипед	vee·la·seep·*yet*
car	машину	ma·*shi*·nu
motorbike	мотоцикл	ma·tat·*sikl*

with …	с …	s …
a driver	шофёром	shaf·*yo*·ram
air conditioning	кондиционером	kan·deet·si·an·*ye*·ram
antifreeze	антифриз	an·tee·*freez*
snow chains	снеговые цепи	snye·*go*·vi·ye tse·pee

How much for … hire?	Сколько стоит … прокат?	skol'·ka sto·eet … pra·*kat*
hourly	часовой	cha·sa·*voy*
daily	однодневный	ad·nad·*nyev*·ni
weekly	недельный	need·*yel*'·ni

air	воздух m	*voz*·dukh
oil	масло n	*mas*·la
petrol	бензин m	been·*zeen*
tyre	шина f	*shi*·na

I need a mechanic.
Мне нужен автомеханик.   mnye *nu*·zhin af·ta·mee·*kha*·neek

I've run out of petrol.
У меня кончился бензин.   u meen·*ya* kon·cheel·sa been·*zeen*

I have a flat tyre.
У меня лопнула шина.   u meen·*ya* lop·*nu*·la *shi*·na

directions

Where's the …?	Где (здесь) …?	gdye (zdyes') …
bank	банк	bank
city centre	центр города	tsentr *go*·ra·da
hotel	гостиница	ga·*stee*·neet·sa
market	рынок	*ri*·nak
police station	полицейский участок	pa·leet·*sey*·skee u·*cha*·stak
post office	почта	*poch*·ta
public toilet	общественный туалет	ap·*shest*·vee·ni tu·al·*yet*

Is this the road to (Kursk)?
Эта дорога ведёт в (Курск)?   *e*·ta da·*ro*·ga veed·*yot* f (kursk)

Can you show me (on the map)?
Покажите мне,   pa·ka·*zhi*·tye mnye
пожалуйста (на карте).   pa·*zhal*·sta (na *kart*·ye)

What's the address?
Какой адрес?   ka·*koy a*·drees

Is it nearby/far away?
Близко/Далеко?   *blees*·ka/da·lee·*ko*

How do I get there?
Как туда попасть?   kak tu·*da* pa·*past'*

Turn ...	Поверните ...	pa·veer·*neet*·ye ...
at the corner	за угол	*za*·u·gal
at the traffic lights	на светофоре	na svee·ta·*for*·ye
left/right	налево/направо	nal·*ye*·va/na·*pra*·va

It's ...		
behind ...	За ...	za ...
far away	Далеко.	da·lee·*ko*
here	Здесь.	zdyes'
in front of ...	Перед ...	*pye*·reet ...
left	Налево.	nal·*ye*·va
near ...	Около ...	*o*·ka·la ...
next to ...	Рядом с ...	*rya*·dam s ...
on the corner	На углу.	na u·*glu*
opposite ...	Напротив ...	na·*pro*·teef ...
straight ahead	Прямо.	*prya*·ma
right	Направо.	na·*pra*·va
there	Там.	tam

by bus	автобусом	af·*to*·bu·sam
by taxi	на такси	na tak·*see*
by train	электричкой	e·leek·*treech*·key
on foot	пешком	peesh·*kom*

north	север	*sye*·veer
south	юг	yuk
east	восток	va·*stok*
west	запад	*za*·pat

ВЪЕЗД/ВЫЕЗД	vyest/vi·yest	**Entrance/Exit**
ОТКРЫТО/ЗАКРЫТО	at·kri·ta/za·kri·ta	**Open/Closed**
СВОБОДНЫЕ МЕСТА	sva·bod·ni·ye mee·sta	**Rooms Available**
МЕСТ НЕТ	myest nyet	**No Vacancies**
ИНФОРМАЦИЯ	een·far·mat·si·ya	**Information**
ОТДЕЛЕНИЕ МИЛИЦИИ	a·deel·ye·nee·ye mee·leet·si	**Police Station**
ЗАПРЕЩЕНО	za·pree·shee·no	**Prohibited**
ТУАЛЕТ	tu·al·yet	**Toilets**
МУЖСКОЙ (М)	mush·skoy	**Men**
ЖЕНСКИЙ (Ж)	zhen·ski	**Women**
ГОРЯЧИЙ/ХОЛОДНЫЙ	ga·rya·chi/kha·lod·ni	**Hot/Cold**

accommodation

finding accommodation

Where's a …?	Где …?	gdye …
camping ground	кемпинг	*kyem*·peeng
guesthouse	пансионат	pan·see·a·*nat*
hotel	гостиница	ga·*stee*·neet·sa
youth hostel	общежитие	ap·shee·*zhi*·tee·ye

Can you	Вы можете	vi *mo*·zhit·ye
recommend	порекомендовать	pa·ree·ka·meen·da·*vat'*
somewhere …?	что-нибудь …?	*shto*·nee·bud' …
cheap	дешёвое	dee·*sho*·va·ye
good	хорошее	kha·*ro*·she·ye
luxurious	роскошное	ras·*kosh*·na·ye
nearby	близко отсюда	*blees*·ka at·*syu*·da

I'd like to book a room, please.

Я бы хотел/хотела   ya bi khat·*yel*/khat·*ye*·la
забронировать номер. m/f   za·bra·*nee*·ra·vat' *no*·meer

I have a reservation.

Я заказал/заказала номер. m/f   ya za·ka·*zal*/za·ka·*za*·la *no*·meer

My surname is …

Моя фамилия …   ma·*ya* fa·*mee*·lee·ya …

Do you have a … room?	У вас есть …?	u vas yest' …
single	одноместный номер	ad·nam·yes·ni no·meer
double	номер с двуспальней кроватью	no·meer z dvu·spaln·yey kra·vat·yu
twin	двухместный номер	dvukh·myes·ni no·meer

How much is it per/for …?	Сколько стоит за …?	skol'·ka sto·eet za …
night	ночь	noch'
two people	двоих	dva·eekh

Can I pay …?	Можно расплатиться …?	mozh·na ras·pla·teet'·sa …
by credit card	кредитной карточкой	kree·deet·nay kar·tach·kay
with a travellers cheque	дорожным чеком	da·rozh·nim che·kam

For (three) nights.
(Трое) суток.   (tro·ye) su·tak

From (5 July) to (8 July).
С (пятого июля) по (восьмое июля).   s (pya·ta·va ee·yul·ya) pa (vas'·mo·ye ee·yul·ya)

Can I see it?
Можно посмотреть?   mozh·na pas·mat·ryet'

Am I allowed to camp here?
Можно устроить стоянку здесь?   mozh·na u·stro·eet' sta·yan·ku zdyes'

Where can I find a camp site?
Где кемпинг?   gdye kyem·peenk

requests & queries

When/Where is breakfast served?
Когда/Где завтрак?   kag·da/gdye zaf·trak

Please wake me at (seven).
Позвоните мне, пожалуйста, в (семь) часов.   paz·va·neet·ye mnye pa·zhal·sta v (syem') chee·sof

Could I have my key, please?

Дайте, пожалуйста ключ
от моего номера.

dayt·ye pa·*zhal*·sta klyuch
at ma·*yee*·*vo* no·*mee*·ra

Can I get another (blanket)?

Дайте, пожалуйста ещё (одеяло).

dayt·ye pa·*zhal*·sta yee·*sho* (a·dee·*ya*·la)

Is there an elevator/a safe?

У вас есть лифт/сейф?

u vas yest' leeft/syeyf

The room is too ...	В комнате очень ...	f *kom*·nat·ye *o*·cheen' ...
cold	холодно	*kho*·lad·na
noisy	шумно	*shum*·na
small	тесно	*tyes*·na

The ... doesn't work.	... не работает.	... nye ra·*bo*·ta·yeet
air conditioner	Кондиционер	kan·deet·si·an·*yer*
heater	Отопление	a·tap·*lye*·nee·ye
toilet	Туалет	tu·al·*yet*

This ... isn't clean.	Эта ... грязная.	*e*·ta ... *gryaz*·na·ya
pillow	подушка	pa·*dush*·ka
sheet	простыня	pra·stin·*ya*

This towel isn't clean.

Это полотенце грязное.

e·ta pa·lat·*yent*·se *gryaz*·no·ye

checking out

What time is checkout?

Когда нужно освободить номер?

kag·*da nuzh*·na as·va·ba·*deet' no*·meer

Can I leave my bags here?

Здесь можно оставлять багаж?

zdyes' *mozh*·na a·stav·*lyat'* ba·*gash*

Could I have my ..., please?	Дайте, пожалуйста ...	*dayt*·ye pa·*zhal*·sta ...
deposit	мой аванс	moy a·*vans*
passport	мой паспорт	moy *pas*·part
valuables	мои ценности	ma·*ee* tse·nas·tee

communications & banking

the internet

Where's the local Internet café?
Где здесь интернет-кафе? · gdye zdyes' een·ter·net·ka·fe

How much is it per hour?
Сколько стоит час? · skol'·ka sto·eet chas

I'd like to ...	Я бы хотел/ хотела ... m/f	ya bi khat·yel/ khat·ye·la ...
check my email	проверить свой и-мэйл	prav·ye·reet' svoy ee·meyl
get Internet access	подключиться к интернету	pat·klyu·cheet'·sa k een·ter·ne·tu
use a printer	воспользоваться принтером	vas·pol'·za·vat'·sa een·ter·ne·tam
use a scanner	воспользоваться сканером	vas·pol'·za·vat'·sa skan·ye·ram

mobile/cell phone

I'd like a ...	Я бы хотел/ хотела ... m/f	ya bi khat·yel/ khat·ye·la ...
mobile/cell phone for hire	взять мобильный телефон напрокат	vzyat' ma·beel'·ni tee·lee·fon nap·ra·kat
SIM card for your network	СИМ-карту для вашей сети	seem·kar·tu dlya va·shey se·tee

What are the rates?
Какие тарифы? · ka·kee·ye ta·ree·fi

telephone

What's your phone number?
Можно ваш номер телефона? · mozh·na vash no·meer tee·lee·fo·na

The number is ...
Телефон ... · tee·lee·fon ...

Where's the nearest public phone?
Где ближайший телефон-автомат? · gdye blee·zhey·shee tee·lee·fon·af·ta·mat

I want to ...	Я бы хотел/	ya bi khat·*yel*/
	хотела ... m/f	khat·ye·la ...
call (Singapore)	позвонить	paz·va·*neet'*
	(в Сингапур)	(v seen·ga·por)
make a local call	сделать местный	sdye·lat' *myest*·ni
	звонок	zva·nok
reverse the charges	позвонить с оплатой	paz·va·*neet'* s a·*pla*·tey
	вызываемого	vi·zi·*va*·yee·ma·va

How much does each minute cost?
Сколько стоит минута?   skol'·ka *sto*·eet mee·*nu*·ta

(Five) roubles per (30) seconds.
(Пять) рублей за (тридцать) секунд.   (pyat') *rub*·lyey za (*treet*·sat') see·*kunt*

I'd like to buy a phonecard.
Я бы хотел/хотела купить   ya bi khat·*yel*/khat·ye·la ku·*peet'*
телефонную карточку. m/f   tee·lee·*fo*·nu·yu *kar*·tach·ku

post office

I want to send a ...	Я хочу послать ...	ya kha·*chu* pas·*lat'* ...
fax	факс	faks
letter	письмо	pees'·*mo*
parcel	посылку	pa·*sil*·ku
postcard	открытку	at·*krit*·ku

I want to buy ...	Я хочу купить ...	yak ha·*chu* ku·*peet'* ...
an envelope	конверт	kan·*vyert*
a stamp	марку	*mar*·ku

Please send it	Пошлите, пожалуйста,	pash·*leet'*·ye pa·*zhal*·sta
(to Australia) by ...	... в (Австралию).	... v (af·*stra*·lee·yu)
airmail	авиа почтой	a·vee·a *poch*·tay
express mail	экспресс почтой	eeks·*pres poch*·tay
registered mail	заказной почтой	za·kaz·*noy poch*·tay
surface mail	обычной почтой	a·*bich*·nay *poch*·tay

| Is there any mail for me? | Есть почта для меня? | yest' *poch*·ta dlya meen·*ya* |

bank

Where's a/an ...?	Где ...?	gdye ...
ATM	банкомат	ban·ka·*mat*
foreign exchange office	обмен валюты	ab·*myen* val·*yu*·ti
Where can I ...?	Где можно ...?	gdye *mozh*·na ...
I'd like to ...	Я бы хотел/ хотела ... m/f	ya bi khat·*yel*/ khat·*ye*·la ...
arrange a transfer	сделать денежный перевод	*sdye*·lat' *dye*·neezh·ni pee·ree·*vod*
cash a cheque	обменять чек	ab·meen·*yat'* chek
change a travellers cheque	обменять дорожный чек	ab·meen·*yat'* da·*rozh*·ni chek
change money	поменять деньги	pa·meen·*yat'* *dyen'*·gee
get a cash advance	снять деньги по кредитной карточке	snyat' *dyen'*·gee pa kree·*deet*·ney *kar*·tach·kye
withdraw money	снять деньги	snyat' *dyen'*·gee

What's the charge for that?
Сколько нужно заплатить?   *skol'*·ka *nuzh*·na za·pla·*teet'*

What's the exchange rate?
Какой курс?   ka·*koy* kurs

It's (12) roubles.
Это будет (двенадцать) рублей.   *e*·ta *bu*·deet (dvee·*nat*·sat') rub·*lyey*

It's free.
Это будет бесплатно.   *e*·ta *bu*·deet bees·*plat*·na

What time does the bank open?
Когда открывается банк?   kag·*da* at·kri·*va*·yeet·sa bank

Has my money arrived yet?
Мои деньги уже пришли?   moy *dyen'*·gee u·*zhe* preesh·*lee*

sightseeing

getting in

What time does it open/close?

Когда открывается/
закрывается?

kag·*da* at·kri·*va*·yeet·sa/
za·kri·*va*·yeet·sa

What's the admission charge?

Сколько стоит входной билет?

skol'·ka *sto*·eet fkhad·*noy* beel·*yet*

Is there a discount for students/children?

Есть скидка для студентов/детей?

yest' *skeet*·ka dlya stud·*yen*·taf/deet·*yey*

I'd like a ...

Я бы хотел/
хотела ... m/f

ya bi khat·*yel*/
khat·*ye*·la ...

catalogue	каталог	ka·ta·*lok*
guide	гида	*gee*·da
local map	карту города	*kar*·tu *go*·ra·da

I'd like to see ...

Я бы хотел/хотела
посетить ... m/f

ya bi khat·*yel*/khat·*ye*·la
pa·see·*teet'* ...

What's that?

Что это?

shto *e*·ta

Can I take a photo?

Можно
сфотографировать?

mozh·na
sfa·ta·gra·*fee*·ra·vat'

tours

When's the next tour?

Когда следующая экскурсия?

kag·*da slye*·du·yu·sha·ya eks·*kur*·see·ya

How long is the tour?

Как долго продолжается
экскурсия?

kag *dol*·ga pra·dal·*zha*·yeet·sa
eks·*kur*·see·ya

What time should we be back?

Когда мы возвращаемся?

kag·*da* mi vaz·vra·*sha*·yeem·sa

Is ... included?

Цена включает ...?

tse·*na* fklyu·*cha*·yeet ...

accommodation	помещение	pa·mee·*she*·nee·ye
the admission charge	входной билет	fkhad·*noy* beel·*yet*
food	обед	ab·*yet*
transport	транспорт	*tran*·spart

castle	замок m	za-mak
cathedral	собор m	sa-bor
church	церковь f	tser-kaf
main square	главная площадь f	glav-na-ya plo-shat'
monastery	монастырь m	ma-na-stir
monument	памятник m	pam-yeet-neek
museum	музей m	muz-yey
old city	старый город m	sta-ri go-rat
palace	дворец m	dvar-yets
ruins	развалины f pl	raz-va-lee-ni
stadium	стадион m	sta-dee-on
statue	статуя f	sta-tu-ya

shopping

enquiries

Where's a ...?	Где ...?	gdye ...
bank	банк	bank
bookshop	книжный магазин	kneezh-ni ma-ga-zeen
camera shop	фотографический магазин	fo-to-gra-fee-chee-skee ma-ga-zeen
department store	универмаг	u-nee-veer-mak
grocery store	гастроном	gast-ra-nom
market	рынок	ri-nak
newsagency	газетный киоск	gaz-yet-ni kee-osk
supermarket	универсам	u-nee-veer-sam

Where can I buy ...?
Где можно купить ...?
gdye mozh-na ku-peet' ...

Can I look at it?
Покажите, пожалуйста.
pa-ka-zhit-ye pa-zhal-sta

Do you have any others?
У вас есть другие?
u vas yest' dru-gee-ye

Does it have a guarantee?
Есть гарантия?
yest' ga-ran-tee-ya

Can I have it sent overseas?
Вы можете переслать
это за границу?
vi mo·zhit·ye pee·rees·lat'
e·ta za gra·neet·su

Can you repair this?
Вы можете это починить?
vi mo·zhit·ye e·ta pa·chee·neet'

It's faulty.
Это браковано.
e·ta z bra·ko·va·na

I'd like ...
Я бы хотел/
хотела ... m/f
ya bi khat·yel/
khat·ye·la ...

a bag	пакет	pak·yet
a refund	получить	pa·lu·cheet'
	обратно деньги	ab·rat·na dyen'·gee
to return this	это возвратить	e·ta vaz·vra·teet'

paying

How much is it?
Сколько стоит?
skol'·ka sto·eet

Can you write down the price?
Запишите, пожалуйста, цену.
za·pee·shit·ye pa·zhal·sta tse·nu

That's too expensive.
Это очень дорого.
e·ta o·cheen' do·ra·ga

Can you lower the price?
Вы можете снизить цену?
vi mo·zhit·ye snee·zeet' tse·nu

I'll give you (100) roubles.
Я вам дам (сто) рублей.
ya vam dam (sto) rub·lyey

There's a mistake in the bill.
Меня обсчитали.
meen·ya ap·shee·ta·lee

Do you accept ...?
Вы принимаете
оплату ...?
vi pri·ni·ma·it·ye
a·pla·tu ...

credit cards	кредитной карточкой	kri·dit·ney kar·tach·key
debit cards	дебитной карточкой	dye·bit·ney kar·tach·key
travellers cheques	дорожным чеком	da·rozh·nihm che·kam

I'd like ...
Я бы хотел/
хотела ... m/f
ya bi khat·yel/
khat·ye·la ...

a receipt	квитанцию	kvee·tant·si·yu
my change	сдачу	zda·chu

clothes & shoes

Can I try it on?	Можно это примерить?	*mozh·na e·ta preem·ye·reet'*
My size is (40).	Мой размер (сорок).	*moy raz·myer (so·*rak)
It doesn't fit.	Это не подходит.	*e·ta nye pat·kho·deet*
small	маленький	*ma·leen'·kee*
medium	средний	*sryed·nee*
large	большой	*bal'·shoy*

books & music

I'd like a ...	Я бы хотел/	*ya bi khat·yel/*
	хотела ... m/f	*khat·ye·la ...*
newspaper	газету	*gaz·ye·tu*
(in English)	(на английском)	*(na an·glee·skam)*
pen	ручку	*ruch·ku*

Is there an English-language bookshop?

Есть магазин английской книги? *yest' ma·ga·zeen an·glee·skey knee·gee*

Can I listen to this?

Можно послушать? *mozh·na pas·lu·shat'*

photography

Can you ...?	Вы можете ...?	*vi mo·zhit·ye ...*
develop this film	проявить эту плёнку	*pra·yee·veet' e·tu plyon·ku*
load this film	вложить эту плёнку	*vla·zhit' e·tu plyon·ku*
transfer photos	перебросить	*pee·ree·bro·seet'*
from my camera	снимки с камеры	*sneem·kee s kam·ye·ri*
to CD	на компакт-диск	*na kam·pakt·deesk*
I need a ... film	Мне нужна ... плёнка	*mnye nuzh·na ... plyon·ka*
for this camera.	на эту камеру.	*na e·tu kam·ye·ru*
B&W	чёрно-белая	*chor·nab·ye·la·ya*
colour	цветная	*tsvet·na·ya*
slide	слайд-овая	*slaid·a·va·ya*
(high) speed	(высоко-)	*(vi·sa·ko·)*
	чувствительная	*chus·vee·teel'·na·ya*
When will it be ready?	Когда она будет готова?	*kag·da a·na bu·deet ga·to·va*

meeting people

greetings, goodbyes & introductions

Hello.	Здравствуйте.	zdrast·vuyt·ye
Hi.	Привет.	preev·yet
Goodbye/Bye.	До свидания/Пока.	da svee·dan·ya/pa·ka
See you later.	До скорой встречи.	da sko·rey fstrye·chee
Mr	господин	ga·spa·deen
Mrs/Miss	госпожа	ga·spa·zha
How are you?	Как дела?	kag dyee·la
Fine, thanks.	Спасибо, хорошо.	spa·see·ba kha·ra·sho
And you?	А у вас?	a u vas
What's your name?	Как вас зовут?	kak vaz za·vut
My name is ...	Меня зовут ...	meen·ya za·vut ...
I'm pleased to meet you.	Очень приятно.	o·cheen' pree·yat·na

This is my ...	Это ...	e·ta ...
boyfriend	мой парень	moy pa·reen
brother	мой брат	moy brat
daughter	моя дочка	ma·ya doch·ka
father	мой отец	moy at·yets
friend	мой друг m	moy druk
	моя подруга f	ma·ya pa·dru·ga
girlfriend	моя девушка	ma·ya dye·vush·ka
husband	мой муж	moy mush
mother	моя мать	ma·ya mat'
partner	мой парень m	moy pa·reen
(intimate)	моя девушка f	ma·ya dye·vush·ka
sister	моя сестра	ma·ya seest·ra
son	мой сын	moy sin
wife	моя жена	ma·ya zhi·na

Here's my ...	Вот мой ...	vot moy ...
What's your ...?	Можно ваш ...?	mozh·na vash ...
address	адрес	a·drees
email address	и-мейл	ee·meyl
fax number	номер факса	no·meer fak·sa
phone number	номер телефона	no·meer tee·lee·fo·na

occupations

What's your occupation?	Кем вы работаете?	kyem vi ra·bo·ta·yeet·ye
I'm a/an ...	Я ...	ya ...
artist	художник m	khu·dozh·neek
	художница f	khu·dozh·neet·sa
businessperson	бизнесмен	beez·nees·myen
farmer	фермер	fyer·meer
office worker	служащий m	slu·zha·shee
	служащая f	slu·zha·shee·ya
scientist	учёный/учёная m/f	u·cho·ni/u·cho·na·ya
student	студент m	stud·yent
	студентка f	stud·yent·ka
tradesperson	ремесленник	reem·yes·lee·neek

background

Where are you from?	Вы откуда?	vi at·ku·da
I'm from ...	Я из ...	ya eez ...
Australia	Австралии	af·stra·lee·ee
Canada	Канады	ka·na·di
England	Англии	an·glee·ee
New Zealand	Новой Зеландии	no·voy zee·lan·dee·ee
the USA	США	se·sha·a
Are you married?	Вы женаты? m	vi zhi·na·ti
	Вы замужем? f	vi za·mu·zhim
I'm married.	Я женат/замужем. m/f	ya zhi·nat/za·mu·zhim
I'm single.	Я холост/холоста. m/f	ya kho·last/kha·la·sta

age

How old ...?	Сколько ... лет?	skol'·ka ... lyet
are you	вам	vam
is your daughter	вашей дочке	va·shey doch·kye
is your son	вашему сыну	va·shi·mu si·nu
I'm ... years old.	Мне ... лет.	mnye ... lyet
He/She is ... years old.	Ему/Ей ... лет.	ye·mu/yey ... lyet

feelings

I'm (not) ...	Я (не) ...	ya (nye) ...
cold	замёрз m	zam·*yors*
	замёрзла f	zam·*yorz*·la
happy	счастлив m	shas·*leef*
	счастлива f	shas·*lee*·va
hot	умираю от жары	u·mee·*ra*·yu ad zha·*ri*
hungry	голоден m	*go*·la·deen
	голодна f	ga·lad·*na*
sad	грущу	gru·*shu*
thirsty	хочу пить	kha·*chu* peet'
What about you?	А вы?	a vih

entertainment

going out

Where can I find ...?	Где находятся ...?	gdye na·*kho*·deet·sa ...
clubs	клубы	*klu*·bi
gay venues	гей-клубы	gyey·*klu*·bi
pubs	пивные	peev·*ni*·ye
I feel like going to a/the ...	Мне хочется пойти ...	mnye *kho*·cheet·sa pey·*tee* ...
concert	на концерт	na kant·*sert*
movies	в кино	v kee·*no*
party	на тусовку	na tu·*sof*·ku
restaurant	в ресторан	v ree·sta·*ran*
theatre	в театр	f tee·*atr*

interests

Do you like ...?	Вам нравится ...?	vam *nra*·veet·sa ...
I (don't) like ...	Мне (не) нравится ...	mnye (nye) *nra*·veet·sa ...
art	искусство	ees·*kust*·va
cooking	готовить	ga·*to*·veet'
movies	кино	kee·*no*
reading	читать	chee·*tat'*
sport	спорт	sport
travelling	путешествовать	pu·tee·*shest*·va·vat'

Do you like to ...?	Вы ...?	vi ...
dance	танцуете	tant·*su*·eet·ye
go to concerts	ходите на	*kho*·deet·ye na
	концерты	kant·*ser*·ti
listen to music	слушаете музыку	*slu*·sha·yeet·ye *mu*·zi·ku

food & drink

finding a place to eat

Can you recommend a ...?	Вы можете порекомендовать ...?	vi mo·*zhit*·ye pa·ree·ka·meen·da·*vat'* ...
bar	бар	bar
café	кафе	ka·*fe*
restaurant	ресторан	ree·sta·*ran*
I'd like ..., please.	Я бы хотел/ хотела ... m/f	ya bi khat·*yel*/ khat·*ye*·la ...
a table for (three)	столик на (троих)	*sto*·leek na (tra·*eekh*)
the nonsmoking section	некурящий	nye·kur·*yash*·chee
the smoking section	курящий	kur·*yash*·chee

ordering food

breakfast	завтрак m	*zaf*·trak
lunch	обед m	ab·*yet*
dinner	ужин m	u·zhin
snack	закуска f	za·*kus*·ka
What would you recommend?	Что вы рекомендуете?	shto vi ree·ka·meen·*du*·eet·ye
I'd like (the) ..., please.	Я бы хотел/ хотела ... m/f	ya bi khat·*yel*/ khat·*ye*·la ...
bill	счёт	shot
drink list	карту вин	*kar*·tu veen
menu	меню	meen·*yu*
that dish	это блюдо	e·ta *blyu*·da

drinks

cup of coffee/tea ...	чашка кофе/чаю ...	*chash*·ka *kof*·ye/*cha*·yu ...
with milk	с молоком	s ma·la·*kom*
without sugar	без сахару	byez *sa*·kha·ru
... water	... вода	... va·*da*
boiled	кипячёная	kee·pee·*cho*·na·ya
(sparkling) mineral	(шипучая)	(shi·*pu*·cha·ya)
	минеральная	mee·nee·*ral*'·na·ya
(orange) juice	(апельсиновый) сок m	(a·*peel*'·*see*·na·vi) sok
soft drink	безалкогольный	bye·zal·ka·*gol*'·ni
	напиток m	na·*pee*·tak

in the bar

I'll have ...	..., пожалуйста.	... pa·*zhal*·sta
I'll buy you a drink.	Я угощаю.	ya u·ga·*sha*·yu
What would you like?	Что вы хотите?	shto vi kha·*tee*·tye
Cheers!	Пей до дна!	pyey da dna
champagne	шампанское n	sham·*pan*·ska·ye
cocktail	коктейль m	kak·*teyl*
vodka	водка f	*vot*·ka
whisky	виски m	*vees*·kee
a ... of beer	... пива	... *pee*·va
bottle	бутылка	bu·*til*·ka
glass	стакан	sta·*kan*
a bottle/glass	бутылка/рюмка	bu·*til*·ka/*ryum*·ka
of ... wine	... вина	... vee·*na*
red	красного	*kras*·na·va
sparkling	шипучего	shi·*pu*·chee·va
white	белого	*bye*·la·va

self-catering

What's the local speciality?
Что типично местное? — shto tee·*peech*·na *myes*·na·ye

What's that?
Что это? — shto *e*·ta

How much (is a kilo of cheese)?
Сколько стоит (кило сыра)? — *skol'*·ka *sto*·eet (kee·*lo si*·ra)

I'd like …	Дайте …	*deyt*·ye …
(200) grams	(двести) грамм	(*dvye*·stee) gram
(two) kilos	(два) кило	(dva) kee·*lo*
(three) pieces	(три) куска	(tree) kus·*ka*
(six) slices	(шесть) ломтика	(shest') *lom*·tee·ka

Less.	Меньше.	*myen'*·shi
Enough.	Достаточно.	da·*sta*·tach·na
More.	Немного.	neem·*no*·ga

special diets & allergies

Is there a vegetarian restaurant nearby?
Здесь есть вегетарианский ресторан? — zdyes' yest' vee·gee·ta·ree·*an*·skee ree·sta·*ran*

Do you have vegetarian food?
У вас есть овощные блюда? — u vas yest' a·vashch·*ni*·ye *blyu*·da

Could you	Вы могли бы	vi ma·*glee* bi
prepare a meal	приготовить	pree·ga·*to*·veet'
without …?	блюдо без …?	*blu*·da byez …
butter	масла	*mas*·la
eggs	яиц	*ya*·eets
meat stock	мясного бульона	myas·*no*·va bu·*lo*·na

I'm allergic to …	У меня аллергия на …	u meen·*ya* a·leer·*gee*·ya na …
dairy produce	молочные продукты	ma·*loch*·ni·ye pra·*duk*·ti
gluten	клейковину	klyey·ka·*vee*·nu
MSG	МНГ	em·en·*ge*
nuts	орехи	ar·*ye*·khee
seafood	морепродукты	mor·ye·pra·*duk*·ti

menu decoder

бефстроганов m	beef·stra·ga·*nof*	braised beef with sour cream & mushrooms
биточки f pl	bee·*toch*·kee	meatballs, often in tomato sauce
блинчики m pl	*bleen*·chee·kee	pancakes with meat, cheese, jam or another sweet filling
борщ московский m	borsh mas·*kof*·skee	beetroot soup with beef & frankfurters
вареники m pl	var·*ye*·nee·kee	dumplings with berries inside
винегрет m	vee·neeg·*ryet*	salad of potatoes, carrots, beetroot, onion & pickles
голубцы m pl	ga·lub·*tsi*	cabbage rolls with meat & rice
грибы в сметане m pl	gree·*bi* f smee·*tan*·ye	mushrooms baked in sour cream
жаркое подомашнему n	zhar·*ko*·ye pa·da·*mash*·nee·mu	meat & vegetables stew
харчо n	zhar·*cho*	lamb soup with cherries, walnuts, rice & vegetables
икра красная f	ee·*kra kras*·na·ya	red caviar (salmon)
икра чёрная f	ee·*kra chor*·na·ya	black caviar (sturgeon)
котлета пожарская f	kat·*lye*·ta pa·*zhar*·ska·ya	minced chicken croquette
котлета по-киевски f	kat·*lye*·ta pa·*kee*·eef·skee	rolled boneless chicken, stuffed with butter, crumbed & deep-fried
кулебяка f	ku·leeb·*ya*·ka	salmon cooked in wine with eggs, rice & vegetables
лапша f	lap·*sha*	chicken noodle soup
манты f pl	*man*·ti	steamed meat dumplings

маринованные грибы m pl	ma·ree·*no*·va·ni·ye gree·*bi*	pickled mushrooms
овощная окрошка f	a·vash·*na*·ya a·*krosh*·ka	cold vegetable soup
овощной пирог m	a·vash·*noy* pee·*rok*	cabbage, mushrooms & cheese pie
окрошка f	a·*krosh*·ka	soup of cucumber, sour cream, potato, egg & meat
оладьи f pl	a·*la*·dee	fritters topped with syrup or sour cream, often fried with fruit
ооливье n	a·lee·*vye*	salad of meat & vegetables with sour cream
пельмени m pl	peelm·*ye*·nee	meat dumplings
пирог из тыквы m	pee·*rok* ees *tik*·vi	baked pumpkin filled with rice, apples, raisins & cherries
пирожки m pl	pee·rash·*kee*	spicy, deep-fried mutton pies
рассольник m	ra·*sol'*·neek	soup with pickles & kidney
салат столичный m	sa·*lat* sta·*leech*·ni	vegetable, beef & egg salad
солёные грибы m pl	sal·yo·ni·ye gree·*bi*	marinated mushrooms
солянка f	sal·*yan*·ka	meat or fish soup with salted cucumbers
табака f	ta·ba·*ka*	seasoned chicken, fried or grilled
уха f	u·*kha*	fish soup with potato & carrot
форшмак m	farsh·*mak*	baked beef & lamb with herrings soaked in milk
хаш m	khash	tripe soup
щи m pl	shee	cabbage, meat & potato soup

emergencies

basics

English	Russian	Pronunciation
Help!	Помогите!	pa·ma·*gee*·tye
Stop!	Прекратите!	pree·kra·*tee*·tye
Go away!	Идите отсюда!	ee·*deet*·ye at·*syu*·da
Thief!	Вор!	vor
Fire!	Пожар!	pa·*zhar*
Watch out!	Осторожно!	a·sta·*rozh*·na
Call ...!	Вызовите ...!	*vi*·za·veet·ye ...
a doctor	врача	vra·*cha*
an ambulance	скорую помощь	*sko*·ru·yu *po*·mash'
the police	милицию	*vi*·za·veet·ye mee·*leet*·si·yu

It's an emergency.
Это срочно!
e·ta *sroch*·na

Could you help me, please?
Помогите, пожалуйста!
pa·ma·*geet*·ye pa·*zhal*·sta

Can I use your phone?
Можно воспользоваться телефоном?
mozh·na vas·*pol*'·za·vat'·sa tee·lee·*fo*·nam

Where are the toilets?
Где здесь туалет?
gdye zdyes' tu·al·*yet*

I'm lost.
Я потерялся/потерялась. m/f
ya pa·teer·*yal*·sa/pa·teer·*ya*·las'

police

Where's the police station?
Где милицейский участок?
gdye mee·leet·*sey*·skee u·*cha*·stak

I want to report an offence.
Я хочу заявить в милицию.
ya kha·*chu* za·ya·*veet*' v mee·*leet*·si·yu

I have insurance.
У меня есть страховка.
u meen·*ya* yest' stra·*khof*·ka

I've been ...	Меня ...	meen·*ya* ...
assaulted	побили	pa·*bee*·lee
raped	изнасиловали	eez·na·*see*·la·va·lee
robbed	ограбили	a·*gra*·bee·lee

I've lost my ...	Я потерял/	ya pa·teer·*yal*/
	потеряла ... m/f	pa·teer·*ya*·la ...
My ... was/were stolen.	У меня украли ...	u meen·*ya* u·*kra*·lee ...
backpack	рюкзак	ryug·*zak*
bags	багаж	ba·*gash*
credit card	кредитную	kree·*deet*·nu·yu
	карточку	*kar*·tach·ku
handbag	сумку	*sum*·ku
jewellery	драгоценности	dra·gat·*se*·na·stee
money	деньги	*dyen'*·gee
passport	паспорт	*pas*·part
travellers cheques	дорожные	da·*rozh*·ni·ye
	чеки	*che*·kee
wallet	бумажник	bu·*mazh*·neek
I want to contact	Я хочу обратиться	ya kha·*chu* a·bra·*teet'*·sa
my ...	в своё ...	f sva·*yo* ...
consulate	консульство	*kan*·sulst·vo
embassy	посольство	pa·*solst*·va

health

medical needs

Where's the nearest ...?	Где здесь ...?	gdye zdyes' ...
dentist	зубной врач	zub·*noy* vrach
doctor	врач	vrach
hospital	больница	bal'·*neet*·sa
(night) pharmacist	(ночная) аптека	(nach·*na*·ya) ap·*tye*·ka

I need a doctor (who speaks English).

Мне нужен врач,
(говорящий на
английском языке).

mnye *nu*·zhin vrach
(ga·var·*ya*·shee na
an·*glee*·skam ya·zik·ye)

Could I see a female doctor?

Можно записаться на
приём к женщине-врачу?

mozh·na za·pee·*sat'*·sa na
pree·*yom* k *zhen*·sheen·ye·vra·*chu*

I've run out of my medication.

У меня кончилось лекарство.

u meen·*ya kon*·chee·las' lee·*karst*·va

symptoms, conditions & allergies

I'm sick.	Я болею.	ya bal·*ye*·yu
It hurts here.	Здесь болит.	zdyes' ba·*leet*
I have (a) ...	У меня ...	u meen·*ya* ...

asthma	астма f	*ast*·ma
bronchitis	бронхит m	bran·*kheet*
constipation	запор m	za·*por*
cough	кашель m	*ka*·shel'
diarrhoea	понос m	pa·*nos*
fever	температура f	teem·pee·ra·*tu*·ra
headache	головная боль f	ga·lav·*na*·ya bol'
heart condition	болезнь сердца f	bal·*yezn*' *syerd*·tsa
nausea	тошнота f	tash·na·*ta*
pain	боль f	bol'
sore throat	болит горло n	ba·*leet gor*·la
toothache	зубная боль f	zub·*na*·ya bol

I'm allergic to ...	У меня аллергия на ...	u meen·*ya* a·leer·*gee*·ya na ...
antibiotics	антибиотики	an·tee·bee·*o*·tee·kee
anti-inflammatories	противо-воспалительные препараты	pra·tee·va·va·spa·*lee*·teel'·ni·ye pree·pa·*ra*·ti
aspirin	аспирин	a·spee·*reen*
bees	пчелиный укус	pchee·*lee*·ni u·kus
codeine	кодеин	kad·ye·*een*
penicillin	пеницилин	pee·neet·*si*·leen

antiseptic	антисептик m	an·tees·*yep*·teek
bandage	бинт m	beent
condoms	презерватив m	pree·zeer·va·*teef*
contraceptives	противозачаточные средства n pl	pra·tee·va·za·*cha*·tach·ni·ye *sryets*·tva
diarrhoea medicine	лекарство от поноса n	li·*karst*·va at pa·*no*·sa
insect repellent	средство от насекомых n	*sryets*·tva at na·see·*ko*·mikh
laxative	слабительное n	sla·*bee*·teel'·na·ye
painkillers	болеутоляющие n pl	bo·lee·u·tal·*ya*·yu·shee·ye
rehydration salts	нюхательная соль m	*nyu*·kha·teel'·na·ya sol'
sleeping tablets	снотворные таблетки f pl	snat·*vor*·ni·ye tab·*lyet*·kee

english–russian dictionary

Russian nouns in this dictionary have their gender indicated by ⓜ masculine, ⓕ feminine or ⓝ neuter. If it's a plural noun you'll also see pl. Adjectives are given in the masculine form only. Words are also marked as a (adjective), v (verb), sg (singular), pl (plural), inf (informal) or pol (polite) where necessary.

A

accident авария ⓕ *a-va-ree-ya*
accommodation помещение ⓝ *pa-mee-she-ee-ye*
adaptor адаптер ⓜ *a-dap-teer*
address адрес ⓜ *a-drees*
after после *pos-lye*
air conditioning кондиционирование ⓝ *kan-deet-si-a-nee-ra-va-nee-ye*
airplane самолёт ⓜ *sa-mal-yot*
airport аэропорт ⓜ *a-e-ra-port*
alcohol алкоголь ⓜ *al-ka-gol'*
all все *fsye*
allergy аллергия ⓕ *al-yer-gee-ya*
ambulance скорая помощь ⓕ *sko-ra-ya po-mash*
and и *ee*
ankle лодыжка ⓕ *la-dish-ka*
arm рука ⓕ *ru-ka*
ashtray пепельница ⓕ *pye-peel'-neet-sa*
ATM банкомат ⓜ *ban-ka-mat*

B

baby ребёнок ⓜ *reeb-yo-nak*
back (body) спина ⓕ *spee-na*
backpack рюкзак ⓜ *ryug-zak*
bad плохой *pla-khoy*
bag мешок ⓜ *mee-shok*
baggage claim выдача багажа ⓕ *vi-da-cha ba-ga-zha*
bank банк ⓜ *bank*
bar бар ⓜ *bar*
bathroom ванная ⓕ *va-na-ya*
battery батарея ⓕ *ba-tar-ye-ya*
beautiful красивый *kra-see-vi*
bed кровать ⓕ *kra-vat'*
beer пиво ⓝ *pee-va*
before до *do*
behind за *za*
bicycle велосипед ⓜ *vee-la-seep-yet*
big большой *bal'-shoy*
bill счёт ⓜ *shot*
black чёрный *chor-ni*
blanket одеяло ⓝ *a-dee-ya-la*
blood group группа крови ⓕ *gru-pa kro-vee*

blue (dark) синий *see-nee*
blue (light) голубой *ga-lu-boy*
boat лодка ⓕ *lot-ka*
book (make a reservation) v заказать *za-ka-zat'*
bottle бутылка ⓕ *bu-til-ka*
bottle opener (beer) открывалка ⓕ *at-kri-val-ka*
bottle opener (wine) штопор ⓜ *shto-par*
boy мальчик ⓜ *mal'-cheek*
brakes (car) тормоза ⓜ pl *tar-ma-za*
breakfast завтрак ⓜ *zaf-trak*
broken (faulty) ошибочный *a-shi-bach-ni*
bus автобус ⓜ *af-to-bus*
business бизнес ⓜ *beez-nees*
buy купить *ku-peet'*

C

café кафе ⓝ *ka-fe*
camera фотоаппарат ⓜ *fo-to-a-pa-rat*
camp site кемпинг ⓜ *kyem-peenk*
cancel отменить *at-mee-neet'*
can opener открывашка ⓕ *at-kri-vash-ka*
car машина ⓕ *ma-shi-na*
cash наличные ⓕ pl *na-leech-ni-ye*
cash (a cheque) v обменять *ab-meen-yat'*
cell phone мобильный телефон ⓜ *ma-beel'-ni tee-lee-fon*
centre центр ⓜ *tsentr*
change (money) v обменять *ab-meen-yat'*
cheap дешёвый *dee-sho-vi*
check (bill) счёт ⓜ *shot*
check-in регистрация ⓕ *ree-geest-rat-si-ya*
chest грудная клетка ⓕ *grud-na-ya klyet-ka*
child ребёнок ⓜ *reeb-yo-nak*
cigarette сигарета ⓕ *see-gar-ye-ta*
city город ⓜ *go-rat*
clean a чистый *chee-sti*
closed закрытый *za-kri-ti*
coffee кофе ⓜ *kof-ye*
coins монеты ⓕ pl *man-ye-ti*
cold a холодный *kha-lod-ni*
collect call звонок по коллекту ⓜ *zva-nok pa kal-yek-tu*
come прийти *pree-tee*
computer компьютер ⓜ *kam-pyu-teer*

condom презерватив ⓜ pree-zeer-va-teef
contact lenses контактные линзы ⓕ pl
  kan-takt-ni-ye leen-zi
cook v готовить ga-to-veet'
cost цена ⓕ tse-na
credit card кредитная карточка ⓕ
  kri-deet-na-ya kar-tach-ka
cup чашка ⓕ chash-ka
currency exchange обмен валюты ⓜ
  ab-myen val-yu-ti
customs (immigration) таможня ⓕ ta-mozh-nya

D

dangerous опасный a-pas-ni
date (time) число ⓝ chees-lo
day день ⓜ dyen'
delay задержка ⓕ zad-yersh-ka
dentist зубной врач ⓜ zub-noy vrach
depart отправиться at-pra-veet'-sa
diaper подгузник ⓜ pad-guz-neek
dictionary словарь ⓜ sla-var'
dinner ужин ⓜ u-zhin
direct прямой pree-moy
dirty грязный gryaz-ni
disabled инвалид ⓜ een-va-leet
discount скидка ⓕ skeet-ka
doctor врач ⓜ vrach
double bed двуспальная кровать ⓕ
  dvu-spal'-na-ya kra-vat'
double room номер на двоих ⓜ no-meer na
  dva-eekh
drink напиток ⓜ na-pee-tak
drive v водить машину va-deet' ma-shi-nu
drivers licence водительские права ⓝ pl
  va-dee-teel'-skee-ye pra-va
drugs (illicit) наркотики ⓕ pl nar-ko-tee-kee
dummy (pacifier) соска ⓕ sos-ka

E

ear ухо ⓝ u-kha
east восток ⓜ va-stok
eat есть yest'
economy class пассажирский класс ⓜ
  pa-sa-zhir-skee klas
electricity электричество ⓝ e-leek-tree-cheest-va
elevator лифт ⓜ leeft
email и-мейл ⓜ ee-meyl
embassy посольство ⓝ pa-solst-va
emergency авария ⓕ a-va-ree-ya
English (language) английский an-glee-skee
entrance вход ⓜ fkhot

evening вечер ⓜ vye-cheer
exchange rate обменный курс ⓜ ab-mye-ni kurs
exit выход ⓜ vi-khat
expensive дорогой da-ra-goy
express mail экспресс почта ⓕ eks-pres poch-ta
eyes глаза ⓕ pl gla-za

F

far далеко da-lee-ko
fast быстрый bist-ri
father отец ⓜ at-yets
film (camera) плёнка ⓕ plyon-ka
finger палец ⓜ pa-leets
first-aid kit санитарная сумка ⓕ
  sa-nee-tar-na-ya sum-ka
first class в первом классе f pyer-vam klas-ye
fish рыба ⓕ ri-ba
food еда ⓕ yee-da
foot нога ⓕ na-ga
fork вилка ⓕ veel-ka
free (of charge) бесплатный bees-plat-ni
friend друг/подруга ⓜ/ⓕ druk/pa-dru-ga
fruit фрукты ⓜ pl fruk-ti
full полный pol-ni
funny смешной smeesh-noy

G

gift подарок ⓜ pa-da-rak
girl (teenage) девушка ⓕ dye-vush-ka
girl (pre-teen) девочка ⓕ dye-vach-ka
glass (drinking) стакан ⓜ sta-kan
glasses очки ⓝ pl ach-kee
go (on foot) идти ee-tee
go (by vehicle) ехать ye-khat'
good хороший kha-ro-shi
green зелёный zeel-yo-ni
guide гид ⓜ geet

H

half половина ⓕ pa-la-vee-na
hand рука ⓕ ru-ka
handbag сумочка ⓕ su-mach-ka
happy счастливый shees-lee-vi
have y ... есть u ... yest'
he он on
head голова ⓕ ga-la-va
heart сердце ⓝ syerd-tsi
heat жара ⓕ zha-ra
heavy тяжёлый tya-zho-li
help v помочь pa-moch'

here здесь zdyes'
high высокий vi-so-kee
highway шоссе ① sha-se
hike v ходить пешком kha-deet' peesh-kom
holiday каникулы ① pl ka-nee-ku-li
homosexual гомосексуалист ⓜ
   go-mo-seek-su-a-leest'
hospital больница ① bol'-neet-sa
hot жаркий zhar-kee
hotel гостиница ① ga-stee-neet-sa
hungry голоден go-la-deen
husband муж ⓜ mush

I

I я ya
identification (card) идентификационная карта ①
   eed-yen-tee-fee-kat-si-o-na-ya kar-ta
ill болен bo-leen
important важный vazh-ni
included включая fklyu-cha-ya
injury травма ① trav-ma
insurance страхование ⓝ stra-kha-va-nee-ye
Internet интернет ⓜ een-ter-net
interpreter переводчик ⓜ pee-ree-vot-cheek

J

jewellery ювелирные изделия ⓝ pl
   yu-vi-leer-ni-ye eez-dye-lee-ya
job работа ① ra-bo-ta

K

key ключ ⓜ klyuch
kilogram килограмм ⓜ kee-la-gram
kitchen кухня ① kukh-nya
knife нож ⓜ nosh

L

laundry (place) прачечная ① pra-cheech-na-ya
lawyer адвокат ⓜ ad-va-kat
left (direction) левый lye-vi
left-luggage office камера хранения ①
   ka-mee-ra khran-ye-nee-ya
leg нога ① na-ga
lesbian лесбиянка ① lees-bee-an-ka
less меньше myen'-she
letter (mail) письмо ⓝ pees'-mo
lift (elevator) лифт ⓜ leeft
light свет ⓜ svyet

like v любить lyu-beet'
lock замок ⓜ za-mok
long длинный dlee-ni
lost пропавший pra-paf-shi
lost-property office бюро находок ⓝ
   byu-ro na-kho-dak
love v любить lyu-beet'
luggage багаж ⓜ ba-gash
lunch обед ⓜ ab-yet

M

mail почта ① poch-ta
man мужчина ⓜ mush-chee-na
map карта ① kar-ta
market рынок ⓜ ri-nak
matches спички ① pl speech-kee
meat мясо ⓝ mya-sa
medicine лекарство ⓝ lee-karst-va
menu меню ⓝ meen-yu
message записка ① za-pees-ka
milk молоко ⓝ ma-la-ko
minute минута ① mee-nu-ta
mobile phone мобильный телефон ⓜ
   ma-beel'-ni tee-lee-fon
money деньги ① pl dyen'-gee
month месяц ⓜ mye-seets
morning утро ⓝ u-tra
mother мать ① mat'
motorcycle мотоцикл ⓜ ma-tat-sikl
motorway шоссе ⓝ sha-se
mouth рот ⓜ rot
music музыка ① mu-zi-ka

N

name (personal) имя ⓝ eem-ya
name (of object) название ⓝ na-zva-nee-ye
napkin салфетка ① salf-yet-ka
nappy подгузник ⓜ pad-guz-neek
near близко blees-ka
neck шея ① she-ya
new новый no-vi
news новости ① pl no-va-stee
newspaper газета ① gaz-ye-ta
night ночь ① noch
no нет nyet
noisy шумный shum-ni
nonsmoking некурящий nee-kur-ya-shee
north север ⓜ sye-veer
nose нос ⓜ nos
now сейчас see-chas
number номер ⓜ no-meer

O

oil (engine) масло ⓝ *mas*-la
old старый *sta*-ri
one-way ticket билет в один конец ⓜ
    beel-*yet* v a-*deen* kan-*yets*
open а открытый at-*kri*-ti
outside снаружи sna-*ru*-zhi

P

package посылка ⓕ pa-*sil*-ka
paper бумага ⓕ bu-*ma*-ga
park (a car) ∨ поставить (машину)
    pa-*sta*-veet' (ma-*shi*-nu)
passport паспорт ⓜ *pas*-part
pay заплатить za-pla-*teet'*
pen ручка ⓕ *ruch*-ka
petrol бензин ⓜ been-*zeen*
pharmacy аптека ⓕ apt-*ye*-ka
phonecard телефонная карточка ⓕ
    tee-lee-*fo*-na-ya *kar*-tach-ka
photo снимок ⓜ *snee*-mak
plate тарелка ⓕ tar-*yel*-ka
police милиция ⓕ mee-*leet*-si-ya
postcard открытка ⓕ at-*krit*-ka
post office почта ⓕ *poch*-ta
pregnant беременная beer-*ye*-mee-na-ya
price цена ⓕ tse-*na*

Q

quiet тихий *ti*-khee

R

rain дождь ⓜ dozht'
razor бритва ⓕ *breet*-va
receipt квитанция ⓕ kvee-*tan*-tsi-ya
red красный *kras*-ni
refund возвращение денег ⓝ
    vaz-vra-*she*-nee-ye *dye*-neek
registered mail заказной za-kaz-*noy*
rent ∨ арендовать a-reen-da-*vat'*
repair ∨ починить pa-chee-*neet'*
reservation заказ ⓜ za-*kas*
restaurant ресторан ⓜ rees-ta-*ran*
return ∨ вернуться veer-*nut'*-sa
return ticket обратный билет ⓜ a-*brat*-ni beel-*yet*
right (direction) правый *pra*-vi
road дорога ⓕ da-*ro*-ga
room (hotel) номер ⓜ *no*-meer
room (house) комната ⓕ *kom*-na-ta
Russia Россия ⓕ ra-*see*-ya

Russian (language) русский ⓜ *rus*-kee
Russian а русский/русская ⓜ/ⓕ *rus*-kee/rus-ka-ya

S

safe а безопасный beez-a-*pas*-ni
sanitary napkin гигиеническая салфетка ⓕ
    gee-gee-ee-*nee*-chee-ska-ya salf-*yet*-ka
seat место ⓝ *myes*-ta
send послать pas-*lat'*
service station заправочная станция ⓕ
    za-*pra*-vach-na-ya *stant*-si-ya
sex секс ⓜ syeks
shampoo шампунь ⓜ sham-*pun'*
share (a dorm) жить в одной комнате
    zhit' v ad-*noy* kom-nat-ye
shaving cream крем для бритья ⓜ
    kryem dlya breet'-*ya*
she она a-*na*
sheet (bed) простыня ⓕ pra-stin-*ya*
shirt рубашка ⓕ ru-*bash*-ka
shoes туфли ⓕ pl *tuf*-lee
shop магазин ⓜ ma-ga-*zeen*
short короткий ka-*rot*-kee
shower душ ⓜ dush
single room одноместный номер ⓜ
    ad-na-*mes*-ni *no*-meer
skin кожа ⓕ *ko*-zha
skirt юбка ⓕ *yup*-ka
sleep ∨ спать spat'
slowly медленно *myed*-lee-na
small маленький *ma*-leen'-kee
smoke (cigarettes) ∨ курить ku-*reet'*
soap мыло ⓝ *mi*-la
some несколько *nye*-skal'-ka
soon скоро *sko*-ra
south юг ⓜ yuk
souvenir shop сувенирный магазин ⓜ
    su-vee-*neer*-ni ma-ga-*zeen*
speak говорить ga-va-*reet'*
spoon ложка ⓕ *losh*-ka
stamp марка ⓕ *mar*-ka
stand-by ticket стенд-бай билет ⓜ
    styend-bai beel-*yet*
station (train) станция ⓕ *stant*-see-ya
stomach желудок ⓜ zhi-*lu*-dak
stop ∨ перестать pee-ree-*stat'*
stop (bus) остановка ⓕ a-sta-*nof*-ka
street улица ⓕ *u*-lee-tsa
student студент/студентка ⓜ/ⓕ
    stud-*yent*/stud-*yent*-ka
sun солнце ⓝ *solnt*-se
sunscreen солнцезащитный крем ⓜ
    sont-se-za-*sheet*-ni kryem
swim ∨ плавать *pla*-vat'

T

tampons тампон ⓜ tam-*pon*
taxi такси ⓜ tak-*see*
teaspoon чайная ложка ⓕ *chey*-na-ya *losh*-ka
teeth зубы ⓜ pl *zu*-bi
telephone телефон ⓜ tee-lee-*fon*
television телевизор ⓜ tee-lee-*vee*-zar
temperature (weather) температура ⓕ
  teem-pee-ra-*tu*-ra
tent палатка ⓕ pa-*lat*-ka
that (one) то to
they они a-*nee*
thirsty (be) хочется пить kho-cheet-sa peet'
this (one) это e-ta
throat горло ⓝ *gor*-la
ticket билет ⓜ beel-*yet*
time время ⓝ *vryem*-ya
tired устал u-*stal*
tissues салфетки ⓕ pl salf-*yet*-kee
today сегодня see-*vod*-nya
toilet туалет ⓜ tu-al-*yet*
tomorrow завтра *zaf*-tra
tonight сегодня вечером see-*vod*-nya vye-chee-ram
toothbrush зубная щётка ⓕ zub-*na*-ya *shot*-ka
toothpaste зубная паста ⓕ zub-*na*-ya *pa*-sta
torch (flashlight) фонарик ⓜ fa-*na*-reek
tour экскурсия ⓕ eks-*kur*-see-ya
tourist office туристическое бюро ⓝ
  tu-rees-*tee*-chee-ska-ye byu-*ro*
towel полотенце ⓝ pa-lat-*yent*-se
train поезд ⓜ *po*-eest
translate перевести pee-ree-vee-*stee*
travel agency бюро путешествий ⓝ
  byu-*ro* pu-tee-*shest*-vee
travellers cheque дорожный чек ⓜ
  da-*rozh*-ni chek
trousers брюки ⓜ pl *bryu*-kee
twin beds две односпальные кровати
  dvye ad-na-*spal*'-ni-ye kra-*va*-tee
tyre шина ⓕ *shi*-na

U

underwear бельё ⓝ beel-*yo*
urgent срочный *sroch*-ni

V

vacant свободный sva-*bod*-ni
vacation каникулы ⓕ pl ka-*nee*-ku-li
vegetable овощ ⓜ *o*-vash
vegetarian вегетарианец/вегетарианка ⓜ/ⓕ
  vee-gee-ta-ree-*a*-neets/vee-gee-ta-ree-*an*-ka
visa виза ⓕ *vee*-za

W

waiter официант/официантка ⓜ/ⓕ
  a-feet-si-*ant*/a-feet-si-*ant*-ka
walk v гулять gul-*yat*'
wallet кошелёк ⓜ ka-she-*lyok*
warm a тёплый *tyop*-li
wash (something) выстирать vi-*stee*-rat'
watch часы ⓜ pl chee-*si*
water вода ⓕ va-*da*
we мы mi
weekend выходные ⓜ pl vi-khad-*ni*-ye
west запад ⓜ *za*-pat
wheelchair инвалидная коляска ⓕ
  een-va-*leed*-na-ya kal-*yas*-ka
when когда kag-*da*
where где gdye
white белый *bye*-li
who кто kto
why почему pa-chee-*mu*
wife жена ⓕ zhi-*na*
window окно ⓝ ak-*no*
wine вино ⓝ vee-*no*
with c s
without без byez
woman женщина ⓕ *zhen*-shee-na
write написать na-pee-*sat*'

Y

yellow жёлтый *zhol*-ti
yes да da
yesterday вчера fchee-*ra*
you sg inf ты ti
you sg pol & pl вы vi

Slovak

slovak alphabet

A a uh	*Á á* *dl·*hair a	*Ä ä* *shi·*ro·kair e	*B b* bair	*C c* tsair	*Č č* ch
D d dair	*Ď ď* dy	*Dz dz* dz	*Dž dž* j	*E e* e	*É é* *dl·*hair air
F f ef	*G g* gair	*H h* ha	*Ch ch* kh	*I i* i	*Í í* *dl·*hair ee
J j yair	*K k* ka	*L l* el	*Ĺ ĺ* *dl·*hair el	*Ľ ľ* ly	*M m* em
N n en	*Ň ň* ny	*O o* o	*Ó ó* *dl·*hair aw	*Ô ô* wo	*P p* pair
Q q quair	*R r* er	*Ŕ ŕ* *dl·*hair er	*S s* es	*Š š* sh	*T t* tair
Ť ť ty	*U u* u	*Ú ú* *dl·*hair oo	*V v* vair	*W w* *dvo·*yi·tair vair	*X x* iks
Y y *ip·*si·lon	*Ý ý* ee	*Z z* zet	*Ž ž* zh		

slovak

SLOVENČINA

introduction

The cosy position of the Slovak language (*slovenčina* slo-ven-chi-na) in Central Europe makes it a perfect base for learning or understanding the languages of other Slavic nations. It shares certain features with its close relatives in the West Slavic group – Czech and Polish. To a lesser extent, Slovak is similar to the South Slavic languages (particularly Slovene, from which it was distanced by the arrival of the Hungarians to their present-day homeland in the 9th century). There are even similarities between Slovak and Ukranian, which represents the East Slavic branch.

Not surprisingly, however, the language that bears the closest resemblance to Slovak is Czech – ties between the two now independent countries date back to the 9th century and the Great Moravian Empire. More recently, the 20th-century Czechoslovakian affair established even closer relations between Czech and Slovak, to the extent that the two languages are mutually intelligible (although less so in the colloquial form or among the younger generation). Hungarian influence on Slovak (mainly in the vocabulary) is a result of the centuries during which Slovaks formed part first of the Kingdom of Hungary and later of the Austro-Hungarian Empire.

The literary standard of Slovak emerged in the mid-19th century, during a national revival movement marked on the linguistic front by the work of Ľudovít Štúr. In earlier times, it was mostly a spoken language, subordinated in writing to Latin and Czech, although texts with elements of Slovak or written entirely in Slovak can be traced back to the 15th century. The Great Moravian Empire was originally the place of St Cyril and Methodius' mission, which for Old Church Slavonic literature used the Glagolitic script, the precursor of the Cyrillic alphabet. However, the West Slavic languages, including Slovak, soon adopted the Roman alphabet due to the influence of the Catholic Church.

Since 1993, Slovak has stepped out of the shadow of its larger neighbour, Czech (with which it shared official status during the Czechoslovakian days). It's now the official language of about 5 million speakers in Slovakia and there are Slovak-speaking minorities in Poland, Hungary, Romania, Ukraine, the northern Serbian province of Vojvodina, and of course, the Czech Republic.

Even if you don't speak Slovak, be sure to look up your name in the official Slovak calendar – in which each day corresponds to a personal name and entitles people to celebrate their 'name day' (*sviatok* svyuh-tok or *meniny* me-nyi-ni) with equal pomp as their birthday!

pronunciation

vowel sounds

Slovak is rich in vowels, including a number of vowel combinations (or 'diphthongs').

symbol	english equivalent	slovak example	transliteration
a	father	*pán*	pan
ai	aisle	*raňajky*	ruh-nyai-ki
air	hair	*voľné*	vol-nair
aw	law	*pól*	pawl
e	bet	*sestra, mäso*	ses-truh, me-so
ee	see	*prosím, bývať*	pro-seem, bee-vuht'
ey	hey	*olej*	o-ley
i	bit	*izba, byt*	iz-buh, bit
o	pot	*meno*	me-no
oh	oh	*zmesou*	zme-soh
oo	zoo	*pavúk*	puh-vook
ow	how	*auto*	ow-to
oy	toy	*ahoj*	a-hoy
uh	run	*matka*	muht-kuh
wo	quote	*môžem*	mwo-zhem

word stress

In Slovak, stress always falls on the first syllable, but it's quite light. Just follow our coloured pronunciation guides, in which the stressed syllable is always in italics.

consonant sounds

Slovak consonants are shown opposite. Most have equivalents in English.

symbol	english equivalent	slovak example	transliteration
b	**bed**	*obed*	*o·*bed
ch	**ch**eat	*večer*	*ve·*cher
d	**d**og	*adresa*	*uh·*dre·suh
dy	**d**uring	*ďaleko, džem*	*dyuh·*le·ko, **dy**em
dz	a**dd**s	*prichádza*	*pri·*kha·**dz**uh
f	**f**at	*fotka*	*fot·*kuh
g	**g**o	*margarin*	*muhr·*guh·reen
h	**h**at	*hlava*	*hluh·*vuh
k	**k**it	*oko*	*o·*ko
kh	lo**ch**	*chorý*	*kho·*ree
l	**l**ot	*lampa*	*luhm·*puh
ly	mi**lli**on	*doľava*	*do·*lyuh·vuh
m	**m**an	*matka*	*muht·*kuh
n	**n**ot	*noviny*	*no·*vi·**ni**
ny	ca**ny**on	*kuchyňa*	*ku·*khi·**nyuh**
p	**p**et	*pero*	*pe·*ro
r	**r**un	*ráno*	*ra·*no
s	**s**un	*sukňa*	*suk·*nyuh
sh	**sh**ot	*štyri*	*shti·*ri
t	**t**op	*tri*	tri
ts	ha**ts**	*anglicky*	*uhng·*lits·ki
ty	**t**utor	*ťava*	*tyuh·*vuh
v	**v**ery	*vízum, watt*	*vee·*zum, vuht
y	**y**es	*ja*	yuh
z	**z**ero	*zub*	zub
zh	plea**s**ure	*manžel*	*muhn·*zhel
'	a slight y sound	*meď*	meď

basics

language difficulties

Do you speak English?
Hovoríte po anglicky?   ho·vo·ree·tye po *uhng*·lits·ki

Do you understand?
Rozumiete?   ro·zu·mye·tye

I understand.
Rozumiem.   ro·zu·myem

I don't understand.
Nerozumiem.   nye·ro·zu·myem

What does (*jablko*) mean?
Čo znamená (jablko)?   cho *znuh*·me·na (*yuh*·bl·ko)

How do you ...?	*Ako sa ...?*	uh·ko suh ...
pronounce this	*toto vyslovuje*	*to*·to *vi*·slo·vu·ye
write (*cesta*)	*píše (cesta)*	pee·she (*tses*·tuh)

Could you please ...?	*Môžete prosím ...?*	mwo·zhe·tye pro·seem ...
repeat that	*to zopakovať*	to zo·puh·ko·vuht'
speak more slowly	*hovoriť pomalšie*	ho·vo·rit' po·muhl·shye
write it down	*to napísať*	to nuh·pee·suht'

essentials

Yes.	*Áno.*	a·no
No.	*Nie.*	ni·ye
Please.	*Prosím.*	pro·seem
Thank you	*Ďakujem*	dyuh·ku·yem
(very much).	*(veľmi pekne).*	(*veľ*·mi *pek*·nye)
You're welcome.	*Prosím.*	pro·seem
Excuse me.	*Prepáčte.*	pre·pach·tye
Sorry.	*Prepáčte.*	pre·pach·tye

0	nula	nu·luh	15	pätnásť	pet·nasť
1	jeden m	ye·den	16	šestnásť	shes·nasť
	jedna f	yed·na	17	sedemnásť	se·dyem·nasť
	jedno n	yed·no	18	osemnásť	o·sem·nasť
2	dva m	dvuh	19	devätnásť	dye·vet·nasť
	dve n/f	dve	20	dvadsať	dvuh·tsuhť
3	tri	tri	21	dvadsať-	dvuh·tsuhť··
4	štyri	shti·ri		jeden	ye·den
5	päť	peť	22	dvadsaťdva	dvuh·tsuhť·dvuh
6	šesť	shesť	30	tridsať	tri·tsuhť
7	sedem	se·dyem	40	štyridsať	shti·ri·tsuhť
8	osem	o·sem	50	päťdesiat	pe·dye·syuht
9	deväť	dye·veť	60	šesťdesiat	shes·dye·syuht
10	desať	dye·suhť	70	sedemdesiat	se·dyem·dye·syuht
11	jedenásť	ye·de·nasť	80	osemdesiat	o·sem·dye·syuht
12	dvanásť	dvuh·nasť	90	deväťdesiat	dye·ve·dye·syuht
13	trinásť	tri·nasť	100	sto	sto
14	štrnásť	shtr·nasť	1000	tisíc	tyi·seets

time & dates

What time is it?	Koľko je hodín?	kol'·ko ye ho·dyeen
It's one o'clock.	Je jedna hodina.	ye yed·nuh ho·dyi·nuh
It's (two) o'clock.	Sú (dve) hodiny.	soo (dve) ho·dyi·ni
Quarter past (one).	Štvrť na (dve).	shtvrť nuh (dve)
Half past (one).	Pól (druhej).	pol (dru·hey)
	(lit: half two)	
Quarter to (eight).	Trištvrte na (osem).	tri·shtvr·tye nuh (o·sem)
At what time ...?	O koľkej ...?	o kol'·key ...
At ...	O ...	o ...
am (before 10)	ráno	ra·no
pm (10 to 12)	dobedu	do·be·du
pm	pobede	po·be·dye

basics – SLOVAK

375

Monday	pondelok	pon·dye·lok
Tuesday	utorok	u·to·rok
Wednesday	streda	stre·duh
Thursday	štvrtok	shtvr·tok
Friday	piatok	pyuh·tok
Saturday	sobota	so·bo·tuh
Sunday	nedeľa	nye·dye·lyuh
January	január	yuh·nu·ar
February	február	feb·ru·ar
March	marec	muh·rets
April	apríl	uhp·reel
May	máj	mai
June	jún	yoon
July	júl	yool
August	august	ow·gust
September	september	sep·tem·ber
October	október	ok·taw·ber
November	november	no·vem·ber
December	december	de·tsem·ber

What date is it today?
  Koľkého je dnes? kol·kair·ho ye dnyes

It's (15 December).
  Je (pätnásteho decembra). ye (pet·nas·te·ho de·tsem·bruh)

since (May)	od (mája)	od (ma·yuh)
until (June)	do (júna)	do (yoo·nuh)
last night	minulú noc	mi·nu·loo nots
last/next ...	minulý/budúci ...	mi·nu·lee/bu·doo·tsi ...
week	týždeň	teezh·dyen'
month	mesiac	me·syuhts
year	rok	rok
yesterday/tomorrow ...	včera/zajtra ...	vche·ruh/zai·truh ...
morning	ráno	ra·no
afternoon	popoludnie	po·po·lud·ni·ye
evening	večer	ve·cher

weather

What's the weather like?	*Aké je počasie?*	*uh*-kair ye po-chuh-si-ye
It's ...		
cloudy	*Je zamračené.*	ye *zuh*-mruh-che-nair
cold	*Je zima.*	ye *zi*-muh
hot	*Je horúco.*	ye *ho*-roo-tso
raining	*Prší.*	*pr*-shee
snowing	*Sneží.*	sne-zhee
sunny	*Je slnečno.*	ye *sl*-nyech-no
warm	*Je teplo.*	ye *tyep*-lo
windy	*Je veterno.*	ye *ve*-tyer-no
spring	*jar* f	yuhr
summer	*leto* n	*le*-to
autumn	*jeseň* f	*ye*-sen'
winter	*zima* f	*zi*-muh

border crossing

I'm here ...	*Som tu ...*	som tu ...
on business	*v obchodnej*	v *ob*-khod-ney
	záležitosti	*za*-le-zhi-tos-tyi
on holiday	*na dovolenke*	nuh *do*-vo-len-ke
I'm here for ...	*Som tu na ...*	som tu nuh ...
(10) days	*(desať) dni*	(*dye*-suht') dnyee
(two) months	*(dva) mesiace*	(dvuh) *me*-syuh-tse
(three) weeks	*(tri) týždne*	(tri) teezhd-nye

I'm going to (Bratislava).
Idem do (Bratislavy).   *i*-dyem do (*bruh*-tyi-sluh-vi)

I'm staying at the (Hotel Grand).
Zostávam v (hoteli Grand).   zo-sta-vuhm v (*ho*-te-li gruhnd)

I have nothing to declare.
Nemám nič na preclenie.   *nye*-mam nyich nuh *prets*-le-ni-ye

I have something to declare.
Mám niečo na preclenie.   mam ni-*ye*-cho nuh *prets*-le-ni-ye

That's (not) mine.
To (nie) je moje.   to (*ni*-ye) ye *mo*-ye

transport

tickets & luggage

Where can I buy a ticket?
Kde si môžem kúpiť cestovný lístok?
kdye si *mwo*-zhem *koo*-pit' tses-tov-nee *lees*-tok

Do I need to book a seat?
Potrebujem si rezervovať miestenku?
po-tre-bu-yem si re-zer-vo-vuht' myes-tyen-ku

One ... ticket (to Poprad), please.
Jeden ... lístok (do Popradu), prosím.
ye-den ... *lees*-tok (do pop-ruh-du) pro-seem
| one-way | jednosmerný | yed-no-smer-nee |
| return | spiatočný | spyuh-toch-nee |

I'd like to ... my ticket, please.
Chcel/Chcela by som ... môj lístok, prosím. m/f
khtsel/*khtse*-luh bi som ... mwoy lees-tok pro-seem
cancel	zrušiť	zru-shit'
change	zmeniť	zme-nyit'
collect	vyzdvihnúť	vizd-vih-noot'
confirm	potvrdiť	po-tvr-dyit'

I'd like a ... seat, please.
Prosím si ... miesto.
pro-seem si ... mye-sto
| nonsmoking | nefajčiarske | nye-fai-chyuhr-ske |
| smoking | fajčiarske | fai-chyuhr-ske |

How much is it?
Koľko to stojí?
kol'-ko to *sto*-yee

Is there air conditioning?
Je tam klimatizácia?
ye tuhm *kli*-muh-ti-za-tsi-yuh

Is there a toilet?
Je tam toaleta?
ye tuhm *to*-uh-le-tuh

How long does the trip take?
Koľko trvá cesta?
kol'-ko tr-va tses-tuh

Is it a direct route?
Je to priamy smer?
ye to *pryuh*-mi smer

I'd like a luggage locker.
Chcel/Chcela by som skrinku na batožinu. m/f
khtsel/*khtse*-luh bi som skrin-ku nuh buh-to-zhi-nu

My luggage has been ...	*Moja batožina ...*	*mo·yuh buh·to·zhi·nuh ...*
damaged	*bola poškodená*	*bo·luh posh·ko·dye·na*
lost	*sa stratila*	*suh struh·tyi·luh*
stolen	*bola ukradnutá*	*bo·luh u·kruhd·nu·ta*

getting around

Where does flight (number 333) arrive?
Kam prilieta let   kuhm *pri*·li·ye·tuh let
(číslo 333)?   (*chees*·lo *tri*·sto·tri·tsat'·tri)

Where does flight (number 333) depart?
Odkiaľ odlieta let   od·kyuhl *od*·li·ye·tuh let
(číslo 333)?   (*chees*·lo *tri*·sto·tri·tsat'·tri)

Where's (the) ...?	*Kde je ...?*	kdye ye ...
arrivals hall	*príletová hala*	*pree*·le·to·va *huh*·luh
departures hall	*odletová hala*	*od*·le·to·va *huh*·luh
duty-free shop	*duty-free obchod*	*dyu*·ti-free *ob*·khod
gate (12)	*vchod (dvanásť)*	vkhod (*dvuh*·nast')

Is this the ...	*Je toto ...*	ye *to*·to ...
to (Komárno)?	*do (Komárna)?*	do (*ko*·mar·nuh)
boat	*loď*	lod'
bus	*autobus*	*ow*·to·bus
plane	*lietadlo*	li·*ye*·tuhd·lo
train	*vlak*	vluhk

What time's the ... bus?	*Kedy príde ... autobus?*	*ke*·di *pree*·dye ... *ow*·to·bus
first	*prvý*	*pr*·vee
last	*posledný*	*po*·sled·nee
next	*nasledujúci*	*nuh*·sle·du·yoo·tsi

At what time does it arrive/leave?
O koľkej prichádza/odchádza?   o *kol'*·key *pri*·kha·dzuh/*od*·kha·dzuh

How long will it be delayed?
Koľko je spozdenie?   *kol'*·ko ye *spoz*·dye·ni·ye

What station/stop is this?
Ktorá stanica/zastávka je toto?   *kto*·ra *stuh*·nyi·tsuh/*zuhs*·tav·kuh ye *to*·to

What's the next station/stop?
Ktorá je nasledujúca   *kto*·ra ye *nuh*·sle·du·yoo·tsuh
stanica/zastávka?   *stuh*·nyi·tsuh/*zuhs*·tav·kuh

Does it stop at (Štúrovo námestie)?
   Stojí to na (Štúrovom námestí)?   *sto·yee to nuh (shtoo·ro·vom na·mes·tyee)*

Please tell me when we get to (Hlavné námestie).
   Môžete ma prosím upozorniť   *mwo·zhe·tye muh pro·seem u·po·zor·nyit'*
   keď budeme na ...   *ked' bu·dye·me nuh ...*

How long do we stop here?
   Ako dlho tu budeme stáť?   *uh·ko dl·ho tu bu·dye·me stat'*

Is this seat available?
   Je toto miesto voľné?   *ye to·to mye·sto voľ·nair*

That's my seat.
   Toto je moje miesto.   *to·to ye mo·ye mye·sto*

I'd like a taxi ...	*Chcel/Chcela by*	*khtsel/khtse·luh bi*
	som taxík na ... m/f	*som tuhk·seek nuh ...*
at (9am)	*(deviatu ráno)*	*(dye·vyuh·tu ra·no)*
now	*teraz*	*te·ruhz*
tomorrow	*zajtra*	*zai·truh*

Is this taxi available?
   Je tento taxík voľný?   *ye ten·to tuhk·seek voľ'·nee*

How much is it to ...?
   Koľko to bude stáť do ...?   *koľ'·ko to bu·dye stat' do ...*

Please put the meter on.
   Zapnite taxameter, prosím.   *zuhp·nyi·tye tuhk·suh·me·ter pro·seem*

Please take me to (this address).
   Zavezte ma (na túto adresu),   *zuh·vez·tye muh (nuh too·to uh·dre·su)*
   prosím.   *pro·seem*

Please ...	*..., prosím.*	*... pro·seem*
slow down	*Spomaľte*	*spo·muhľ'·tye*
stop here	*Zastavte tu*	*zuhs·tuhv·tye tu*
wait here	*Počkajte tu*	*poch·kai·tye tu*

car, motorbike & bicycle hire

I'd like to hire a ...	*Chcel/Chcela by som si*	*khtsel/khtse·luh bi som si*
	prenajať ... m/f	*pre·nuh·yuhť ...*
bicycle	*bicykel*	*bi·tsi·kel*
car	*auto*	*ow·to*
motorbike	*motorku*	*mo·tor·ku*

with ...	s ...	s ...
a driver	*šoférom*	*sho*·fair·rom
air conditioning	*klimatizáciou*	*kli*·muh·ti·za·tsi·oh
antifreeze	*protimrazovou*	*pro*·tyi·mruh·zo·voh
	zmesou	*zme*·soh
snow chains	*snehovými*	*snye*·ho·vee·mi
	reťazami	*re*·tyuh·zuh·mi
How much for	*Koľko stojí*	*koľ*·ko *sto*·yee
... hire?	*prenájom na ...?*	*pre*·na·yom nuh ...
hourly	*hodinu*	*ho*·dyi·nu
daily	*deň*	dyen'
weekly	*týždeň*	*teezh*·dyen'
air	*stlačený vzduch* m	*stluh*·che·nee vzdukh
oil	*olej* m	*o*·ley
petrol	*benzín* m	*ben*·zeen
tyres	*pneumatiky* f pl	*pne*·u·muh·ti·ki

I need a mechanic.
Potrebujem automechanika. *po*·tre·bu·yem *ow*·to·me·khuh·ni·kuh

I've run out of petrol.
Minul sa mi benzín. *mi*·nul suh mi *ben*·zeen

I have a flat tyre.
Dostal/Dostala som defekt. m/f *dos*·tuhl/*dos*·tuh·luh som de·fekt

directions

Where's the ...?	*Kde je ...?*	kdye ye ...
bank	*banka*	*buhn*·kuh
city centre	*mestské centrum*	*mes*·kair tsen·trum
hotel	*hotel*	*ho*·tel
market	*trh*	trh
police station	*policajná stanica*	*po*·li·tsai·na *stuh*·nyi·tsuh
post office	*pošta*	*posh*·tuh
public toilet	*verejný záchod*	*ve*·rey·nee *za*·khod
tourist office	*turistická*	*tu*·ris·tits·ka
	kancelária	*kuhn*·tse·la·ri·yuh

Is this the road to ...? *Je toto cesta na ...?* ye *to*·to *tses*·tuh nuh ...

| Can you show me (on the map)? | | |
| Môžete mi ukázať (na mape)? | | mwo·zhe·tye mi u·ka·zuht' (nuh muh·pe) |

What's the address?
Aká je adresa? uh·ka ye uh·dre·suh

How far is it?
Ako je to ďaleko? uh·ko ye to dyuh·le·ko

How do I get there?
Ako sa tam dostanem? uh·ko suh tuhm dos·tuh·nyem

Turn ...	Zabočte ...	zuh·boch·tye ...
at the corner	na rohu	nuh ro·hu
at the traffic lights	na svetelnej križovatke	nuh sve·tyel·ney kri·zho·vuht·ke
left	doľava	do·lyuh·vuh
right	doprava	do·pruh·vuh

It's ...	Je to ...	ye to ...
behind ...	za ...	zuh ...
far away	ďaleko	dyuh·le·ko
here	tu	tu
in front of ...	pred ...	pred ...
left	vľavo	vlyuh·vo
near (to ...)	blízko (k ...)	bleez·ko (k ...)
next to ...	vedľa ...	ved·lyuh ...
on the corner	na rohu	nuh ro·hu
opposite ...	oproti ...	o·pro·tyi ...
right	vpravo	vpruh·vo
straight ahead	rovno	rov·no
there	tam	tuhm

by bus	autobusom	ow·to·bu·som
by taxi	taxíkom	tuhk·see·kom
by train	vlakom	vluh·kom
on foot	peši	pe·shi

north	sever	se·ver
south	juh	yooh
east	východ	vee·khod
west	západ	za·puhd

Vchod/Východ	vkhod/*vee*·khod	**Entrance/Exit**
Otvorené/Zatvorené	*ot*·vo·re·nair/*zuht*·vo·re·nair	**Open/Closed**
Ubytovanie	u·bi·to·vuh·ni·ye	**Rooms Available**
Plne obsadené	pl·nye *ob*·suh·dye·nair	**No Vacancies**
Informácie	*in*·for·ma·tsi·ye	**Information**
Policajná stanica	po·li·tsai·na *stuh*·nyi·tsuh	**Police Station**
Zakázané	*zuh*·ka·zuh·nair	**Prohibited**
Záchody/WC/Toalety	*za*·kho·di/*vair*·tsair/*to*·uh·le·ti	**Toilets**
Páni	*pa*·nyi	**Men**
Dámy	*da*·mi	**Women**
Horúca/Studená	*ho*·roo·tsuh/*stu*·dye·na	**Hot/Cold**

accommodation

finding accommodation

Where's a ...?	*Kde je ...?*	kdye ye ...
camping ground	*táborisko*	ta·bo·ris·ko
guesthouse	*penzión*	pen·zi·awn
hotel	*hotel*	ho·tel
youth hostel	*nocľaháreň pre mládež*	nots·lyuh·ha·ren' pre mla·dyezh
Can you recommend somewhere ...?	*Môžete odporučiť niečo ...?*	mwo·zhe·tye *od*·po·ru·chit' ni·ye·cho ...
cheap	*lacné*	*luhts*·nair
good	*dobré*	dob·rair
nearby	*nablízku*	nuh·bleez·ku
I have a reservation.	*Mám rezerváciu.*	mam re·zer·va·tsi·yu
My name's ...	*Volám sa ...*	*vo*·lam suh ...
Do you have a twin room?	*Máte dve oddelené postele?*	ma·tye dve *od*·dye·le·nair pos·tye·le
Do you have a single room?	*Máte jednoposteľovú izbu?*	ma·tye yed·no·pos·tye·lyo·voo *iz*·bu
Do you have a double room?	*Máte izbu s manželskou posteľou?*	ma·tye *iz*·bu s muhn·zhels·koh *pos*·tye·lyoh

How much is it per ...?	*Kolko to stojí na ...?*	kol'·ko to *sto*·yee nuh ...
night	*noc*	nots
person	*osobu*	o·*so*·bu

Can I pay by ...?	*Môžem platiť ...?*	*mwo*·zhem *pluh*·tyit' ...
credit card	*kreditnou kartou*	kre·dit·noh *kuhr*·toh
travellers cheque	*cestovnými šekmi*	tses·tov·nee·mi *shek*·mi

I'd like to stay for (two) nights.
Chcel/Chcela by som   khtsel/*khtse*·luh bi som
zostať (dve) noci. **m/f**   zos·tuhť (dve) *no*·tsi

From (2 July) to (6 July).
Od (druhého júla)   od (*dru*·hair·ho *yoo*·luh)
do (šiesteho júla).   do (*shyes*·te·ho *yoo*·luh)

Can I see it?
Môžem to vidieť?   *mwo*·zhem to *vi*·di·yeť

Am I allowed to camp here?
Môžem tu stanovať?   *mwo*·zhem tu *stuh*·no·vuhť

Is there a camp site nearby?
Je tu nablízku táborisko?   ye tu *nuh*·blees·ku *ta*·bo·ris·ko

requests & queries

When/Where is breakfast served?
Kedy/Kde sa podávajú   ke·di/kdye suh *po*·da·vuh·yoo
raňajky?   *ruh*·nyai·ki

Please wake me at (seven).
Zobuďte ma o (siedmej), prosím.   zo·buď·tye muh o (*syed*·mey) *pro*·seem

Could I have my key, please?
Prosím si môj kľúč.   *pro*·seem si mwoy klyooch

Can I get another (blanket)?
Môžem dostať inú (prikrývku)?   *mwo*·zhem *dos*·tuhť *i*·noo (*pri*·kreev·ku)

Is there a/an ...?	*Je tam ...?*	ye tuhm ...
elevator	*výťah*	*vee*·tyah
safe	*bezpečnostný trezor*	bez·pech·nos·nee *tre*·zor

The room is too ...	*Izba je príliš ...*	*iz*·buh ye *pree*·lish ...
expensive	*drahá*	*druh*·ha
noisy	*hlučná*	*hluch*·na
small	*malá*	*muh*·la

The ... doesn't work.	... nefunguje.	... nye·fun·gu·ye
air conditioning	Klimatizácia	kli·muh·ti·za·tsi·yuh
fan	Ventilátor	ven·ti·la·tor
toilet	Toaleta	to·uh·le·tuh

This ... isn't clean.	Tento ... nie je čistý.	ten·to ... ni·ye ye chis·tee
pillow	vankúš	vuhn·koosh
towel	uterák	u·tye·rak

This sheet isn't clean.
Táto plachta nie je chistaa.   ta·to pluhkh·tuh ni·ye ye chis·ta

checking out

What time is checkout?
O kolkej sa odhlasuje?   o kol'·key suh od·hluh·su·ye

Can I leave my luggage here?
Môžem si tu nechať batožinu?   mwo·zhem si tu nye·khuht' buh·to·zhi·nu

Could I have my ...?	Poprosím vás o ...	po·pro·seem vas o ...
deposit	moju zálohu	mo·yu za·lo·hu
passport	môj cestovný pas	mwoy tses·tov·nee puhs
valuables	moje cennosti	mo·ye tsen·nos·tyi

communications & banking

the internet

Where's the local Internet café?
Kde je miestne internet café?   kdye ye myes·ne in·ter·net kuh·fair

How much is it per hour?
Koľko stojí na hodinu?   kol'·ko sto·yee nuh ho·dyi·nu

I'd like to ...	Chcel/Chcela by som ... m/f	khtsel/khtse·luh bi som ...
check my email	si skontrolovať email	si skon·tro·lo·vuht' ee·meyl
get Internet access	sa pripojiť na internet	suh pri·po·yit' nuh in·ter·net
use a printer	použiť tlačiareň	po·u·zhit' tluh·chyuh·ren'
use a scanner	použiť scanner	po·u·zhit' ske·ner

mobile/cell phone

I'd like a …	Chcel/Chcela	khtsel/khtse·luh
	by som … m/f	bi som …
mobile/cell phone	si prenajať	si pre·nuh·yuhť
for hire	mobilný telefón	mo·bil·nee te·le·fawn
SIM card for your	SIM kartu pre vašu	sim kuhr·tu pre vuh·shu
network	sieť	syeť

| What are the rates? | Aké sú poplatky? | uh·kair soo pop·luht·ki |

telephone

What's your phone number?
Aké je vaše telefónne číslo?   uh·kair ye *vuh*·she te·le·faw·ne *chees*·lo

The number is …
Číslo je …   *chees*·lo ye …

Where's the nearest public phone?
Kde je najbližší verejný telefón?   kdye ye *nai*·blizh·shee *ve*·rey·nee te·le·fawn

I'd like to buy a phonecard.
Chcel/Chcela by som si kúpiť   khtsel/*khtse*·luh bi som si *koo*·piť
telefónnu kartu. m/f   te·le·faw·nu *kuhr*·tu

I want to …	Chcem …	khtsem …
call (Singapore)	volať	vo·luhť
	(do Singapúru)	(do sin·guh·poo·ru)
make a local call	volať miestne číslo	vo·luhť myes·ne chees·lo
reverse the	hovor na účet	ho·vor nuh oo·chet
charges	volaného	vo·luh·nair·ho

How much does … cost?	Koľko …?	koľ·ko …
a (three)-minute	stoja (tri) minúty	sto·yuh (tri) mi·noo·ti
call	volania	vo·luh·ni·yuh
each extra	stojí každá	sto·yee kuhzh·da
minute	ďalšia minúta	dyuhl·shyuh mi·noo·tuh

(One) euro per minute.
(Jedno) euro za minútu.   (yed·no) e·u·ro zuh mi·noo·tu

post office

I want to send a ...	*Chcel/Chcela by som poslať ...* m/f	khtsel/*khtse*-luh bi som *pos*-luhť ...
fax	*fax*	fuhks
letter	*list*	list
parcel	*balík*	*buh*-leek
postcard	*pohľadnicu*	po-hlyuhd-nyi-tsu

I want to buy a/an ...	*Chcel/Chcela by som si kúpiť ...* m/f	khtsel/*khtse*-luh bi som si *koo*-piť ...
envelope	*obálku*	o-bal-ku
stamp	*známku*	znam-ku

Please send it (to Australia) by ...	*Prosím pošlite to (do Austrálie) ...*	pro-seem posh-li-tye to (do ows-tra-li-ye) ...
airmail	*leteckou poštou*	le-tyets-koh posh-toh
express mail	*expresne*	eks-pres-nye
registered mail	*doporučene*	do-po-ru-che-nye
surface mail	*obyčajnou poštou*	o-bi-chai-noh posh-toh

Is there any mail for me?
Je tam nejaká pošta pre mňa?   ye tuhm nye-yuh-ka posh-tuh pre mnyuh

bank

Where's a/an ...?	*Kde je ...?*	kdye ye ...
ATM	*nejaký bankomat*	nye-yuh-kee buhn-ko-muht
foreign exchange office	*nejaká zmenáreň*	nye-yuh-ka zme-na-reň

I'd like to ...	*Chcel/Chcela by som ...* m/f	khtsel/*khtse*-luh bi som ...
Where can I ...?	*Kde môžem ...?*	kdye mwo-zhem ...
arrange a transfer	*zariadiť prevod*	zuh-ryuh-dyiť pre-vod
cash a cheque	*preplatiť šek*	pre-pluh-tyiť shek
change a travellers cheque	*zameniť cestovný šek*	zuh-me-nyiť tses-tov-nee shek
change money	*zameniť peniaze*	zuh-me-nyiť pe-ni-yuh-ze
get a cash advance	*dostať vopred hotovosť*	dos-tuhť vo-pred ho-to-vosť
withdraw money	*vybrať peniaze*	vib-ruhť pe-ni-yuh-ze

What's the ...?	_Aký je ...?_	_uh·kee ye ..._
charge for that	_za to poplatok_	_zuh to pop·luh·tok_
exchange rate	_výmenný kurz_	_vee·men·nee kurz_

It's ...	_Je to ..._	_ye to ..._
(12) euros	_(dvanásť) euro_	_(dvuh·nast') e·u·ro_
free	_zadarmo_	_zuh·duhr·mo_

What's the commission?
Aká je provízia?   _uh·ka ye pro·vee·zi·yuh_

What time does the bank open?
O koľkej otvára banka?   _o koľ·key ot·va·ruh buhn·kuh_

Has my money arrived yet?
Prišli už moje peniaze?   _prish·li uzh mo·ye pe·ni·yuh·ze_

sightseeing

getting in

What time does it open/close?
O koľkej otvárajú/   _o koľ·key ot·va·ruh·yoo/_
zatvárajú?   _zuht·va·ruh·yoo_

What's the admission charge?
Koľko je vstupné?   _koľ·ko ye vstup·nair_

Is there a discount for students/children?
Je nejaká zľava pre   _ye nye·yuh·ka zľyuh·vuh pre_
študentov/deti?   _shtu·den·tov/dye·tyi_

I'd like a ...	_Chcel/Chcela_	_khtsel/khtse·luh_
	by som ... m/f	_bi som ..._
catalogue	_katalóg_	_kuh·tuh·lawg_
guide	_sprievodcu_	_sprye·vod·tsu_
local map	_miestnu mapu_	_myest·nu muh·pu_

I'd like to see ...	_Rád/Rada by som_	_rad/ruh·duh bi som_
	videl/videla ... m/f	_vi·dyel/vi·dye·luh ..._
What's that?	_Čo je to?_	_cho ye to_
Can I take a photo?	_Môžem_	_mwo·zhem_
	fotografovať?	_fo·to·gruh·fo·vuht'_

tours

When's the next ...?	Kedy je ďalší ...?	ke·di ye dyuhl·shee ...
day trip	celodenný výlet	tse·lo·den·nee vee·let
tour	zájazd	za·yuhzd

Is ... included?	Je zahrnuté ...?	ye zuh·hr·nu·tair ...
accommodation	ubytovanie	u·bi·to·vuh·ni·ye
the admission charge	vstupné	vstup·nair
food	jedlo	yed·lo

Is transport included?
Je zahrnutá doprava?   ye zuh·hr·nu·ta do·pruh·vuh

How long is the tour?
Koľko trvá zájazd?   koľ·ko tr·va za·yuhzd

What time should we be back?
O koľkej by sme mali byť späť?   o koľ·key bi sme muh·li biť speť

sightseeing

castle	zámok m	za·mok
cathedral	katedrála f	kuh·ted·ra·luh
church	kostol m	kos·tol
main square	hlavné námestie n	hluhv·nair na·mes·ti·ye
monastery	kláštor m	klash·tor
monument	pamätník m	puh·met·nyeek
museum	múzeum n	moo·ze·um
old city	staré mesto n	stuh·rair mes·to
palace	palác m	puh·lats
ruins	zrúcaniny pl	zroo·tsuh·nyi·ni
stadium	štadión m	shtuh·di·awn
statue	socha f	so·khuh

shopping

enquiries

Where's a ...?	Kde je ...?	kdye ye ...
bank	banka	buhn-kuh
bookshop	kníhkupectvo	knyeeh-ku-pets-tvo
camera shop	fotografický obchod	fo-to-gruh-fits-kee ob-khod ob-khod
department store	obchodný dom	ob-khod-nee dom
grocery store	potraviny	po-truh-vi-ni
market	trh	trh
newsagency	predajňa novín	pre-dai-nyuh no-veen
supermarket	samoobsluha	suh-mo-ob-slu-huh

Where can I buy (a padlock)?
Kde si môžem kúpiť
(visiaci zámok)?
kdye si mwo-zhem koo-pit'
(vi-syuh-tsi za-mok)

I'm looking for ...
Hľadám ...
hlyuh-dam ...

Can I look at it?
Môžem sa na to pozrieť?
mwo-zhem suh nuh to poz-ryet'

Do you have any others?
Máte nejaké iné?
ma-tye nye-yuh-kair i-nair

Does it have a guarantee?
Je na to záruka?
ye nuh to za-ru-kuh

Can I have it sent abroad?
Môžem si to dať poslať do
zahraničia?
mwo-zhem si to duht' pos-luht' do
zuh-hruh-nyi-chyuh

Can I have my ... repaired?
Môžem si dať opraviť môj ...?
mwo-zhem si duht' o-pruh-vit' mwoy ...

It's faulty.
Je to pokazené.
ye to po-kuh-ze-nair

I'd like ..., please.	Poprosil/Poprosila by som ... m/f	po-pro-sil/po-pro-si-luh bi som ...
a bag	tašku	tuhsh-ku
a refund	vrátenie peňazí	vra-tye-ni-ye pe-nyuh-zee
to return this	toto vrátiť	to-to vra-tyit'

paying

How much is it?
Koľko to stojí? — koľ·ko to sto·yee

Can you write down the price?
Môžete napísať cenu? — mwo·zhe·tye nuh·pee·suht' tse·nu

That's too expensive.
To je príliš drahé. — to ye pree·lish druh·hair

What's your lowest price?
Aká je vaša najnižšia cena? — uh·ka ye vuh·shuh nai·nizh·shyuh tse·nuh

I'll give you (five) euros.
Dám vám (päť) euro. — dam vam (pet') e·u·ro

There's a mistake in the bill.
V účte je chyba. — v ooch·tye ye khi·buh

Do you accept ...? — *Prijmate ...?* — pree·muh·tye ...
  credit cards — *kreditné karty* — kre·dit·nair kuhr·ti
  debit cards — *debetné karty* — de·bet·nair kuhr·ti
  travellers cheques — *cestovné šeky* — tses·tov·nair she·ki

I'd like ..., please. — *Prosím si ...* — pro·seem si ...
  a receipt — *potvrdenie* — pot·vr·dye·ni·ye
  my change — *môj výdavok* — mwoy vee·duh·vok

clothes & shoes

Can I try it on? — *Môžem si to vyskúšať?* — mwo·zhem si to vis·koo·shuht'
My size is (42). — *Moja velkosť je (štyridsaťdva).* — mo·yuh vel'·kost' ye (shti·rid·suht'·dvuh)
It doesn't fit. — *Nesedí mi to.* — nye·se·dyee mi to

small — *malý* — muh·lee
medium — *stredný* — stred·nee
large — *veľký* — vel'·kee

books & music

I'd like a ...	*Môžem dostať ...*	*mwo*-zhem dos-tuht' ...
newspaper	*noviny*	*no*-vi-ni
(in English)	*(v angličtine)*	(v *uhn*-glich-tyi-nye)
pen	*pero*	*pe*-ro

Is there an English-language bookshop?
Je tu anglické kníhkupectvo?   ye tu *uhn*-glits-kair *kneeh*-ku-pets-tvo

I'm looking for something by (Milan Lasica/Boris Filan).
Hľadám niečo od (Milana Lasicu/   *hlyuh*-dam ni-*ye*-cho od (*mi*-luh-nuh *luh*-si-tsu/
Borisa Filana).   bo-ri-suh *fi*-luh-nuh)

Can I listen to this?
Môžem si to vypočuť?   *mwo*-zhem si to *vi*-po-chut'

photography

Can you ...?	*Mohli by ste ...?*	*mo*-hli bi stye ...
burn a CD from	*napáliť CD z*	*nuh*-pa-lit' *tsair*-dair z
my memory card	*mojej pamäťovej*	*mo*-yey puh-me-tyo-vey
	karty	*kuhr*-ti
develop this film	*vyvolať tento film*	*vi*-vo-luht' *ten*-to film
load my film	*zaviesť môj film*	zuh-*vyest'* mwoy film

I need a/an ... film	*Potrebujem ... film*	po-tre-bu-yem ... film
for this camera.	*do tohto fotoaparátu.*	do *to*-hto *fo*-to-uh-puh-ra-tu
APS	*APS*	a pair es
B&W	*čiernobiely*	*chyer*-no-bye-li
colour	*farebný*	*fuh*-reb-nee
slide	*navíjací*	*nuh*-vee-yuh-tsee
(200) speed	*(dvestovku) citlivosť*	(*dve*-stov-ku) *tsit*-li-vost'

When will it be ready?	*Kedy to bude hotové?*	*ke*-di to *bu*-dye *ho*-to-vair

meeting people

greetings, goodbyes & introductions

Hello/Hi.	Dobrý deň/Ahoj.	do·bree dyen'/uh·hoy
Good night.	Dobrú noc.	do·broo nots
Goodbye/Bye.	Do videnia/Ahoj.	do vi·dye·ni·yuh/uh·ho

| Mr/Mrs | pán/pani | pan/puh·nyi |
| Miss | slečna | slech·nuh |

How are you?	Ako sa máte/máš? pol/inf	uh·ko suh ma·tye/mash
Fine, thanks.	Dobre, ďakujem.	do·bre dyuh·ku·yem
And you?	A vy/ty? pol/inf	uh vi/ti
What's your name?	Ako sa voláte/ voláš? pol/inf	uh·ko suh vo·la·tye/ vo·lash
My name is ...	Volám sa ...	vo·lam suh ...
I'm pleased to meet you.	Teší ma.	tye·shee muh

This is my ...	Toto je môj/moja ... m/f	to·to ye mwoy/mo·yuh ...
boyfriend	priateľ	pryuh·tyel'
brother	brat	bruht
daughter	dcéra	tsair·ruh
father	otec	o·tyets
friend	kamarát m	kuh·muh·rat
	kamarátka f	kuh·muh·rat·kuh
girlfriend	priateľka	pryuh·tyel'·kuh
husband	manžel	muhn·zhel
mother	matka	muht·kuh
partner (intimate)	partner/partnerka m/f	part·ner/part·ner·kuh
sister	sestra	ses·truh
son	syn	sin
wife	manželka	muhn·zhel·kuh

What's your ...?	Aká je vaša ...?	uh·ka ye vuh·shuh ...
address	adresa	uhd·re·suh
email address	emailová adresa	ee·mey·lo·va uhd·re·suh

Here's my ...	Tu je môj ...	tu ye mwoy ...
What's your ...?	Aké je vaše ...?	uh·kair ye vuh·she ...
fax number	faxové číslo	fuhk·so·vair chees·lo
phone number	telefónne číslo	te·le·fuhwn·ne chees·lo

occupations

What's your occupation?
    Aké je vaše povolanie?   *uh·kair ye vuh·she po·vo·luh·ni·ye*

I'm a/an ...	Som ...	som ...
artist	*umelec/umelkyňa* m/f	*u·me·lets/u·mel·ki·nyuh*
businessperson	*podnikateľ* m	*pod·nyi·kuh·tyel'*
	podnikateľka f	*pod·nyi·kuh·tyel'·kuh*
farmer	*pestovateľ* m	*pes·to·vuh·tyel'*
	pestovateľka f	*pes·to·vuh·tyel'·ka*
manual worker	*robotník* m	*ro·bot·nyeek*
	robotníčka f	*ro·bot·nyeech·kuh*
office worker	*úradník* m	*oo·ruhd·nyeek*
	úradníčka f	*oo·ruhd·nyeech·kuh*
scientist	*vedecký*	*ve·dyets·kee*
	pracovník m	*pruh·tsov·nyeek*
	vedecká	*ve·dets·ka*
	pracovníčka f	*pruh·tsov·nyeech·kuh*
student	*študent/študentka* m/f	*shtu·dent/shtu·dent·kuh*
tradesperson	*živnostník* m	*zhiv·nos·nyeek*
	živnostníčka f	*zhiv·nos·nyeech·kuh*

background

Where are you from?	Odkiaľ ste?	od·kyuhl' stye

I'm from ...	Som z ...	som z ...
Australia	*Austrálie*	*ows·tra·li·ye*
Canada	*Kanady*	*kuh·nuh·di*
England	*Anglicka*	*uhng·lits·kuh*
New Zealand	*Nového Zélandu*	*no·vair·ho zair·luhn·du*
the USA	*USA*	*oo·es·a*

Are you married?	Ste ženatý/vydatá? m/f	stye zhe·nuh·tee/vi·duh·ta

I'm ...	Som ...	som ...
married	*ženatý/vydatá* m/f	*zhe·nuh·tee/vi·duh·ta*
single	*slobodný* m	*slo·bod·nee*
	slobodná f	*slo·bod·na*

age

How old ...?	Koľko ... rokov?	koľ·ko ... ro·kov
are you	máte/máš pol/inf	ma·tye/mash
is your daughter	má vaša dcéra	ma vuh·shuh tsair·ruh
is your son	má váš syn	ma vash sin

| I'm ... years old. | Ja mám ... rokov. | yuh mam ... ro·kov |
| He/She is ... years old. | On/Ona má ... rokov. | on/onuh ma ... ro·kov |

feelings

I'm (not) ...	(Nie) Je mi ...	(ni·ye) ye mi ...
Are you ...?	Je vám ...?	ye vam ...
cold	zima	zi·muh
hot	teplo	tye·plo

I'm (not) ...	(Nie) Som ...	(ni·ye) som ...
Are you ...?	Ste ...?	stye ...
happy	šťastný/šťastná m/f	shtyuhs·nee/shtyuhs·na
hungry	hladný/hladná m/f	hluhd·nee/hluhd·na
sad	smutný/smutná m/f	smut·nee/smut·na
thirsty	smädný/smädná m/f	smed·nee/smed·na

entertainment

going out

Where can I find ...?	Kde nájdem ...?	kdye nai·dyem ...
clubs	kluby	klu·bi
gay venues	podniky pre homosexuálov	pod·nyi·ki pre ho·mo·sek·su·a·lov
pubs	krčmy	krch·mi

I feel like going to a/the ...	Mám chuť ísť ...	mam khuť eesť ...
concert	na koncert	nuh kon·tsert
movies	do kina	do ki·nuh
restaurant	do reštaurácie	do resh·tow·ra·tsi·ye
theatre	do divadla	do dyi·vuhd·luh

interests

Do you like ...?	*Máte radi ...?*	*ma·tye ruh·di ...*
I like ...	*Mám rád/rada ... m/f*	mam rad/*ruh·duh ...*
I don't like ...	*Nemám rád/*	*nye·*mam rad/
	rada ... m/f	*ruh·duh ...*
art	*umenie*	*u·*me·ni·ye
cooking	*varenie*	*vuh·*re·ni·ye
movies	*filmy*	*fil·*mi
nightclubs	*nočné kluby*	*noch·*nair *klu·*bi
reading	*čítanie*	*chee·*tuh·ni·ye
shopping	*nakupovanie*	*nuh·*ku·po·vuh·ni·ye
sport	*šport*	shport
travelling	*cestovanie*	*tses·*to·vuh·ni·ye
Do you like to ...?	*Radi ...?*	*ruh·*dyi ...
dance	*tancujete*	*tuhn·*tsu·ye·tye
go to concerts	*chodíte na*	*kho·*dyee·tye nuh
	koncerty	*kon·*tser·ti
listen to music	*počúvate hudbu*	*po·*choo·vuh·tye *hud·*bu

food & drink

finding a place to eat

Can you	*Môžete mi*	*mwo·*zhe·tye mi
recommend a ...?	*odporučiť ...?*	*od·*po·ru·chit' ...
bar	*bar*	buhr
café	*kaviareň*	*kuh·*vyuh·ren'
restaurant	*reštauráciu*	*resh·*tow·ra·tsi·yu
I'd like ..., please.	*Chcel/Chcela by som*	khtsel/*khtse·*luh bi som
	..., prosím. m/f	... *pro·*seem
a table for (four)	*stôl pre (štyroch)*	stwol pre (*shti·*rokh)
the nonsmoking	*nefajčiarsku časť*	*nye·*fai·chyuhr·sku chuhst'
section		
the smoking section	*fajčiarsku časť*	*fai·*chyuhr·sku chuhst'

ordering food

breakfast	*raňajky* pl	*ruh*·nyai·ki
lunch	*obed* m	*o*·bed
dinner	*večera* f	*ve*·che·ruh
snack	*občerstvenie* n	*ob*·cherst·ve·ni·ye
What would you recommend?	*Čo by ste mi odporučili?*	cho bi stye mi *od*·po·ru·chi·li
I'd like (the) ..., please.	*Prosím si ...*	*pro*·seem si ...
bill	*účet*	*oo*·chet
drink list	*nápojový lístok*	*na*·po·yo·vee *lees*·tok
menu	*jedálny lístok*	*ye*·dal·ni *lees*·tok
that dish	*toto jedlo*	*to*·to *yed*·lo

drinks

(cup of) coffee/tea ...	*(šálka) kávy/čaju ...*	*(shal*·kuh) ka·vi/*chuh*·yu ...
with milk	*s mliekom*	s *mlye*·kom
without sugar	*bez cukru*	bez *tsuk*·ru
(orange) juice	*(pomarančový) džús* m	*(po*·muh·ruhn·cho·vee) dyoos
soft drink	*nealkoholický nápoj* m	nye·uhl·ko·ho·lits·kee *na*·poy
(boiled/mineral) water	*(prevarená/minerálna) voda* f	*(pre*·vuh·re·na/*mi*·ne·ral·nuh) *vo*·duh

in the bar

I'll have ...	*Dám si ...*	dam si ...
I'll buy you a drink. inf/pol	*Kúpim ti/vám drink.*	*koo*·pim tyi/vam drink
What would you like? inf/pol	*Čo si dáš/dáte?*	cho si dash/*da*·tye
Cheers!	*Nazdravie!*	*nuhz*·druh·vi·ye
a shot of (whisky)	*štamperlík (whisky)*	*shtuhm*·per·leek (*vis*·ki)
a bottle/glass of beer	*fľaša/pohár piva*	*flyuh*·shuh/*po*·har *pi*·vuh
a bottle/glass of ...wine	*fľaša/pohár ... vína*	*flyuh*·shuh/*po*·har ... *vee*·nuh
red	*červeného*	*cher*·ve·nair·ho
sparkling	*šumivého*	*shu*·mi·vair·ho
white	*bieleho*	*bye*·le·ho

self-catering

What's the local speciality?
Čo je miestna špecialita?   cho ye *myes*·nuh *shpe*·tsyuh·li·tuh

What's that?
Čo je to?   cho ye to

How much is (a kilo of cheese)?
Koľko stojí (kilo syra)?   *koľ*·ko sto·yee (*ki*·lo *si*·ruh)

I'd like ...	*Môžem dostať ...*	mwo·zhem *dos*·tuhť ...
(100) grams	*(sto) gramov*	(sto) *gruh*·mov
(two) kilos	*(dve) kilá*	(dve) *ki*·la
(three) pieces	*(tri) kusy*	(tri) *ku*·si
(six) slices	*(šesť) plátkov*	(shesť) *plat*·kov

Less.	*Menej.*	me·nyey
Enough.	*Stačí.*	*stuh*·chee
More.	*Viac.*	vyuhts

special diets & allergies

Is there a vegetarian restaurant near here?
Je tu nablízku vegetariánska   ye tu *nuh*·bleez·ku ve·ge·tuh·ri·yan·skuh
reštaurácia?   resh·tow·ra·tsi·yuh

Do you have vegetarian food?
Máte vegetariánske jedlá?   ma·tye ve·ge·tuh·ri·yan·ske *yed*·la

Could you prepare	*Mohli by ste pripraviť*	mo·hli bi stye *pri*·pruh·viť
a meal without ...?	*jedlo bez ...?*	*yed*·lo bez ...
butter	*masla*	*muhs*·luh
eggs	*vajec*	*vuh*·yets
meat stock	*mäsového vývaru*	me·so·vair·ho *vee*·vuh·ru

I'm allergic to ...	*Som alergický/*	som uh·*ler*·gits·kee/
	alergická na ... m/f	uh·*ler*·gits·ka nuh ...
dairy produce	*mliečne produkty*	mlyech·ne pro·*duk*·ti
gluten	*lepok*	*le*·pok
MSG	*zvýrazňovač*	zvee·*ruhz*·nyo·vuhch
	chute	*khu*·tye
nuts	*orechy*	o·*re*·khi
seafood	*dary mora*	*duh*·ri mo·ruh

menu decoder

balkánský šalát m	*buhl-*kan-ski *shuh-*lat	lettuce, tomato, onion & cheese salad
bravčové pečené s rascou n	*bruhv-*cho-vair *pe-*che-nair s *ruhs-*tsoh	roast pork with caraway seeds
držková polievka f	*drzh-*ko-va *po-*lyev-kuh	sliced tripe soup
dusené hovädzie na prírodno n	*du-*se-nair *ho-*ve-dzye nuh *pree-*rod-no	braised beef slices in sauce
guláš m	*gu-*lash	thick, spicy beef & potato soup
hovädzí guláš m	*ho-*ve-dzee *gu-*lash	beef chunks in brown sauce
hovädzí vývar m	*ho-*ve-dzee *vee-*vuhr	beef in broth
hrachová polievka f	*hruh-*kho-va *po-*lyev-kuh	thick pea soup with bacon
jablkový závin m	*yuh-*bl-ko-vee *za-*vin	apple strudel
kapor na víne m	*kuh-*por nuh *vee-*nye	carp braised in wine
koložvárska kapusta f	*ko-*lozh-var-skuh *kuh-*pus-tuh	goulash with beef, pork, lamb & sauerkraut in a cream sauce
krokety m pl	*kro-*ke-ti	deep-fried mashed potato
kuracia polievka f	*ku-*ruh-tsyuh *po-*lyev-kuh	chicken soup
kurací paprikáš m	*ku-*ruh-tsee *puhp-*ri-kash	chicken braised in red (paprika) sauce
kyslá uhorka f	*kis-*la *u-*hor-kuh	dill pickle (gherkin)
opékané zemiaky f pl	*o-*pe-kuh-nair *ze-*myuh-ki	fried potatoes
ovocné knedle f pl	*o-*vots-nair *kned-*le	fruit dumplings
palacinky f pl	*puh-*luh-tsin-ki	pancakes
paradajková polievka s cibuľkou f	*puh-*ruh-dai-ko-va *po-*lyev-kuh s *tsi-*buľ-koh	tomato & onion soup

pečené zemiaky f pl	pe-che-nair ze-myuh-ki	roast potatoes
plnená paprika v paradajkovej omáčke f	pl-nye-na puhp-ri-kuh v puh-ruh-dai-ko-vey o-mach-ke	capsicum stuffed with minced meat & rice, served with tomato sauce
polievka z bažanta f	po-lyev-kuh z buh-zhuhn-tuh	pheasant soup
praženica f	pruh-zhe-nyi-tsuh	scrambled eggs
prírodný rezeň m	pree-rod-nee re-zen'	unbreaded pork or veal schnitzel
rizoto n	ri-zo-to	mixture of pork, onion, peas & rice
ruské vajcia n pl	rus-kair vai-tsyuh	hard-boiled egg, potato & salami, with mayonnaise
rybacia polievka f	ri-buh-tsyuh po-lyev-kuh	fish soup
ryžový nákup m	ri-zho-vee na-kip	rice soufflé
salámový tanier s oblohou m	suh-la-mo-vee tuh-nyer s ob-lo-hoh	salami platter with fresh or pickled vegetables
sviečková na smotane f	svyech-ko-va nuh smo-tuh-nye	roast beef with sour cream sauce & spices
špenát m	shpe-nat	finely chopped spinach, cooked with onion, garlic & cream
šunka pečená s vajcom f	shun-kuh pe-che-na s vai-tsom	fried ham with egg
tatárska omáčka f	tuh-tar-skuh o-mach-kuh	creamy tartar sauce
tatársky biftek m	tuh-tar-ski bif-tek	raw steak
teľacie pečené n	tye-lyuh-tsye pe-che-nair	roast veal
tlačenka s octom a cibuľou f	tluh-chen-kuh s ots-tom uh tsi-bu-loh	jellied meat loaf with vinegar & onion
vyprážané rybacie filé n	vi-pra-zhuh-nair ri-buh-tsye fi-lair	fillet of fish fried in breadcrumbs

emergencies

basics

English	Slovak	Pronunciation
Help!	*Pomoc!*	*po*·mots
Stop!	*Stoj!*	stoy
Go away!	*Choďte preč!*	*khod'*·tye prech
Thief!	*Zlodej!*	*zlo*·dyey
Fire!	*Oheň!*	*o*·hen'
Watch out!	*Pozor!*	*po*·zor
Call a doctor!	*Zavolajte lekára!*	zuh·vo·lai·tye *le*·ka·ruh
Call an ambulance!	*Zavolajte záchranku!*	zuh·vo·lai·tye *zakh*·ruhn·ku
Call the police!	*Zavolajte políciu!*	zuh·vo·lai·tye *po*·lee·tsi·yu

It's an emergency!
Je to pohotovostný prípad! — ye to *po*·ho·to·vos·nee *pree*·puhd

Could you help me, please?
Môžete mi prosím pomôcť? — *mwo*·zhe·tye mi *pro*·seem *po*·mwotst'

I have to use the telephone.
Potrebujem telefón. — *po*·tre·bu·yem *te*·le·fawn

I'm lost.
Stratil/Stratila som sa. m/f — *struh*·tyil/*struh*·tyi·luh som suh

Where are the toilets?
Kde sú tu záchody? — kdye soo tu *za*·kho·di

police

Where's the police station?
Kde je policajná stanica? — kdye ye *po*·li·tsai·na *stuh*·nyi·tsuh

I want to report an offence. (serious/minor)
Chcem nahlásiť zločin/priestupok. — khtsem nuh·hla·sit' *zlo*·chin/*prye*·stu·pok

I've been ...	*Bol/Bola som ...* m/f	bol/*bo*·luh som ...
assaulted	*prepadnutý* m	*pre*·puhd·nu·tee
	prepadnutá f	*pre*·puhd·nu·ta
raped	*znásilnený* m	*zna*·sil·nye·nee
	znásilnená f	*zna*·sil·nye·na
robbed	*okradnutý* m	*o*·kruhd·nu·tee
	okradnutá f	*o*·kruhd·nu·ta

I've lost my ...	Stratil/Stratila som ... m/f	struh·tyil/struh·tyi·luh som ...
My ... was/were stolen.	Ukradli mi ...	u·kruhd·li mi ...
backpack	plecniak	plets·ni·yuhk
bags	batožinu	buh·to·zhi·nu
credit card	kreditnú kartu	kre·dit·noo kuhr·tu
handbag	kabelku	kuh·bel·ku
jewellery	šperky	shper·ki
money	peniaze	pe·nyuh·ze
passport	cestovný pas	tses·tov·nee puhs
travellers cheques	cestovné šeky	tses·tov·nair she·ki
wallet	peňaženku	pe·nyuh·zhen·ku
I want to contact my ...	Chcem sa spojiť s ...	khtsem suh spo·yit' s ...
consulate	mojím konzulátom	mo·yeem kon·zu·la·tom
embassy	mojou ambasádou	mo·yoh uhm·buh·sa·doh

health

medical needs

Where's the nearest ...?	Kde je najbližší/ najbližšia ...? m/f	kdye ye nai·blizh·shee/ nai·blizh·shyuh ...
dentist	zubár m	zu·bar
doctor	doktor m	dok·tor
hospital	nemocnica f	ne·mots·nyi·tsuh
(night) pharmacist	(pohotovostná) lekáreň f	(po·ho·to·vost·na) le·ka·ren'

I need a doctor (who speaks English).
Potrebujem lekára,
(ktorý hovorí po anglicky).
po·tre·bu·yem le·ka·ruh
(kto·ree ho·vo·ree po uhng·lits·ki)

Could I see a female doctor?
Mohla by som navštíviť
ženského lekára?
mo·hluh bi som nuhv·shtyee·vit'
zhen·skair·ho le·ka·ruh

I've run out of my medication.
Minuli sa mi lieky.
mi·nu·li suh mi li·ye·ki

symptoms, conditions & allergies

| I'm sick. | Som chorý/chorá. m/f | som kho·ree/kho·ra |
| It hurts here. | Tu ma to bolí. | tu muh to bo·lee |

I have (a) ...		
asthma	Mám astmu.	mam uhst·mu
bronchitis	Mám zápal priedušiek.	mam za·puhl prye·du·shyek
constipation	Mám zápchu.	mam zap·khu
cough	Mám kašeľ.	mam kuh·shel
diarrhoea	Mám hnačku.	mam hnuhch·ku
fever	Mám horúčku.	mam ho·rooch·ku
headache	Bolí ma hlava.	bo·lee muh hluh·vuh
heart condition	Mám srdcovú príhodu.	mam srd·tso·voo pree·ho·du
nausea	Je mi nazvracanie.	ye mi nuhz·vruh·tsuh·ni·ye
pain	Mám bolesti.	mam bo·les·tyi
sore throat	Bolí ma hrdlo.	bo·lee muh hrd·lo
toothache	Bolí ma zub.	bo·lee muh zub

I'm allergic to ...	Som alergický/ alergická na... m/f	som uh·ler·gits·kee/ uh·ler·gits·ka nuh ...
antibiotics	antibiotiká	uhn·ti·bi·o·ti·ka
anti-inflammatories	protizápalové lieky	pro·ti·za·puh·lo·vair lye·ki
aspirin	aspirín	uhs·pi·reen
bees	včely	fche·li
codeine	kodeín	ko·de·een
penicillin	penicilín	pe·ni·tsi·leen

antiseptic	antiseptikum n	uhn·ti·sep·ti·kum
bandage	obväz m	ob·vez
condoms	kondómy m pl	kon·daw·mi
contraceptives	antikoncepcia f	uhn·ti·kon·tsep·tsi·yuh
diarrhoea medicine	lieky proti hnačke m	li·ye·ki pro·tyi hnuhch·ke
insect repellent	repelent proti hmyzu m	re·pe·lent pro·tyi hmi·zu
laxatives	preháňadlá n pl	pre·ha·nyuhd·la
painkillers	analgetiká n pl	uh·nuhl·ge·ti·ka
rehydration salts	rehydratujúce soli f pl	re·hid·ruh·tu·yoo·tse so·li
sleeping tablets	tabletky na spanie f pl	tuhb·let·ki nuh spuh·ni·ye

english–slovak dictionary

Slovak nouns in this dictionary have their gender indicated by ⓜ (masculine), ⓕ (feminine) or ⓝ (neuter). If it's a plural noun, you'll also see pl. Adjectives are given in the masculine form only. Words are also marked as a (adjective), v (verb), sg (singular), pl (plural), inf (informal) or pol (polite) where necessary.

A

accident *nehoda* ⓕ nye-ho-duh
accommodation *ubytovanie* ⓝ u-bi-to-vuh-ni-ye
adaptor *rozvodka* ⓕ roz-vod-kuh
address *adresa* ⓕ uh-dre-suh
after *po* po
air-conditioned *klimatizovaný* klí-muh-ti-zo-vuh-nee
airplane *lietadlo* ⓝ li-ye-tuhd-lo
airport *letisko* ⓝ le-tis-ko
alcohol *alkohol* ⓜ uhl-ko-hol
all (everything) *všetko* fshet-ko
allergy *alergia* ⓕ uh-ler-gi-yuh
ambulance *ambulancia* ⓕ uhm-bu-luhn-tsi-yuh
and *a* uh
ankle *členok* ⓜ chle-nok
arm *rameno* ⓝ ruh-me-no
ashtray *popolník* ⓜ po-pol-nyeek
ATM *bankomat* ⓜ buhn-ko-muht

B

baby *dieťatko* ⓝ di-ye-tyuht-ko
back (body) *chrbát* ⓜ khr-baat
backpack *ruksak* ⓜ ruk-suhk
bad *zlý* zlee
bag *taška* ⓕ tuhsh-kuh
baggage claim *úložňa batožiny* ⓕ oo-lozh-nyuh buh-to-zhi-ni
bank *banka* ⓕ buhn-kuh
bar *bar* ⓜ buhr
bathroom *kúpeľňa* ⓕ koo-peľ-nyuh
battery *batéria* ⓕ buh-tair-ri-yuh
beautiful *krásny* kras-ni
bed *posteľ* ⓕ pos-tyeľ
beer *pivo* ⓝ pi-vo
before *pred* pred
behind *za* zuh
bicycle *bicykel* ⓜ bi-tsi-kel
big *veľký* veľ-kee
bill *účet* ⓜ oo-chet
black *čierny* chyer-ni
blanket *prikrývka* ⓕ pri-kreev-kuh

blood group *krvná skupina* ⓕ krv-na sku-pi-nuh
blue *modrý* mod-ree
boat *loď* ⓕ loď
book (make a reservation) v *rezervovať* re-zer-vo-vuhť
bottle *fľaša* ⓕ fľyuh-shuh
bottle opener *otvárač na fľašu* ⓜ ot-va-ruhch nuh fľyuh-shu
boy *chlapec* ⓜ khluh-pets
brakes (car) *brzdy* ⓕ pl brz-di
breakfast *raňajky* pl ruh-nyai-ki
broken (faulty) *pokazený* po-kuh-ze-nee
bus *autobus* ⓜ ow-to-bus
business *obchod* ⓜ ob-khod
buy *kúpiť* koo-piť

C

café *kaviareň* ⓕ kuh-vyuh-ren'
camera *fotoaparát* ⓜ fo-to-uh-puh-rat
camp site *táborisko* ⓝ ta-bo-ris-ko
cancel *zrušiť* zru-shiť
can opener *otvárač na konzervu* ⓜ ot-va-ruhch nuh kon-zer-vu
car *auto* ⓝ ow-to
cash *hotovosť* ⓕ ho-to-vosť
cash (a cheque) v *preplatiť (šek)* prep-luh-tyiť (shek)
cell phone *mobil* ⓜ mo-bil
centre *centrum* ⓝ tsen-trum
change (money) v *zameniť (peniaze)* zuh-me-nyiť (pe-ni-yuh-ze)
cheap *lacný* luhts-nee
check (bill) *účet* ⓜ oo-chet
check-in *registrácia* ⓕ re-gis-tra-tsi-yuh
chest *hruď* ⓕ hruď
child *dieťa* ⓝ di-ye-tyuh
city *mesto* ⓝ mes-to
cigarette *cigareta* ⓕ tsi-guh-re-tuh
clean a *čistý* chis-tee
closed *zatvorený* zuht-vo-re-nee
coffee *káva* ⓕ ka-vuh
coins *mince* ⓕ pl min-tse
cold a *studený* stu-dye-nee

collect call *hovor na účet volaného* ⓜ
ho-vor nuh oo-chet vo-luh-nair-ho
come *prísť* 'preest'
computer *počítač* ⓜ po-chee-tuhch
condom *kondóm* ⓜ kon-duhwm
contact lenses *kontaktné šošovky* ⓕ pl
kon-tuhkt-nair sho-shov-ki
cook v *variť* vuh-rit'
cost *cena* ⓕ tse-nuh
credit card *kreditná karta* ⓕ kre-dit-na kuhr-tuh
cup *šálka* ⓕ shaal-ka
currency exchange *výmena peňazí* ⓕ
vee-me-nuh pe-nyuh-zee
customs (immigration) *colnica* ⓕ tsol-nyi-tsuh

D

dangerous *nebezpečný* ne-bez-pech-nee
date (time) *dátum* ⓜ da-tum
day *deň* dyen'
delay *meškanie* ⓝ mesh-kuh-ni-ye
dentist *zubár* ⓜ zu-bar
depart *odchádzať* od-kha-dzat'
diaper *plienka* ⓕ pli-yen-kuh
dictionary *slovník* ⓜ slov-nyeek
dinner *večera* ⓕ ve-che-ruh
direct a *priamy* pryuh-mi
dirty *špinavý* shpi-nuh-vee
disabled *postihnutý* pos-tyih-nu-tee
discount *zľava* ⓕ zlyuh-vuh
doctor *lekár* ⓜ le-kar
double bed *dvojitá posteľ* ⓕ dvo-yi-ta pos-tyel'
double room *dvojposteľová izba* ⓕ
dvoy-pos-tye-lyo-va iz-buh
drink *nápoj* ⓜ na-poy
drive v *riadiť* ryuh-dyit'
drivers licence *vodičský preukaz* ⓜ
vo-dyich-skee pre-u-kuhz
drug (illicit) *droga* ⓕ dro-guh
dummy (pacifier) *cumeľ* ⓜ tsu-mel'

E

ear *ucho* ⓝ u-kho
east *východ* vee-khod
eat *jesť* yest'
economy class *ekonomická trieda* ⓕ
e-ko-no-mits-ka trye-duh
electricity *elektrika* ⓕ e-lek-tri-kuh
elevator *výťah* ⓜ vee-tyah
email *email* ⓜ ee-meyl
embassy *veľvyslanectvo* ⓝ veľ-vis-luh-nyets-tvo
emergency *pohotovosť* ⓕ po-ho-to-vost'

English (language) *angličtina* ⓕ uhng-lich-tyi-nuh
entrance *vchod* ⓜ vkhod
evening *večer* ⓜ ve-cher
exchange rate *výmenný kurz* vee-men-nee kurz
exit *východ* ⓜ vee-khod
expensive *drahý* druh-hee
express mail *expresná pošta* ⓕ eks-pres-na posh-tuh
eye *oko* ⓝ o-ko

F

far *ďaleko* dyuh-le-ko
fast *rýchly* reekh-li
father *otec* ⓜ o-tyets
film (camera) *film* ⓜ film
finger *prst* ⓜ prst
first-aid kit *lekárnička* ⓕ le-kar-nyich-kuh
first class *prvá trieda* ⓕ pr-va trye-duh
fish *ryba* ⓕ ri-buh
food *jedlo* ⓝ yed-lo
foot *noha* ⓕ no-huh
fork *vidlička* ⓕ vid-lich-kuh
free (of charge) *zadarmo* zuh-duhr-mo
friend *priateľ/priateľka* ⓜ/ⓕ pryuh-teľ/prya-tyeľ-ka
fruit *ovocie* ⓝ o-vo-tsye
full *plný* pl-nee
funny *smiešny* smyesh-ni

G

gift *dar* ⓜ duhr
girl *dievča* ⓝ di-yev-chuh
glass (drinking) *pohár* ⓜ po-har
glasses *okuliare* pl o-ku-lyuh-re
go *ísť* eest'
good *dobrý* dob-ree
green *zelený* ze-le-nee
guide *sprievodca* ⓜ sprye-vod-tsuh

H

half *polovica* ⓕ po-lo-vi-tsuh
hand *ruka* ⓕ ru-kuh
handbag *kabelka* ⓕ kuh-bel-kuh
happy *šťastný* shtyuhs-nee
have *mať* muht'
he *on* on
head *hlava* ⓕ hluh-vuh
heart *srdce* ⓝ srd-tse
heat *teplo* ⓝ tyep-lo
heavy *ťažký* tyuhzh-kee
help v *pomôcť* pom-wotst'

here *tu* tu
high *vysoký* vi-so-kee
highway *diaľnica* ① di-yuhl-nyi-tsuh
hike v *ísť na turistiku* eesť nuh tu-ris-ti-ku
holiday *dovolenka* ① do-vo-len-kuh
homosexual *homosexuál* ⓜ ho-mo-sek-su-al
hospital *nemocnica* ① ne-mots-nyi-tsuh
hot *horúci* ho-roo-tsi
hotel *hotel* ⓜ ho-tel
hungry *hladný* hluhd-nee
husband *manžel* ⓜ muhn-zhel

I

I *ja* yuh
identification (card) *občiansky preukaz* ⓜ
  ob-chyuhns-ki pre-u-kuhz
ill *chorý* kho-ree
important *dôležitý* dwo-le-zhi-tee
included *zahrnutý* zuh-hr-nu-tee
injury *poranenie* ⓝ po-ruh-nye-ni-ye
insurance *poistenie* ⓝ po-is-tye-ni-ye
Internet *internet* ⓜ in-ter-net
interpreter *tlmočník* ⓜ tl-moch-nyeek

J

jewellery *šperky* ⓜ pl shper-ki
job *zamestnanie* ⓝ zuh-mest-nuh-ni-ye

K

key *kľúč* ⓜ kľooch
kilogram *kilogram* ⓜ ki-log-ruhm
kitchen *kuchyňa* ① ku-khi-nyuh
knife *nôž* ⓜ nwozh

L

laundry (place) *práčovňa* ① pra-chov-nyuh
lawyer *právnik* ⓜ prav-nyik
left (direction) *vľavo* vluh-vo
left-luggage office *úschovňa batožiny* ①
  oos-khov-nyuh buh-to-zhi-ni
leg *noha* ① no-huh
lesbian *lesbia* ① les-bi-yuh
less *menej* me-nyey
letter (mail) *list* ⓜ list
lift (elevator) *výťah* ⓜ vee-tyah
light *svetlo* ⓝ svet-lo
like v *mať rád* muhť rad

lock *zámok* ⓜ za-mok
long *dlhý* dl-hee
lost *stratený* struh-tye-nee
lost-property office *straty a nálezy* ①
  struh-ti uh na-le-zi
love v *ľúbiť* lyoo-biť
luggage *batožina* ① buh-to-zhi-nuh
lunch *obed* ⓜ o-bed

M

mail *pošta* ① posh-tuh
man *muž* ⓜ muzh
map *mapa* ① muh-puh
market *trh* ⓜ trh
matches *zápalky* ① pl za-puhl-ki
meat *mäso* ⓝ me-so
medicine *liek* ⓜ li-yek
menu *jedálny lístok* ⓜ ye-dal-ni lees-tok
message *správa* ① spra-vuh
milk *mlieko* ⓝ mli-ye-ko
minute *minúta* ① mi-noo-tuh
mobile phone *mobil* ⓜ mo-bil
money *peniaze* ⓜ pl pe-ni-yuh-ze
month *mesiac* ⓜ me-syuhts
morning *ráno* ⓝ ra-no
mother *matka* ① muht-kuh
motorcycle *motorka* ① mo-tor-kuh
motorway *hlavná cesta* ① hluhv-na tses-tuh
mouth *ústa* pl oos-tuh
music *hudba* ① hud-buh

N

name *meno* ⓝ me-no
napkin *obrúsok* ⓜ ob-roo-sok
nappy *plienka* ① plyen-kuh
near *blízko* bleez-ko
neck *krk* ⓜ krk
new *nový* no-vee
news *správy* ① pl spra-vi
newspaper *noviny* pl no-vi-ni
night *noc* ① nots
no *nie* ni-ye
noisy *hlučný* hluch-nee
nonsmoking *nefajčiarsky* ne-fai-chyuhr-ski
north *sever* se-ver
nose *nos* ⓜ nos
now *teraz* te-ruhz
number *číslo* ⓝ chees-lo

O

oil (engine) *olej* ⓜ o-ley
old *starý* stuh-ree
one-way ticket *jednosmerný lístok* ⓜ
    yed-no-smer-nee lees-tok
open a *otvorený* ot-vo-re-nee
outside *vonku* von-ku

P

package *balík* ⓜ buh-leek
paper *papier* ⓜ puh-pyer
park (car) v *zaparkovať* zuh-puhr-ko-vuhť
passport *cestovný pas* ⓜ tses-tov-nee puhs
pay *platiť* pluh-tyiť
pen *pero* ⓝ pe-ro
petrol *benzín* ⓜ ben-zeen
pharmacy *lekáreň* ⓕ le-ka-reň
phonecard *telefónna karta* ⓕ
    te-le-fuhwn-nuh kuhr-tuh
photo *fotografia* ⓕ fo-to-gruh-fi-yuh
plate *tanier* ⓜ tuh-ni-yer
police *polícia* ⓕ po-lee-tsi-yuh
postcard *pohľadnica* ⓕ poh-lyuhd-nyi-tsuh
post office *pošta* ⓕ posh-tuh
pregnant *tehotná* tye-hot-na
price *cena* ⓕ tse-nuh

Q

quiet *tichý* tyi-khee

R

rain *dážď* ⓜ dazhď
razor *žiletka* ⓕ zhi-let-kuh
receipt *potvrdenie* ⓝ pot-vr-dye-ni-ye
red *červený* cher-ve-nee
refund *vrátenie peňazí* ⓝ
    vra-tye-ni-ye pe-nyuh-zee
registered mail *doporučená pošta* ⓕ
    do-po-ru-che-na posh-tuh
rent v *prenajať* pre-nuh-yuhť
repair v *opraviť* o-pruh-viť
reservation *rezervácia* ⓕ
    re-zer-va-tsi-yuh
restaurant *reštaurácia* ⓕ resh-tow-ra-tsi-yuh
return v *vrátiť* vra-tyiť
return ticket *spiatočný lístok* ⓜ
    spyuh-toch-nee lees-tok
right (direction) *vpravo* vpruh-vo

road *cesta* ⓕ tses-tuh
room *izba* ⓕ iz-buh

S

safe a *bezpečný* bez-pech-nee
sanitary napkin *dámska vložka* ⓕ dams-kuh
    vlozh-kuh
seat *sedadlo* ⓝ se-duhd-lo
send *poslať* pos-luhť
service station *benzínová stanica* ⓕ
    ben-zee-no-va stuh-nyi-tsuh
sex *sex* ⓜ seks
shampoo *šampón* ⓜ shuhm-puhwn
share (a dorm) *deliť sa (o izbu)*
    dye-liť suh (o iz-bu)
shaving cream *krém na holenie* ⓜ
    krairm nuh ho-le-ni-ye
she *ona* o-nuh
sheet (bed) *plachta* ⓕ pluhkh-tuh
shirt *košeľa* ⓕ ko-she-lyuh
shoes *topánky* ⓕ pl to-pan-ki
shop *obchod* ⓜ ob-khod
short *krátky* krat-ki
shower *sprcha* ⓕ spr-khuh
single room *jednoposteľová izba* ⓕ
    yed-no-pos-tye-lyo-va iz-buh
skin *koža* ⓕ ko-zhuh
skirt *sukňa* ⓕ suk-nyuh
sleep v *spať* spuhť
Slovakia *Slovensko* ⓝ slo-vens-ko
Slovak (language) *slovenčina* ⓕ slo-ven-chi-na
Slovak a *slovenský* slo-vens-kee
slowly *pomaly* po-muh-li
small *malý* muh-lee
smoke (cigarettes) v *fajčiť* fai-chiť
soap *mydlo* ⓝ mid-lo
some *nejaký* nye-yuh-kee
soon *skoro* sko-ro
south *juh* yooh
souvenir shop *obchod so suvenírmi* ⓜ
    ob-khod zo su-ve-neer-mi
speak *hovoriť* ho-vo-riť
spoon *lyžica* ⓕ li-zhi-tsuh
stamp *známka* ⓕ znam-kuh
stand-by ticket *lístok na čakacom zozname* ⓜ
    lees-tok nuh chuh-kuh-tsom zoz-nuh-me
station (train) *železničná stanica* ⓕ
    zhe-lez-nich-na stuh-ni-tsuh
stomach *žalúdok* ⓜ zhuh-loo-dok
stop v *stáť* stať

english–slovak

O

407

stop (bus) *autobusová zastávka* ⓕ
  ow-to-bu-so-va *zuhs*-tav-kuh
street *ulica* ⓕ u-li-tsuh
student *študent/študentka* ⓜ/ⓕ
  shtu-dent/shtu-dent-ka
sun *slnko* ⓝ *sln*-ko
sunscreen *ochranný faktor* ⓜ o-khruhn-nee *fuhk*-tor
swim v *plávať* pla-*vuht'*

T

tampons *tampóny* ⓜ pl tuhm-puhw-ni
taxi *taxík* ⓜ *tuhk*-seek
teaspoon *lyžička* ⓕ li-zhich-ku
teeth *zuby* ⓜ pl zu-bi
telephone *telefón* ⓜ te-le-fuhwn
television *televízia* ⓕ te-le-vee-zi-yuh
temperature (weather) *teplota* ⓕ tep-lo-tuh
tent *stan* ⓜ stuhn
that (one) *to* to
they *oni* o-nyi
thirsty *smädný* smed-nee
this (one) *toto* to-to
throat *hrdlo* ⓝ hrd-lo
ticket *lístok* ⓜ lees-tok
time *čas* ⓜ chuhs
tired *unavený* u-nuh-ve-nee
tissues *servítky* ⓕ pl ser-veet-ki
today *dnes* dnyes
toilet *záchod* ⓜ za-khod
tomorrow *zajtra* zai-truh
tonight *dnes večer* dnyes ve-cher
toothbrush *zubná kefka* ⓕ zub-na *kef*-kuh
toothpaste *zubná pasta* ⓕ zub-na puhs-tuh
torch (flashlight) *baterka* ⓕ buh-ter-kuh
tour *zájazd* ⓜ za-yuhzd
tourist office *turistická kancelária* ⓕ
  tu-ris-tits-ka kuhn-tse-la-ri-yuh
towel *uterák* ⓜ u-tye-rak
train *vlak* ⓜ vluhk
translate *prekladať* pre-kluh-duht'
travel agency *cestovná kancelária* ⓕ
  tses-tov-na kuhn-tse-la-ri-yuh
travellers cheque *cestovný šek* ⓜ tses-tov-nee shek
trousers *nohavice* pl no-huh-vi-tse
twin beds *dve oddelené postele* ⓕ pl
  dve od-dye-le-nair pos-tye-le
tyre *pneumatika* ⓕ pne-u-muh-ti-kuh

U

underwear *spodné prádlo* ⓝ spod-nair prad-lo
urgent *súrny* soor-ni

V

vacant *voľný* voly-nee
vacation *dovolenka* ⓕ do-vo-len-kuh
vegetable *zelenina* ⓕ ze-le-nyi-nuh
vegetarian a *vegetariánsky* ve-ge-tuh-ri-yans-ki
visa *vízum* ⓝ vee-zum

W

waiter *čašník* ⓜ chuhsh-nyeek
walk v *kráčať* kra-chuht'
wallet *peňaženka* ⓕ pe-nyuh-zhen-kuh
warm a *teplý* tep-lee
wash (something) *umývať* u-mee-vuht'
watch *hodinky* pl ho-dyin-ki
water *voda* ⓕ vo-duh
we *my* mi
weekend *víkend* ⓜ vee-kend
west *západ* za-puhd
wheelchair *invalidný vozík* ⓜ in-vuh-lid-nee vo-zeek
when *kedy* ke-di
where *kde* kdye
white *biely* bye-li
who *kto* kto
why *prečo* pre-cho
wife *manželka* ⓕ muhn-zhel-kuh
window *okno* ⓝ ok-no
wine *víno* ⓝ vee-no
with *s* s
without *bez* bez
woman *žena* ⓕ zhe-nuh
write *písať* pee-suht'

Y

yellow *žltý* zhl-tee
yes *áno* a-no
yesterday *včera* vche-ruh
you sg inf *ty* ti
you sg pol & pl *vy* vi

Slovene

slovene alphabet

A a a	*B b* buh	*C c* tsuh	*Č č* chuh	*D d* duh
E e e	*F f* fuh	*G g* guh	*H h* huh	*I i* ee
J j yuh	*K k* kuh	*L l* luh	*M m* muh	*N n* nuh
O o o	*P p* puh	*R r* ruh	*S s* suh	*Š š* shuh
T t tuh	*U u* oo	*V v* vuh	*Z z* zuh	*Ž ž* zhuh

slovene

SLOVENŠČINA

introduction

The language spoken by about 2 million people 'on the sunny side of the Alps', Slovene (*slovenščina* slo-*vensh*-chee-na) is sandwiched between German, Italian and Hungarian, against the backdrop of its wider South Slavic family. Its distinctive geographical position parallels its unique evolution, beginning with Slav settlement in this corner of Europe back in the 6th century, then becoming the official language of Slovenia – first as a part of Yugoslavia and since 1991 an independent republic.

Although Croatian and Serbian are its closest relatives within the South Slavic group, Slovene is nevertheless much closer to Croatia's northwestern and coastal dialects. It also shares some features with the more distant West Slavic languages (through contact with a dialect of Slovak, from which it was later separated by the arrival of the Hungarians to Central Europe in the 9th century). Unlike any other modern Slavic language, it has preserved the archaic Indo-European dual grammatical form, which means, for example, that instead of *pivo* pee·vo (a beer) or *piva* pee·va (beers), you and a friend could simply order *pivi* pee·vee (two beers).

German, Italian and Hungarian words entered Slovene during the centuries of foreign rule (in the Austro-Hungarian Empire or under the control of Venice), as these were the languages of the elite, while the common people spoke one of the Slovene dialects. Croatian and Serbian influence on Slovene was particularly significant during the 20th century when all three countries coexisted within the Yugoslav state.

For a language with a relatively small number of speakers, Slovene abounds in regional variations – eight major dialect groups have been identified, which are further divided into fifty or so regional dialects. Some of these cover the neighbouring areas of Austria, Italy and Hungary. The modern literary language is based largely on the central dialects and was shaped through a gradual process that lasted from the 16th to the 19th century.

Slovenia has been called 'a nation of poets', and what better way to get immersed in that spirit than to plunge into this beautiful language first? While you're soaking up the atmosphere of the capital, Ljubljana (whose central square is graced with a monument in honour of the nation's greatest poet, France Prešeren), remember that its name almost equals 'beloved' (*ljubljena* lyoob·lye·na) in Slovene!

pronunciation

vowel sounds

The vowels in Slovene can be pronounced differently, depending on whether they're stressed or unstressed, long or short. Don't worry about these distinctions though, as you shouldn't have too much trouble being understood if you follow our coloured pronunciation guides. Note that we've used the symbols oh and ow to help you pronounce vowels followed by the letters *l* and *v* in written Slovene – when they appear at the end of a syllable, these combinations sometimes produce a sound similar to the 'w' in English.

symbol	english equivalent	slovene example	transliteration
a	father	*dan*	dan
ai	aisle	*srajca*	srai·tsa
e	bet	*center*	tsen·ter
ee	see	*riba*	ree·ba
o	pot	*oče*	o·che
oh	oh	*pol, nov*	poh, noh
oo	zoo	*jug*	yoog
ow	how	*ostal, prav*	os·tow, prow
uh	ago	*pes*	puhs

word stress

Slovene has free stress, which means there's no general rule regarding which syllable the stress falls on – it simply has to be learned. You'll be fine if you just follow our coloured pronunciation guides, in which the stressed syllable is always in italics.

consonant sounds

Most Slovene consonant sounds are pronounced more or less as they are in English. Don't be intimidated by the vowel-less words such as *trg* tuhrg (square) or *vrt* vuhrt (garden) — we've put a slight 'uh' sound before the *r*, which serves as a semi-vowel between the two other consonants.

symbol	english equivalent	slovene example	transliteration
b	**b**ed	*brat*	brat
ch	**ch**eat	*hči*	hchee
d	**d**og	*datum*	*da*·toom
f	**f**at	*telefon*	te·le·*fon*
g	**g**o	*grad*	grad
h	**h**at	*hvala*	*hva*·la
k	**k**it	*karta*	*kar*·ta
l	**l**ot	*ulica*	oo·lee·tsa
m	**m**an	*mož*	mozh
n	**n**ot	*naslov*	nas·*loh*
p	**p**et	*pošta*	*po*·shta
r	**r**un (rolled)	*brez*	brez
s	**s**un	*sin*	seen
sh	**sh**ot	*tuš*	toosh
t	**t**op	*sto*	sto
ts	ha**ts**	*cesta*	*tse*·sta
v	**v**ery	*vlak*	vlak
y	**y**es	*jesen*	ye·*sen*
z	**z**ero	*zima*	*zee*·ma
zh	plea**s**ure	*žena*	*zhe*·na
'	a slight y sound	*kašelj, manj*	ka·shel', man'

basics

language difficulties

Do you speak English?
Ali govorite angleško?
a·lee go·vo·*ree*·te ang·*lesh*·ko

Do you understand?
Ali razumete?
a·lee ra·*zoo*·me·te

I (don't) understand.
(Ne) Razumem.
(ne) ra·*zoo*·mem

What does (*danes*) mean?
Kaj pomeni (danes)?
kai po·*me*·nee (*da*·nes)

Could you repeat that?
Lahko ponovite?
lah·*ko* po·no·*vee*·te

How do you ...?
  pronounce this word
  write (*hvala*)

Kako se ...?
  izgovori to besedo
  napiše (hvala)

ka·*ko* se ...
  eez·go·vo·*ree* to be·*se*·do
  na·*pee*·she (*hva*·la)

Could you please ...?
  speak more slowly
  write it down

Prosim ...
  govorite počasneje
  napišite

pro·seem ...
  go·vo·*ree*·te po·cha·*sne*·ye
  na·*pee*·shee·te

essentials

Yes.	*Da.*	da
No.	*Ne.*	ne
Please.	*Prosim.*	*pro*·seem
Thank you (very much).	*Hvala (lepa).*	*hva*·la (*le*·pa)
You're welcome.	*Ni za kaj.*	nee za kai
Excuse me.	*Dovolite.*	do·vo·*lee*·te
Sorry.	*Oprostite.*	op·ros·*tee*·te

0	*nula*	*noo*-la	16	*šestnajst*	*shest*-naist	
1	*en/ena* m/f	*en/e*-na	17	*sedemnajst*	*se*-dem-naist	
2	*dva/dve* m/f	*dva/dve*	18	*osemnajst*	*o*-sem-naist	
3	*trije/tri* m/f	*tree*-ye/tree	19	*devetnajst*	*de*-vet-naist	
4	*štirje* m	*shtee*-rye	20	*dvajset*	*dvai*-set	
	štiri f	*shtee*-ree	21	*enaindvajset*	*e*-na-een-dvai-set	
5	*pet*	pet	22	*dvaindvajset*	*dva*-een-dvai-set	
6	*šest*	shest				
7	*sedem*	*se*-dem	30	*trideset*	*tree*-de-set	
8	*osem*	*o*-sem	40	*štirideset*	*shtee*-ree-de-set	
9	*devet*	de-*vet*	50	*petdeset*	*pet*-de-set	
10	*deset*	de-*set*	60	*šestdeset*	*shest*-de-set	
11	*enajst*	e-*naist*	70	*sedemdeset*	*se*-dem-de-set	
12	*dvanajst*	*dva*-naist	80	*osemdeset*	*o*-sem-de-set	
13	*trinajst*	*tree*-naist	90	*devetdeset*	*de*-*vet*-de-set	
14	*štirinajst*	*shtee*-ree-naist	100	*sto*	sto	
15	*petnajst*	*pet*-naist	1000	*tisoč*	*tee*-soch	

time & dates

What time is it?	*Koliko je ura?*	*ko*-lee-ko ye *oo*-ra
It's one o'clock.	*Ura je ena.*	*oo*-ra ye e-na
It's (10) o'clock.	*Ura je (deset).*	*oo*-ra ye (de-*set*)
Quarter past (one).	*Četrt čez (ena).*	che-*tuhrt* chez (e-na)
Half past (one).	*Pol (dveh).* (lit: half two)	pol (dveh)
Quarter to (one).	*Petnajst do (enih).*	*pet*-naist do (e-neeh)
At what time ...?	*Ob kateri uri ...?*	ob ka-*te*-ree *oo*-ree ...
At ...	*Ob ...*	ob ...
am	*dopoldne*	do-*poh*-dne
pm	*popoldne*	po-*poh*-dne
Monday	*ponedeljek*	po-ne-*del*-yek
Tuesday	*torek*	*to*-rek
Wednesday	*sreda*	*sre*-da
Thursday	*četrtek*	che-*tuhr*-tek
Friday	*petek*	*pe*-tek
Saturday	*sobota*	so-*bo*-ta
Sunday	*nedelja*	ne-*del*-ya

January	januar	ya-noo-ar
February	februar	feb-roo-ar
March	marec	ma-rets
April	april	ap-reel
May	maj	mai
June	junij	yoo-neey
July	julij	yoo-leey
August	avgust	av-goost
September	september	sep-tem-ber
October	oktober	ok-to-ber
November	november	no-vem-ber
December	december	de-tsem-ber

What date is it today?
Katerega smo danes?   ka-te-re-ga smo da-nes

It's (18 October).
Smo (osemnajstega oktobra).   smo (o-sem-nai-ste-ga) ok-tob-ra

| since (May) | od (maja) | od (ma-ya) |
| until (June) | do (junija) | do (yoo-nee-ya) |

last ...

night	prejšnji večer	preysh-nyee ve-cher
week	prejšnji teden	preysh-nyee te-den
month	prejšnji mesec	preysh-nyee me-sets
year	prejšnje leto	preysh-nye le-to

next ...

week	naslednji teden	nas-led-nyee te-den
month	naslednji mesec	nas-led-nyee me-sets
year	naslednje leto	nas-led-nye le-to

yesterday/tomorrow ...   *včeraj/jutri ...*   vche-rai/yoot-ree ...

morning	zjutraj	zyoot-rai
afternoon	popoldne	po-poh-dne
evening	zvečer	zve-cher

weather

What's the weather like?	Kakšno je vreme?	kak·shno ye vre·me
It's raining/snowing.	Dežuje/Sneži.	de·zhoo·ye/sne·zhee

It's	... je.	... ye
cloudy	Oblačno	ob·lach·no
cold	Mrzlo	muhr·zlo
hot	Vroče	vro·che
sunny	Sončno	sonch·no
warm	Toplo	top·lo
windy	Vetrovno	vet·roh·no

spring	pomlad f	pom·lad
summer	poletje n	po·let·ye
autumn	jesen f	ye·sen
winter	zima f	zee·ma

border crossing

I'm here ...	Tu sem ...	too sem ...
on business	poslovno	pos·lov·no
on holiday	na počitnicah	na po·cheet·nee·tsah

I'm here for ...	Ostanem ...	os·ta·nem ...
(10) days	(deset) dni	(de·set) dnee
(two) months	(dva) meseca	(dva) me·se·tsa
(three) weeks	(tri) tedne	(tree) ted·ne

I'm going to ...
Namenjen/Namenjena sem v ... m/f na·men·yen/na·men·ye·na sem v ...

I'm staying at the (Slon).
Stanujem v (Slonu). sta·noo·yem v (slo·noo)

I have nothing to declare.
Ničesar nimam za prijaviti. nee·che·sar nee·mam za pree·ya·vee·tee

I have something to declare.
Nekaj imam za prijaviti. ne·kai ee·mam za pree·ya·vee·tee

That's mine.
To je moje. to ye mo·ye

That's not mine.
To ni moje. to nee mo·ye

transport

tickets & luggage

Where can I buy a ticket?
Kje lahko kupim vozovnico?
kye lah-*ko* koo-peem vo-*zov*-nee-tso

Do I need to book a seat?
Ali moram rezervirati sedež?
a-lee mo-ram re-zer-vee-ra-tee se-dezh

One ... ticket to (Koper), please.	... vozovnico do (Kopra), prosim.	... vo-*zov*-nee-tso do (*ko*-pra) *pro*-seem
one-way	Enosmerno	e-no-*smer*-no
return	Povratno	pov-*rat*-no

I'd like to ... my ticket, please.	Želim ... vozovnico, prosim.	zhe-*leem* ... vo-*zov*-nee-tso *pro*-seem
cancel	preklicati	prek-*lee*-tsa-tee
change	zamenjati	za-*men*-ya-tee
collect	dvigniti	*dveeg*-nee-tee
confirm	potrditi	po-tuhr-*dee*-tee

I'd like a ... seat, please.	Želim ... sedež, prosim.	zhe-*leem* ... se-dezh *pro*-seem
nonsmoking	nekadilski	ne-ka-*deel*-skee
smoking	kadilski	ka-*deel*-skee

How much is it?
Koliko stane?
ko-lee-ko *sta*-ne

Is there air conditioning?
Ali ima klimo?
a-lee ee-*ma klee*-mo

Is there a toilet?
Ali ima stranišče?
a-lee ee-*ma* stra-*neesh*-che

How long does the trip take?
Kako dolgo traja potovanje?
ka-*ko dol*-go *tra*-ya po-to-*van*-ye

Is it a direct route?
Je to direktna proga?
ye to dee-*rekt*-na *pro*-ga

I'd like a luggage locker.
Želim garderobno omarico.
zhe-*leem* gar-de-*rob*-no o-*ma*-ree-tso

My luggage has been ...	*Moja prtljaga je ...*	*mo*·ya puhrt·*lya*·ga ye ...
damaged	*poškodovana*	posh·ko·do·*va*·na
lost	*izgubljena*	eez·goob·*lye*·na
stolen	*ukradena*	oo·*kra*·de·na

getting around

Where does flight (AF 46) arrive/depart?
Kje pristane/odleti let — kye pree·*sta*·ne/od·le·*tee* let
številka (AF 46)? — shte·*veel*·ka (a fuh *shtee*·ree shest)

Where's (the) ...?	*Kje je/so ...? sg/pl*	kye ye/so ...
arrivals hall	*prihodi pl*	pree·*ho*·dee
departures hall	*odhodi pl*	od·*ho*·dee
duty-free shop	*brezcarinska*	brez·tsa·*reen*·ska
	trgovina sg	tuhr·go·*vee*·na
gate (12)	*izhod (dvanajst) sg*	eez·*hod* (*dva*·naist)

Is this the ... to (Venice)?	*Je to ... za (Benetke)?*	ye to ... za (be·*net*·ke)
boat	*ladja*	*lad*·ya
bus	*avtobus*	*av*·to·boos
plane	*letalo*	le·*ta*·lo
train	*vlak*	vlak

What time's the ... bus?	*Kdaj odpelje ... avtobus?*	kdai od·*pel*·ye ... *av*·to·boos
first	*prvi*	*puhr*·vee
last	*zadnji*	*zad*·nyee
next	*naslednji*	nas·*led*·nyee

At what time does it arrive/leave?
Kdaj prispe/odpelje? — kdai prees·*pe*/od·*pel*·ye

How long will it be delayed?
Koliko je zamujen? — *ko*·lee·ko ye za·moo·*yen*

What station is this?
Katera postaja je to? — ka·*te*·ra pos·*ta*·ya ye to

What stop is this?
Katero postajališče je to? — ka·*te*·ro pos·ta·ya·*leesh*·che ye to

What's the next station?
Katera je naslednja postaja? — ka·*te*·ra ye nas·*led*·nya pos·*ta*·ya

What's the next stop?
Katero je naslednje postajališče? — ka·*te*·ro ye nas·*led*·nye pos·ta·ya·*leesh*·che

| Does it stop at (Postojna)? | | |
| *Ali ustavi v (Postojni)?* | *a·lee oos·ta·vee v (pos·toy·nee)* | |

Please tell me when we get to (Kranj).		
Prosim povejte mi,	*pro·seem po·vey·te mee*	
ko prispemo v (Kranj).	*ko prees·pe·mo v (kran)*	

| How long do we stop here? | | |
| *Kako dolgo stojimo tu?* | *ka·ko dol·go sto·yee·mo too* | |

| Is this seat available? | | |
| *Je ta sedež prost?* | *ye ta se·dezh prost* | |

| That's my seat. | | |
| *To je moj sedež.* | *to ye moy se·dezh* | |

I'd like a taxi ...	*Želim taksi ...*	*zhe·leem tak·see ...*
at (9am)	*ob (devetih dopoldne)*	*ob (de·ve·teeh do·poh·dne)*
now	*zdaj*	*zdai*
tomorrow	*jutri*	*yoot·ree*

| Is this taxi available? | | |
| *Je ta taksi prost?* | *ye ta tak·see prost* | |

| How much is it to ...? | | |
| *Koliko stane do ...?* | *ko·lee·ko sta·ne do ...* | |

| Please put the meter on. | | |
| *Prosim, vključite taksimeter.* | *pro·seem vklyoo·chee·te tak·see·me·ter* | |

| Please take me to (this address). | | |
| *Prosim, peljite me na (ta naslov).* | *pro·seem pel·yee·te me na (ta nas·loh)* | |

Please ...	*Prosim ...*	*pro·seem ...*
slow down	*vozite počasneje*	*vo·zee·te po·chas·ne·ye*
stop here	*ustavite tukaj*	*oos·ta·vee·te too·kai*
wait here	*počakajte tukaj*	*po·cha·kai·te too·kai*

car, motorbike & bicycle hire

I'd like to hire a ...	*Želim najeti ...*	*zhe·leem na·ye·tee ...*
bicycle	*kolo*	*ko·lo*
car	*avto*	*av·to*
motorbike	*motor*	*mo·tor*

with ...	s ...	s ...
a driver	*šoferjem*	sho-*fer*-yem
air conditioning	*klimo*	*klee*-mo
antifreeze	*sredstvom proti*	*sreds*-tvom *pro*-tee
	zmrzovanju	zmuhr-zo-*van*-yoo
snow chains	*snežnimi*	*snezh*-nee-mee
	verigami	ve-*ree*-ga-mee
How much for	*Koliko stane najem*	ko-*lee*-ko *sta*-ne na-*yem*
... hire?	*na ...?*	na ...
hourly	*uro*	*oo*-ro
daily	*dan*	dan
weekly	*teden*	*te*-den
air	*zrak* m	zrak
oil	*olje* n	*ol*-ye
petrol	*bencin* m	ben-*tseen*
tyres	*gume* f	*goo*-me

I need a mechanic.
Potrebujem mehanika. — pot-re-*boo*-yem me-*ha*-nee-ka

I've run out of petrol.
Zmanjkalo mi je bencina. — zman'-ka-lo mee ye ben-*tsee*-na

I have a flat tyre.
Počila mi je guma. — po-*chee*-la mee ye *goo*-ma

directions

Where's the ...?	*Kje je ...?*	kye ye ...
bank	*banka*	*ban*-ka
city centre	*center mesta*	*tsen*-ter *mes*-ta
hotel	*hotel*	ho-*tel*
market	*tržnica*	*tuhrzh*-nee-tsa
police station	*policijska*	po-lee-*tseey*-ska
	postaja	pos-*ta*-ya
post office	*pošta*	*posh*-ta
public toilet	*javno stranišče*	*yav*-no stra-*neesh*-che
tourist office	*turistični*	too-*rees*-teech-nee
	urad	*oo*-rad

Is this the road to (Ptuj)?
Pelje ta cesta do (Ptuja)?   *pel·ye ta tses·ta do (ptoo·ya)*

Can you show me (on the map)?
Mi lahko pokažete   mee lah·ko po·ka·zhe·te
(na zemljevidu)?   (na zem·lye·vee·doo)

What's the address?
Na katerem naslovu je?   na ka·te·rem nas·lo·voo ye

How far is it?
Kako daleč je?   ka·ko da·lech ye

How do I get there?
Kako pridem tja?   ka·ko pree·dem tya

Turn ...	*Zavijte ...*	za·veey·te ...
at the corner	*na vogalu*	na vo·ga·loo
at the traffic lights	*pri semaforju*	pree se·ma·for·yoo
left/right	*levo/desno*	le·vo/des·no

It's ...		
behind ...	*Za ...*	za ...
far away	*Daleč.*	da·lech
here	*Tukaj.*	too·kai
in front of ...	*Pred ...*	pred ...
left	*Levo.*	le·vo
near (to ...)	*Blizu ...*	blee·zoo ...
next to ...	*Poleg ...*	po·leg ...
on the corner	*Na vogalu.*	na vo·ga·loo
opposite ...	*Nasproti ...*	nas·pro·tee ...
right	*Desno.*	des·no
straight ahead	*Naravnost naprej.*	na·rav·nost na·prey
there	*Tam.*	tam

by bus	*z avtobusom*	z av·to·boo·som
by taxi	*s taksijem*	s tak·see·yem
by train	*z vlakom*	z vla·kom
on foot	*peš*	pesh

north	*sever*	se·ver
south	*jug*	yoog
east	*vzhod*	vzhod
west	*zahod*	za·hod

signs

Vhod/Izhod	*vhod/eez·hod*	**Entrance/Exit**
Odprto/Zaprto	*od·puhr·to/za·puhr·to*	**Open/Closed**
Proste sobe	*pros·te so·be*	**Rooms Available**
Ni prostih mest	*nee pros·teeh mest*	**No Vacancies**
Informacije	*een·for·ma·tsee·ye*	**Information**
Policijska postaja	*po·lee·tseey·ska pos·ta·ya*	**Police Station**
Prepovedano	*pre·po·ve·da·no*	**Prohibited**
Stranišče	*stra·neesh·che*	**Toilets**
Moški	*mosh·kee*	**Men**
Ženske	*zhen·ske*	**Women**
Vroče/Mrzlo	*vro·che/muhr·zlo*	**Hot/Cold**

accommodation

finding accommodation

Where's a ...?	*Kje je ... ?*	kye ye ...
camping ground	*kamp*	kamp
guesthouse	*gostišče*	gos·teesh·che
hotel	*hotel*	ho·tel
youth hostel	*mladinski hotel*	mla·deen·skee ho·tel
Can you recommend a ... hotel?	*Mi lahko priporočite ... hotel?*	mee lah·ko pree·po·ro·chee·te ... ho·tel
cheap	*poceni*	po·tse·nee
good	*dober*	do·ber

Can you recommend a hotel nearby?
Mi lahko priporočite hotel v bližini?
mee lah·ko pree·po·ro·chee·te ho·tel oo blee·zhee·nee

I'd like to book a room, please.
Želim rezervirati sobo, prosim.
zhe·leem re·zer·vee·ra·tee so·bo pro·seem

I have a reservation.
Imam rezervacijo.
ee·mam re·zer·va·tsee·yo

My name's ...
Ime mi je ...
ee·me mee ye ...

Do you have a twin room?
Imate sobo z ločenima posteljama?   ee-*ma*-te *so*-bo z *lo*-che-nee-ma *pos*-tel-ya-ma

Do you have a … room?   *Ali imate … sobo?*   a-lee ee-*ma*-te … *so*-bo
   single   *enoposteljno*   e-no-*pos*-tel'-no
   double   *dvoposteljno*   dvo-*pos*-tel'-no

How much is it per …?   *Koliko stane na …?*   ko-lee-ko *sta*-ne na …
   night   *noč*   noch
   person   *osebo*   o-*se*-bo

Can I pay by …?   *Lahko plačam s …?*   lah-*ko pla*-cham s …
   credit card   *kreditno kartico*   kre-*deet*-no *kar*-tee-tso
   travellers cheque   *potovalnim čekom*   po-to-*val*-neem *che*-kom

I'd like to stay for (three) nights.
Rad bi ostal (tri) noči. m   ra-da bee os-*tow* (tree) no-*chee*
Rada bi ostala (tri) noči. f   *ra*-da bee os-*ta*-la (tree) no-*chee*

From (2 July) to (6 July).
Od (drugega julija).   od (droo-ge-ga *yoo*-lee-ya)
do (šestega julija).   do (shes-te-ga *yoo*-lee-ya)

Can I see the room?
Lahko vidim sobo?   lah-ko vee-deem *so*-bo

Am I allowed to camp here?
Smem tu kampirati?   smem too kam-*pee*-ra-tee

Is there a camp site nearby?
Je v bližini kakšen kamp?   ye v blee-*zhee*-nee *kak*-shen kamp

requests & queries

When/Where is breakfast served?
Kdaj/Kje strežete zajtrk?   kdai/kye *stre*-zhe-te *zai*-tuhrk

Please wake me at (seven).
Prosim, zbudite me ob (sedmih).   pro-seem zboo-*dee*-te me ob (*sed*-meeh)

Could I have my key, please?
Lahko prosim dobim ključ?   lah-ko pro-sim do-*beem* klyooch

Can I get another (blanket)?
Lahko dobim drugo (odejo)?   lah-ko do-*beem droo*-go (o-*de*-yo)

Is there an elevator/a safe?
Imate dvigalo/sef?   ee-*ma*-te dvee-*ga*-lo/sef

The room is too...	Soba je ...	*so*·ba ye ...
expensive	predraga	pre·*dra*·ga
noisy	prehrupna	pre·*hroop*·na
small	premajhna	pre·*mai*·hna

This ... isn't clean.	Ta ... ni čista.	ta ... nee *chees*·ta
pillow	blazina	bla·*zee*·na
sheet	rjuha	ryoo·ha
towel	brisača	bree·*sa*·cha

The fan doesn't work.
Ventilator je pokvarjen.   ven·tee·*la*·tor ye pok·*var*·yen

The air conditioning doesn't work.
Klima je pokvarjena.   *klee*·ma ye pok·*var*·ye·na

The toilet doesn't work.
Stranišče je pokvarjeno.   stra·*neesh*·che ye pok·*var*·ye·no

checking out

What time is checkout?
Kdaj se moram odjaviti?   kdai se *mo*·ram od·*ya*·vee·tee

Can I leave my luggage here?
Lahko pustim prtljago tu?   lah·*ko* poos·*teem* puhrt·*lya*·go too

Could I have my ..., please?	Lahko prosim dobim ...?	lah·*ko* pro·seem do·*beem* ...
deposit	moj polog	moy *po*·log
passport	moj potni list	moy *pot*·nee leest
valuables	moje dragocenosti	mo·ye dra·go·*tse*·nos·tee

communications & banking

the internet

Where's the local Internet café?
Kje je najbližja internetna kavarna?   kye ye nai·*bleezh*·ya een·ter·*net*·na ka·*var*·na

How much is it per hour?
Koliko stane ena ura?   *ko*·lee·ko *sta*·ne e·na *oo*·ra

I'd like to ...	Želim ...	zhe·leem ...
check my email	preveriti elektronsko pošto	pre·ve·ree·tee e·lek·tron·sko posh·to
get Internet access	dostop do interneta	dos·top do een·ter·ne·ta
use a printer	uporabiti tiskalnik	oo·po·ra·bee·tee tees·kal·neek
use a scanner	uporabiti optični čitalnik	oo·po·ra·bee·tee op·teech·nee chee·tal·neek

mobile/cell phone

I'd like a ...	Želim ...	zhe·leem ...
mobile/cell phone for hire	najeti mobilni telefon	na·ye·tee mo·beel·nee te·le·fon
SIM card for your network	SIM kartico za vaše omrežje	seem kar·tee·tso za va·she om·rezh·ye

What are the rates?	Kakšne so cene?	kak·shne so tse·ne

telephone

What's your phone number?
Lahko izvem vašo telefonsko številko?
lah·ko eez·vem va·sho te·le·fon·sko shte·veel·ko

The number is ...
Številka je ...
shte·veel·ka ye ...

Where's the nearest public phone?
Kje je najbližja govorilnica?
kye ye nai·bleezh·ya go·vo·reel·nee·tsa

I'd like to buy a phonecard.
Želim kupiti telefonsko kartico.
zhe·leem koo·pee·tee te·le·fon·sko kar·tee·tso

I want to ...	Želim ...	zhe·leem ...
call (Singapore)	poklicati (Singapur)	pok·lee·tsa·tee (seen·ga·poor)
make a local call	klicati lokalno	klee·tsa·tee lo·kal·no
reverse the charges	klicati na stroške klicanega	klee·tsa·tee na strosh·ke klee·tsa·ne·ga

How much does ... cost?	Koliko stane ...?	ko·lee·ko sta·ne ...
a (three)-minute call	(tri)minutni klic	(tree·)mee·noot·nee kleets
each extra minute	vsaka dodatna minuta	vsa·ka do·dat·na mee·noo·ta

post office

I want to send a ...	*Želim poslati ...*	zhe·*leem* pos·*la*·tee ...
letter	*pismo*	*pees*·mo
parcel	*paket*	pa·*ket*
postcard	*razglednico*	raz·*gled*·nee·tso
I want to buy a/an ...	*Želim kupiti ...*	zhe·*leem* koo·*pee*·tee ...
envelope	*kuverto*	koo·*ver*·to
stamp	*znamko*	*znam*·ko
Please send it by ...	*Prosim, pošljite ...*	*pro*·seem posh·*lyee*·te ...
airmail	*z letalsko pošto*	z le·*tal*·sko *posh*·to
express mail	*s hitro pošto*	s *heet*·ro *posh*·to
registered mail	*s priporočeno pošto*	s pree·po·ro·*che*·no *posh*·to
surface mail	*z navadno pošto*	z na·*vad*·no *posh*·to

bank

Where's a/an ...?	*Kje je ...?*	kye ye ...
ATM	*bankomat*	ban·ko·*mat*
foreign exchange office	*menjalnica*	men·*yal*·nee·tsa
I'd like to ...	*Želim ...*	zhe·*leem* ...
Where can I ...?	*Kje je mogoče ...?*	kye ye mo·*go*·che ...
cash a cheque	*unovčiti ček*	oo·*nov*·chee·tee chek
change a travellers cheque	*zamenjati potovalni ček*	za·*men*·ya·tee po·to·*val*·nee chek
change money	*zamenjati denar*	za·*men*·ya·tee de·*nar*
withdraw money	*dvigniti denar*	*dveeg*·nee·tee de·*nar*
What's the ...?	*Kakšen/Kakšna je ...?* m/f	*kak*·shen/*kak*·shna ye ...
commission	*provizija* f	pro·*vee*·zee·ya
exchange rate	*menjalni tečaj* m	men·*yal*·nee te·*chai*

Can I arrange a transfer of money?
Lahko uredim prenos denarja?   lah·ko oo·re·*deem* pre·*nos* de·*nar*·ya

What time does the bank open?
Kdaj se banka odpre?   kdai se *ban*·ka od·*pre*

Has my money arrived yet?
Je moj denar že prispel?   ye moy de·*nar* zhe prees·*pe*·oo

sightseeing

getting in

What time does it open/close?
Kdaj se odpre/zapre?   kdai se od-*pre*/za-*pre*

What's the admission charge?
Koliko stane vstopnica?   ko-lee-ko *sta*-ne *vstop*-nee-tsa

Is there a discount for students/children?
Imate popust za   ee-*ma*-te po-*poost* za
študente/otroke?   shtoo-*den*-te/ot-*ro*-ke

I'd like a ...	*Želim ...*	zhe-*leem* ...
catalogue	*katalog*	ka-ta-*log*
guide	*vodnik*	vod-*neek*
local map	*zemljevid kraja*	zem-lye-*veed kra*-ya

I'd like to see ...   *Želim videti ...*   zhe-*leem vee*-de-tee ...
What's that?   *Kaj je to?*   kai ye to
Can I take a photo?   *Ali lahko fotografiram?*   *a*-lee lah-*ko* fo-to-gra-*fee*-ram

tours

When's the next ...?	*Kdaj je naslednji ...?*	kdai ye nas-*led*-nyee ...
boat trip	*izlet s čolnom*	eez-*let* s *choh*-nom
day trip	*dnevni izlet*	*dnev*-nee eez-*let*
tour	*izlet*	eez-*let*

Is ... included?	*Je ... vključena?*	ye ... *vklyoo*-che-na
accommodation	*nastanitev*	nas-ta-*nee*-tev
the admission charge	*vstopnina*	vstop-*nee*-na
food	*hrana*	*hra*-na

Is transport included?
Je prevoz vključen?   ye pre-*voz vklyoo*-chen

How long is the tour?
Koliko časa traja izlet?   ko-lee-ko *cha*-sa *tra*-ya eez-*let*

What time should we be back?
Kdaj naj se vrnemo?   kdai nai se *vuhr*-ne-mo

castle	*grad* m	grad
cathedral	*stolnica* f	*stol*-nee-tsa
church	*cerkev* f	*tser*-kev
main square	*glavni trg* m	*glav*-nee tuhrg
monastery	*samostan* m	sa-mos-*tan*
monument	*spomenik* m	spo-me-*neek*
museum	*muzej* m	moo-*zey*
old city	*staro mesto* n	*sta*-ro *mes*-to
palace	*palača* f	pa-*la*-cha
ruins	*ruševine* f	roo-she-*vee*-ne
stadium	*stadion* m	*sta*-dee-on
statue	*kip* m	keep

shopping

enquiries

Where's a ...?	*Kje je ...?*	kye ye ...
bank	*banka*	*ban*-ka
bookshop	*knjigarna*	knyee-*gar*-na
camera shop	*trgovina s*	tuhr-go-*vee*-na s
	fotografsko opremo	fo-to-*graf*-sko op-*re*-mo
department store	*blagovnica*	bla-*gov*-nee-tsa
grocery store	*trgovina s*	tuhr-go-*vee*-na s
	špecerijo	shpe-tse-*ree*-yo
market	*tržnica*	*tuhrzh*-nee-tsa
newsagency	*kiosk*	*kee*-osk
supermarket	*trgovina*	tuhr-go-*vee*-na

Where can I buy (a padlock)?
Kje lahko kupim (ključavnico)? kye lah-*ko* koo-peem (klyoo-*chav*-nee-tso)

I'm looking for ...
Iščem ... *eesh*-chem ...

Can I look at it?
Lahko pogledam? lah-*ko* pog-*le*-dam

Do you have any others?
Imate še kakšnega/kakšno? m/f — ee-*ma*-te she *kak*-shne-ga/*kak*-shno

Does it have a guarantee?
Ali ima garancijo? — *a*-lee ee-*ma* ga-ran-*tsee*-yo

Can I have it sent abroad?
Mi lahko pošljete v tujino? — mee lah-*ko* posh-lye-te v too-*yee*-no

Can I have my ... repaired?
Mi lahko popravite ...? — mee lah-*ko* po-*pra*-vee-te ...

It's faulty.
Ne deluje. — ne de-*loo*-ye

I'd like ..., please.
Želim ..., prosim. — zhe-*leem* ... *pro*-seem
  a bag — *vrečko* — *vrech*-ko
  a refund — *vračilo denarja* — vra-*chee*-lo de-*nar*-ya
  to return this — *vrniti tole* — vr-*nee*-tee *to*-le

paying

How much is this?
Koliko stane? — ko-*lee*-ko *sta*-ne

Can you write down the price?
Lahko napišete ceno? — lah-*ko* na-*pee*-she-te *tse*-no

That's too expensive.
To je predrago. — to ye pre-dra-*go*

What's your lowest price?
Povejte vašo najnižjo ceno. — po-*vey*-te *va*-sho nai-*neezh*-yo *tse*-no

I'll give you (five) euros.
Dam vam (pet) evrov. — dam vam (pet) *ev*-roh

There's a mistake in the bill.
Na računu je napaka. — na ra-*choo*-noo ye na-*pa*-ka

Do you accept ...?
Ali sprejemate ...? — *a*-lee spre-*ye*-ma-te ...
  credit cards — *kreditne kartice* — kre-*deet*-ne *kar*-tee-tse
  debit cards — *debetne kartice* — de-*bet*-ne *kar*-tee-tse
  travellers cheques — *potovalne čeke* — po-to-*val*-ne *che*-ke

I'd like ..., please.
Želim ..., prosim. — zhe-*leem* ... *pro*-seem
  a receipt — *račun* — ra-*choon*
  my change — *drobiž* — dro-*beezh*

clothes & shoes

Can I try it on?	Lahko pomerim?	lah·ko po·me·reem
My size is (42).	Nosim številko	no·seem shte·veel·ko
	(dvaištirideset).	(dva·een·shtee·ree·de·set)
It doesn't fit.	Ni mi prav.	nee mee prow
... size	... številka	... shte·veel·ka
small	majhna	mai·hna
medium	srednja	sred·nya
large	velika	ve·lee·ka

books & music

I'd like a ...	Želim ...	zhe·leem ...
newspaper	časopis	cha·so·pees
(in English)	(v angleščini)	(v ang·lesh·chee·nee)
pen	pisalo	pee·sa·lo

I'm looking for an English-language bookshop.
Iščem angleško knjigarno.   eesh·chem ang·lesh·ko knyee·gar·no

I'm looking for a book/music by (Miha Mazzini/Zoran Predin).
Iščem knjigo/glasbo   eesh·chem knyee·go/glaz·bo
(Mihe Mazzinija/Zorana Predina).   (mee·he ma·tsee·nee·ya/zo·ra·na pre·dee·na)

Can I listen to this?
Lahko tole poslušam?   lah·ko to·le pos·loo·sham

photography

Can you ...?	Lahko ...?	lah·ko ...
burn a CD from	zapečete CD z moje	za·pe·che·te tse·de z mo·ye
my memory card	spominske kartice	spo·meen·ske kar·tee·tse
develop this film	razvijete ta film	raz·vee·ye·te ta feelm
load this film	vstavite ta film	vsta·vee·te ta feelm
I need a/an ... film	Potrebujem ... film	pot·re·boo·yem ... feelm
for this camera.	za ta fotoaparat.	za ta fo·to·a·pa·rat
APS	APS	a·pe·es
B&W	črno-bel	chuhr·no·be·oo
colour	barvni	barv·nee
(200) speed	(dvesto) ASA	(dve·sto) a·sa

I need a slide film for this camera.

Potrebujem film za diapozitive   pot·re·*boo*·yem feelm za dee·a·po·zee·*tee*·ve
za ta fotoaparat.   za ta fo·to·a·pa·*rat*

When will it be ready?

Kdaj bo gotovo?   kdai bo go·*to*·vo

meeting people

greetings, goodbyes & introductions

Hello/Hi.	*Zdravo.*	*zdra*·vo
Good night.	*Lahko noč.*	*lah*·ko noch
Goodbye/Bye.	*Na svidenje/Adijo.*	na *svee*·den·ye/a·*dee*·yo
See you later.	*Se vidiva.*	se *vee*·dee·va
Mr/Mrs	*gospod/gospa*	gos·*pod*/gos·*pa*
Miss	*gospodična*	gos·po·*deech*·na
How are you?	*Kako ste/si?* **pol/inf**	ka·*ko* ste/see
Fine, thanks.	*Dobro, hvala.*	*dob*·ro hva·la
And you?	*Pa vi/ti?* **pol/inf**	pa vee/tee
What's your name?	*Kako vam/ti je ime?* **pol/inf**	ka·*ko* vam/tee ye ee·*me*
My name is …	*Ime mi je …*	ee·*me* mee ye …
I'm pleased to	*Veseli me, da sem vas*	ve·se·*lee* me da sem vas
meet you.	*spoznal/spoznala.* **m/f**	spoz·*now*/spoz·*na*·la
This is my …	*To je moj/moja …* **m/f**	to ye moy/*mo*·ya …
boyfriend	*fant*	fant
brother	*brat*	brat
daughter	*hči*	hchee
father	*oče*	*o*·che
friend	*prijatelj* m	pree·*ya*·tel'
	prijateljica f	pree·*ya*·tel·yee·tsa
girlfriend	*punca*	*poon*·tsa
husband	*mož*	mozh
mother	*mama*	*ma*·ma
partner (intimate)	*partner/partnerka* **m/f**	*part*·ner/*part*·ner·ka
sister	*sestra*	*ses*·tra
son	*sin*	seen
wife	*žena*	*zhe*·na

Here's my phone number.
Tu je moja telefonska številka.   too ye mo·ya te·le·fon·ska shte·veel·ka

What's your phone number?
Mi poveste vašo telefonsko številko?   mee po·ves·te va·sho te·le·fon·sko shte·veel·ko

Here's my ...	*Tu je moj/moja ...* m/f	too ye moy/mo·ya ...
What's your ...?	*Kakšen je vaš ...?* m	kak·shen ye vash ...
	Kakšna je vaša ...? f	kak·shna ye va·sha ...
(email) address	*(elektronski) naslov* m	(e·lek·tron·skee) nas·loh
fax number	*številka faksa* f	shte·veel·ka fak·sa

occupations

What's your occupation?	*Kaj ste po poklicu?*	kai ste po pok·lee·tsoo
I'm a/an ...	*... sem.*	... sem
artist	*Umetnik* m	oo·met·neek
	Umetnica f	oo·met·nee·tsa
farmer	*Kmet/Kmetica* m/f	kmet/kme·tee·tsa
office worker	*Uradnik* m	oo·rad·neek
	Uradnica f	oo·rad·nee·tsa
scientist	*Znanstvenik* m	znans·tve·neek
	Znanstvenica f	znans·tve·nee·tsa
student	*Študent/Študentka* m/f	shtoo·dent/shtoo·dent·ka
tradesperson	*Trgovec/Trgovka* m/f	tuhr·go·vets/tuhr·gov·ka

background

Where are you from?	*Od kod ste?*	od kod ste
I'm from ...	*Iz ... sem.*	eez ... sem
Australia	*Avstralije*	av·stra·lee·ye
Canada	*Kanade*	ka·na·de
England	*Anglije*	an·glee·ye
New Zealand	*Nove Zelandije*	no·ve ze·lan·dee·ye
the USA	*Združenih držav*	zdroo·zhe·neeh dr·zhav
Are you married?	*Ste poročeni?*	ste po·ro·che·nee
I'm married.	*Poročen/Poročena*	po·ro·chen/po·ro·che·na
	sem. m/f	sem
I'm single.	*Samski/Samska sem.* m/f	sam·skee/sam·ska sem

age

How old ...?	Koliko ...?	ko·lee·ko ...
are you	si star/stara m/f inf	see star/sta·ra
are you	ste stari m&f pol	ste sta·ree
is your daughter	je stara vaša hči	ye sta·ra va·sha hchee
is your son	je star vaš sin	ye star vash seen

| I'm ... years old. | Imam ... let. | ee·mam ... let |
| He/She is ... years old. | ... let ima. | ... let ee·ma |

feelings

I'm ...	... sem.	... sem
hungry	Lačen/Lačna m/f	la·chen/lach·na
thirsty	Žejen/Žejna m/f	zhe·yen/zhey·na
tired	Utrujen m	oot·roo·yen
	Utrujena f	oot·roo·ye·na

I'm not ...	Nisem ...	nee·sem ...
hungry	lačen/lačna m/f	la·chen/lach·na
thirsty	žejen/žejna m/f	zhe·yen/zhey·na
tired	utrujen/utrujena m/f	oot·roo·yen/oot·roo·ye·na

Are you ... ?	Ste ...?	ste ...
hungry	lačni	lach·nee
thirsty	žejni	zhey·nee
tired	utrujeni	oot·roo·ye·nee

I'm ...	... mi je.	... mee ye
hot	Vroče	vro·che
well	Dobro	dob·ro

I'm not ...	Ni mi ...	nee mee ...
Are you ...?	Vam je ...?	vam ye ...
hot	vroče	vro·che
well	dobro	dob·ro

| I'm (not) cold. | (Ne) Zebe me. | ne ze·be me |
| Are you cold? | Vas zebe? | vas ze·be |

entertainment

going out

Where can I find ...?	Kje je kakšen ...?	kye ye *kak*·shen ...
clubs	klub	kloob
gay venues	homoseksualski bar	ho·mo·sek·soo·*al*·skee bar
pubs	bar	bar

I feel like going to a/the ...	Želim iti	zhe·*leem* ee·tee ...
concert	na koncert	na kon·*tsert*
movies	v kino	oo *kee*·no
party	na zabavo	na za·*ba*·vo
restaurant	v restavracijo	oo res·tav·*ra*·tsee·yo
theatre	v gledališče	oo gle·da·*leesh*·che

interests

Do you like ...?	Vam je všeč ...?	vam ye vshech ...
I like ...	Všeč mi je ...	vshech mee ye ...
I don't like ...	Ni mi všeč ...	nee mee vshech ...
art	umetnost	oo·*met*·nost
cooking	kuhanje	*koo*·han·ye
reading	branje	*bran*·ye
shopping	nakupovanje	na·koo·po·*van*·ye
sport	šport	shport

Do you like ...?	So vam všeč ...?	so vam vshech ...
I like ...	Všeč so mi ...	vshech so mee ...
I don't like ...	Niso mi všeč ...	*nee*·so mee vshech ...
movies	filmi	*feel*·mee
nightclubs	nočni bari	*noch*·nee *ba*·ree
travelling	potovanja	po·to·*van*·ya

Do you like to ...?	Ali radi ...?	a·lee ra·dee ...
dance	plešete	*ple*·she·te
go to concerts	hodite na koncerte	ho·dee·te na kon·*tser*·te
listen to music	poslušati glasbo	pos·*loo*·sha·te *glas*·bo

food & drink

finding a place to eat

Can you recommend a ...?	Mi lahko priporočite ...?	mee lah·ko pree·po·ro·chee·te ...
bar	bar	bar
café	kavarno	ka·var·no
restaurant	restavracijo	res·tav·ra·tsee·yo
I'd like ..., please.	Želim ..., prosim.	zhe·leem ... pro·seem
a table for (five)	mizo za (pet)	mee·zo za (pet)
the (non)smoking section	prostor za (ne)kadilce	pros·tor za (ne·)ka·deel·tse

ordering food

breakfast	zajtrk m	zai·tuhrk
lunch	kosilo n	ko·see·lo
dinner	večerja f	ve·cher·ya
snack	malica f	ma·lee·tsa
today's special	danes nudimo	da·nes noo·dee·mo
What would you recommend?	Kaj priporočate?	kai pree·po·ro·cha·te
I'd like (the) ..., please.	Želim ..., prosim.	zhe·leem ... pro·seem
bill	račun	ra·choon
drink list	meni pijač	me·nee pee·yach
menu	jedilni list	ye·deel·nee leest
that dish	to jed	to yed

drinks

cup of coffee ...	skodelica kave ...	sko·de·lee·tsa ka·ve ...
cup of tea ...	skodelica čaja ...	sko·de·lee·tsa cha·ya ...
with milk	z mlekom	z mle·kom
without sugar	brez sladkorja	brez slad·kor·ya

(orange) juice	(pomarančni) sok m	(po·ma·ranch·nee) sok
soft drink	brezalkoholna	brez·al·ko·hol·na
	pijača f	pee·ya·cha
... water	... voda	... vo·da
boiled	prekuhana	pre·koo·ha·na
(sparkling)	mineralna	mee·ne·ral·na
mineral	(gazirana)	(ga·zee·ra·na)

in the bar

I'll have ...
Jaz bom ... yaz bom ...

I'll buy you a drink.
Povabim te na pijačo. inf po·va·beem te na pee·ya·cho

What would you like?
Kaj boš? inf kai bosh

Cheers!
Na zdravje! na zdrav·ye

brandy	vinjak m	veen·yak
champagne	šampanjec m	sham·pan·yets
cocktail	koktajl m	kok·tail
cognac	konjak m	kon·yak
a shot of (whisky)	kozarček (viskija)	ko·zar·chek (vees·kee·ya)
a ... of beer	... piva	... pee·va
glass	kozarec	ko·za·rets
jug	vrč	vuhrch
pint	vrček	vuhr·chek
a bottle/glass	steklenica/kozarec	stek·le·nee·tsa/ko·za·rets
of ... wine	... vina	... vee·na
red	rdečega	rde·che·ga
sparkling	penečega	pe·ne·che·ga
white	belega	be·le·ga

self-catering

What's the local speciality?
Kaj je lokalna specialiteta?   kai ye lo-*kal*-na spe-tsee-a-lee-*te*-ta

What's that?
Kaj je to?   kai ye to

How much is (a kilo of cheese)?
Koliko stane (kila sira)?   ko-lee-ko *sta*-ne (*kee*-la *see*-ra)

I'd like ...	*Želim ...*	zhe-*leem* ...
(200) grams	*(dvesto) gramov*	(dve-sto) *gra*-mov
(two) kilos	*(dva) kilograma*	(dva) kee-lo-*gra*-ma
(three) pieces	*(tri) kose*	(tree) *ko*-se
(six) slices	*(šest) rezin*	(shest) re-*zeen*

Less.	*Manj.*	man'
Enough.	*Dovolj.*	do-*vol*
More.	*Več.*	vech

special diets & allergies

Is there a vegetarian restaurant near here?
Je tu blizu vegetarijanska   ye too *blee*-zoo ve-ge-ta-ree-*yan*-ska
restavracija?   res-tav-*ra*-tsee-ya

Do you have vegetarian food?
Ali imate vegetarijansko hrano?   a-lee ee-*ma*-te ve-ge-ta-ree-*yan*-sko *hra*-no

Could you prepare	*Lahko pripravite*	lah-*ko* pree-*pra*-vee-te
a meal without ...?	*obed brez ...?*	o-*bed* brez ...
butter	*masla*	*mas*-la
eggs	*jajc*	yaits
meat stock	*mesne osnove*	*mes*-ne os-*no*-ve

I'm allergic to ...	*Alergičen/Alergična*	a-*ler*-gee-chen/a-*ler*-geech-na
	sem na ... m/f	sem na ...
dairy produce	*mlečne izdelke*	*mlech*-ne eez-*del*-ke
gluten	*gluten*	gloo-*ten*
MSG	*MSG*	em es ge
nuts	*oreške*	o-*resh*-ke
seafood	*morsko hrano*	*mor*-sko *hra*-no

menu decoder

bograč m	*bog*-rach	beef goulash
brancin na maslu m	bran-*tseen* na *mas*-loo	sea bass in butter
čebulna bržola f	che-*bool*-na br-*zho*-la	braised beef with onions
čevapčiči m	che-*vap*-chee-chee	spicy beef or pork meatballs
drobnjakovi štruklji m	drob-*nya*-ko-vee *shtrook*-lyee	dumplings of cottage cheese & chives
dunajski zrezek m	doo-nai-skee *zre*-zek	breaded veal or pork cutlet
francoska solata f	fran-*tsos*-ka so-*la*-ta	diced potatoes & vegetables with mayonnaise
gobova kremna juha f	*go*-bo-va *krem*-na *yoo*-ha	creamed mushroom soup
goveja juha z rezanci f	go-*ve*-ya *yoo*-ha z *re*-zan-tsee	beef broth with little egg noodles
jota f	*yo*-ta	beans, sauerkraut & potatoes or barley cooked with pork
kisle kumarice f	*kees*-le *koo*-ma-ree-tse	pickled cucumbers
kmečka pojedina f	*kmech*-ka po-*ye*-dee-na	smoked meats with sauerkraut
kranjska klobasa z gorčico f	*kran'*-ska klo-*ba*-sa z gor-*chee*-tso	sausage with mustard
kraški pršut z olivami m	*krash*-kee puhr-*shoot* z o-*lee*-va-mee	air-dried ham with black olives
krofi m	*kro*-fee	jam-filled doughnuts
kuhana govedina s hrenom f	*koo*-ha-na go-*ve*-dee-na s *hre*-nom	boiled beef with horseradish
kuhana postrv f	*koo*-ha-na pos-*tuhrv*	boiled trout
kumarična solata f	*koo*-ma-reech-na so-*la*-ta	cucumber salad
ljubljanski zrezek m	lyoob-*lyan*-skee *zre*-zek	breaded cutlet with cheese

mešano meso na žaru n	me-sha-no me-so na zha-roo	mixed grill
ocvrt oslič m	ots-vuhrt os-leech	fried cod
ocvrt piščanec m	ots-vuhrt peesh-cha-nets	fried chicken
orada na žaru f	o-ra-da na zha-roo	grilled sea bream
palačinke f	pa-la-cheen-ke	thin pancakes with marmalade, nuts or chocolate
pečena postrv f	pe-che-na pos-tuhrv	grilled trout
pečene sardele f	pe-che-ne sar-de-le	grilled sardines
pleskavica f	ples-ka-vee-tsa	spicy meat patties
pariški zrezek m	pa-reesh-kee zre-zek	cutlet fried in egg batter
puranov zrezek s šampinjoni m	poo-ra-nov zre-zek s sham-peen-yo-nee	turkey steak with white mushrooms
ražnjiči m	razh-nyee-chee	shish kebab
riba v marinadi f	ree-ba v ma-ree-na-dee	marinated fish
ričet m	ree-chet	barley stew with smoked pork ribs
rižota z gobami f	ree-zho-ta z go-ba-mee	risotto with mushrooms
sadna kupa f	sad-na koo-pa	fruit salad with whipped cream
srbska solata f	suhrb-ska so-la-ta	salad of tomatoes & green peppers with onions & cheese
svinjska pečenka f	sveen'-ska pe-chen-ka	roast pork
škampi na žaru m	shkam-pee na zha-roo	grilled prawns
školjke f	shkol'-ke	clams
zelena solata f	ze-le-na so-la-ta	lettuce salad
zelenjavna juha f	ze-len-yav-na yoo-ha	vegetable soup

emergencies

basics

Help!	Na pomoč!	na po-*moch*
Stop!	Ustavite (se)!	oos-*ta*-vee-te (se)
Go away!	Pojdite stran!	poy-*dee*-te stran
Thief!	Tat!	tat
Fire!	Požar!	po-*zhar*
Watch out!	Pazite!	pa-*zee*-te

Call ...!	Pokličite ...!	pok-*lee*-chee-te ...
a doctor	zdravnika	zdrav-*nee*-ka
an ambulance	rešilca	re-*sheel*-tsa
the police	policijo	po-lee-*tsee*-yo

It's an emergency.
Nujno je. — *nooy*-no ye

Could you help me, please?
Pomagajte mi, prosim. — po-*ma*-gai-te mee *pro*-seem

I have to use the telephone.
Poklicati moram. — pok-*lee*-tsa-tee *mo*-ram

I'm lost.
Izgubil/Izgubila sem se. m/f — eez-*goo*-beew/eez-goo-*bee*-la sem se

Where are the toilets?
Kje je stranišče? — kye ye stra-*neesh*-che

police

Where's the police station?
Kje je policijska postaja? — kye ye po-lee-*tseey*-ska pos-*ta*-ya

I want to report an offence.
Želim prijaviti prestopek. — zhe-*leem* pree-*ya*-vee-tee pres-*to*-pek

I have insurance.
Zavarovan/Zavarovana sem. m/f — za-va-ro-*van*/za-va-ro-*va*-na sem

I've been ...	... so me.	... so me
assaulted	Napadli	na-*pad*-lee
raped	Posilili	po-*see*-lee-lee
robbed	Oropali	o-*ro*-pa-lee

I've lost my ...	Izgubil/Izgubila sem ... m/f	eez-goo-beew/eez-goo-bee-la sem ...
My ... was/were stolen.	Ukradli so mi ...	ook-rad-lee so mee ...
backpack	nahrbtnik	na-huhrbt-neek
bags	torbe	tor-be
credit card	kreditno kartico	kre-deet-no kar-tee-tso
handbag	ročno torbico	roch-no tor-bee-tso
jewellery	nakit	na-keet
money	denar	de-nar
passport	potni list	pot-nee leest
travellers cheques	potovalne čeke	po-to-val-ne che-ke
wallet	denarnico	de-nar-nee-tso
I want to contact my ...	Želim poklicati ... svoj/svojo ... m/f	zhe-leem pok-lee-tsa-tee ... svoy/svo-yo ...
consulate	konzulat m	kon-zoo-lat
embassy	ambasado f	am-ba-sa-do

health

medical needs

Where's the nearest ...?	Kje je najbližji/ najbližja ... ? m/f	kye ye nai-bleezh-yee/ nai-bleezh-ya ...
dentist	zobozdravnik m	zo-bo-zdrav-neek
doctor	zdravnik m	zdrav-neek
hospital	bolnišnica f	bol-neesh-nee-tsa
(night) pharmacist	(nočna) lekarna f	(noch-na) le-kar-na

I need a doctor (who speaks English).
Potrebujem zdravnika (ki govori angleško).
pot-re-boo-yem zdrav-nee-ka (kee go-vo-ree ang-lesh-ko)

Could I see a female doctor?
Bi me lahko pregledala zdravnica?
bee me lah-ko preg-le-da-la zdrav-nee-tsa

I've run out of my medication.
Zmanjkalo mi je zdravil.
zman'-ka-lo mee ye zdra-veel

symptoms, conditions & allergies

| I'm sick. | Bolan/Bolna sem. m/f | bo-lan/boh-na sem |
| It hurts here. | Tu me boli. | too me bo-lee |

I have (a) ...	Imam ...	ee-mam ...
asthma	astmo	ast-mo
bronchitis	bronhitis	bron-hee-tees
constipation	zapeko	za-pe-ko
diarrhoea	drisko	drees-ko
fever	vročino	vro-chee-no
headache	glavobol	gla-vo-bol
heart condition	srčno bolezen	suhr-chno bo-le-zen
toothache	zobobol	zo-bo-bol
pain	bolečine	bo-le-chee-ne

I'm nauseous.	Slabo mi je.	sla-bo mee ye
I'm coughing.	Kašljam.	kash-lyam
I have a sore throat.	Boli me grlo.	bo-lee me guhr-lo

I'm allergic to ...	Alergičen/Alergična sem na ... m/f	a-ler-gee-chen/a-ler-geech-na sem na ...
antibiotics	antibiotike	an-tee-bee-o-tee-ke
anti-inflammatories	protivnetna zdravila	pro-teev-net-na zdra-vee-la
aspirin	aspirin	as-pee-reen
bees	čebelji pik	che-bel-yee peek
codeine	kodein	ko-de-een
penicillin	penicilin	pe-nee-tsee-leen

antiseptic	razkužilo n	raz-koo-zhee-lo
bandage	obveza f	ob-ve-za
condoms	kondomi m pl	kon-do-mee
contraceptives	kontracepcija f	kon-tra-tsep-tsee-ya
diarrhoea medicine	zdravilo za drisko n	zdra-vee-lo za drees-ko
insect repellent	sredstvo proti mrčesu n	sreds-tvo pro-tee muhr-che-soo
laxatives	odvajala n pl	od-va-ya-la
painkillers	analgetiki m pl	a-nal-ge-tee-kee
rehydration salts	sol za rehidracijo f	sol za re-heed-ra-tsee-yo
sleeping tablets	uspavalne tablete f pl	oos-pa-val-ne tab-le-te

english–slovene dictionary

Slovene nouns in this dictionary have their gender indicated by ⓜ (masculine), ⓕ (feminine) or ⓝ (neuter).
If it's a plural noun, you'll also see pl. Adjectives are given in the masculine form only. Words are also marked
as a (adjective), v (verb), sg (singular), pl (plural), inf (informal) or pol (polite) where necessary.

A

accident *nesreča* ⓕ nes-re-cha
accommodation *nastanitev* ⓕ na-sta-*nee*-tev
adaptor *adapter* ⓜ a-*dap*-ter
address *naslov* ⓜ nas-*loh*
after *po* po
air-conditioned *klimatiziran* klee-ma-tee-*zee*-ran
airplane *letalo* ⓝ le-*ta*-lo
airport *letališče* ⓝ le-ta-*leesh*-che
alcohol *alkohol* ⓜ al-ko-*hol*
all *vse* vse
allergy *alergija* ⓕ a-ler-*gee*-ya
ambulance *rešilni avto* ⓜ re-*sheel*-nee av-to
and *in* een
ankle *gleženj* ⓜ *gle*-zhen'
arm *roka* ⓕ *ro*-ka
ashtray *pepelnik* ⓜ pe-*pel*-neek
ATM *bankomat* ⓜ ban-ko-*mat*

B

baby *dojenček* ⓜ do-*yen*-chek
back (body) *hrbet* ⓜ *huhr*-bet
backpack *nahrbtnik* ⓜ na-*huhrbt*-neek
bad *slab* slab
bag *torba* ⓕ *tor*-ba
baggage *prtljaga* ⓕ puhrt-*lya*-ga
baggage claim *prevzem prtljage* ⓕ
  prev-*zem* puhrt-*lya*-ge
bank *banka* ⓕ *ban*-ka
bar *bar* bar
bathroom *kopalnica* ⓕ ko-*pal*-nee-tsa
battery *baterija* ⓕ ba-te-*ree*-ya
beautiful *lep* lep
bed *postelja* ⓕ *pos*-tel-ya
beer *pivo* ⓝ *pee*-vo
before *prej* prey
behind *zadaj* za-dai
bicycle *bicikel* ⓜ bee-*tsee*-kel
big *velik* ve-leek
bill *račun* ⓜ ra-*choon*
black *črn* chuhrn

blanket *odeja* ⓕ o-*de*-ya
blood group *krvna skupina* ⓕ *kuhrv*-na skoo-*pee*-na
blue *moder* mo-der
boat (ship) *ladja* ⓕ *lad*-ya
boat (small) *čoln* chohn
book (make a reservation) v *rezervirati*
  re-zer-vee-ra-tee
bottle *steklenica* ⓕ stek-le-*nee*-tsa
bottle opener *odpirač* ⓜ od-pee-*rach*
boy *fant* ⓜ fant
brakes (car) *zavore* ⓕ pl za-*vo*-re
breakfast *zajtrk* ⓜ *zai*-tuhrk
broken (faulty) *pokvarjen* pok-*var*-yen
bus *avtobus* ⓜ av-to-*boos*
business *posel* ⓜ po-se-oo
buy *kupiti* koo-*pee*-tee

C

café *kavarna* ⓕ ka-*var*-na
camera *fotoaparat* ⓜ fo-to-a-pa-*rat*
camera shop *trgovina s fotografsko opremo* ⓕ
  tr-go-*vee*-na s fo-to-*graf*-sko o-*pre*-mo
campsite *kamp* ⓜ kamp
cancel *preklicati* prek-*lee*-tsa-tee
can opener *odpirač za pločevinke* ⓜ
  od-pee-*rach* za plo-che-*veen*-ke
car *avtomobil* ⓜ av-to-mo-*beel*
cash *gotovina* ⓕ go-to-*vee*-na
cash (a cheque) v *unovčiti (ček)* oo-*nov*-chee-tee (chek)
cell phone *mobilni telefon* ⓜ mo-*beel*-nee te-le-*fon*
centre *center* ⓜ *tsen*-ter
change (money) v *menjati (denar)* men-*ya*-tee (de-*nar*)
cheap *poceni* po-*tse*-nee
check (bill) *račun* ⓜ ra-*choon*
check-in *prijava za let* ⓕ pree-*ya*-va za let
chest *prsni koš* ⓜ *puhr*-snee kosh
child *otrok* ⓜ ot-*rok*
cigarette *cigareta* ⓕ tsee-ga-*re*-ta
city *mesto* ⓝ *mes*-to
clean a *čist* cheest
closed *zaprt* za-*puhrt*
coffee *kava* ⓕ *ka*-va
coins *kovanci* ⓜ pl ko-*van*-tsee

cold a *hladen* hla-den
collect call *klic na stroške klicanega* ⓜ
  kleets na strosh-ke klee-tsa-ne-ga
come *priti* pree-tee
computer *računalnik* ⓜ ra-choo-nal-neek
condom *kondom* ⓜ kon-dom
contact lenses *kontaktne leče* ① pl kon-takt-ne le-che
cook v *kuhati* koo-ha-tee
cost *strošek* ⓜ stro-shek
credit card *kreditna kartica* ① kre-deet-na kar-tee-tsa
cup *skodelica* ① sko-de-lee-tsa
currency exchange *menjava* ① men-ya-va
customs (immigration) *carina* ① tsa-ree-na

D

dangerous *nevaren* ne-va-ren
date (time) *datum* ⓜ da-toom
day *dan* ⓜ dan
delay *zamuda* ① za-moo-da
dentist *zobozdravnik* ⓜ zo-boz-drav-neek
depart *oditi* o-dee-tee
diaper *plenica* ① ple-nee-tsa
dictionary *slovar* ⓜ slo-var
dinner *večerja* ① ve-cher-ya
direct *direkten* dee-rek-ten
dirty *umazan* oo-ma-zan
disabled (person) *invaliden* een-va-lee-den
discount *popust* ⓜ po-poost
doctor *zdravnik* ⓜ zdrav-neek
double bed *dvojna postelja* ① dvoy-na pos-tel-ya
double room *dvoposteljna soba* ①
  dvo-pos-tel'-na so-ba
drink *pijača* ① pee-ya-cha
drive v *voziti* vo-zee-tee
drivers licence *vozniško dovoljenje* ⓜ
  voz-neesh-ko do-vol-yen-ye
drug (illicit) *mamilo* ⓜ ma-mee-lo
dummy (pacifier) *duda* ① doo-da

E

ear *uho* ⓝ oo-ho
east *vzhod* ⓜ vzhod
eat *jesti* yes-tee
economy class *turistični razred* ⓜ
  too-rees-teech-nee raz-red
electricity *elektrika* ① e-lek-tree-ka
elevator *dvigalo* ⓝ dvee-ga-lo
email *elektronska pošta* ① e-lek-tron-ska posh-ta
embassy *ambasada* ① am-ba-sa-da
emergency *nujen primer* ⓜ noo-yen pree-mer
English (language) *angleščina* ① ang-lesh-chee-na

entrance *vhod* ⓜ vhod
evening *večer* ⓜ ve-cher
exchange rate *menjalni tečaj* ⓜ men-yal-nee te-chai
exit *izhod* ⓜ eez-hod
expensive *drag* drag
express mail *hitra pošta* ① heet-ra posh-ta
eye *oko* ⓝ o-ko

F

far *daleč* da-lech
fast *hitro* heet-ro
father *oče* ⓜ o-che
film (camera) *film* ⓜ feelm
finger *prst* ⓜ puhrst
first-aid kit *komplet za prvo pomoč* ⓜ
  kom-plet za puhr-vo po-moch
first class *prvi razred* ⓜ puhr-vee raz-red
fish *riba* ① ree-ba
food *hrana* ① hra-na
foot *stopalo* ⓝ sto-pa-lo
fork *vilice* ① pl vee-lee-tse
free (of charge) *brezplačen* brez-pla-chen
friend *prijatelj/prijateljica* ⓜ/①
  pree-ya-tel/pree-ya-tel-yee-tsa
fruit *sadje* ⓝ pl sad-ye
full *poln* poln
funny *smešen* sme-shen

G

gift *darilo* ⓝ da-ree-lo
girl *dekle* ⓝ dek-le
glass (drinking) *kozarec* ⓜ ko-za-rets
glasses *očala* ⓝ pl o-cha-la
go *iti* ee-tee
good *dober* do-ber
green *zelen* ze-len
guide *vodnik* ⓜ vod-neek

H

half *pol* poh
hand *roka* ① ro-ka
handbag *ročna torbica* ① roch-na tor-bee-tsa
happy *srečen* sre-chen
have *imeti* ee-me-tee
he *on* ⓜ on
head *glava* ① gla-va
heart *srce* ⓝ suhr-tse
heat *vročina* ① vro-chee-na
heavy *težek* te-zhek

help v *pomagati* po-*ma*-ga-tee
here *tukaj* too-*kai*
high *visok* vee-*sok*
highway *hitra cesta* ① *heet*-ra *tses*-ta
(go on a) hike v *iti na pohod* ee-tee na po-*hod*
holidays *počitnice* ① pl po-*cheet*-nee-tse
homosexual *homoseksualec* ⓜ ho-mo-sek-soo-*a*-lets
hospital *bolnišnica* ① bol-*neesh*-nee-tsa
hot *vroč* vroch
hotel *hotel* ⓜ ho-*tel*
hungry *lačen* la-chen
husband *mož* ⓜ mozh

I

I *jaz* yaz
identification (card) *osebna izkaznica* ①
o-*seb*-na eez-*kaz*-nee-tsa
ill *bolan* bo-*lan*
important *pomemben* po-*mem*-ben
included *vključen* vklyoo-chen
injury *poškodba* ① posh-*kod*-ba
insurance *zavarovanje* ⓝ za-va-ro-*van*-ye
Internet *internet* ⓜ een-ter-net
interpreter *tolmač* ⓜ tol-*mach*

J

jewellery *nakit* ⓜ na-*keet*
job *služba* ① *sloozh*-ba

K

key *ključ* ⓜ klyooch
kilogram *kilogram* ⓜ *kee*-lo-gram
kitchen *kuhinja* ① koo-*heen*-ya
knife *nož* ⓜ nozh

L

laundry (place) *pralnica* ① *pral*-nee-tsa
lawyer *odvetnik* ⓜ od-*vet*-neek
left (direction) *levo* le-vo
left-luggage office *garderoba* ① gar-de-*ro*-ba
leg *noga* ① *no*-ga
lesbian *lezbijka* ① lez-*beey*-ka
less *manj* man'
letter (mail) *pismo* ⓝ *pees*-mo
lift (elevator) *dvigalo* ⓝ dvee-*ga*-lo
light *svetloba* ① svet-*lo*-ba
like v *všeč biti* vshech bee-tee

lock *ključavnica* ① klyoo-*chav*-nee-tsa
long *dolg* dohg
lost *izgubljen* eez-goob-*lyen*
lost-property office *urad za izgubljene predmete* ⓜ
oo-rad za eez-goob-*lye*-ne pred-*me*-te
love v *ljubiti* lyoo-bee-tee
luggage *prtljaga* ① puhrt-*lya*-ga
lunch *kosilo* ⓝ ko-*see*-lo

M

mail *pošta* ① *posh*-ta
man *moški* ⓜ *mosh*-kee
map *zemljevid* ⓜ zem-lye-*veed*
market *tržnica* ① tuhrzh-nee-tsa
matches *vžigalice* ① pl vzhee-*ga*-lee-tse
meat *meso* ⓝ me-*so*
medicine *zdravilo* ⓝ zdra-*vee*-lo
menu *jedilni list* ⓜ ye-*deel*-nee leest
message *sporočilo* ⓝ spo-ro-*chee*-lo
milk *mleko* ⓝ *mle*-ko
minute *minuta* ① mee-*noo*-ta
mobile phone *mobilni telefon* ⓜ mo-*beel*-nee te-le-*fon*
money *denar* ⓜ de-*nar*
month *mesec* ⓜ *me*-sets
morning *dopoldne* ① do-*pol*-dne
mother *mama* ① *ma*-ma
motorcycle *motorno kolo* ⓝ mo-*tor*-no ko-*lo*
motorway *motorna cesta* ① mo-*tor*-na *tses*-ta
mouth *usta* ⓝ *oos*-ta
music *glasba* ① *glaz*-ba

N

name *ime* ⓝ ee-*me*
napkin *prtiček* ⓜ puhr-*tee*-chek
nappy *plenica* ① ple-*nee*-tsa
near *blizu* blee-zoo
neck *vrat* ⓜ vrat
new *nov* noh
news *novice* ① pl no-*vee*-tse
newspaper *časopis* ⓜ cha-so-*pees*
night *noč* ① noch
no *ne* ne
noisy *hrupen* hroo-pen
nonsmoking *nekadilski* ne-ka-*deel*-skee
north *sever* ⓜ *se*-ver
nose *nos* ⓜ nos
now *zdaj* zdai
number *število* ⓝ shte-*vee*-lo

O

oil (engine) *olje* ⓝ ol-ye
old *star* star
one-way ticket *enosmerna vozovnica* ⓕ
e·no·*smer*·na vo·*zov*·nee·tsa
open a *odprt* od·*puhrt*
outside *zunaj* zoo·nai

P

package *paket* ⓜ pa·*ket*
paper *papir* ⓜ pa·*peer*
park (car) v *parkirati* par·*kee*·ra·tee
passport *potni list* ⓜ *pot*·nee leest
pay *plačati* pla·*cha*·tee
pen *pisalo* ⓝ pee·*sa*·lo
petrol *bencin* ⓜ ben·*tseen*
pharmacy *lekarna* ⓕ le·*kar*·na
phonecard *telefonska kartica* ⓕ
te·le·*fon*·ska *kar*·tee·tsa
photo *fotografija* ⓕ fo·to·gra·*fee*·ya
picnic *piknik* ⓜ *peek*·neek
plate *krožnik* ⓜ *krozh*·neek
police *policija* ⓕ po·lee·*tsee*·ya
postcard *razglednica* ⓕ raz·*gled*·nee·tsa
post office *pošta* ⓕ *posh*·ta
pregnant *noseča* no·*se*·cha
price *cena* ⓕ *tse*·na

Q

quiet *tih* teeh

R

rain *dež* ⓜ dezh
razor *brivnik* ⓜ *breev*·neek
receipt *račun* ⓜ ra·*choon*
red *rdeč* rdech
refund *vračilo denarja* ⓝ vra·*chee*·lo de·*nar*·ya
registered mail *priporočena pošta* ⓕ
pree·po·ro·*che*·na *posh*·ta
rent v *najeti* na·ye·tee
repair v *popraviti* pop·*ra*·vee·tee
reservation *rezervacija* ⓕ re·zer·*va*·tsee·ya
restaurant *restavracija* ⓕ res·tav·*ra*·tsee·ya
return v *vrniti* vr·*nee*·tee

return ticket *povratna vozovnica* ⓕ
pov·*rat*·na vo·*zov*·nee·tsa
right (direction) *desno* des·no
road *cesta* ⓕ *tses*·ta
room *soba* ⓕ *so*·ba

S

safe a *varen* va·ren
sanitary napkins *damski vložki* ⓜ pl
dam·skee *vlozh*·kee
seat *sedež* ⓜ se·dezh
send *poslati* pos·*la*·tee
service station *servis* ⓜ *ser*·vees
sex *seks* ⓜ seks
shampoo *šampon* ⓜ sham·*pon*
share (a dorm) *deliti (sobo)* de·lee·tee (so·bo)
shaving cream *krema za britje* ⓕ *kre*·ma za *breet*·ye
she *ona* ⓕ o·na
sheet (bed) *rjuha* ⓕ *ryoo*·ha
shirt *srajca* ⓕ *srai*·tsa
shoes *čevlji* ⓜ pl *chev*·lyee
shop *trgovina* ⓕ tuhr·go·*vee*·na
short *kratek* *kra*·tek
shower *prha* ⓕ *puhr*·ha
single room *enoposteljna soba* ⓕ
e·no·*pos*·tel'·na *so*·ba
skin *koža* ⓕ *ko*·zha
skirt *krilo* ⓕ *kree*·lo
sleep v *spati* *spa*·tee
Slovenia *Slovenija* ⓕ slo·*ve*·nee·ya
Slovene (language) *slovenščina* ⓕ slo·*vensh*·chee·na
Slovene a *slovenski* slo·*ven*·skee
slowly *počasi* po·*cha*·see
small *majhen* *mai*·hen
smoke (cigarettes) v *kaditi* ka·*dee*·tee
soap *milo* ⓝ *mee*·lo
some *nekaj* *ne*·kai
soon *kmalu* *kma*·loo
south *jug* ⓜ yoog
souvenir shop *trgovina s spominki* ⓕ
tuhr·go·*vee*·na s spo·*meen*·kee
speak *govoriti* go·vo·*ree*·tee
spoon *žlica* ⓕ *zhlee*·tsa
stamp *znamka* ⓕ *znam*·ka
stand-by ticket *stand-by vozovnica* ⓕ
stend·bai vo·*zov*·nee·tsa
station (train) *postaja* ⓕ *pos*·ta·ya
stomach *želodec* ⓜ zhe·*lo*·dets

stop v *ustaviti* oos-*ta*-vee-tee
stop (bus) *postajališče* ⓝ pos-ta-ya-*leesh*-che
street *ulica* ⓕ oo-lee-tsa
student *študent/študentka* ⓜ/ⓕ
shtoo-*dent*/shtoo-*dent*-ka
sun *sonce* ⓝ *son*-tse
sunscreen *krema za sončenje* ⓕ *kre*-ma za *son*-chen-ye
swim v *plavati* *pla*-va-tee

T

tampons *tamponi* ⓜ pl tam-*po*-nee
taxi *taksi* ⓜ *tak*-see
teaspoon *čajna žlička* ⓕ *chai*-na *zhleech*-ka
teeth *zobje* ⓜ *zob*-ye
telephone *telefon* ⓜ te-le-*fon*
television *televizija* ⓕ te-le-*vee*-zee-ya
temperature (weather) *temperatura* ⓕ
tem-pe-ra-*too*-ra
tent *šotor* ⓜ *sho*-tor
that (one) *tisti* *tees*-tee
they *oni/one* ⓜ/ⓕ *o*-nee/*o*-ne
thirsty *žejen* *zhe*-yen
this (one) *ta* ta
throat *grlo* ⓝ *guhr*-lo
ticket (entrance) *vstopnica* ⓕ *vstop*-nee-tsa
ticket (travel) *vozovnica* ⓕ vo-*zov*-nee-tsa
time *čas* ⓜ chas
tired *utrujen* oo-*troo*-yen
tissues *robčki* ⓜ pl *rob*-chkee
today *danes* *da*-nes
toilet *stranišče* ⓝ stra-*neesh*-che
tomorrow *jutri* *yoot*-ree
tonight *nocoj* no-*tsoy*
toothbrush *zobna ščetka* ⓕ *zob*-na *shchet*-ka
toothpaste *zobna pasta* ⓕ *zob*-na *pas*-ta
torch (flashlight) *baterija* ⓕ ba-te-*ree*-ya
tour *izlet* ⓜ *eez*-let
tourist office *turistični urad* ⓜ too-*rees*-teech-nee oo-*rad*
towel *brisača* ⓕ bree-*sa*-cha
train *vlak* ⓜ vlak
translate *prevesti* pre-*ves*-tee
travel agency *potovalna agencija* ⓕ
po-to-*val*-na a-*gen*-tsee-ya
travellers cheque *potovalni ček* ⓜ po-to-*val*-nee chek
trousers *hlače* ⓝ pl *hla*-che
twin beds *ločeni postelji* ⓕ pl *lo*-che-nee *pos*-tel-yee
tyre *guma* ⓕ *goo*-ma

U

underwear *spodnje perilo* ⓝ *spod*-nye pe-*ree*-lo
urgent *nujen* noo-yen

V

vacant *prost* prost
vacation *počitnice* ⓕ pl po-*cheet*-nee-tse
vegetable *zelenjava* ⓕ ze-len-*ya*-va
vegetarian a *vegetarijanski* ve-ge-ta-ree-*yan*-skee
visa *viza* ⓕ *vee*-za

W

waiter *natakar* ⓜ na-*ta*-kar
walk v *hoditi* ho-*dee*-tee
wallet *denarnica* ⓕ de-*nar*-nee-tsa
warm a *topel* to-pe-oo
wash (something) *prati* *pra*-tee
watch *zapestna ura* ⓕ za-*pest*-na *oo*-ra
water *voda* ⓕ *vo*-da
we *mi* mee
weekend *vikend* ⓜ *vee*-kend
west *zahod* ⓜ za-*hod*
wheelchair *invalidski voziček* ⓜ
een-va-*leed*-skee vo-*zee*-chek
when *kdaj* kdai
where *kje* kye
white *bel* be-oo
who *kdo* kdo
why *zakaj* za-*kai*
wife *žena* ⓕ *zhe*-na
window *okno* ⓝ *ok*-no
wine *vino* ⓝ *vee*-no
with *z/s* z/s
without *brez* brez
woman *ženska* ⓕ *zhen*-ska
write *pisati* *pee*-sa-tee

Y

yellow *rumen* roo-men
yes *da* da
yesterday *včeraj* *vche*-rai
you sg inf/pol *ti/vi* tee/vee
you pl *vi* vee

INDEX

451

INDEX

453

festivals in eastern europe

The Tirana International Film Festival in December is the first and only short film festival in **Albania**. Gjirokastra is the home of the Albanian Folklore Festival, usually held in September every four years to celebrate the national traditions, folk music and dance.

The renowned Varna Summer International Festival in **Bulgaria** features all sorts of music between May and October. Locals in full costume prepare for weeks to bring history to life in the Re-enactment of the 1876 April Uprising in Koprivshtitsa.

In July and August, a programme of theatre, concerts and dance is presented on open-air stages at the prestigious Dubrovnik Summer Festival in **Croatia**. The Rijeka Carnival in February is a week of partying with plenty of parades and street dances.

The Prague Spring in May, one of Europe's biggest festivals of classical music, kicks off the summer in the **Czech Republic**. Prachatice goes fairly wild during the mid-June Gold Trail Festival with medieval costumes, fencing tournaments and fireworks.

People from all over Europe camp and party at the Sziget Festival in **Hungary**, a week-long world music bash in early August on Budapest's Óbuda Island. The Gyula Theatre Festival has spectacular performances in the castle courtyard during July and August.

In July, a village in **Macedonia** hosts very popular and wildly romantic traditional weddings during the Galichnik Wedding Festival. Poets from around 50 countries take part at the Struga Poetry Evenings in August, complete with food and drink in the streets.

The Dominican Fair in Gdansk is the oldest shopping fair in **Poland**, held in August and accompanied by street theatre, concerts, parades and races. The May Juvenalia in Kraków is a student carnival with fancy dress, masquerades and dancing in the street.

The Medieval Festival of the Arts in late July brings music, arts, crafts, and colourful costumes to the streets of Sighişoara, **Romania**. The Juni Pageant in Braşov (in May) is a centuries-old tradition with a riding parade, elaborate costumes and folk dancing.

In late June, the hedonistic crowds celebrate the longest days of the year during the White Nights in St Petersburg. The Golden Mask Festival, featuring **Russia**'s premier drama, opera, dance and musical performers, brightens up March and April in Moscow.

In July, artists from all over Europe come to Kežmarok for the biggest Craft Fair in **Slovakia**, with food, drinks and live music. Rumours that the Bojnice Castle is haunted are kept alive by the International Festival of Spirits and Ghosts, held in early May.

Kurentovanje, a rite of spring celebrated in February, is the most extravagant folklore event in **Slovenia**, held in Ptuj. Maribor hosts both the International Puppet Festival in July and August and a renowned theatre festival in the second half of October.

3 7242 00236 5448